INTERNET Insider

Ruffin Prevost

Osborne **McGraw-Hill**
Berkeley New York St. Louis San Francisco
Auckland Bogotá Hamburg London Madrid
Mexico City Milan Montreal New Delhi Panama City
Paris São Paulo Singapore Sydney

Osborne **McGraw-Hill**
2600 Tenth Street
Berkeley, California 94710
U.S.A.

For information on translations or book distributors outside of the U.S.A., please write to Osborne **McGraw-Hill** at the above address.

Internet Insider

1a 234567890 DOC 998765

ISBN 0-07-882084-7

Publisher
Lawrence Levitsky

Acquisitions Editor
Scott Rogers

Project Editor
Cindy Brown

Copy Editor
Carl Wikander

Proofreaders
Margaret Dodd
Stephanie Otis

Indexer
David Heiret

Computer Designer
Peter F. Hancik

Illustrators
Lance Ravella
Joe Scuderi

Cover Design
Soto Associates

Table of Contents

Special Reports

ELVIS BIRD

FIRST TIME EVER !!

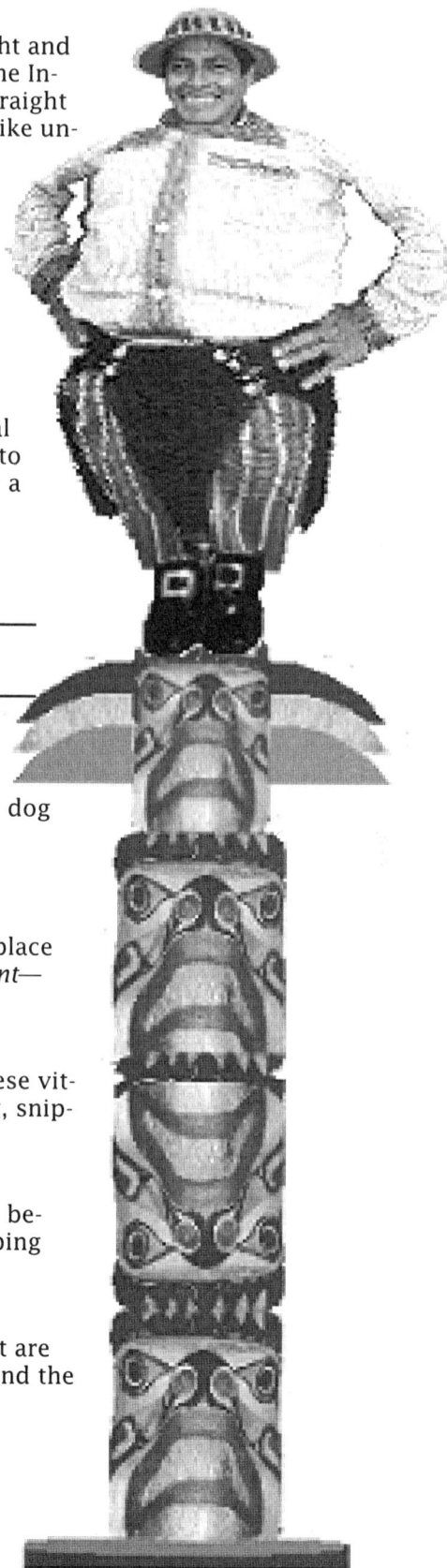

Features

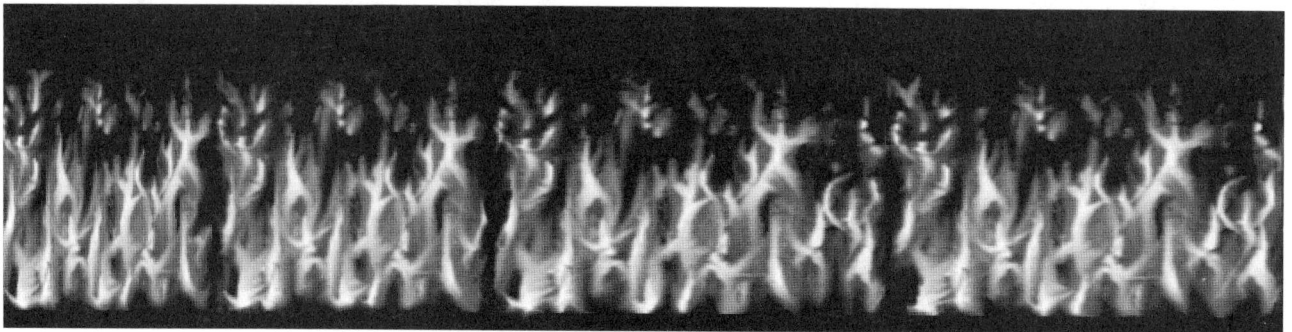

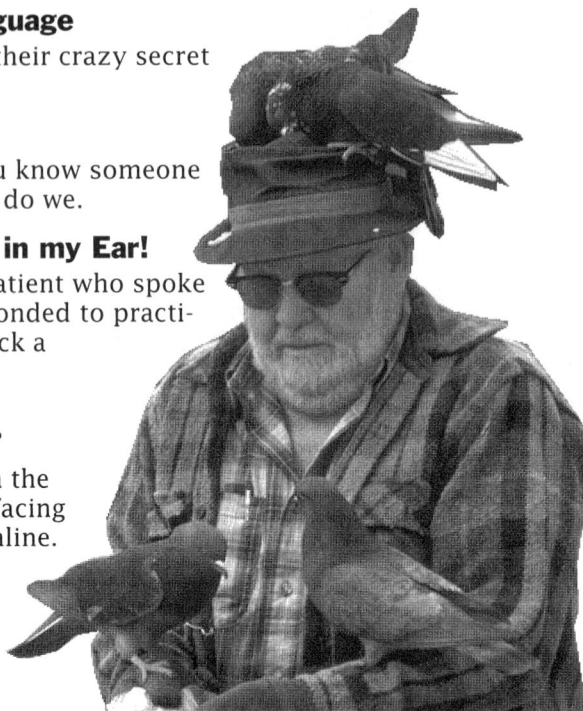

Departments

The following departments are spread throughout the book. Page numbers are listed for their first appearance only.

Acknowledgments

While the process of writing most books is typically a solitary endeavor, putting together a book like the *Internet Insider* has been something more akin to a grand collaboration. On behalf of the entire *Internet Insider* staff, from the metro editors to the mailroom clerks to the summer interns, I'd like to extend my sincere gratitude to a number of people who helped make the *Insider* possible.

First and foremost, thanks to all those individuals who graciously gave their permission for their work to be reprinted in these pages. They are the real stars of this book, and I hope they receive the recognition they deserve. If you're pleased by a particular article, don't hesitate to e-mail the author (e-mail addresses generally appear next to bylines) and let him or her know how much you liked it.

Thanks to all the folks at Osborne McGraw-Hill for their hard work and dedication in helping to make the *Insider* a unique and singularly unrivaled book amongst a sea of Internet contenders. Special thanks to Lance "Alot" Ravella (my co-conspirator), Joe Scuderi, and Peter "Paste-up" Hancik, also to Roberta Steele, Leslee Bassin, Jani Beckwith, Marcela Hancik, and everyone in the production department who worked long hours to bring the authentically outrageous look and feel of the world of trashy tabloids to the *Insider*. Their skill at simulating tastelessness and sleaze is truly disturbing.

Thanks also to Osborne publisher Larry "Done Deal" Levitsky for agreeing to such a hair-brained idea in the first place and for giving me the freedom and support to create a book that lesser publishers might fear or renounce. Editors "Downtown" Cindy Brown and Jeff "Red Hot Chili" Pepper offered invaluable insight, advice, and assistance. Extra-special thanks to my editor, Scott "the Hammer" Rogers, who not only spent nights and weekends editing copy but was instrumental in championing the cause of the *Insider's* existence. His hard work and dedication to every aspect of this project is greatly appreciated.

My thanks to Kelly Vogel, Patty Mon, Lisa Kissinger, Kendall Anderson, and everyone else at Osborne who helped out.

Thanks also to Diane and Bruce Rogers, without whose burst of creative insight this book might have been called "The Internet Pajama Party." Also, thanks for the courteous, swift, and efficient service (Ha!) from the fine folks at Jerry's, Art's, and Solley's Delis, as well as the folks at the aptly named Insomnia Cafe. I hope I never have to drink that much 4 a.m. coffee again in my life.

Special thank-yous go to Steve Kinzler, custodian of the fabled Usenet Oracle for his gracious permission to reprint oracularities as well as his long and careful work in helping choose, compile, and credit the various excerpts; Tim Bowden, manager of the Nerdnosh mailing list and all those members of Nerdnosh who allowed their works to be reprinted—thanks for letting the world in on your dream-sired high-wired campfire choir; and Juan Bootsie (and friends) for providing us with the best of the outrageous *Bootsie Reports* and allowing *Insider* readers to experience life "from the edge of credibility."

To a number of other individuals, I offer my sincere gratitude, especially to Kent England, Pushpendra Mohta, Carlos Robles, and Meg Jahnke of CERFnet; Professor Larry Press of Computer Information Systems at Cal-State Dominguez Hills; Guy Stevens of Intercon, makers of the excellent (and highly recommended) TCP/Connect II Integrated Internet Software for the Macintosh; and the dozens of writers who compiled FAQ files for various newsgroups and many netizens who helped ferret out information for inclusion in this book. Special thanks to CorelDraw and Walnut Creek Software for providing many of the original images used in this book.

To the following Internet tipsters, info scouts and online prospectors, I'm proud to bestow the title of honorary *Internet Insider* correspondent: Charles Overbeck (National Affairs Desk), Rob Terrell (Science & Technology Desk), Craig Stinson (International Affairs Desk), Shea Tisdale (Political Analyst), John Hedtke (Cultural Affairs Desk), Harold Deen McClure (Military Analyst), and Donald Trull (Literary Critic). Thanks also to Trey Prevost and all the middle-management dorks at Novaplex, Inc. for their patience and understanding in dealing with a beleaguered creative services department.

Finally, thanks to all those celebrities, luminaries, and just plain common folks who answered the ridiculous and aggravating e-mail queries sent to them by K. Johnson, who, we're told, is still beaming out letters to unsuspecting dupes up and down the infobahn.

read.me.first

Sometime after Nixon left the White House and before Al Gore became the second-most-powerful cyber-wonk on the planet, a revolution took place. The world became wired while no one was watching. The trend-mongers and consultants were predicting a massive change in the way we work and play. The psychics and tabloids were spouting off about all the incredible changes that would be upon us "by the year 2000." Meanwhile, the Net came of age.

Well, sort of.

A collection of thousands of networks and hundreds of thousands of computers scattered across the globe, the *Internet*—the world's largest computer network—is the daily stomping grounds of millions of explorers along the electronic frontier. Long before the Internet graced the cover of *Time* magazine or became Oprah's topic *du jour*, millions of people were spending a significant portion of their lives carving the Internet out of the electronic ether.

The *Internet Insider* is a testament to their efforts. Insofar as such a thing is possible, its purpose is to present a fleeting picture of what the Internet is like today—how it touches the lives of the people who use it and how it must appear to people who've never witnessed it first-hand. Ten years ago, a book about the Internet would have interested few readers beyond a handful of scientists, scholars, and defense contractors. Ten years hence, the Internet may scarcely be recognizable as a descendant of what it is today.

Today—right now—the Internet has taken an early shape, but has not yet fully metamorphosed. It's in the midst of an awkward but hugely compelling adolescence that will soon vanish. Consider the *Internet Insider* to be a slightly overexposed prom-night snapshot of an Internet too old for training wheels but scarcely old enough for the keys to the family car. The Internet is a real place where real people spend precious seconds and idle days on plaintive epistles and outrageous rants.

More than any other physical place or material or electronic medium on the planet, the Internet is an unregulated, egalitarian marketplace of ideas where the attention given to any thought or comment is in direct proportion to its merit, popularity, or true mass appeal. It's a forum where heads of state share the spotlight with heads in altered states, where captains of industry argue semantics with the captains of galactic starships, and where planetary pundits are shown their place by the global village idiots.

It would take volumes of books and a battleship full of researchers, academicians, and digital know-it-alls to present a fair, accurate, and complete picture of the Internet. Luckily, it's possible for a single smartass to offer a personal view that's nearly as enlightening and probably a bit more fun.

> *Consider the* **Internet Insider** *to be a slightly overexposed prom-night snapshot of an Internet too old for training wheels but scarcely old enough for the keys to the family car.*

The *Internet Insider* is a rough attempt to show veteran Net-dwellers their favorite haunts from a fresh perspective and to give Internet newbies a whirlwind tour of some of the Net's more intriguing and enlightening attractions.

Because of the Net's incomprehensible scope, any attempt to categorize, analyze, or otherwise cross-reference its contents is not only futile from a logistical standpoint, but counterproductive from an aesthetic one. The Internet is about as neatly categorized as a sophomore dorm room and as easily navigable as the Roman catacombs. Consequently, the *Insider* follows the time-tested organizational scheme of the city dump: things appear where they are pretty much because that's where they were put.

But perhaps more noteworthy than *where* items of interest appear is *how* they appear. No doubt, some of you are saying to yourselves: "A book full of the best stuff on the Internet! I love it. But what's all this tabloid nonsense?" My response is, of course, "Why not?" In an age when the art of hype has supplanted nearly everything else of relevance in modern existence, I've decided it's easier to join 'em than to try and beat 'em.

Besides, what single topic has suffered under more speculation, myth, legend, rumor, conjecture, distortion, misrepresentation, oversimplification, and outright hype than the Internet, progenitor-to-be of the fabled infotainment suprahypeway? It takes the single-minded, outrageous,

and . . . well . . . *gonzo* approach of the tabloid to shed light on the humanity and reality of the Internet, heretofore portrayed as a high-tech digital wonderland where information giblets whiz around cyberspace like sentient photon-bugs.

Whether you're a confessed Internet junkie, just a "casual user," or a bona fide netaphobe, you'll find something of interest in the Insider's many departments. Keep an eye out for the following regular features:

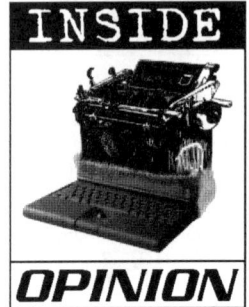

When your brain is swollen and aching from straining to comprehend the complex underlying forces and subtle nuances of how the Internet works, there's only one place to go for relief. Find out *what it all means* and see the Net clearly, from a fresh and enlightened perspective via the Inside Opinion. Written exclusively by the top journalists at the *Internet Insider*, the Inside Opinion is the final word on whatever you might be pondering. Accept it as gospel.

For the hard-core Net ramblers, you'll find priceless contact information in each Net Resources section. Unlike your typical tabloid, the *Insider* is only too happy to share its sources—well, *most* of its sources—with everyone. Get the straight dope straight from the Net via FTP, e-mail, the World-Wide Web, and more by checking the Net Resources sections. But remember, once you leave the comfort of our tawdry pages, you're on your own . . . we're not coming after you!

Net Resources

Hey, let's face it—rumors abound on the Net. There's no way to avoid them, so we all may as well learn to deal with them. The problem is, of course, separating fact from fiction. Enter Rumor Control. Drawing on scores of well-placed sources throughout the Net, our Rumor Control staff helps you filter out the gossip and hearsay, casting a knowing light on fantasy and reality alike. But be forewarned, even our crack staff makes mistakes. Nevertheless, while not everything in Rumor Control can be assumed 100% factual, can you afford not to believe it?

Some folks can't stand to waste a single second dilly-dallying on the filigree and lace of everyday life. They want the facts, and *just* the facts. They are, quite simply, bottom-liners. List Service will no doubt appeal to hard-core bottom-liners. Why waste time on unneeded verbs, adjectives, gerunds, and such nonsense? With List Service, it's typically just nouns, nouns, and nouns, and plenty of them!

List Service

Everybody knows that the construction crew working on the Tower of Babel had a communications gap, but that was nothing. Imagine how tough it must be for 25 million people in dozens of countries to converse via their computers. To make matters worse, these damn kids with their goofy slang and wacky lingo keep inventing new words. But don't dismay—just check out net.speak for the real meaning behind the latest jargon online.

He's the most well-connected man on the Net and he's sharing his privileged information with readers of the *Insider*. Juan Bootsie—the man who got the exclusive interview with Lisa Marie, the man who went inside the camp at Guantanamo Bay, the man who almost married Liz Taylor, comes to us by special arrangement. Read his columns here or catch him on the Net, where he faithfully reports "from the edge of credibility."

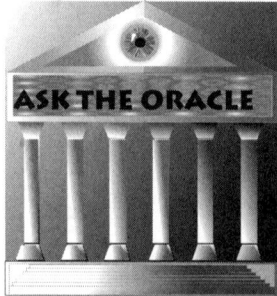

Bootsie Report

ASK THE ORACLE

In ancient Greece, the Oracle at Delphi offered advice, predictions, and sage wisdom to faithful supplicants. In the digital age, the faithful around the globe can submit their queries to the Usenet Oracle via electronic mail. Miraculously, the Usenet Oracle responds in a timely manner, dispensing well-informed insight with sardonic wit. By special arrangement, a number of outstanding excerpts representing the collected wisdom of the Oracle appear in the *Internet Insider* for the benefit of a new assemblage of supplicants.

Life on the Net is different than the real world. Trying to take in the "big picture" of Internet culture is easier said than done. Don't make the mistake of searching for a single truth that sums it all up. Life@Large brings you bit-sized chunks of the politics, customs, rituals, and culture of the Net, serving up a kernel of truth in every offering.

LIFE@LARGE

The articles included in the *Insider* were chosen through a carefully controlled process involving arbitrary impulses, luck, laziness, convenience, serendipity, and voodoo. If you don't find your favorite "net.thing" in this book, you're certainly not alone. You're encouraged to send along your personal Internet obsession for inclusion in the second edition and the *Internet Insider* online (see back page for details.).

But for now, kick back and relax while you enjoy the best of the Net from the safety and comfort of your LA-Z-Boy. Turn off your modem, shut down your computer, and let go of that damned mouse! Let the expert staff of the Internet's first tabloid newspaper bring you the news and views of the infobahn. Consider this book the hometown paper for the first settlers in cyberspace—it's The *Internet Insider*.

Ruffin Prevost
ruffin@cerf.net
November, 1994
Los Angeles, Calif.

What Is the Internet?

INTERNET
INFORMATION HIGHWAY

Ask a dozen people what the Internet is, and you're likely to get a dozen different answers. Actually, if the *Internet Insider's* field research and highly scientific polling data is any indication, you're more likely to get an answer like, "The enterwhat?" or "Whatever it is, I don't wanna buy any! Get lost!"

So perhaps in the great tradition of those 4 out of 5 dentists who recommend gum for their patients who chew gum, we should more accurately state that of the five peo-

> **EXTRA!**
> **Internet Alleged to Be Fabled Info Highway**

ple who at least *claim* to know what the Internet is, four describe it as a global collection of computer networks linked together by a common protocol.

Well, one of our interns here at the *Insider* is the son of that fifth dentist, and he's a pretty good indicator of the kind of people who make up the *Insider*. He has a few more interesting theories about exactly what the Internet is:

1. A subversive plot by the commies to distract us from the one thing that made America great: TV.
2. An alien experiment in which 25 million earthlings are compelled to peck randomly at keyboards in hopes of producing the complete works of Jvyyvnz Funxrfcrner, the greatest playwright in the galaxy!

3. Just another way for AT&T to eventually push our monthly phone bills into the triple-digit range.
4. A handy way for Elvis to keep in touch with Lisa Marie and Michael when he's on the road, far from home.
5. The worst thing to happen to male-female relationships since Monday Night Football.
6. The most media-hyped, misunderstood, anxiety-inducing buzzword of the last decade of the 20th century.
7. The thing that makes that little box next to the computer screech and hiss like a bird caught in a snake's throat.
8. The place to go if you want to meet a bunch of Star Trek-obsessed, eyeglasses-wearing, slightly overweight, technically inclined, British-comedy-loving, maladjusted, friendless white guys with too much time on their hands.
9. That place that's like the super info highway or cypress-space or something like that, right?
10. The best excuse for ignoring someone since "I didn't get your voice mail."

Fortunately, our intern is wrong, and while the list above represents some of the popular stereotypes and misconceptions about the Internet, it's something that can't be so easily defined.

The Internet is a computer network, to be sure. It spans the globe, delivers millions of pieces of electronic mail every day, and more or less forms what is known as the much-touted info highway. But it's also a place where people spend time with other people on the other end of a long wire, sharing thoughts and communicating ideas. More than anything else, for at least the short term, the Internet is a community of people exploring their similarities and differences via the written word.

Whose Idea Was the Internet, Anyway?

The history of the Internet is long and, unfortunately, not all that interesting. As a service to our readers, the *Insider* would like to offer the true but wildly ironic tale of how the Internet developed. To be able to understand it all, we'll return to that pivotal time in the 20th century, the Second World War.

In World War II, a U.S. destroyer used a peaceful tuber—the potato—to make war. Through a strange twist of fate that no historian could predict, nearly half a century later Soviet citizens would use an implement of war—the Internet—to wage peace and procure potatoes.

It seems that in 1943, the U.S.S. O'Bannon, patrolling the area around the Solomon Islands, came upon a Japanese submarine. After their conning tower was shot off, the Japanese were unable to dive, lest they flood their damaged sub. So rather than subject themselves to the huge guns of the O'Bannon, the Japanese commander pulled his sub alongside the destroyer, so close that the big ship's guns couldn't be angled down to fire on the sub.

The Japanese came topside (perhaps in an attempt to raid the O'Bannon), but the crew of the O'Bannon (which was apparently low on ammunition) was ready—they tossed scores of potatoes at the Japanese, who were convinced they were being subjected to an intense grenade attack. The Japanese crew quickly scrambled back inside and submerged their sub, which promptly sank.

Shortly afterwards, the U.S. dropped the first atomic bombs on Japan, ending the war. Realizing the devastating effect a nuclear war would have on a country's communications infrastructure, U.S. military engineers took the destruction of Hiroshima and Nagasaki to heart when they were instructed by the Pentagon to construct a communications network over which military, research, and educational institutions could communicate, even after an all-out nuclear assault.

The Internet was born in 1969 (then called ARPAnet), and it quickly became the communications method of choice amongst cyber-inclined geeks, wonks, professors, and technocrats throughout the land—including lands across the sea and around the globe. That's right, by August 1991, when hard-line coup plotters made their move in Moscow to oust Mikhail Gorbachev from power, the Internet was a full-fledged global telecommunications network.

During the August Coup, reliable information inside the Soviet Union was scarce, as partisans battled for control of the media. Prices soared as frightened citizens hoarded everything from gasoline to goulash, including potatoes. Fearing they might never again eat an affordable potato if the coup wasn't derailed, Net-savvy Russian patriots put the inside story of the coup out across the Internet, in a last-ditch attempt to inform the public of what was really going on.

The strategy worked. The hardline media blackout and propaganda campaign was derailed, and the coup plotters were ousted from power.

In large part, thanks to the Internet—a communications network designed to help the U.S. fight and win a nuclear war with the Soviet Union—an entire nation was saved, Soviet communism soon dissolved, and potato prices stabilized, making the world safe for democracy, e-mail, and those golden McDonald's fries—even in Moscow.

Internet, Potatoes, Play Role in Fall of Communism

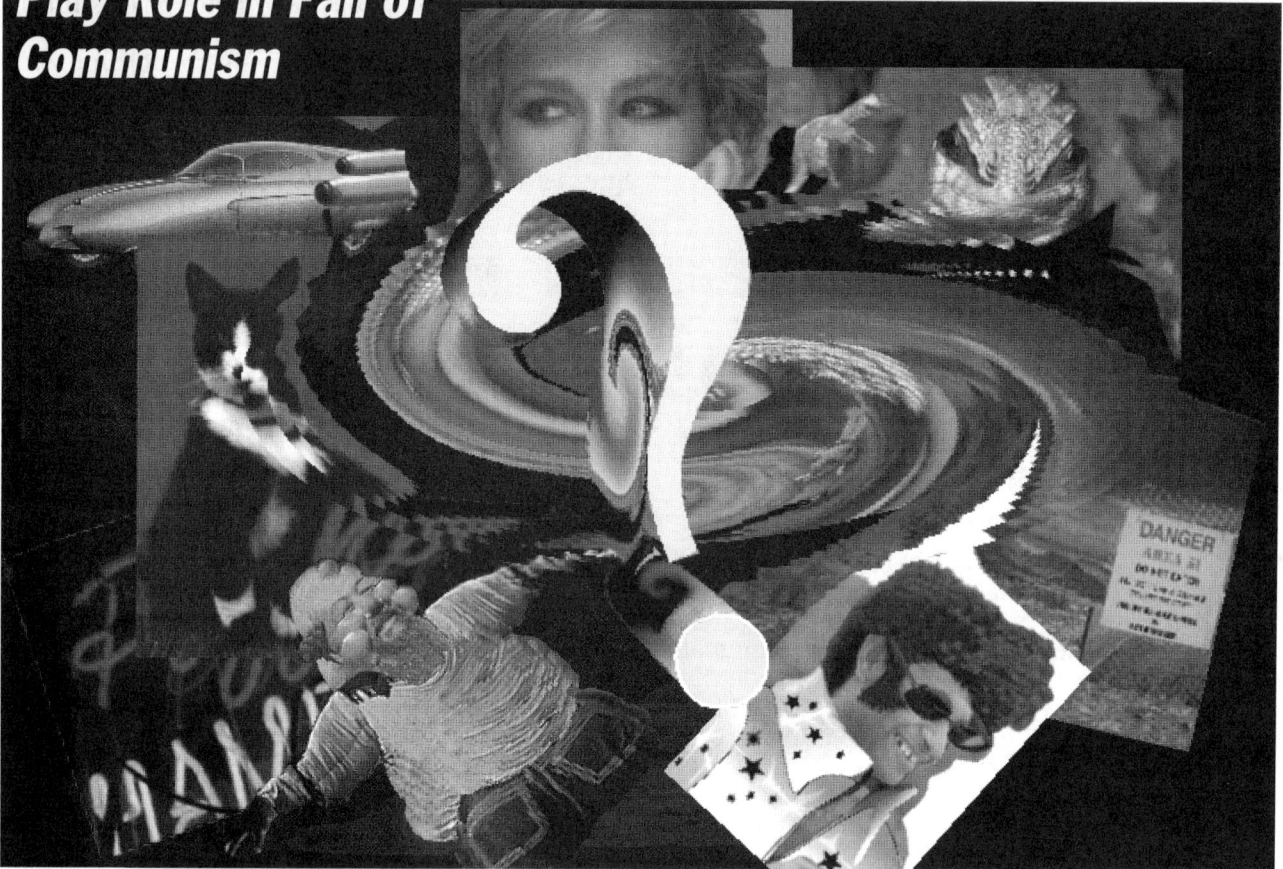

Why Join the Net?

So now that you know what the Internet is and how it came to be, you might be asking yourself, "Yeah, so, what's in it for me?" (If you still don't know what the Internet is or how it got started, then you're obviously a stickler for details. We suggest you go buy one of the thousands of Internet books out there with long, boring descriptions of how the TCP/IP protocol functions and why the NSFNet backbone is arranged in the particular configuration that it is. But don't say we didn't warn you!)

If, after reading this book, you're still wondering why you should get online, there's not much else we here at the *Insider* can say or do to convince you. Besides the wild, wacky, and gonzo side of the Net, some poor souls try to use it for serious informa-

Millions Scream: "I Can't Live Without the Internet"

tion and communication applications. A scant few of them actually succeed at this task.

If you're anxious to discover and explore a new world of ideas and information, written and composed by the people and for the people, then you already know why the Internet is growing at a rate roughly parallel to the national debt. For many, logging onto the Net goes beyond a hobby or a tool—it's an outright addiction. Who hasn't seen an e-mail deprived cyber-weenie writhe in high anxiety after four days without logging on?

Addictions aside, the Internet offers a number of clear and obvious benefits to its users, many of which are covered in this book:

☆ **Electronic mail (e-mail)**—You can send and receive messages to millions of people all over the world, including users of the most popular commercial online service. A growing number of companies and organizations are also using e-mail.

☆ **USENET newsgroups**—You can read and post messages across a huge network of newsgroups, a collection of special- and general-interest areas where millions of users swap

information and opinions on countless subjects.

☆ **Mailing lists**—Mailing lists are specialized groups of people who use private e-mail to discuss specific topics of interest. A number of public and private interest groups also use mailing lists to keep their members informed.

☆ **File archives**—Hundreds of universities and businesses offer large archives of highly useful text, graphics, and application files. You can find everything from priceless shareware to archives of fascinating political documents archived on the Net, and you can download it all via anonymous file transfer protocol (FTP) for next to nothing.

☆ **Electronic magazine (e-zine)**—The Internet's answer to the office photocopier and a screaming obsession, e-zines offer a cheap and effective way for anyone to "publish" his or her ideas and spew them out into the electronic ether. They range from the slick and professional to the crude and practically unreadable, but they all offer something of value to patient readers.

¶ **World-Wide Web**—In a race to live up to its unrequited media hype, the Web features tons of useful and frivolous information that you can explore and search for via Mosaic or another web browser. Web sites are cropping up by the thousands, and, like zines, they vary in their style and substance, but they are a vast world waiting to be discovered.

Experts Warn of Internet Addiction

These are the high points of what the Internet has to offer. If the Internet were Disneyland, they would be Space Mountain and Pirates of the Caribbean—in other words, the *main* attractions. While there are a number of other resources and attractions online, most are little more than spinning teacups or overpriced souvenirs.

Why Not to Join the Net

For too many digi-phobic yuppies struggling to stay afloat in a rising tide of complicated new technologies and perplexing cyber-trends, the Internet is a frightening monolith that they "ought" to learn how to use. Forget it. Setting up an Internet account isn't a diet, an exercise program, a worthy cause, or a phone call to your mother—in short, it isn't something you "should" do. It's not a task to be undertaken, nor is it a membership at the country club. It's not that impressive or helpful (yet), and it's by no means necessary for doing business or "keeping up" with the average person in the world.

(*continues*)

"I'd Rather Be Fishing"

net.speak

Worried about being new online? You should be. Like the new kid at school, if you're new to the Net, there are always those who will waste no time in letting you know they were there first. Here are a few words and phrases likely to confuse Net newcomers:

eager beaver—a long-winded or enthusiastic newcomer, particularly to a sex-oriented area on the Internet (drawn from old C.B. radio slang).

flame—any vitriolic debate between two or more people, usually centered around a meaningless point of contention and marked by personal slurs and insults.

John Hancock—someone with an Internet account used simply for sending and receiving mail, and nothing more.

lurker—someone who frequently hangs around a particular spot but seldom (or never) contributes to the discussion.

newbie—one who's new to the Net or a particular corner of the Net.

person of no account—one who has no e-mail account at all.

spam—to post an irrelevant message (usually an advertisement) to dozens (or sometimes thousands) of newsgroups, forcing, for instance, readers of biochemistry news in Sacramento to endure a question about a lost dog in Cleveland.

troll—to post a message aimed solely at eliciting an excited response or inciting a flame war; for instance, posting a "Windows is better than Macs" message in a Macintosh newsgroup.

(Why Not to Join, continued)

Although electronic mail is quickly becoming as essential as the phone or fax machine for business use, you don't need an Internet account to use e-mail. America Online, CompuServe, Prodigy, GEnie, and all the other major online services offer full e-mail service to the Net and all points in-between.

Finally, if you're anxious to get onto the Net just to find out what the hype is all about, the *Insider* is a much quicker, cheaper, and far less painless solution. So unless you're sure you'll use the Internet and can justify the cost, don't go blowing a big chunk of change on an Internet account just for the sake of status or prestige or to assuage techno-slacker-induced guilt.

Getting Connected

Q: How many psychiatrists does it take to change a light bulb?
A: One, but the bulb has to really *want* to change.

Getting connected to the Net is a little like being that light bulb—you have to really *want* to be a part of the Internet. No one is going to come along and make it happen, and there are often a number of complicated steps involved, so you have to be prepared to endure a good deal of

Getting Connected at the Net

hassle to make your Internet dreams become a reality.

Sadly, setting up an Internet account isn't quite as easy as screwing in a light bulb. In fact, in most cases, it's not as easy as logging onto a commercial service or a Bulletin Board System. Hell, let's be honest—sometimes it's easier to calculate the atomic weight of a cesium isotope than set up an Internet account. But the good news is that it's getting easier.

The first thing you'll need to find in your quest for Net access is a service provider. An Internet service provider is a little like a cable TV company, offering different levels and packages of service at varying prices. To find out about Internet service providers, you can start by calling the InterNIC (619-455-4600), a non-

profit organization designed to help individuals and businesses make the most of the Net. Ask them for a list of Internet Service providers.

The simplest Internet connection, a dial-up account, is fairly painless to obtain and use. They usually cost approximately $15 per month and provide a large chunk (or unlimited amount) of access time. If you are a university student or faculty member or part of a large corporation, you can probably get a free dial-up account. In addition, many cities have established "free nets," which are local phone numbers offering dial-up access that individuals can use (for free) to log onto the Net with any standard telecommunications software.

More advanced and powerful accounts include SLIP accounts (a dial-up account that offers the benefits of a direct connection to the Net but at a cost of approximately $30 per month) and dedicated connections that can cost between $150 and $500 per month. If you're not sure what kind of connection you need, start with the simplest and cheapest you can get and build from there if necessary. For more information, talk to someone at the InterNIC or pick up one of the many books or kits available offering advice on getting connected to the Internet.

Things to Do, People to See, Places to Go

Life on the Internet can be daunting. There are so many attractions to see and people to meet, you might begin to think you'll never take it all in. Have you ever been on a vacation with one of those annoying people that insists on doing *something* every single minute until there's nothing left to do? Ugh! Need we remind you of how utterly unrestful those vacations are?

Surely you recall: It's rise-and-shine first thing in the morning for a sunrise walk on the beach. Poolside breakfast starts at 7:30: melons, bagels, juice, fruit, high-energy

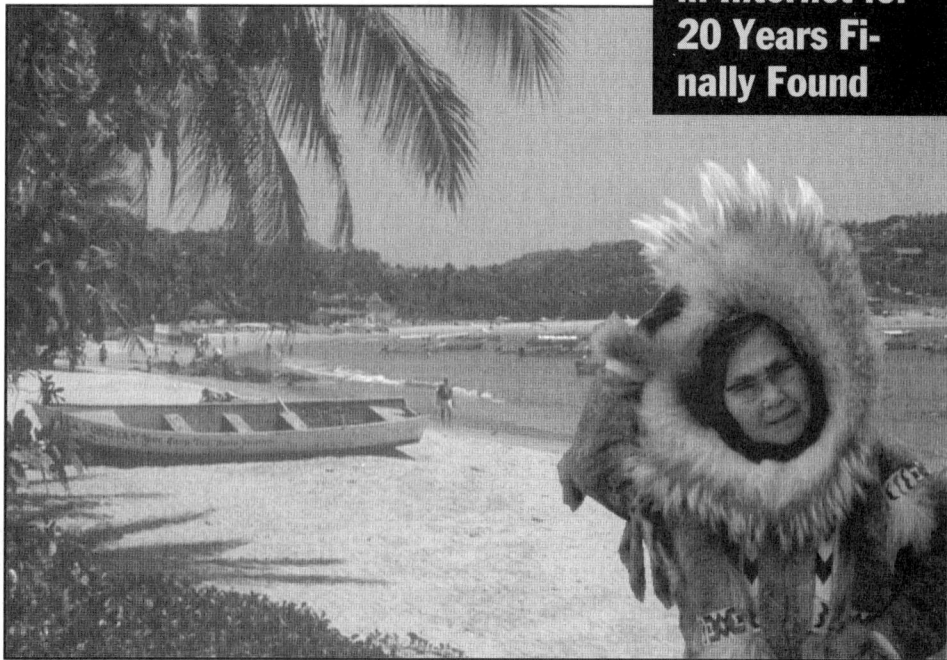

Explorer Lost in Internet for 20 Years Finally Found

bran muffins and a little low-fat yogurt. Dressed by 8:30 and ready for a morning of shopping in the quaint town square. Four-and-a-half frantic hours of intense haggling—"600 zlotveeys? I'll give you 200 zlotveeys! That's 18 cents. I'm not paying 54 cents!"—for the best deals on all the straw mats, bottle-cap earrings, and hand-carved teakwood cigarette lighter holders you can carry. Finally, around 1:00 p.m., it's time for a quick lunch of mystery gyro-meat and tandori-curry sauce on a bed of scary looking "lettuce" and other "local vegetables" before climbing onto the quaint city bus

for the 90-minute ride to the other side of town, where you spend another four hours dickering in the "peasant's bazaar" for a good deal on straw handbags, bot-

Internet Offers Impossible Dream to Info Junkies

tle-cap bracelets, and hand-carved teakwood knick-knack boxes. Then it's a jaunty taxi hop back to the hotel where you grab a drink before the donkey ride down to the marina to watch the sunset and look for sand dollars on the beach. Back to the

hotel for a shower and quick clothes change before the "full-moon feast" at the Hilton on the other side of town: all-you-can-eat deep sea bass in a lemon-jalap-

eno-bean gravy with a side of "gambi-riko-naki," or "leftover rice and shrimp tails with extra MSG and pig fat." A little post-dinner dancing (the limbo or other humiliating-to-tourists-dance) before a romantic walk along the beach at midnight. By 1:00 a.m.,

you're ready for a quick 6-hour nap before embarking on another day of rest and relaxation. (You did remember to send off a few postcards, didn't you?)

Take our advice: don't approach the Internet the same way. Relax! Take it easy. Sure, there's lots to see and do, but no matter how willy-nilly you scramble around, you won't be able to do it all. But since we know you'll try anyway, here are a few places to start:

InterNIC Scouting Report
New Web Sites
List of Mailing Lists
Zine areas
Cyberscope
Netsurf

Millions Surf Net Aimlessly

Tools of the Trade

Internet newcomers often have a bit of a problem conceptualizing exactly what the Internet is and how it works. This problem isn't helped any by the fact that the Net isn't a single, coherent "place" where you can go to find everything. In fact, if the "information highway" model of the Net were to be accurately described in realistic terms, it would involve a lot of switching from car to bus to plane to boat to pack burro as your travels take you from one region to another and from eight-lane freeways to overgrown swamp trails.

Luckily, we're not going to try to accurately describe things in realistic terms. For the sake of simplicity, we'll stick to the familiar uninformative and unrepresentative flawed analogies.

Internet veterans know what Net newcomers don't—there are a number of popular tools you can use to get around the Net more quickly and easily:

Net Vets Use Secret Weapons

Mail readers range from simple typing and mailing programs to complex applications that filter and sort e-mail. People use mail readers to send and receive e-mail and to obtain text documents from *mail servers*, automated "mail robots" that respond to specific requests issued via e-mail.

News readers are programs used for reading and/or subscribing to messages posted to the thousands of USENET newsgroups. (While lots of techno-weenies will argue that USENET isn't really an official part of the Net, we advise you to ignore them.) With a news reader, you can search, read, and post messages on thousands of topics ranging from the politics of the Pacific Rim to holiday recipes to how to build a pipe bomb.

FTP clients allow you to download all kinds of files, including text, sound, and graphics files. You can search and download from thousands of archives full of hundreds of thousands of files, including countless free and low-cost software programs.

Web Browsers are client software programs that let you search and explore the World-Wide Web, a global collection of information sites established by individuals, businesses, universities, and other organizations and institutions. You can browse all or parts of the Web using any number of popular client software programs, including Gopher clients and the ubiquitous Mosaic.

Other client software programs range from special applications that let you search for a specific file to custom tools that allow you to hop from one point to another across the Internet. There are dozens of tools, protocols, and standards used on the Net, each with a bizarre, humorous, or downright confusing name.

List Service

There are many programs and protocols on the Net that have been developed and named by college students at major research universities. Consequently, these kooky kollege kreations sport names that are a bit more . . . *creative* than the standard business software names. Rather than being saddled with a moniker like InterPlot, VisiMail, or MegaSprawl, these homegrown resources bear elaborate acronym or mascot names, like Veronica, Archie, Gopher, and so on. Here are a few suggestions from *Insider* interns on names for Net protocols, resources, and programs that we may see in the coming years:

ESOPHAGUS (Electronic Sentry Overseeing Private Household Aggregate Goods in the United States) Protocol used by the Internal Revenue Service for tracking income and automatically e-mailing tax bills to all citizens.

SERVICE (Separate Electronic Router for Virtual Information on Civil Enterprise) Back-up protocol for ESOPHAGUS.

VOMIT (Vital Official Manager of Information Tags) Tool used by low-level bureaucrats in charge of managing mundane and unimportant municipal data.

HERNIA (Hemispheric Engineering Regulations for National and International Administrations) Standard but useless protocols issued to control growth of Internet throughout U.S. and the rest of the world; largely ignored by all Net administrators.

SPASM (Standard Protocol for Attenuated Standard Mechanisms) Protocol adapted to ensure that devices attached to the Net for providing "virtual feedback" to remote users do not result in physical harm to the operators or users of those devices.

PILLAGE (Private Information and Litigation Language for Administrative and Government Endeavors) Encrypted Internet communication standard used by federal government and big business when filing threatening and abusive lawsuits against private citizens.

SUPPORT (Second Underlying Principle for Posting Overt Rants and Tirades) Net-wide standard that all upset netizens must use when posting rants, raves, and flames.

When it comes to Internet software, even the most adept power users can proudly proclaim, "I've never paid for it in my life!" That's because there are tons of free or low-cost shareware programs available for every Internet task you're likely to encounter. So when you're shopping for special Internet software, don't automatically assume that you get what you pay for. Some of the best things in life are free, especially when it comes to Internet client applications.

These Internet People Are Weird and Scary

The Net is full of weird people. And not just your ordinary weird folks, either. For instance, do you remember the weird kids from your high school? We're not talking about the odd ones that pretty much kept to themselves or "just didn't seem to fit in." We're talking about the complete square pegs that were way over the deep end. Kids like Ricky Dale McClure, who went to the high school of one *Insider* staffer who will remain nameless.

Like all true hardcore weirdos, Ricky Dale was so far out there, he was blissfully unaware that folks thought of him as . . . well, *different*. As far as he was concerned, he was just fine, and it was the rest of the world that was screwed up. Ricky Dale drove a hearse to school every day, and on the days when he didn't eat his brown-bag lunch from his usual spot in the apple tree outside the lunchroom, he would lie down in the back of his hearse and eat.

Ricky Dale wore a long, black cape with a red lining (of course) because it tended to lend a dra-

matic flare to his entrances and exits (not that they needed any extra flare at all). Unlike your ordinary, garden variety fruit, Ricky Dale was vocal and outspoken and assumed the other kids were dying to hear his opinions and ideas. If you said something to Ricky Dale that he vehemently disagreed with (which included pretty much anything you might say), he would scoop up a handful of dirt and stick it in his mouth, then spit it high into the air. We can only guess this was his special way of expressing his distaste for what you had to say.

Then there was the time he climbed the fire escape to the second-story landing outside Mr. Parker's shop class and pulled his pants down and . . . well, never mind. You get the picture. Ricky Dale was a free spirit, unfettered by the normal social conventions that bind the rest of us—refusing to serve as a slave to the demands of conformity. Needless to say, Ricky Dale would be right at home on the Internet, roaming the info highways with an online nickname like "DarkDale" and spouting off his opinions at the drop of a hat, spitting virtual dirt at anyone who dares to disagree.

Without the social pressures and instant feedback of face-to-face interaction, the Internet tends to serve as a gathering place (or perhaps a breeding ground) for people who don't do so well in the interpersonal interaction department. Not surprisingly, they don't do much better online. Without the visual cues of facial expressions or subtleties of verbal timing and intonation, a lot of what's "said" on the Net comes across with all the wit and grace of a dying mackerel.

We're by no means trying to suggest that the Internet is populated entirely by maladjusted lunatics with a lust for confrontation and the social graces of a constipated yak. In fact, only about *half* the folks online are like that, the other half are quite pleasant. OK, maybe not half of all netizens are goofballs, but there's certainly a higher percentage of strange birds online than in your average movie line or office elevator. Our advice is simple—don't make any sudden moves, ignore any attempts aimed at inciting your ire, and just remember that very few Internet death threats are ever carried out.

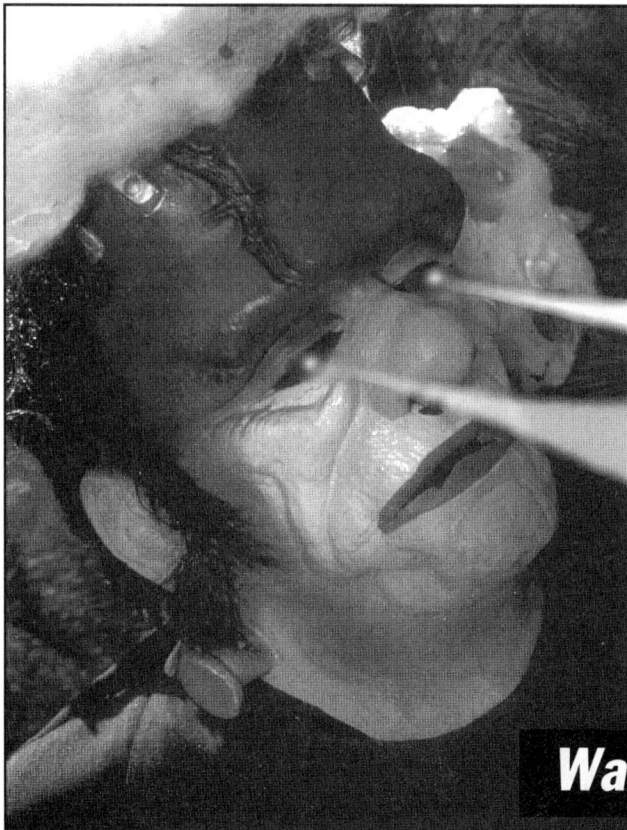

Watch Out for Internuts!

In all seriousness, the Internet has its share of scary people, but there are plenty of great, friendly, engaging people online also. If you never take the time to get to know them, then you'll never know what you're missing.

The Scary World of Internet Nuts

To help you integrate seamlessly into the strange new world of the Net, we're proud to offer a few humble suggestions on what to do and what not to do while online. While these tips hold true for any online communications, they're especially helpful for those engaged in newsgroup and mailing list discussions.

List Service

DO	DON'T
State your points calmly and clearly	Rant and rave at the drop of a hat
Criticize the logic or facts behind a statement	Attack the person who made the statement
Express your points clearly and succinctly	Ramble on for the joy of hearing yourself type
Check the FAQ files for obvious information	Ask a question that has been answered 1,000 times already
Keep your comments aimed at the topic at hand	Discuss Arena football on the bagpipe mailing list
Ignore folks who are simply trying to irk you	Let yourself be sucked into unresolvable debates

Cyberspace Populated With Scary Weirdos

I Still Haven't Found What I'm Looking for

The same goes for the huge collections of resources and information on the Net. If you can't find what you're looking for online, then it's likely to be because you haven't looked in the right place, not because the information isn't there. But you can't expect to just stumble on what you're looking for. Browsing and grazing for information is fun, but not particularly productive.

If you're serious about finding useful information on the Internet, spend a few bucks and spring for one of the many excellent books available offering hundreds of pages of listings of Internet information and resources. *The Internet Yellow Pages, Second Edition* ($29.95, by Harley Hahn and Rick Stout, published by Osborne McGraw-Hill) is the well-thumbed, dog-eared choice of most members of the *Insider* staff, but there are plenty of fine books available on the subject.

Finally, if you decide the Internet is not for you, that's OK too. Don't feel compelled to bow to the peer pressure and techno-snobbery of the digital elite. Like the wilds of the great outdoors, the fabled electronic frontier of the Internet is not for everyone. Besides, with resources like the *Internet Insider* around to bring you the best of the Net in convenient book form, there's hardly a need to log on. Feel free to sit back, relax and ignore the Internet completely. Just don't be upset when folks start calling you "informationally challenged" or "telecommunications-deprived," and don't say we didn't warn you. ■

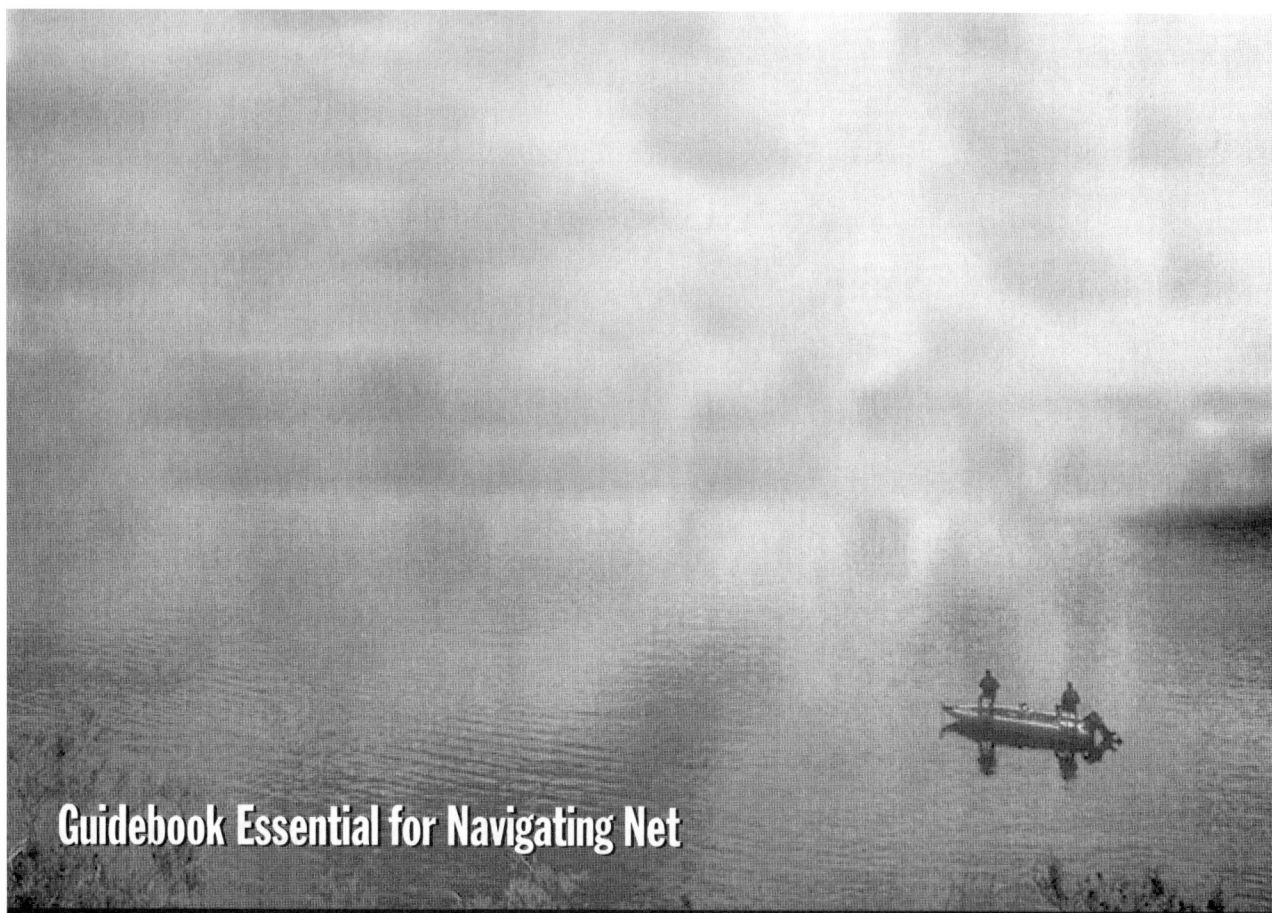

Guidebook Essential for Navigating Net

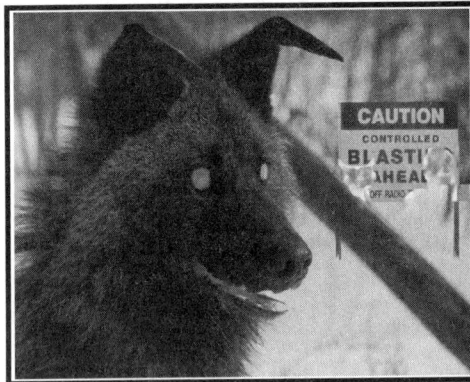

WANTED

DEAD OR ALIVE!

Lucky

Identifying features:
Cataracts in both eyes
Answers to most four-letter words

$10,000

REWARD

They Call Him Lucky– But He's Not!

A lot of strange dog stories float around the **rec.pets.dogs newsgroup**, and the folks in **talk.politics.animal** have a long list of tales

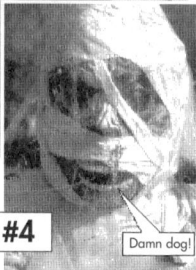

"LUCKY"

VICTIM #4

Damn dog!

about mistreated mutts, but the hottest pet rumor of late concerns a dog with the unlikely name of Lucky. The scuttlebutt on Lucky was that he was a guide dog who ended up leading two former masters to their deaths.

The *Insider* is proud to report that this rumor is false. Lucky is actually responsible for the deaths of four former blind owners. According to an October 1993 report in the *Europa Times*, Lucky has been involved in at least four unfortunate, yet unrelated accidents.

VICTIM #5

"Lucky is basically a damn good guide dog," dog trainer Ernst Gerber told reporters at a press conference. "He just needs a little brush-up on some elementary skills, that's all."

Regarding the disturbing news that all of Lucky's owners had died, Gerber stated, "I admit it's not an impressive record on paper. He led his first owner in front of a bus, and the second off the end of a pier. He actually pushed his third owner off a railway platform just as the Cologne to Frankfurt express was approaching, and he walked his fourth owner into heavy traffic, before abandoning him and running away to safety. But, apart from epileptic fits, he has a lovely temperament. And guide dogs are difficult to train these days."

Gerber stated Lucky's fifth owner would not be informed of the dog's track record. "It would make him nervous,

VICTIM #2

and would make Lucky nervous. And when Lucky gets nervous, he's liable to do something silly." ■

Santa, Parents Conspire to Deceive Girl with Clone Dog

By Pamela Templin (mustang8@pangea.ohionet.org)

When I was young, I had a stuffed Snoopy. Snoopy was my best companion—we did everything together—I told him all my secrets. Even Santa Claus knew how important Snoopy was to me. Every Christmas, when Santa stopped by, he gave Snoopy a bath and a new bright red ribbon. Snoopy must've snuck out of bed to greet Santa, because he would always be patiently waiting under the tree every Christmas morning (guarding all my booty, no doubt).

At least . . . that's what I was led to believe.

A few years ago, I returned from college for a visit with my parents, and one evening as we were talking at dinner, Snoopy was mentioned. I began talking of my fond memories of my beloved Snoopy. And how it was amazing that my parents (a.k.a. Santa) were able to find a red ribbon that was such a perfect match *and* use the washing machine without waking me up (the washing machine was on the other side of my wall). My parents just smiled. I was to dis-

Skeptics abound on the Net. For every kook who has a wild accusation, crackpot theory, or noodle-brained idea, there's always an anti-kook close at hand to debunk, deride, or simply debase the idea or (more often) the person behind the idea.

Field research by *Internet Insider* research assistants, summer interns, and automated phone-response info-bots have indicated that 11.7 percent of all postings to newsgroups involve either 1) crackpot ideas, 2) rebuttals to crackpot ideas, or 3) personal attacks on those who post or rebut crackpot ideas. (This number is even higher—14.2 percent—following holiday weekends.)

But once in a while, you'll find someone who posts something on the Net that reads like a crackpot idea at first, but on closer examination turns out to have a kernel of truth that speaks to the very core of your being. That's how the *Internet Insider* Conspiracy Assessment Staff felt when they read Pamela Templin's "Snoopy Incident."

If you've ever been betrayed by your so-called parents, hoodwinked by your alleged friends, or bamboozled by a purported confidante, you'll no doubt experience a sick and twisted feeling of *déjà vu* when you read Templin's bizarre and shocking tale. And remember, our motto here at the *Internet Insider* : Trust everyone, then cut the cards.

INSIDE OPINION

Parents Seize Child's Best Friend, Replace with Duplicate

cover it was a smile of guilt.

"We didn't," my mother stated. Dad continued, "We bought a new one every year and threw the old one away."

"You what?!" I shouted in disbelief. "So you mean, every year I was confid-

ing in and sharing my life with . . . an *impostor Snoopy* !?"

"Well . . . yes," my father replied. "Finally, though, you went on to something else before they stopped making those. Good thing, too, or who knows what your mother and I would've had to come up with." They smiled, and we went on with my visit. But all the way back to school, I couldn't help thinking about the Impostor Snoopy.

I suppose you can imagine how this Snoopy Incident has severely affected my life. I am suspicious of waiters who say they are taking my glass for a refill. Is that *really* my glass when he returns it? While my husband showers, I check to make sure he is really the man I married. And what about my car? I am the only one I allow to wash it, and I watch while any repairs are made.

I wonder if anyone else has experienced such a conspiracy. Beware. The Snoopy Incident could be happening to you! When your friends come over, are you sure that they are really the same friends who visited yesterday? When you return home from work, are you positive those are really the exact same children you left that morning? Always write down all serial numbers. Fingerprint everyone you know.

I love my parents dearly, and in some ways, I have even forgiven them for the Snoopy Incident. But every time I go for a visit, I wonder: Is that really them?

My real parents would never have done such a thing. ∎

For years, young Pamela Templin never suspected she was the victim of a conspiracy!

Mysterious Entity Knows All, Has E-Mail Account

As a general rule, kids aren't allowed around the offices of the *Internet Insider*. They get in the way, spill things, whine, complain and—perhaps most unnerving—have an annoying habit of always asking "Why?"

That's one question no self-respecting tabloid has time to answer. Who cares why? People want to know who, what, when, where, and how, but not *why*. Never *why*! Life is complicated enough without focusing on underlying reasons, worrying about root causes, pondering subconscious motivations, or exploring *why* anything happens—or doesn't happen!

We here at the *Insider* will tell you all about the blood and carnage at a crime scene, we'll fill you in on when the senator was cheating on his wife, we'll explain exactly how the train jumped its tracks, and

Investigators claim this mysterious photo shows the Usenet Oracle in action

INSIDE

OPINION

we'll cover in detail who stole the pension fund money from the bricklayers' union. But forget about knowing *why*. That's a job for scientists, priests, and spiritual entities.

Like the Usenet Oracle, for instance. In a quiet little corner of the Net (in a university computer lab in Indiana, if you must know), a mystical, all-knowing being toils night and day, every day, to answer the really big questions of our time. Many of them are variations of one kind or another on the dreaded question, "Why?"

Why did the chicken cross the road? Why did God invent relativity? Why isn't the earth flat? Why don't they give planes more interesting names

that the 747 or F1? Why does a fierce green snake always bar the way? Why is it that once you get what you've been longing for, it suddenly loses its fascination? Even the infamous query "Why ask why?" has been among the list of unknowable truths and unanswerable questions answered by the all-knowing Usenet Oracle.

Created by Steve Kinzler, the Usenet Oracle (known by most as simply "the Oracle") is indeed one of the wonders of the digital world. It is a living, thinking, self-perpetuating electronic entity with its own personality and attributes, sustained by thousands of volunteers who are connected to the Oracle only through the tenuous strands that link one part of cyberspace to another.

The Usenet Oracle is only the latest modern incarnation of an ancient tradition of all-knowing sources of wisdom. As Kinzler states in the Oracle's FAQ file:

> *"Throughout the history of mankind, there have been many Oracles who have been consulted by many mortals, and some immortals. The great Hercules was told by the Delphic Oracle to serve Eurystheus, king of Mycenae, for twelve years to atone for the murder of his own children. It was the Oracle of Ammon who told King Cepheus to chain his daughter Andromeda to the rocks of Joppa to appease the terrible sea monster that was ravaging the coasts. That solution was never tested, though, as Perseus saved the girl in the nick of time. With the advent of the electronic age, and especially high-speed e-mail communication, the spirit of the Oracles found a new outlet, and we now recognize another great Oracle, the Usenet Oracle."*

The Oracle's workings, while apparently shrouded in mystery to the many thousands who have sought its advice, are revealed in print here for perhaps the first time, exclusively by the *Internet Insider*. The Oracle works on a surprisingly simple principle. Submit a question to the Oracle (via e-mail) and a response magically and mysteriously is returned to you (via e-mail), often before the sun rises and sets again.

The "trick" behind the Oracle is simplicity itself: all those who *ask* questions are eventually called on by the Oracle to *answer* a question. Unlike many other Net-based resources, the Oracle *thrives* on heavy traffic, meaning that a flood of questions is more likely to widen the Oracle's horizons than swamp it with a seemingly impossible list of queries to answer. In fact, according to Kinzler, "it works better the larger its community of users."

But what would motivate someone to create an Internet entity that answers questions—an electronic version of the Oracle at Delphi of ancient Greece? In short, why create the Oracle? In breaking with our policy, the *Insider* has worked to piece together *why* Steve Kinzler created the Oracle.

And in case you're still wondering "why," we're sorry to inform you that even the mighty Oracle sometimes declines to answer questions that begin with "Why," as evidenced in the oracularity below.

THE USENET ORACLE HAS PONDERED YOUR QUESTION DEEPLY. YOUR QUESTION WAS:

Why is it that once you get what you've been longing for, it suddenly loses its fascination?

AND IN RESPONSE, THUS SPAKE THE ORACLE:

I'd answer you, but then you wouldn't want to know anymore.

(answer by Evan Hunt; evanh@sco.com)

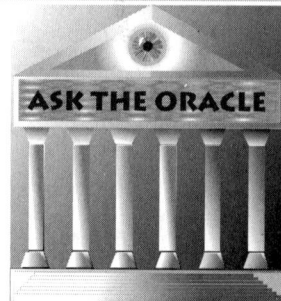

ASK THE ORACLE

As of August 17, 1994, the Oracle:

- has been asked more than 106,000 questions.
- has produced answers that are gathered into "best of" collections that have been compiled and published in 671 digests (with 10 oracularities in each digest).
- reaches some 1,900 subscribers via e-mail on a regular basis.
- reaches an estimated 81,000 readers via the rec.humor.oracle newsgroup.
- has touched the lives of some 22,000 different participants who have asked a question or given an answer.
- penetrated the borders of just about every country that has e-mail, including people on every continent except Antarctica.

List Service

Net Resources

Provided you have e-mail, you can ask the Oracle any pressing question by simply typing up your question and e-mailing it to: oracle@cs.indiana.edu. (Please don't ask "How much wood could a woodchuck chuck?" That one's been asked and answered 1,000 times.) Be sure to include the words "tell me" (as in "please tell me why we drive on a parkway and park on a driveway") somewhere in the *subject* of your message.

The Oracle will soon answer your question, automatically sending the precious revelation directly to your e-mail address. In return for answering your urgent plea, the Oracle may ask you to answer another "supplicant's" question. (A *supplicant* is anyone who asks a question of the Oracle.)

For details on how the entire process works, you can request the Oracle's Frequently Asked Questions file by sending e-mail to oracle@cs. indiana.edu with the word "help" in the subject line. Send a message with "ask me" in the subject line, and the Oracle will forward an unanswered question to you for you to answer.

But before you ask a question (and certainly before you write an answer), you should check out a few oracularities (combined questions and answers). The best ones are posted each month to the **rec.humor.oracle** newsgroup. (Posting questions to this moderated newsgroup has the same effect as e-mailing a question directly to the Oracle.) For a general, unmoderated discussion about the Oracle and oracularities, check out the **rec.humor.oracle.d** newsgroup.

To automatically receive the best oracularities via e-mail, send a message with the word "subscribe" in the subject line to oracle-request@cs.indiana.edu and send a message with "unsubscribe" in the subject line to cancel your subscription.

To read "back issues" of the best oracularities, you can download various collections archived in the /pub/oracle directory via anonymous FTP at: cs.indiana.edu. For details on accessing the archives via e-mail rather than FTP, send e-mail to mailserv@cs.indiana.edu with the word "help" in the *body* of the message.

RUMOR CONTROL

There are a number of goofy rumors surrounding the Oracle. Some, like all rumors, are roughly based in fact, some are wildly off the mark.

Steve Kinzler, the creator of the Oracle, does *not*, as some have suggested, personally write the scores of responses the Oracle issues daily. Nor is the Oracle an artificial-intelligence-style info-bot that spits back silly responses based on the content of your question, as is obvious from reading any of the "oracularities" excerpted throughout this book.

The Oracle is not a CIA project designed to surreptitiously compile a list of "known subversives" with access to e-mail. (Although that's not a bad idea . . .) One rumor suggests that oracularities have become required readings for a college course. Not exactly.

Kinzler explains: "A couple of times, a professor of an introductory computer class in Texas asked me if he could use the Oracle as an assignment to his class to learn e-mail. This resulted in a minor bombardment of the Oracle with pretty lame questions, all signed something like 'Joe Freshman, Student,' since that's what their mail software automatically appended. This started a temporary Oracle convention of characterizing Oracle losers as '<Name>, Student.'"

And what about the rumor of the Oracle actually solving problems for strangers in strange lands? Again, Kinzler explains: "There was a guy in Argentina (if I recall) who used the Oracle to ask favors of people in the U.S.—for example to call a certain toll-free number to ask a question for him and forward the answer via the Oracle—it worked, he got his answer!"

"I started the Oracle because I thought it was a really cool idea that just deserved to be done," Kinzler told the *Insider* in an exclusive interview. "It had 'hack value,' to use hacker's jargon. Once it was going, my involvement became an exercise in creating a self-sustaining system. If I could set it up so that it mostly ran itself, there'd be no reason the Oracle couldn't be a permanent fixture of cyberspace."

In fact, a thorough investigation by the *Insider* has proven Kinzler has been wildly successful in his goal, with the Oracle having answered more than 100,000 questions in about five years, with sometimes as many as 200 questions being asked of and answered by the Oracle in a single day. The magic of matching questions to answers is handled by software written by Kinzler and others—software that is always being revised and fine-tuned for optimum efficiency, though Kinzler maintains he doesn't spend much time at all ("only a few spare minutes a day") maintaining the Oracle, which is essentially a self-sustaining entity.

A vast folklore and host of stylistic and creative conventions have grown up (and continue to evolve) around the Oracle, which will become evident as you read the excerpts throughout this book. A "priesthood" of assistants helps Kinzler screen the writings of the Oracle. (A question paired with its answer is known as an *oracularity*.) While there are a number of regular contributors, the vast majority of oracularities are written by "casual" or "one-time" Oracle browsers who are drafted to write a response.

The Oracle's popularity continues to grow steadily as its fame spreads and the general population of the Net grows. "Franchise" Oracles have sprouted up for German- and Finnish-language oracularities, and Kinzler envisions the Oracle adapting to the changing face of the Net in ways that include new question-and-answer routing software and World-Wide Web compatibility.

The *Insider* is proud to bring you a handful of the best oracularities, scattered throughout this book under the heading "Ask the Oracle." While the Oracle guarantees anonymity for its contributors, those who are credited here chose to have their names included. See the "Net Resources" sidebar for details on contacting the Oracle.

Whatever the future holds for the Oracle, you can expect it to continue a thriving existence as one of the most interesting and provocative Net resources. ∎

THE USENET ORACLE HAS PONDERED YOUR QUESTION DEEPLY. YOUR QUESTION WAS:

Oracle oh wise, I'm stressing real hard! Should I get a trip to Europe or a "nice" NeXT computer for graduation?

AND IN RESPONSE, THUS SPAKE THE ORACLE:

My son, let us compare the two options systematically and the choice will become clear . . .

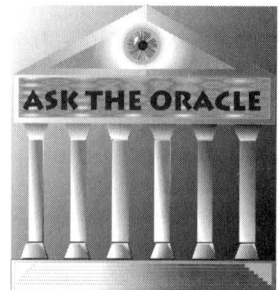

ASK THE ORACLE

Options	NeXT	Europe
Voltage	110V	220V
Storage	CD-ROM	Two bags plus carryon
Operating System	Windows/UNIX	Socialism
Speed	10.5 Hz	2 cappucinos/day
Standard languages	C/Pascal/Fortran	No standard
Expandability	Unlimited	Unlikely
M.T.B.F.	24,000 hours	24 hours
Displays	VGA-plus	Museums, nude beaches
Networking	LAN-ready	EEC
Documentation	3-volume manual	Fodor's
Portability	With special case	Not hardly
Expected date of obsolescence	1992	1992

SPONTANEOUS

Some people are *so* stupid

Haven't you ever wanted to just kill some blabber-mouth know-it-all who won't shut up? Hey, let's face it, sometimes shooting someone is the only way to settle things once and for all. Take Alexander Hamilton, for instance: Hamilton was a no-good, power-mad Federalist aristocrat who advocated a strict and merciless central government that would trample the liberties and siphon the wealth of the masses straight into the pockets of the elite. Plus, he had a bad habit of letting his flapping gums blab him into trouble with the populist heroes of the day.

In fact, in 1804, Vice President Aaron Burr was fed up with Hamilton's constantly gibbering donut-trap. Hamilton with his fat mouth had kept Burr from being voted president in 1800 (forcing him to settle for vice president—argh!), and calling Burr "a dangerous man" had cost him his chance at governor of New York in 1804. Burr exercised his only option: he challenged that sputtering moron Hamilton to a duel. The fool accepted, and they met in Weehawken Heights, N.J. Hamilton died of wounds he suffered from dueling with Burr. That shut the old guy up.

Alas, most folks throughout the modern world tend to pooh-pooh dueling as a "barbaric" ritual, calling it an "ineffective" way of settling disputes. (Ask Hamilton how effective it was!) In this high-tech age of digital bickering, we're reduced to hiring overpaid peacocks called lawyers to settle our petty disputes. Unless we have an Internet account.

On the Net, if someone rubs you the wrong way, just "flame" him or her. Unload with a written barrage of insults, snipes, put-downs, and witty rejoinders. It's OK. Honest. In fact, like dueling in the 19th century, it's a time-honored, socially acceptable custom. So the next time you feel like shooting some yabbering idiot who has written an annoying bit of nonsense, leave your gun in its holster and flame him instead.

While this section features a few of the common, everyday personal flames that crop up between embittered combatants, it also offers a look at a number of rants, raves, and diatribes that, while technically not flames, share the vitriolic spirit of a good flame, and thus deserve to be highlighted here.

Just remember, as in dueling, every flame-war has its winner and its loser, so if you intend to flame someone, make sure you flame with all your power, wit, skill, and energy.

You don't want to end up like Alexander Hamilton.

INSIDE

OPINION

COMBUSTION

net.speak

Listen up, newbies. If you expect to survive the **alt.flame** news-group without being roasted to a crisp, you'd better study these terms from the FAQ file. Don't say we didn't warn you.

:-D—*(unknown)* Secret Masonic signal indicating that someone is laughing at you behind your back.

auto-flame—*(n.)* self-deprecatory post or argument that makes poster look like an idiot.

BZZZT!—*(v.)* Sign that flamer has run out of ideas. (similar to "zzzzzzz".)

IKYABWAI—*(n.)* "I know you are but what am I?" A lame comeback flame that copies the original in-sult.

luser-*(n., derogatory)* Also "loser," "looser," and "loooooooooser."

net cop—*(n. extreme derogatory)* A whiny stool-pigeon.

spanked—*(v.)* A false claim of vic-tory. (Ex: "I spanked Pinhead off of the net!")

spank-list—*(n.)* A list of combat-ants the flamer has supposedly conquered.

List Service

Think you're bad? Think you've got the hot stuff? Ready to flame the snot out of someone? Wondering how to get started on a long and prosperous career as a flamer? Well, as the **alt.flame** FAQ file states, "Don't bother. There are too many newbies here already." But if you insist on making a fool of yourself, here are a few do's and don'ts:

☆ Don't flame by e-mail (why bother behaving like an idiot in private?)

☆ Never e-mail someone's system administrator because of something they said in **alt.flame**.

☆ Don't be a net.cop.

☆ Never apologize in **alt.flame**.

☆ Never post from an anonymous account (unless you like being called a "coward").

☆ Don't be a net.cop.

☆ Don't whine if people ignore you.

☆ Don't be a net.cop.

☆ Choose your enemy carefully.

☆ Pick on someone who is really stupid and weak (not as hard as it sounds).

☆ Don't be surprised if it turns out that you are more stupid and weak.

☆ Remember: everyone is out to get you.

☆ Don't be a net.cop.

The Twelve Commandments of Flaming

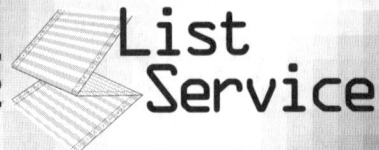

List Service

1 Make things up about your opponent: It's important to make your lies sound true. Preface your argument with the word "clearly." As in, "Clearly, Joe Bloe is a racist, and a dirtball to boot."

2 Be an armchair psychologist: You're a smart person. You've heard of Freud. You took a psychology course in college. Clearly, you're qualified to psychoanalyze your opponent. "Peach Pshawski (God Bless You!), by using the word "zucchini" in her posting, shows she has a bad case of . . .

3 Cross-post your flames: Everyone on the net is just waiting for the next literary masterpiece to leave your terminal. They're all holding their breaths until your next flame. Therefore, post everywhere.

4 Conspiracies abound: If everyone's against you, the reason can't *possibly* be that you're a jerk. There's obviously a conspiracy against you, and you will be doing the entire net a favor by exposing it.

5 Lawsuit threats: This is the reverse of Rule #4 (sort of like the Yin & Yang of flaming). Threatening a lawsuit is always considered to be in good form. "By saying that I've posted to the wrong group, B. Didley has libeled me, slandered me, and sodomized me. See you in court, B. Didley."

6 Force them to document their claims: Even if Ralph Gagliano states outright that he likes tomato sauce on his pasta, you should demand documentation. If *Newsweek* hasn't written an article on Ralph's pasta preferences, then Ralph's obviously lying.

7 Use foreign phrases: French is good, but Latin is the *lingua franca* of flaming. You should use the words "ad hominem" at least three times per article. Other favorite Latin phrases are "ad nauseum," "vini, vidi, vinci," and "fetuccini alfredo."

8 Tell 'em how smart you are: Why use intelligent arguments to convince them you're smart, when all you have to do is tell them? State that you're a member of Mensa or Mega Dorks of America. Tell them the scores you received on every exam since high school. "I got an 800 on my SATs, LSATs, GREs, MCATs, and I can also spell the word *premeiotic*."

9 Accuse your opponent of censorship: It is your right as an American citizen to post whatever the hell you want to the Net (as guaranteed by the 37th Amendment, I think). Anyone who tries to limit your cross-posting or squelch a flame war is either a communist, a fascist, or both.

10 Doubt their existence: You've never actually seen your opponent, have you? And since you're the center of the universe, you should have seen them by now, shouldn't you? Therefore, *they don't exist*! This is the beauty of flamers' logic.

11 Lie, cheat, steal, leave the toilet seat up.

12 When in doubt, insult: If you forget the other 11 rules, remember this one. At some point during your wonderful career as a flamer, you will undoubtedly end up in a flame war with someone who is better than you. This person will expose your lies, tear apart your arguments, make you look generally like a bozo. At this point, there's only one thing to do: insult the dirtbag! "Oh yeah? Well, your mother does strange things with . . . "

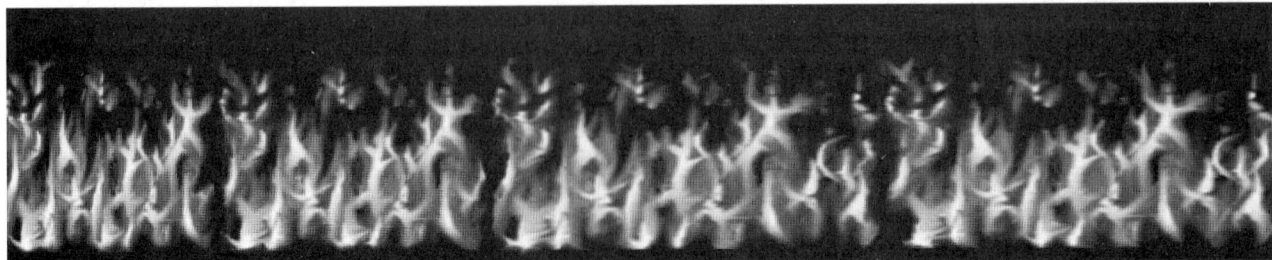

LIFE @ LARGE

MARKETING . . . FLAME ON!

From: Harold Deen McClure (HDMcClure@gibbs.oit.unc.edu)

I drink Sprite because I'm thirsty, not because I want to be part of the crowd.

I'm getting really sick of being marketed to. I don't mind someone trying to sell me something, that's capitalism. But lately, I'm convinced that I'm nothing more than a blatantly obvious demographic profile waiting to be exploited—separated from my "disposable" income.

Take, for instance, all those commercials that are trying to get "Generation X" (whatever that is) to buy Product X. For instance: Sprite's "Obey Your Thirst" campaign, in which the guy says, "I don't drink it to be cool, I drink Sprite because I'm thirsty, not because I want to be part of the in crowd. I drink Sprite because I like it." The commercial only mentions Sprite 57 times, as if "Gen X" were too stupid to pick up on the product, and as if we're too stupid to know when we're being blatantly marketed to.

Same with those ridiculous "Coors Lite Channel" commercials, featuring this snippet: "Tonight on the Coors Light Channel: Buying A Flannel, on Joe the Slacker." Is Coors so stupid it doesn't get it that "we" hate being called "slacker." And if a 38-year-old ad exec—who just got divorced and upgraded from his BMW to a Lexus to compensate for his shortcomings—is just now figuring out that "slackers wear flannel," then does he really think he's smart enough to trick us into thinking: "Hey, I'm a flannel-wearing slacker just like Joe. I'll drink Coors!"

You see a lot of the same thing in technical advertising and promotional crap, where whoever writes the ad copy knows nothing about either the details of how the technology works, or the truth about how it's used, or the culture surrounding it. Cruise the Net. Surf the Highway. Spank the Mon-

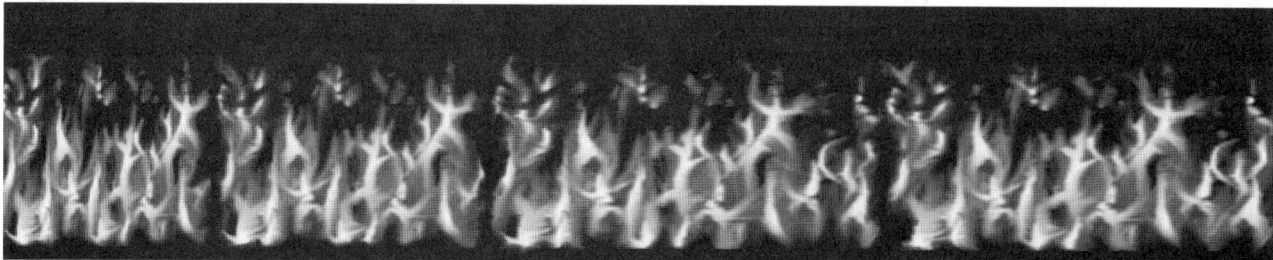

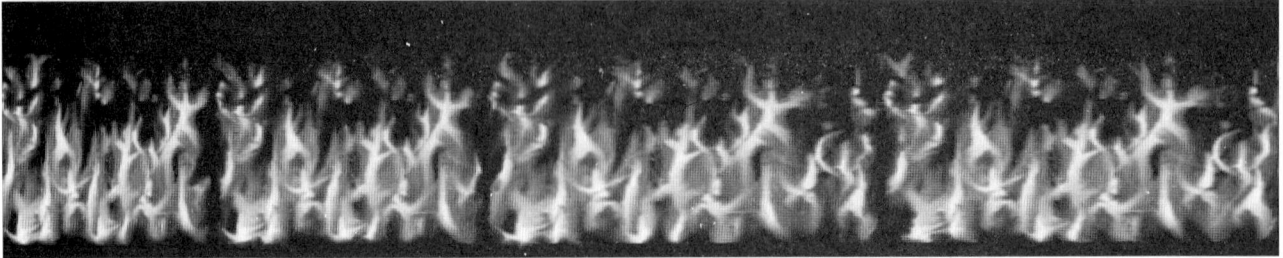

key. Fork the Cash Over to Us. "Purchase the Product," they might as well just say. How's this for a shoe-selling slogan: "Just Buy It."

And what about those GEnie ads (really now, an online service owned by General Electric!?!?!), painting AOL and CompuServe as services for nerds? And I suppose GEnie is where the kewl dudes hang out? Who gives a crap what's cool? How much does it cost and what's on the service? (Notice that's exactly what they don't tell you.)

And don't even get me started on those damned AT&T commercials. I was watching Sumo wrestling on the Japanese channel the other night (the Hawaiian guy is still the champ and is 12-0 for this "season"), and one of those "You Will" commercials came on, only it was in Japanese and featured Japanese actors. And instead of sending a fax from the beach, or tucking in the baby via the videophone, the people in these commercials were doing some very cyberjizzbotic stuff, like conference-calling each other over their car-computer-video-phone-map-geo-positioning terminals. Obviously, AT&T is dumbing-down what "We Will" be doing in America and teching-up what "They Will" be doing in Japan. Jacking up or down the cyberjizzbot quotient depending on the demographic. How very demographically correct!

I'm reaching critical mass, so I think I'll end this diatribe now before it spins out of control and becomes too much to stop. Remember, Just Do It and Obey Your Thirst for that which is Always Coca-Cola, because You Will!

From: Sedar Cockwekk (sera@elec.apana.org.au)

In a previous article, rimshotg@aol.com wrote:
> There's no description of this newsgroup [**alt.flame**], so I was wondering what's it for?

First of all, Rimshot, let me welcome you on behalf of this newsgroup. I speak for all of us when I say we're glad you joined us!! This newsgroup is for the discussion of flames, fires, barbecues, and gas cooktops and other forms of combustion. Unfortunately a few people have started disrupting this newsgroup with petty bickering and arguments, and endless, highly offensive sexual innuendo, but don't let that discourage you. Please make a few test postings to make sure your messages are getting through before you make proper posts.

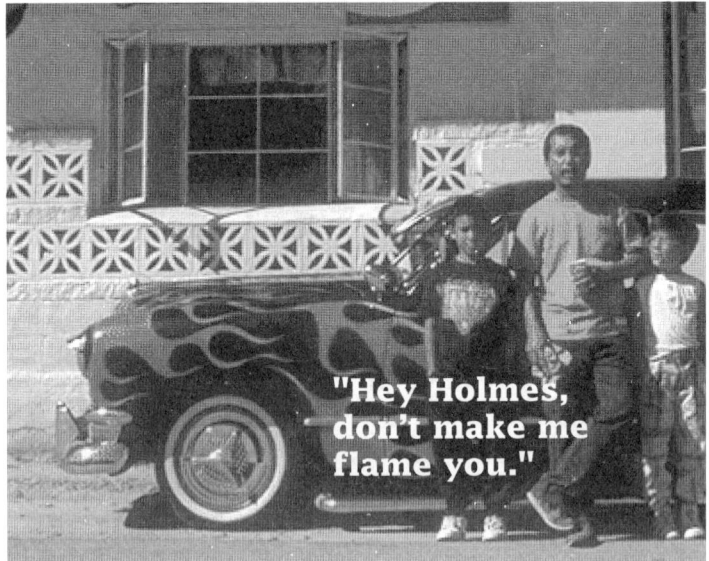

"Hey Holmes, don't make me flame you."

If you think the **alt.flame** newsgroup is a merry, happy playground where silly college kids post goofy insults to each other, think again. These guys mean war. They take their flaming seriously. And they don't want new recruits like you fouling up their area. (**Point #1** in the **alt.flame** FAQ is "*Go away, newbie. Nobody wants you here.*")

Here's some simple advice. Because you're a newbie (a newcomer to the group), others will try to suck you into a *flame war* (a protracted and

LIFE @ LARGE

heated exchange of flames). Don't fall for their *flame bait* (messages tossed out in hopes of suckering in and inflaming a newbie or other easily manipulated mark). By all means, this doesn't mean you shouldn't flame. Just pick your flames carefully, know what you're getting into, and remember: flame smart and flame safe.

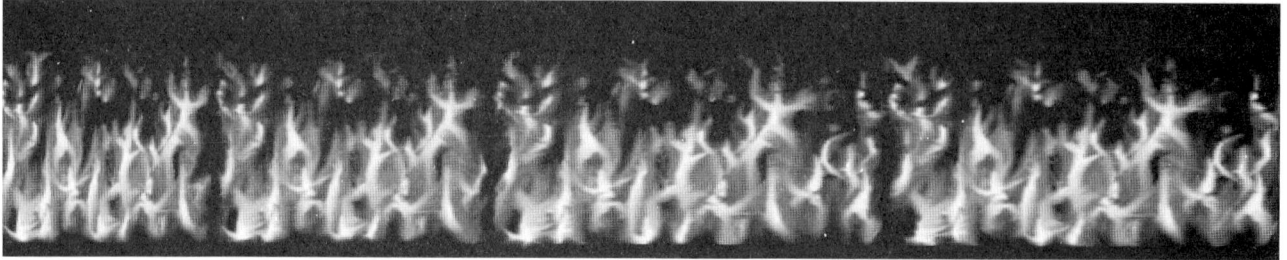

MEAT FLAMED ON NET!

From: "Mastermind" (Krempel@stpc.wi.LeidenUniv.nl)

There seems to be some commotion about people who eat meat. Well, I eat meat and I'm proud of it. Why do I eat meat, you say?? Well, isn't it obvious? To continue my existence and, at the same time, to minimize the amount of suffering I inflict upon the world. Let me explain: If you kill a cow, that's enough meat for me to live on for days, weeks even. Do you guys have any idea how many patatoes will have to die horribly by being boiled in water (or frying oil, on weekends and holidays) to provide that kind of nourishment?

Also, if you shoot a cow through the head, it's dead. No more pain, no more suffering. If you cut a potato in half, it's not dead. With some effort, both halves could grow into full-vegged potato plants. Instead of getting the mercifully quick death of a cow, *billions* of potatoes are being skinned alive, cut into little pieces, and boiled in

Mmmooo!

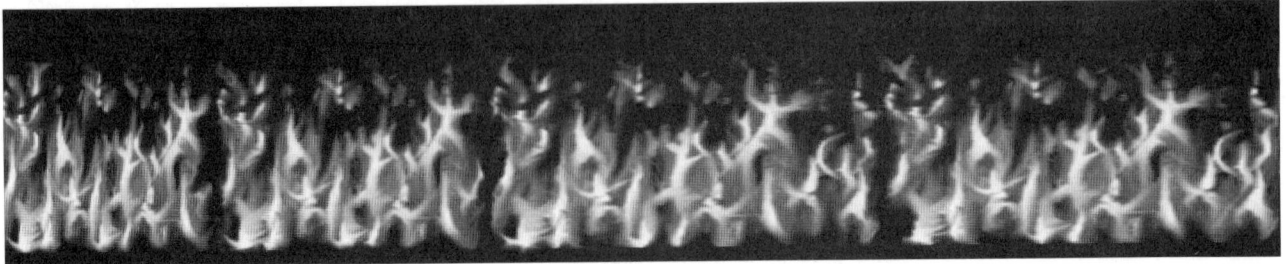

hot water or oil. The same goes for countless other species of vegetables.

So, what does this tell us about vegetarians? Well, for one thing they're mass murderers and psychopaths who can think of nothing better to do than invent new ways to bring innocent vegetables to a horrible end. Some go even as far as to swallow them alive! Imagine the death cry of a small, innocent Brussels sprout, calling for its parent while being slowly dissolved in stomach acid.

I do not object to people who eat vegetables in general. I know that sometimes they can be a necessary addition to one's diet. However, I cannot see why anyone would want to eat more than is strictly necessary for his/her well-being. Why then all this unnecessary suffering? Why then—when a diet of meat, milk, vitamin pills, and the occasional carrot will suffice—do they persist in slaughtering so many vegetables every day? I'll tell you why. Because they're nothing but a bunch of neo-fascist pigs who enjoy the torture and needless suffering of other beings.

They hide behind a facade of morality and good intentions, like so many of their kind, but in the privacy of their own kitchen their distorted minds come out and turn ordinary household appliances into instruments of torture. Merely killing the victims is not enough. No, they continue to experiment with them. "Let's try smothering them." "Let's try frying." "Let's try baking them in oil." These are only some of the methods used by these degenerate mutants of the human race. And they even advertise their religion! They actively defend their way of life and try to persuade others to join them. They have even infiltrated the Net, and use it to further their habits and ideas.

No more, I say! Let the crusade against these poor excuses for human beings begin! Join the Anti-Veggie Nazi Lobby (AVNL). Join your local Vegetables Rights Group (VRG). For those of us who prefer action above words, join the Flora Liberation Front! (FLF) Take action *now*! ∎

When **"Fighting O.J. Simpson"** was offered up as a topic of discussion in the **rec.martial-arts** newsgroup, one upset reader wrote:

"Get real! What type of subject is this to be put under martial arts? Do any of you have a life?"

To which Robert Agar-Hutton (robert@winghigh.demon.co.uk) responded:

"No, but when you get one, buy a spare for me."

"(This is my first flame! Sorry it's not very good.)"

LIFE @ LARGE

Sources at NASA report that at 12:05 p.m. EDT on July 24, 1994, for no apparent reason, the Earth suddenly slipped off its axis and plunged into the sun. Then, oddly, it resumed its orbit as though nothing had happened. Scientists were amazed that no apparent damage was caused by this incident and that no one on Earth seems to have noticed. Said one guy in Houston, "I guess with all this O.J. stuff on TV, no one's paying much attention to anything else."

Reporting from the edge of credibility, I'm Juan Bootsie. Contact Juan Bootsie at: an31291@anon.penet.fi or check out his archives via FTP in the /pub/hamlet directory at ftp.netcom.com.

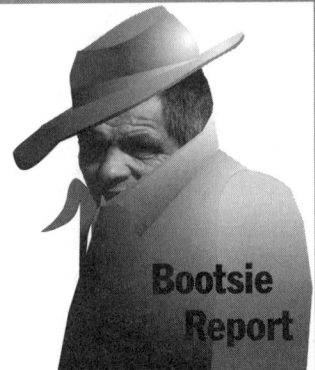

Bootsie Report

Bootsie Report

Just as I was preparing to dig into my swordfish (lunch at Spago is such a well-deserved break in my hectic day) who should walk in but Johnny Carson himself. I wanted to find out the real deal behind this supposed feud between him and successor Jay Leno, so I stepped over to his table. Mr. Carson seemed in excellent spirits when I appeared tableside, then he gave me a sidelong glance and said, "I'd like to see a menu, Pancho!"

Well, let me tell you, it's been a long time since anyone got away with mistaking me for a waiter. Let's just say I taught Johnny a few Spanish phrases you won't be hearing on TeleMundo anytime soon! He wasn't too happy with the impromptu Español tutoring, so needless to say,

A lot of fuss is made these days over the high ideals of "responsible journalism" and the "role of the media" and all that sort of nonsense. Well, we here at the *Insider* don't live our lives in a vacuum (however much we'd like to), and we're not insensitive to complaints of the tabloid press sensationalizing and exploiting the news to turn a quick buck.

But let's be honest. A robust and engaged spin on the news is a tradition that goes back to before the turn of the century in America. Has the world forgotten the likes of William Randolph Hearst (founding father of so-called "yellow journalism"), who built an empire of 18 newspapers and nine magazines? The Hearst papers' wild-eyed accounts of events in Cuba helped bring about the Spanish-American War in 1898.

Hearst loved fearless, bombastic, no-holds-barred journalists who followed a lead to the ends of the earth—reporters like Juan Bootsie. If Hearst were alive today, there's no doubt Juan Bootsie would be his ace reporter.

Juan's column, "The Bootsie Report," appears regularly in a number of newsgroups—including **talk.rumors**, **talk.bizarre**, **alt.showbiz.gossip**, **alt.timewasters** and **misc.misc**—with an estimated readership larger than that of the *Chicago Tribune*. His column is picked up and carried by a number of commercial online services, including America Online and Delphi, and his fans inhabit every corner of the globe, with regular readers in Europe, Africa, Asia, and Australia.

By special arrangement, the *Internet Insider* is pleased to present the best of Juan Bootsie's reports, originally published throughout the Internet. You'll no doubt notice that Juan pulls no punches and spares no details in casting the harsh light of truth on the darkest corners of showbiz, global politics, and high finance. Juan tells it like it is, and isn't afraid to . . . er, *embellish* his reports with the details we know you crave.

So, if you find Juan's reporting "at the edge of credibility" and you're dying to hear us admit that we may have bent the truth or exaggerated a few details now and then (we prefer to think of it as creating a "virtual account" of our own perceived reality), we'll plead "guity as charged." But c'mon, we've never started a war!

this reporter had to request a doggy bag for the swordfish.

And Wolfgang was none too happy to oblige, either. Said something about a tab I had no idea I was running. Well, excuuuuse me for leaving home without my American Impress cárd, Mr. Puck! Stuck me back in the kitchen, where I made a none too grand an exit as soon as his fry cook looked the other way.

Oh, well, I thought the swordfish was a little dry anyway. ■

Reporting from the edge of credibility, I'm Juan Bootsie.

Contact Juan Bootsie at: an31291@anon.penet.fi or check out his archives via FTP in the /pub/hamlet directory at ftp.netcom.com.

Canadian Love Slaves Devoted to Gemütlichkeit

There are times when you're searching for a specific word to capture a thought or feeling or state of mind, but either because you ignored your vocabulary homework throughout high school or because you're simply left hanging by the shallowness of the English language (probably the former), you just can't think of

INSIDE

OPINION

the right word. A thesaurus is no help—for instance, have you ever tried to find another word for "thesaurus?"—it's not even in there!

That's when we here at the *Insider* like to fall back on a fancy-sounding foreign word or phrase. And if we can't think of a real foreign word, then, hell, we just make one up. Who'll ever know the difference? Well, the Germans, for starters. Those people have words for *everything*, including that cozy sense of secure well-being you get when you're comfortable and relaxed amidst familiar surroundings: *gemütlichkeit*. (Look it up. It's really a real word.)

Apparently, the home economics curriculum in Canada in the 1950s placed a very high priority on *gemütlichkeit*. An excerpt from an Ontario school home econ text recently turned up on the Internet describing how the faithful homemaker can achieve an atmosphere of perfect *gemütlichkeit* for her hard-toiling hubby. Incidentally, isn't it funny how the Internet works that way sometimes, like some stupid, three-legged dog that digs up fossilized information and plops it in your lap with a moronic, self-satisfied doggy-grin.

In a piece originally called "The Fascinating Womanhood Way to Welcome a Man When He Comes Home From Work," would-be subservient housewives are given strict and specific instructions on how to treat their husbands and create the perfect post-work atmosphere of total and complete *gemütlichkeit*. Leave it to a modern technology to resurrect and offer up for public ridicule the dogma of the past. Techno-*déjà vu*? Digiresurrectiscorn? There's gotta be a word for that.

GET YOUR WORK DONE: Plan your tasks with an eye on the clock. Finish or interrupt them an hour before he is expected. Your anguished cry, "Are you home already?" is not exactly a warm welcome.

HAVE THE DINNER READY: Plan ahead, even the night before to have a delicious meal, on time. This is a way of letting him know that you have been thinking about him and are concerned about his needs. Most men are hungry when they come home and the prospects of a good meal are part of the warm welcome needed.

PREPARE YOURSELF: Take 15 minutes to rest so you will be refreshed when he arrives. This will also make you happy to see him instead of too tired to care.

Turn off the worry and be glad to be alive and grateful for the man who is going to walk in. While you are resting you can be thinking about your Fascinating Womanhood assignment and all you can do to make him happy and give his spirits a lift. When you arise, take care of your appearance. Touch up your makeup, put a ribbon in your hair and be fresh looking. He has just been with a lot of work-weary people. Be a little gay and a little more interesting. His boring day may need a lift.

CLEAR AWAY THE CLUTTER: Make one last trip through the main part of the house just before your husband arrives, gathering up school books, toys, paper, etc. in a bucket or wastebasketandputthem in the back bedroom for sorting later. Then run a dustclothoverthetables. Yourhusbandwillfeelhe has reached a haven of rest and order and it will giveyoualifttoo.Having the house in order is another way of letting him know that you care and have planned for this homecoming.

PREPARE THE CHILDREN: Take just a few minutes to wash the children's hands and faces (if they are small), comb their hair, and if necessary change their clothes. They are little treasures and he would like to see them look the part.

to see him. Tell him that it is good to have him home. This may make his day worthwhile. If there is any romance left in you, he needs it now.

SOME DON'TS: Don't greet him with problems and complaints. Solve the problems you can before he gets home and save those you must discuss with him until later in the evening. Also, don't complain if he is late for dinner. Count this as a minor problem when compared with what he might have gone through that day. Don't allow the children to rush at him with problems or requests. Allow them to briefly greet their father but save demands for later.

LISTEN TO HIM: You may have a dozen things to tell him, but the moment of his arrival is not the time. Let him talk first, then he will be a more responsive listener later.

MAKE THE EVENING HIS: Never complain if he does not take you out to dinner or to other places of entertainment. Instead, try to understand his world of strain and pressure, his need to be home and to relax. If he is cross or irritable, never fight back. Again, try to understand his world of strain.

THE GOAL: Try to make your home a place of peace and order where your husband can renew himself in body and spirit. Then add to this the application of all the

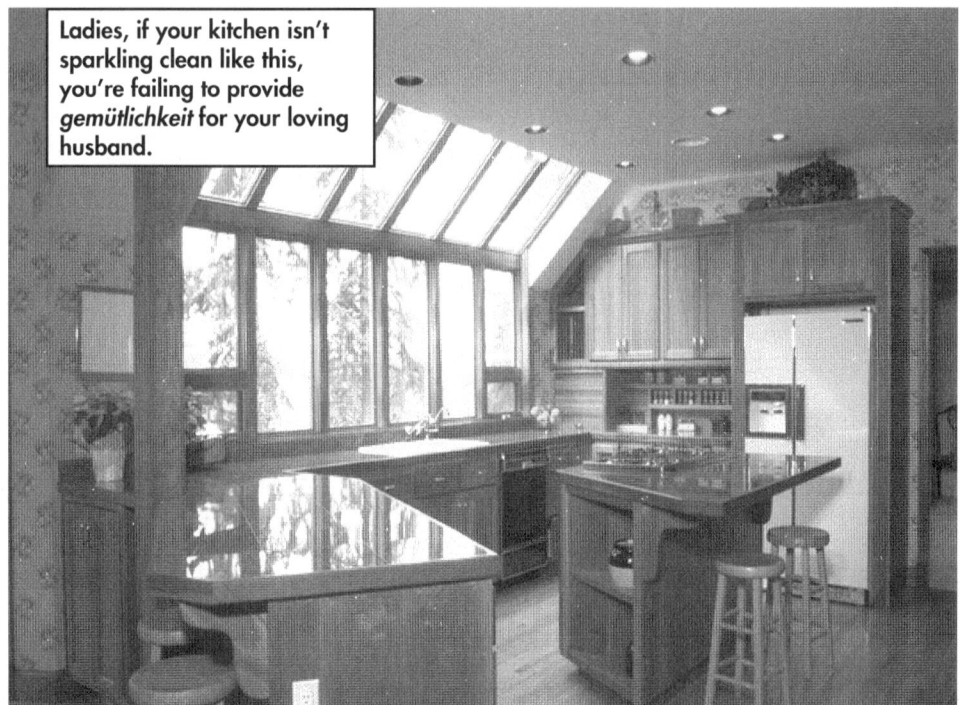

Ladies, if your kitchen isn't sparkling clean like this, you're failing to provide *gemütlichkeit* for your loving husband.

MINIMIZE ALL NOISE: Especially give heed to this if your husband has to join rush-hour traffic. At the time of his arrival, eliminate noise of washer, dryer, dishwasher or vacuum. Try to encourage the children to be quiet at the time of their father's arrival. Let them be a little noisy beforehand to get it out of their system.

BE HAPPY TO SEE HIM: Greet him with a warm smile and act glad

MAKE HIM COMFORTABLE: Have him lean back into a comfortable chair or suggest he lie down in the bedroom. Have a cool or warm drink ready for him. Arrange his pillow and offer to massage his neck and shoulders and take off his shoes. Don't insist on this however. Turn on music if it is one of his pleasures. Speak in a soft, soothing, pleasant voice. Allow him to relax—to unwind.

principles of Fascinating Womanhood and your husband *will want to come home.* He will rather be with you than with anyone else in the world and will spend whatever time he can possibly spare with you. Try living all of these rules for his homecoming and see what happens. This is the way to bring a man home to your side, not by pressure, persuasion or moral obligation. ∎

The Socks Chronicles

In this ongoing series of behind-the-scenes looks at the inner workings of the White House, the *Internet Insider* follows Socks, America's First Cat, through another harrowing press conference. In this official White House document obtained exclusively by the *Insider*, you'll see how the White House press corps is once again sidetracked from the real issues facing our government to consider the life and times of that lovable kitty, Socks.

Why the media obsession with the President's cat? Is there something the White House doesn't want us to know? Is "Socks" a secret code word that sends reporters into a trance of distraction and diversion? Why does the press offer only a 30-second sound bite from a 30-minute meeting? Does Socks prefer frolicking in the Lincoln Bedroom or on the South Lawn? These questions and more are answered as we present the first installment of: *The Socks Chronicles.*

The place: The White House Briefing Room.

The time: March 23, 1993; 9:49 a.m. E.S.T.

The players: Clinton Administration spokesperson Dee Dee Myers and the White House press corps.

In this episode, Dee Dee Myers discusses the possibility that Ambassador Caputo and Special Envoy Pezzullo can help bring peace to poverty-stricken Haiti. Meanwhile, the media questions whether Socks gave President Clinton a nasty gash across the face. Will the dictators surrender power in Haiti? Will Socks be punished for scratching? Let's listen.

Ms. Myers: Today's press conference will begin at 1:02 p.m. for you broadcast folks. We are going to work really hard to start it right at 1:02 p.m.

Q: That means he starts the walk or he opens his mouth, or what?

Q: That's Central time or Eastern time?

Ms. Myers: Well, that's a good question. I would like to have him at the podium ready to start speaking at 1:02 p.m.

Q: Have you told the President this?

Ms. Myers: Yes, and we will continue to reinforce that. I think it might be interesting to start a pool to see exactly when he might arrive. No, we will try very hard to have him standing at the podium at 1:02 p.m., which means he'll start the walk 30 seconds before that.

Q: Will there be an opening statement, Dee Dee?

Ms. Myers: Very brief opening statement.

Q: About?

Q: Foreign or domestic?

Ms. Myers: Domestic.

Q: Geared toward the Senate vote or—

Ms. Myers: Yes, geared toward the economic plan generally.

Q: Dee Dee, in terms of the President's schedule and jogging, three days have elapsed that we haven't seen him jogging. Is he jogging? Is he jogging on the track? What's happening?

Ms. Myers: I don't know. I think maybe he's just been tired and has been sleeping in a little in the morning. I don't think there's any major policy implications.

Q: Has he used the track yet?

Ms. Myers: No. It was completed over the weekend but I don't believe he's used it yet.

Q: Dee Dee, do we have a final list of contributors to that?

Ms. Myers: Pardon me?

Q: Do you have a final list of contributors to the track? I mean is that public?

Ms. Myers: I'll double-check on that.

Q: Did you have an explanation for the gash? Was that Socks?

Ms. Myers: No, no. I believe the President cut himself shaving yesterday.

Q: What do you do now to pressure Aristide to give in and accept some form of amnesty?

Ms. Myers: Ambassador Caputo and Special Envoy Pezzullo are continuing to work down there. I believe they're making progress and we're encouraged by the process. Other than that, we'll continue to work through the process.

Q: Do you have any state visits planned at all? We haven't had any yet.

Ms. Myers: We haven't had any yet. I don't know of any that are on the schedule.

Q: Does he travel next week?

Ms. Myers: Unclear.

Q: Is he trying to save money by having working visits?

Ms. Myers: No, but you can only have one state visit per country per administration.

Q: Is there going to be a dedication of the jogging track?

Ms. Myers: I don't expect any formal ceremony.

Q: Why not?

Ms. Myers: Helen, you can plan one and host it, jog on it. (*Laughter.*) Only if you jog will we have a formal ceremony. (*Laughter.*)

Q: All right, it's a deal.

photo courtesy of The White House

What's Your Takeaway?

By Terry Bjork (73754.3076@compuserve.com)

When my grandparents transferred to Thompson Falls in 1960, my father bought Heap Far Lodge from my grandfather for $100, and it became *our* cabin. Eighty-nine miles, exactly, over Rogers Pass from our house in Great Falls, it was a world away from work and school and the city and the heat of the plains. We grew up there, in the Rockies, on weekends, and summer vacations, among the Ponderosa pines, and shooting stars and lupine and beargrass, creeks full of cutthroat trout and frogs, unpeopled trails to mountain lakes and lookout towers and alpine meadows, and night skies clear and brilliant with the Milky Way and the Big Dipper and the Pleiades and Orion the Hunter, and sometimes the Northern Lights.

In the evenings, my dad lit the Coleman lantern and we'd play cards, Shanghai and 31 and hearts. Then, when it was time for bed, my mom would read us a story, usually "The Terrible Ollie," and when

There is a popular and widely believed myth in American history that Abraham Lincoln composed his Gettysburg Address on the back of an envelope during the train ride to Gettysburg. Despite the hope and promise this pervasive falsehood offers to procrastinating speechwriters everywhere, it is entirely untrue.

Having been roundly criticized months earlier by a hostile press for delivering a speech deemed too informal and inappropriate at a ceremony in Antietam, Lincoln was determined to silence his critics with his speech at Gettysburg. He worked on the Gettysburg Address for two weeks, writing five drafts and releasing a mostly final version to the Associated Press before delivering it at the dedication of the national cemetery at Gettysburg.

The unfortunate truth is that most any written work scribbled on an envelope during a train ride is likely to be singularly inferior to something that has been crafted and polished for two weeks. Unfortunately, too much of what is written and posted to the Internet is the digital-age equivalent of a frantic, train-bound envelope-scribble.

While we at the *Insider* are the first to admit that we love a good frantic envelope-scribble, we also can't help asking ourselves: what are the places on the Net where the truly *serious* writers hang out? From the looks of things, Nerdnosh is one of those places.

The *Nerdnosh Story Digest* is a mailing list where folks exchange stories about themselves and their lives. Most are true, some are fictional, but almost all of them are engaging and make for great reading. Understandably, the members of Nerdnosh were slightly apprehensive when the *Insider* approached them about covering their mailing list.

They felt, and rightly so, that the Nerdnosh was something worth protecting from the more savage members of the electronic frontier. The misgivings of the group, Nerdnosh list-supervisor Tim Bowden told the *Insider*, were "similar to the citizens of a remote and scenic hamlet fearing the deluge of tourists if the travel column goes into the papers."

Consider Terry Bjork's "What's Your Takeaway?"—in which he discusses one of those "takeaway" moments of life, one you'll cherish and take with you everywhere—to be a native-written travel column on the Nerdnosh mailing list. And there are several other pieces from the "Nosh" covered by the *Insider*, so after reading these samples, you should come away with a strong impression of what life around the Nosh's storytelling campfire is like.

If you're interested in sharing good stories with good friends, you might stop by the Nerdnosh campfire. But be sure to honor the local customs, and if you're going to share a story of your own, try to spend a little more time and effort writing it than Lincoln is alleged to have spent on the Gettysburg Address.

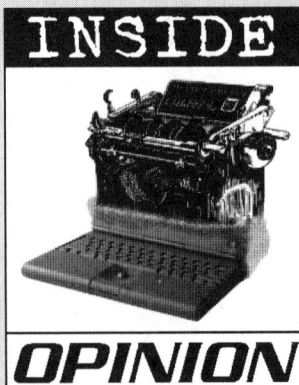

INSIDE

OPINION

she was done, my dad would throw a few last pieces of wood into the stove and turn down the lantern, and we'd watch in the dark as the lantern slowly went down until there was only the glow of two "panther eyes."

**A June blanket
of snow — a "takeaway moment."**

And when we went to the cabin, it was just us, my family, away from all the other relatives and friends and neighbors. But as we grew up, and moved away, the trips to the cabin were more often alone, or with friends, and finally with families of our own.

In May of one year, I was talking to my sister long distance, and she told me that she and her boyfriend, my parents, my friend Kevin, and my brother and his family were all going to meet at the cabin for my brother's birthday in June. "It would sure be nice if you two could come up and join us,"

she said, and I agreed, but didn't think it very likely, two airfares from Phoenix, with a new house payment and all. "I hope you all have a good time," I wished her.

I talked it over with the wife, though (the boss of the money), and she surprised me, saying yes, we could afford it, and furthermore, she thought it was great idea, which really surprised me. So I called Frontier Airlines, and made reservations, but to my brother's home town, not my parents'. I'd called him the night before; we'd decided on a *surprise* birthday gathering.

Anyhow, the big family reunion at the cabin was a big success, and a big surprise for my parents and sister, and a little bit cramped with all those people jammed in a one-room cabin. But we didn't care—we had fun playing cards, and all held our breath when my sister's boyfriend said "Shit!" in front of my mom, but she laughed, and then later, before my dad put more wood in the stove (it was a cold weekend, even in June), and before he turned down the lantern to make panther eyes, we talked my mom into reading us "The Terrible Ollie" from the storybook on the shelf, and she read it, how Ollie managed to steal all the treasures from the troll across the lake, and how Ollie fooled the troll into chopping off his own daughters' heads, and how Ollie fooled the troll's wife into baking herself in the oven, and finally, how Ollie made the troll look into the rising sun, and he exploded.

The next morning, June 12, my brother's birthday, was really cold, and no one wanted to be the first out of bed to build the fire, but finally my brother got up and took his two-year-old son outside with him for a trip to the outhouse, or to the truck for new diapers, or something. And then, we assumed hopefully, back in to make the fire so none of us would have to get up. But he didn't come back in right away, and we started wondering what was going on, so finally I got up and pulled back the curtains on the front window to see what was happening.

It had snowed overnight, even in June, and there were about three inches of beautiful, wet snow perched on the pine branches and the green meadow grass in front of the cabin, and on my brother's red pickup. And as we shivered, and watched through the window, my brother was having a snowball fight with his two-year-old son.

Originally published in the Nerdnosh Story Digest *mailing list. Reprinted here by permission.* ■

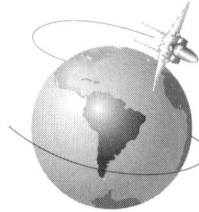

Net Resources

Unlike many places on the Net, Nerdnosh is fairly private and, in many ways, intimate. If you're not willing to share something real of yourself, you're not likely to appreciate the works published in Nerdnosh. But if you're interested in reading more works from Nerdnosh, subscribing to the mailing list, or submitting your own stories, here's how:

To subscribe, send an e-mail message to **listserv@clovis.felton.ca.us** with the word "join" as the body of the message.

For more information about the list, send the message "help" to the same address.

Back issues are available for downloading via FTP at ftp.infonet.net in the /showcase/dmorris/nerdnosh directory.

Finally, keep in mind that many of the writers who contribute to Nerdnosh are working or aspiring writers who struggle to make a living from what they write. Their works are copyrighted, each by its author, and aren't for widespread distribution or commercial reproduction without permission.

ELVIS SIGHTINGS

Everyone has an Elvis story. (You didn't think you'd make it through an entire tabloid book of Internet material without a section on Elvis, did you?) Just as practically anyone can tell you an anecdote about high school or a friend or relative's wedding, most everyone has a story about how Elvis touched his or her life—perhaps indirectly, but in a real way, just the same.

Take Craig Stinson, of Nogales, Arizona. Craig (who resembles the young Elvis in a vaguely familiar way) was all too happy to send us a letter about his Uncle James, who used to cut the King's hair. No lie. Craig will even have Uncle James pull out the scissors and show them to you, as he did for one *Insider* reporter. As far as scissors go, they don't look like anything special, but you can tell by the way Uncle James holds them (he carries them everywhere) that they're the real thing.

Then there's Betty Rathbone, of Clyde, North Carolina, a huge Elvis fan. Years ago, she had front-row seats to see the King when he came to the Asheville Civic Center. She took her camera and got a few great shots (these were of Elvis during the "later" years) before catching one of the leis the King tossed to the crowd. Her boss—a small-town dentist—was so jealous for missing the concert that he made copies of the photos and forged Presley's autograph on the back. He still shows them to his more gullible patients.

For most people on the Internet, including those who were too young to ever see the King in person or experience him at his peak, their "Elvis Moments" are limited to an "Elvis sighting." That's what keeps the **alt.elvis.sighting newsgroup** going. We may love and remember Elvis for his eccentricities: shooting the TV, dining on peanut butter and banana sandwiches, even dying on the commode, but we continue to honor him by "sighting" him everywhere, from the car care section of K-Mart to the bar at the Waldorf-Astoria.

C'mon. Admit it. You've had an "Elvis Moment" too, haven't you? Maybe you thought you saw him coming out of a crowded theater, or heard his voice on the next aisle over in the grocery store. Don't be afraid, share your moment with the rest of the world. Post it on the Net, where the King himself can read it.

INSIDE

OPINION

Could this man, gas station attendant, Norris K. Dimsdale, be the King?

ELVIS SIGHTINGS

NK NUCLEAR FACILITY

Sources indicate this shadowy figure may, in fact, be the King himself.

From: Claire Jarmey Swan (jarmeyswan@bchm.unp.ac.za)

Elvis was seen in Pietermaritzburg, Natal, South Africa last night at a seedy joint called "**Drifters**" where he was drinking beer and smoking heavily. He looked a bit "shagged out." Rumor has it he will change his hair style to avoid further recognition.

From: Chris Lugo (lugo0001@gold.tc.umn.edu)

Elvis came by my house today to fix my television set. But when he turned it on to see if it worked, the show **Hard Copy** was on proclaiming the "truth about **Michael** and **Lisa Marie**." He fell down dead right there of a heart attack and I had to put him in the garbage bin. Now Elvis is recycled newspaper somewhere in Tuba City, AZ. The King is really dead.

From: Richard Karch (rkarch@mhs.mendocino.k12.ca.us)

If you watch the opening to the **McNeil-Lehrer News Hour**, you will notice the word *Elvis* as the titles rotate from thin to thick. I also notice there is a person on the credits who has all the letters in Elvis in his name. Check it out!

From: Paul Arthur (paular@Eng.Sun.COM)

Elvis has been seen visiting **Carlos the Jackal** in Paris. Thus far, the Jackal's only visitor has been the King. Seems only right. No word on what they discussed. Elvis did mention his disappointment over the pay-per-view price for Woodstock 2, but said that **Red Hot Chili Peppers** bassist Flea was "just too damn funky."

From: Shawn Yeul
(yeul@ac.dal.ca)

Some time ago, I realized that when the King passed on (supposedly, hah!) he was too young to die and too fat to live. So where would a man of this stature go after faking his own death?

After weeks of careful research and study, I came upon a startling discovery. The real reason the North Koreans won't let anyone inspect their nuclear facilities isn't that they are hiding weapons; the answer is far more insidious than that. They are hiding Elvis. In fact, Elvis is making nuclear weapons for the North Koreans.

Ludicrous? I think not. Have you ever played "**Love Me Tender**" backwards? When you do, you will begin to learn of the depths that the King was beginning to spiral downwards into.

I think the King must be stopped. Fine, let the Communists have their little nukes, but the time has come to eliminate the King once and for all!

From: Scott R. Webb
(SRW@MED.UMICH.EDU)

The **CIA** is already working on this. Operative Jackson has deployed a story about marrying his daughter in hopes that he will return to the U.S. to save his little girl.

From: Joshua Wright
(jwright@wimsey.com)

Yeah, that's right, I saw Elvis at my local **London Drugs**. He was working the checkout. I told him that there is a newsgroup about him on the Internet and he laughed. He then told me that he likes his new life here in Vancouver, and is married with new children, living in a nice little apartment over on the east side near Hastings and Main.

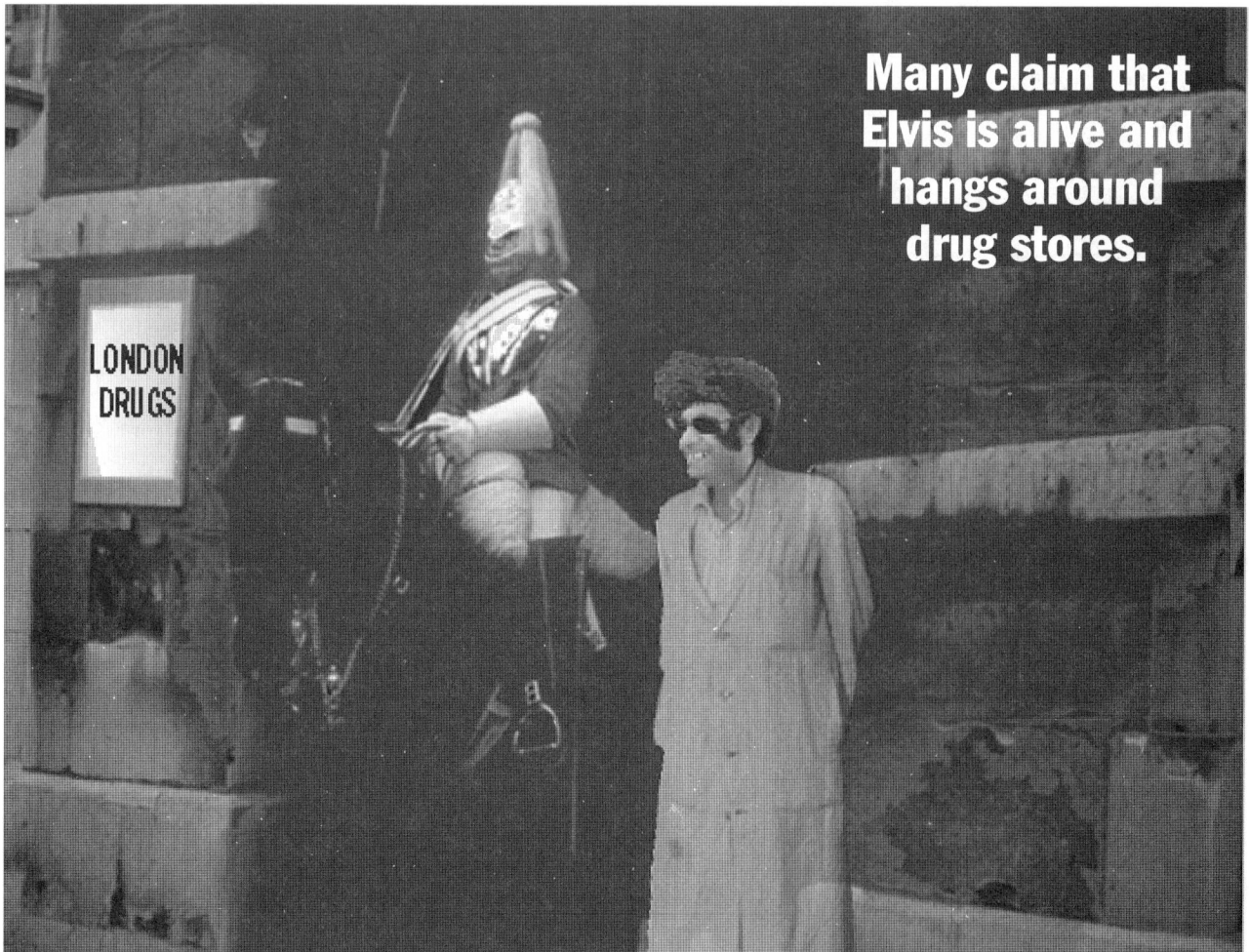

Many claim that Elvis is alive and hangs around drug stores.

LONDON DRUGS

From: acoustic4@aol.com

Have I seen Elvis? I've got a one word clue for you guys: Biosphere.

From: Kevin J. Deroos (kderoos@iastate.edu)

I saw "**Forrest Gump**" this evening, and I have one question. Was that the King doing the scene with the young Forrest? I could not help but notice that they kept the Elvis "character" somewhat blurry. I realize that he was rather slim, but he could be on some type of exercise program, like Chico-metrics or something. If it was him, then maybe that was Elvis in "**True Romance**"—the Elvis "character" was shot from behind and blurry then too.

Perhaps this is his way of reentering Hollywood.

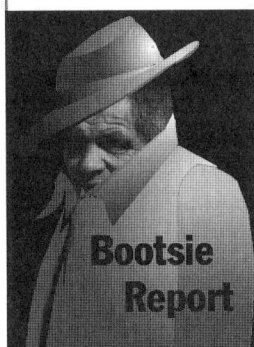

ELVIS BIRD

FIRST TIME EVER !!

Could this be Elvis's feathered friend "the Colonel?"

Bootsie Report

A collector in Newark, NJ, Thursday paid nearly a billion dollars for a messy napkin said to have been used once by Elvis Presley. The authenticity of the artifact is dubious, however, owing to the fact that the napkin is from Domino's Pizza, a chain that did not exist at the time of Elvis's death in 1977. Despite this, the collector paid for it anyway. When asked for an explanation, the collector replied, "I'm crazy!"

Reporting from the edge of credibility, I'm Juan Bootsie. Contact Juan Bootsie at: an31291@anon.penet.fi or check out his archives via FTP in the /pub/hamlet directory at ftp.netcom.com.

RUMOR CONTROL

There have been persistent rumors floating around claiming that Elvis Presley is dead. Clearly, these rumors are just that—the idle gossip of the ill-informed and the malicious lies of jealous party-poopers. Just ask anyone in **alt.elvis.sighting** and you'll find out right away that the King never died, despite what "they" say.

Imagine the shockwave of disgust that tore through the Net when *Time* magazine pronounced in September 1994: "Once again it's official: the king of rock 'n' roll died of heart disease. The Tennessee health department confirmed the 1977 coroner's report and announced it had found no evidence of falsity on the singer's death certificate." How right the conspiring media barons at *Time* were when they glibly proclaimed that "the finding probably will not put an end to the theorizing that . . . the putative father-in-law of **Michael Jackson** might not be dead at all."

In another example of the big-money media attempting to hoodwink the faithful masses, Reuters news service announced that "**the King**" is dead. Really." The blasphemy continued: "'It's typical foolishness,'" **Jack Soden**, chief executive officer of Elvis Presley Enterprises Inc., says of the latest report that Presley is alive and enrolled in a witness protection program. Mr. Presley is dead and buried at his **Graceland** mansion, thank you very much."

Maybe. Maybe not. If the report isn't true, could someone please explain why one of the *Insider's* interns recently spotted federal agents carrying a platter of peanut butter and banana sandwiches into the **Graceview Hotel** in Van Nuys?

Finally, one highly reliable source from a ranch in Santa Barbara has informed the *Insider* that not only is the King alive and well, he prowls cyberspace regularly, checking his e-mail four or five times a day. Oh, and in case you're wondering, that same source informs us that Elvis prefers Macs.

THE USENET ORACLE HAS PONDERED YOUR QUESTION DEEPLY.
YOUR QUESTION WAS:

O Oracle most wise, O Oracle most witty,
I cannot understand you 'cause my mind is itty-bitty.
Although I am unworthy, I really must inquire:
Is the singular of scissors sciss? and of pliers plier?

(question by Chris Weider; clw@bunyip.com)

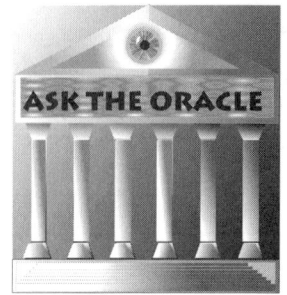

AND IN RESPONSE, THUS SPAKE THE ORACLE:

Tis true you are unworthy, with this adolescent question.
Your poetry is awful, too, but here is a suggestion:
When coming up with questions, I'd appreciate your trying
A query on the dulcet tones of The Sound of One Plier Plying.
And the singular of scissors? I must keep you in the dark
You see, I never end a poem with any cutting remark.

Your poetic license is hereby revoked.
You owe the Oracle One Grecian Urn.

(answer by Scott Minkin; sminkin@bbn.com)

... *quo vadis, Rex?*

On August 18, 1991, Soviet Defense Minister Dmitri Yazov, Vice President Gennady Yanayev, and top leaders from the KGB confined Mikhail Gorbachev at his dacha in the Crimea. The leaders of what would come to be known as the August Coup aimed to prevent Gorbachev from signing a treaty giving greater power and autonomy to the Union's member republics, an act he was scheduled to perform in two days. Instead, three days later, the attempted coup disintegrated, and by midnight on December 31 of that year, the last flags of the Soviet Union were removed forever from capitals throughout the now former Union of Soviet Socialist Republics.

When the hard-line military leaders and politicians attempted to oust Gorbachev from power, the world watched, transfixed by the drama of the unfolding events. But on the Internet, both in the U.S. and throughout the Soviet Union, Americans and Soviets were exchanging information with each other in an attempt to keep the world—but especially the Soviet people—informed of the horrifying chain of events.

At the time of the attempted coup, the Soviet Union didn't have (and still does not) a network equivalent to the Internet in the United States. While the Soviet network followed essentially the same protocols, it operated on much less sophisticated equipment and via communications lines that were far less reliable.

One of the primary Soviet networks was RELCOM, which was managed by a cooperative called Demos. The members of Demos—including Vadim and Polina Antonov, whose messages appear in this report—were instrumental in disseminating information throughout Russia and to people around the world. In some instances, people on the outside helped keep the members of Demos (and, in turn, the rest of the USSR) up to date on events inside their own country. Prof. Larry Press was one of those people on the outside feeding information and moral support to the members of Demos.

"We are witnessing a revolution of international relations toward increasingly open and mass-scale communication. And this greatly increases the role of creative and positive policies. But equally, it raises the price of mistakes—the price we must pay for adherence to outdated dogmas, routine and old thinking."

—Mikhail S. Gorbachev, address at Stanford University, Summer, 1990

☆FOILS☆COUP☆

Press, a professor of Computer Information Systems at California State University at Dominguez Hills, offered immeasurable assistance to the *Insider* in preparing this report. The week before the coup, Press co-chaired a conference on human-computer interaction in Moscow. While there, he spent several days visiting the Demos Cooperative. During the coup, Press kept in close contact with Vadim and Polina Antonov of Demos.

Monday Aug. 19, 1991
From: Vadim Antonov

". . . I've seen the tanks with my own eyes. I hope we'll be able to communicate during the next few days. Communists cannot rape the Mother Russia once again!"

About that message, Press stated that it "was sent from Moscow at 5:01 a.m. and was written by Vadim Antonov, a senior programmer at the Demos Cooperative in the Soviet Union. Demos operates a computer-based communication network which spans the Soviet Union, and within a few hours, Vadim's message had been relayed to computers in 70 Soviet cities from Leningrad in the West to Vladivostok in the East."

From that moment onward, the genie was out of the bottle, and Antonov and his countrymen exploited the Internet to their every advantage. The use of the Internet to organize the resistance and pass along vital information has been called both "an information bucket-brigade" and a "democracy wall," both of which are accurate.

Soon, the whole world was watching the events unfold, and while most people could only tune to CNN for a sketchy picture of each day's events, those with Internet access did their part to fan the flames of democracy. Luckily, Jie Liang had Internet access, and decided to post a message. He sent advice based on his experience at Tiananmen Square and called for "a *campaign to let people inside the USSR to know the truth and how the world is reacting . . . At this heavy historic moment, the Chinese people are standing by the Soviet people."*

Unfortunately, not all messages were so inspiring or helpful. In fact, while members of the Soviet resistance were trying to use the Internet to organize their movements and transfer intelligence information, the digital equivalent of the "ugly American" was clogging the communications lines, exercising his sovereign right to remote-controlled, armchair-accessed, spectator voyeurism toward the plights of the world. Here are a few examples of this type of special-interest coup-related message:

"I'd like to get an article to put in our newsletter . . . a national computer network for senior citizens . . . about the resistance using their computer networks."

And:

"I wonder if anyone who can read this message has any news on how the recent Soviet coup has affected the nascent lesbian/gay/bisexual liberation movement in the Soviet Union."

In response to a deluge of annoying and channel-clogging postings, Antonov issued this message:

"Please stop flooding the only narrow channel with bogus messages with silly questions. Note that it's neither a toy nor a means to reach your relatives or friends. We need the bandwidth to help organize the resistance. Please, do not (even unintentionally) help these fascists!"

In spite of Antonov's message, traffic rose to a high of 13,159 messages on August 21, more than twice the usual volume.

Nevertheless, news and details of events surrounding the coup attempt leaked out of the Soviet Union via the Internet, where they were picked up by the world press, including the BBC, which broadcast reports back into Russia, where, among others, Mikhail Gorbachev listened transfixed to the reports on a portable radio.

The members of Demos no doubt wondered why no one in power had pulled the plug on their network.

"At the beginning, we had no idea what was happening. We were preparing for long-term under-

---

"Political power comes from the barrel of a gun."
—Mao Tse-Tung

ground activity," Antonov said. He and his associates understood that RELCOM was the key to keeping communications alive inside the USSR. *"Computer communications are more democratic by nature than mass media like TV or newspapers, simply because they don't belong to a single entity. There's no central authority over the network. We all realized it was the only chance for us to survive."*

Ironically, the Demos headquarters was located less than a mile from KGB headquarters. The members of Demos weren't taking any chances, though, and within a short while, they had decentralized the organization of the network to make it even more difficult—if not impossible—to close down completely.

As Antonov explained to Doug Jones at the University of Iowa:

"Yes, we already prepared to shift to underground; you know—reserve nodes, backup channel, hidden locations. They'll have a hard time catching us! Anyway, our main communication line is still open and it makes us more optimistic."

Clearly, the KGB realized the power of the Internet too late to shut it down. *"During the last night of the coup, we got a strange phone call to our headquarters,"* Antonov said. *"The caller said, 'We are your users. Please give us your modem phone number.'"* Antonov knew he was on the other end of a KGB fishing expedition, since his associates obviously knew the relevant phone numbers. Instead of information on how to connect to RELCOM, Antonov states that *"we said to them rude words."*

The speed with which information raced across the Internet was astonishing. In one instance, a copy of the speech Boris Yeltsin delivered from a tank turret in front of the Russian Parliament building was forwarded throughout the Net and translated into English in a matter of hours.

"The Demos staff had learned of the coup around 6 a.m. on the 19th, and immediately began sending political information to the Soviet Union and the outside world," Prof. Larry Press said. "By 12:30 p.m., Moscow time, I was reading news releases from the independent Soviet news agency Interfax. Although outlawed [via normal media transmission] by the junta, news from Interfax, the Radio Moscow World Service, the Russian Information Agency, Northwest Information Agency (Leningrad), and Baltfax was disseminated by RELCOM throughout the coup attempt."

The raw drama of the role of the Net in foiling the coup, however, is most evident in the messages between Vadim and Polina Antonov of Demos and Prof. Larry Press, as well as others inside and outside the Soviet Union. And while the messages in this report—compiled and passed along to the *Insider* by Press—offer only a partial view of the crucial role the Internet played in thwarting the coup, they make compelling reading.

The drama of the situation is revealed in the following messages that reached Press.

The Laptop Is Mightier than the Tank

Monday Aug. 19
From: Vadim Antonov, Demos Software Cooperative

". . . I've seen the tanks with my own eyes. I hope we'll be able to communicate during the next few days. Communists cannot rape the Mother Russia once again!"

Other messages followed, and Press kept in close contact with Vadim Antonov and his wife, Polina, who is also a Demos staff member.

From Polina:

". . . maybe you'd write me what do they say on your TV about the situation, as we can't watch CNN now."

After receiving news from Press, Polina wrote:

"You can't even imagine how grateful we are for your help and support in this terrible time! The best thing is to know that we aren't alone.

"This paid me 1,000 times for time spent on-line during the coup."

Press was concerned about the safety of Vadim and Polina, and he waited anxiously for news that they were all right:

From Polina:

"Hi! Don't worry, we're OK, though frightened and angry. Moscow is full of tanks and military machines; I hate them. They try to close all mass media, they shutted up CNN an hour ago, Soviet TV transmits opera and old movies. But, thanks Heaven, these cretins don't consider RELCOM mass media or they simply forgot about it. Now we transmit information enough to put us in prison for the rest of our life :-). Hope all will turn out well at long last."

Also from Polina:

"Don't worry; the only danger for us is if they catch and arrest us, as we are sitting at home (Valera is at Demos) and distributing all the information we have. I can only hear these tanks, and, it seems, aircraft."

Vadim sent this message:

"If these dogs win, for certain they'll throw us in prison—we distributed the proclamation from Yeltsin and the Moscow and Leningrad Soviets throughout the entire Soviet Union, together with the forbidden communiqués from Interfax . . . Greetings from the underground."

Other messages, to Press and others, and even no one in particular included:

From Nizhniy Novgorod:

"Yesterday at 17:00 a rally in support of Yeltsin was held; regional deputies participated. Today at 17:00 there will be a rally in the city center where a strike committee will be formed . . . The atmosphere is calm in the city, there are no troops to be seen."

A message from Kiev:

"It is relatively quiet in Kiev as it all seems like a silly joke from here. On top of this, relevant information is not being supplied on the TV. I was on the central square at 12:30. A group of about 100 people was discussing the news."

From Enn Tyugu:

"Estonia has survived until this hour. The troops are near Tallinn and more are coming, but they have not yet got to the TV and radio centers. Latvia and Lithuanian mass media are already in the hands of the troops. Many people are around our vulnerable buildings protecting them and building barricades. Mostly heavy trucks are being used as barricades.

"Thanks for your support."

From Anonymous:

"To all people of good will! We want you to know that the democracy of the USSR is in great danger. . . Right now the center of Moscow is surrounded by tanks and soldiers . . . We need your moral support! . . . Down with the Communist tyranny!"

Eventually, that's exactly what would happen, but for the time being, the Soviet people and the members of Demos were exulting in the news that their brave and brilliant work had helped unravel a sinister attempt to enslave a nation.

From Polina:

"Really good news. Right now we're listening to the Radio Russia (without any jamming!); they told that the Eight left Moscow, no one knows where . . . Hard to believe . . . Maybe, they really run away? Radio asks for information about their location."

Also from Polina:
"Thank you, Larry!

"Now all information media are on, CNN transmits our 'Time' TV program, and I can watch them both!"

"Microprocessors and PCs are the stuff of revolutions."
—*Paul Saffo*, research fellow at Institute for the Future, Menlo Park, Calif.

"*I've heard (maybe it was CNN) that they withdraw armed forces from Baltic cities. I'm not near the parliament, I'm still at the computer, but the situation on the net became lighter now and I hope to sleep a little; it was my dream during last two days. You can't even imagine how grateful we are for your help and support in this terrible time! The best thing is to know, that we aren't alone.*

"*Cheers, Polina.*"

From George Tereshko:

"*When the dark night fell upon Moscow, RELCOM was one source of light for us. Thanks to all these brave people, we could get information and hope. I would also like to thank the people running Soviet BBSs who provided another net for information flow.*"

From Polina:

"*Dear Larry,*

"*Now Vadim and I have to do our usual work (that's so nice!) and Valera and Mike Korotaev went to sleep. They were on duty the whole night. Now there is celebration in Moscow. We just watched president Gorbachev on TV.*

"*Greetings from Natasha.*

"*Cheers, Polina.*"

But perhaps this single message best sums up the euphoria and jubilation present on the Net after the coup disintegrated.

From Dimitri Rakitin:

WE WON !!!

According to Larry Press, RELCOM, the major Soviet computer communications

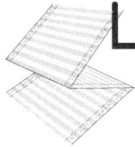

List Service

network, was crucial to a number of organizations within the former Soviet Union, not just the underground fighting the attempted coup. A look at the list of organizations that rely on RELCOM may explain why it was impossible to close down this communications link during the days of the coup attempt. The list of organizations with RELCOM computers includes

11 government agencies, including the USSR and Russian Finance Ministries,

15 foreign and domestic publications and news services including AP, UPI, the German Press Agency, and Financial Times,

20 commodity, raw material and stock exchanges,

26 universities and university departments, including several machines at Moscow State and Leningrad Universities,

96 limiteds, corporations, enterprises, companies, firms or banks, joint ventures or small ventures, and

117 scientific and research institutes, nearly all in technical fields such as mathematics and physics.

Net Foils Coup, Helps Bring Fall of Communism

Russia is a country rife with rumors, even during times of relative peace and normality. So it was no surprise that rumors spread like wildfire during the coup. Word had it that Gorbachev was dead, or had fled to safety elsewhere in Europe, or perhaps in the U.S.

The presence of the Internet inside the Soviet Union no doubt helped dispel many of these rumors, but now, years after the failed coup, a couple of irresistible rumors still linger.

One popular rumor puts forth the seemingly outrageous claim that Gorbachev anticipated just such a coup, and prepared for it by upgrading the Soviet Union's communications infrastructure. While it's difficult to credit Gorbachev with such a specific prescience, his former science advisor Yevgeny Velikhov has stated that during the first days of Perestroika, he and Gorbachev undertook a concerted campaign to install satellite dishes across the USSR. Their thinking, which history has proved correct, was that the low-cost global

Curious about how Russians communicate over the Internet without typing in English? An excerpt from a file of Russian e-mail addresses shows you how Cyrillic script looks translated to standard ASCII characters. Remember, we're trained professionals, don't try this at home.

LIFE @ LARGE

<R>sANKTPETERBURGSKIJ gOSUDARSTWENNYJ pEDAGOGI^ESKIJ iNSTITUT<L>

Leningr*adskij Gosud*arstvennyj Pedagog*icheskij Instit*ut

St. Petersburg State Pedagogical Institute

<R>191186 sANKTPETERBURG/ nABEREVNAQ rEKI mOJKI, 48<L>

48 Mojka River Embankment/ St. Petersburg 191186

#N	ila.spb.su
#S	PC/AT; MS DOS
#O	Joint Venture Interlacs
#C	Klaus Peter Meyer
#E	meyer@ila.spb.su
#T	+7 812 272 5204
#P	Chajkovskogo Ul. 43, SU-191194, Leningrad, USSR
##	¡_"'_/_-_-_-'_"'_-_-_/_' _ÿ_"_'_"_ /__ÏÓ_'_ÎÂ _ÿ_'

"Information Technology and Stalinism Don't Mix"
—InfoWorld ed*itorial headline*

RUMOR CONTROL

communications facilitated by satellite dishes would make it impossible to undo the changes they began.

Another widespread report claims that, in his efforts to foil the coup, Boris Yeltsin kept in close contact with the world from deep inside his blockaded parliament building via a borrowed cellular phone. Later reports seem to substantiate this rumor, stating that it was American business executive Paul Tatum, visiting Moscow to negotiate financing for a new hotel in Moscow, who loaned Yeltsin the cellular phone.

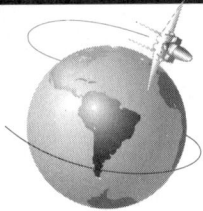

Net Resources

Interested in keeping up with Russia and the Commonwealth Republics via the Internet? Although they aren't always easy to navigate, there are a number of helpful resources available.

You can start by keeping an eye on the following newsgroups:

soc.culture.soviet,
alt.current-events,
alt.activism
soc.rights.human.

"We pretend to work and they pretend to pay us."
—old Soviet worker joke

For daily news updates via e-mail (in digest form) on events in Russia, central Asia, and central and eastern Europe, you'll want to check out the RFE/RL Daily Report. Send e-mail to: rferl-daily-report-request@Admina.rferl.org.

For the full text of Russian laws, decrees, edicts, statutes, and other official documents, check out the LABAS database. For more information, write to: Ross Teasley, Holingshead and Harris, 71740.637@compuserve.com.

For information on GlasNet, the first non-profit, non-governmental telecommunications network to be established in the Soviet Union, send e-mail to David Caulkins, GlasNet USA,dcaulkins@igc.org.

For access to a large number of files about Russia and the former Soviet Union—including information on Russian apartment prices, e-mail addresses, consumer goods prices, a copy of the Russian constitution, an English-Russian dictionary, travel tips, and even timetables for the trains in Moscow—check out the /pub/cyrillic directory at: ftp.cs.umd.edu. While many of these files are actually written in Cyrillic (Russian script), many are in English.

For more information on the ongoing work of connecting Russia and the Commonwealth states to the Internet, subscribe to the SUEARN-L mailing list. Send e-mail to: suearn-l@ubvm.bitnet. ■

THE USENET ORACLE HAS PONDERED YOUR QUESTION DEEPLY. YOUR QUESTION WAS:

Oracle of wonders, I want to marry my girlfriend Cathy. What does our future look like? Children? Money? Affairs?

AND IN RESPONSE, THUS SPAKE THE ORACLE:

Your future looks bleak, oh young hormone-infested mortal. Your inability to communicate in complete sentences will be nothing but trouble for you. You will drive Cathy crazy saying things like, "How are the wedding invitations coming? Envelopes? Stamps? Post?" Later, after you are married, Cathy will become increasingly irritable after being exposed to your odd mannerism for a month or two. "Honey, where are my socks? Argyle? Sweat? Dark?" Unfortunately, things will only go downhill from there. "Cathy, why don't we have any friends? Turtle? Banana? Apocalypse?" You will become increasingly moody and withdrawn.

"Dammit, don't let the Kaiser steal my string! Swingtown! Megaphone? Grunties!" As a last ditch effort, Cathy will dunk your head in a vat of strawberry yogurt to shake this affliction from you. Ultimately, you will die a solitary man, feeble and wrinkled. Your last words being, "Curse you Red Baron! You and all your ugly kin! Greenspan? Rosebud! Phlegm." Hey, you asked.

You owe the Oracle a Sears Mediterranean-style color console television set with 25" screen and real simulated woodgrain finish. (Mine is on the fritz.)

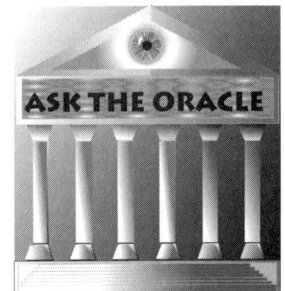

ASK THE ORACLE

America's Love Affair with Hate

A**mericans love laughing *with* famous people, but we much prefer laughing *at* them.

Which is something that lies at the root of what must be one of the hardest lessons for celebrities to learn: we don't draw much of a distinction between loving them and hating them. Instead, it seems enough to be merely obsessed with a star. A corollary to that lesson is the realization that the press can just as easily tear you to shreds as dip you in gold. Some celebs are foolish enough to actually believe the old show biz maxim that "even bad press is better than no press." Well, not necessarily: just ask Helmut Jahn. Or O.J. Simpson, for that matter. (More on Helmut later.)

Alas, the O.J. debacle features everything Americans (and especially the press) have always loved in a sleazy story: a bloody and violent crime, a sexy blond woman, intrigue, rank exploitation, shocking accusations and equally shocking denials, celebrities, betrayal, fools, fall guys, mystery witnesses, racial tension, car chases, big-money legal wranglings, and live action footage. Throw in virtual reality, rap music, abortion and Rush Limbaugh and we'd have a story no American could ignore.

But we here at the *Insider* are convinced that it's the spectacle of public failure—the shocking fall from such a dazzling height by such a beloved celebrity—that has most focused our attention on The Juice. (Trust us, we're in the tabloid business: it's our job to know these things.) Besides, O.J. isn't the only fallen angel to be devoured by the same media that made him—he's just the latest in a long list ranging from Charlie Chaplin to Joe McCarthy to Roseanne.

But forget the power of the press and instead consider: what do the people think? Only the Internet reflects what the general public *really* wants to know about the O.J. affair. Namely, what Marcia Clark will wear to court, how fast Ben & Jerry's ice cream melts, and whether Libyan Col. Muammar Qaddafi had anything to do with the impound-lot break-in of the white Ford Bronco. O.J. himself (**O.J.@aol.com**) even made a brief but decisive appearance in the **alt.fan.O.J.simpson** newsgroup when he "confessed" to millions of Internet users.

At least O.J. has the background and training of an actor, sports star, and overall celebrity to help him deal with the situation. He could have been like poor Helmut Jahn—finally, we get to Helmut—completely unprepared to handle the public spotlight. Oh, sure, Helmut was expecting a *little* media attention. After all, nearly a thousand architects had gathered to see him receive a special award from the president of the American Institute of Architects. They were honoring Helmut Jahn at the opening of Kansas City's $20 million Kemper Arena, which he designed. Unfortunately, Helmut got more attention than he bargained for when, during the event, the roof literally caved in.

We're not laughing *with* you, Helmut (or O.J.), we're laughing *at* you.

INSIDE

OPINION

51

Getting the VIP Treatment in L.A. County Lock-Up

By Stan Noffler (Snofledog@aol.com)

Boy am I really getting sick of reading all the junk you people post on this group. Do you actually think you have a single new thought to add to the legal debate or matters of evidence? As an example of the kind of stuff you ought to be writing, and since I'm a native Los Angeleno, I'd like to touch on a few things about this whole O.J. affair that are so exclusively L.A. that it couldn't happen anywhere else.

First of all, you've got a celebrity suspect. And not just a sports star, but a former sports star who's only remained in the public eye because he's "made it" as a broadcaster, pitchman, and movie straight man. This kind of junk isn't just an L.A. thing—it's invented, patented, and bred out here.

Second, there's the whole "surrender on your own terms" nonsense. If a celebrity was wanted for murder in New York, Cincinnati, or Spartanburg, the cops would go extra-tough on the guy just to prove they aren't swayed by the suspect's celebrity status. But not here. Just as there are VIP rooms in all the L.A. night clubs where only Jack Nicholson and Tori Spelling can sit around and look cool, there is apparently a VIP program for celebrity fugitives ranging from Sean Penn to Chàrles Keating, both of whom were locked down in L.A. In fact, there's a special wing in the L.A. county lockup where celebrities, rotten cops, and snitches are kept "for their own protection."

Third, there's the commuter escape. O.J. couldn't just head for Mexico or get on a plane and jet off to Argentina. I thought for a while he was headed for Canada. (By the way, here's a handy tip: Canada has no death penalty and will not extradite a fugitive facing a possible death penalty to any state or nation that has the death penalty until the convicting state or nation makes a binding promise to not prosecute the suspect for murder in the first degree—i.e., no death penalty threat). At any rate, O.J. chose to wander aimlessly around the L.A. freeways in rush hour traffic.

Fourth, let's note the cellular phone. You never hear of suspects in *Iowa* cutting deals on the cell phone while they're still fleeing pursuit. Can you imagine O.J.'s conversations with SWAT guys?! I'd love to go into the recording studio and do a prO.J.ect along the lines of "The O.J. Tapes," where we "recreate" what "might have been said" in those cell calls. Probably O.J. calling his agent to see what kind of offers he's had on the TV-movie rights before he decides whether to call it a day or add another bizarre chapter to his story.

Finally, there's "the media." Now I'm not denying that "the media" descends on anything that even *smells* like a lead-off for "Inside Copy" or "Hard Edition." I haven't forgotten Baby Jessica or those whales trapped in the Arctic ice. But if O.J. had been a farmer in South Dakota fleeing justice in his Ford pickup, you'd be lucky to have the local Action 7 news crew chasing him in the Chevy Suburban Action 7-Mobile. You sure as hell wouldn't have five or six choppers offering live coverage of the "escape" effort. I was watching that junk on TV, and there were 8 channels *plus* Larry King showing O.J. and the Bronco rolling along the 405.

So, I'm a little upset that:

1 that jerk decided to pick rush hour on a Friday evening to clog up the 5 and 405 (which, according to Cal-Trans are the two busiest roads in the *world* under normal circumstances) to go driving around like a freaked-out lunatic.

2 he can afford a flock of mouthpieces in three-piece suits to argue he was a victim of a dysfunction-of-the-week and get off like Lyle and Eric.

3 O.J. is being held in the VIP wing of county lock-down. (Hey, we could all argue that we need special protection in prison, but the solution isn't to quarantine the rich, famous, and former cops, the answer is to make prisons safer.)

4 he wasn't arrested and convicted and locked down and put through some serious rehabilitation the first 9 times he beat his wife. (The cops responded to domestic violence calls 8 times at O.J.'s, the ninth she had to be hospitalized so the cops had little choice but to arrest him. He pleaded "no contest.")

But I suppose I'm most upset about the whole traffic situation. During the freeway chase, I turned on the scanner to try to catch a little background chatter and maybe a snatch of what O.J. might be chatting about on his cell phone. All I got was people talking about O.J. on their cell phones. I checked the cop bands, and what I got was cops chattering about how funny, messed up and bizarre it all was. Two of them were laughing about having to close off the on-ramps to the 405 freeway and giggled about how funny it was when people complained to them about not being able to get home or whatever.
Ugh.

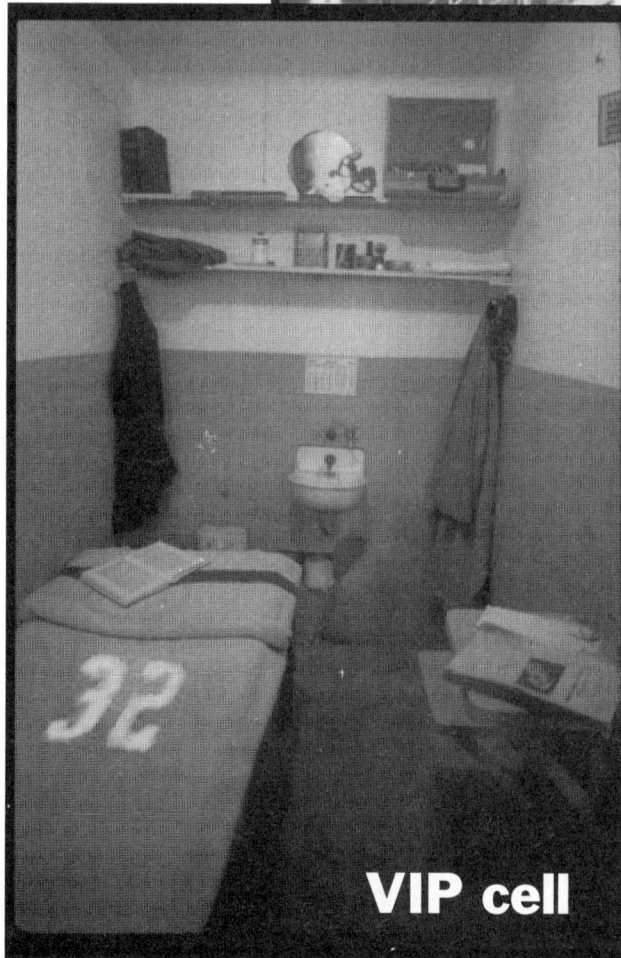

VIP cell

Los Angeles Gives O.J. the Star Treatment

In case you're wondering what in the world members of the **alt.fan.O.J.-simpson** newsgroup talk about, here's a list of the subject lines to postings culled from a single day's traffic. Imagine what you must be missing now!

ice cream melt rate
Marcia Clark—UGLY?
Howard Stern's remarks—racist?
multiple DNA tests match O.J.'s at scene
my evil twin in LAKGB
mystery car
Naked Gun defense tactic
NB's phone call to mother ends at 9:42
NB has phone call with friend
NY Daily news scenario
O.J. DID IT
O.J. quaking
O.J. and many of us

O.J. filmography
O.J. CD-ROM
O.J. buys a disguise
O.J. on airplane
O.J. IS INNOCENT!!!
O.J. fact of the day
O.J. offers to take lie detector test
O.J. at least partly innocent
Shapiro.....UGLY
Shapiro plans defense based on racism
Some thoughts on football
Spin doctors
I know who did it!
Is Kato lying
Grand Jury evidence
Candles in the bathroom
age of the blood trail
another possibility

List Service

FLASH: Rain Forest Crunch Melts Fastest!

By barbgrn@crl.com (Barbara Greene)

I can't believe I'm doing this—and the State of California has asked Judge Ito to recess the O.J. case for 2 days in November so people will VOTE vs. stay home and watch the trial . . .

Last night a talk show on KGO (radio) with an attorney as host had an Expert Witness on: a clerk from the local Ben & Jerry's. They preset the studio temp to 60-65 degrees F, and then, live, on radio, observed various flavors of B&Js melting.

The local (San Francisco) B&J guy knows the L.A. B&J guy and had a talk with him before this show—before the L.A. guy was swamped with calls and offers by various tabloids to pay him for his exclusive story.

Factoids:
* B&J stores ice cream at -10 to 0 degrees in the freezer and 0 to +10 degrees in the store.
* LA store closes at 10 PM/11 PM (I am not sure what he said, but it may be important).
* Ice cream/frozen yogurt purchased was in 4 oz cups. All B&Js use same kind and they probably would "hold" fingerprints.
* The "mystery blond guy" was apparently just another customer in store at the time, not with Nicole Brown. (A friend of NB's was also there and said they were not together.)
* All 4 oz samples "melted" ("got zoopy") in 45 minutes to 1 hour. Rain Forest Crunch melts

Latest tests reveal that .143 cubic liters of Rainforest Crunch melts in 27 seconds.

fastest, followed by Cherry Garcia.
* He thinks NB bought frozen yogurt.

Quibbles:
* The radio hosts ate most of the evidence during the "trial." (Hey, isn't this illegal or something? Destruction of evidence?) This proves talk shows are not good Triers of Fact.
* The cups were on a nice warm desk near all the nice warm electronics equipment.

Skepticism:
I find it amazing that we have run on with all this speculation based on virtually *nothing*. Like WHO found WHAT, WHERE, WHEN, and in what condition (melted/frozen/partially melted/zoopy). Good grief already!

Six Degrees of Separation From O.J.

By tbevan@wo.erim.org

My wife's friend is a flight attendant for American. She knows one of the flight attendants on O.J.'s flight from Chicago to L.A. She said that O.J. was very thirsty and drank lots of water. He used all of the Band Aids on the plane for himself. She asked him if something was wrong and he said, "You don't know the half of it."

By Tom Huber (thuber@netcom.com)

My God! I almost fell off my chair when I noticed your organization [**erim.org**], recalling my days in Ann Arbor Michigan, working as a fast-food delivery person. I once delivered a hamburger to the company where the man works whose wife has a friend who is a flight attendant who knows another flight attendant who served O.J. a drink the day after his wife was killed. I had better buy a suit. I might have to testify!

What's Black and White and Green All Over?

By elshark@aol.com

My company has made a T-shirt showing an orange in an electric chair. We are going to have an ad in the next issue of *Rolling Stone* magazine. If you would like a copy of the artwork, please feel free to E-mail me at the above address. The shirts sell for $15 + $3 S&H. You can also write for a copy of the artwork or just order the shirts. Send to Venture Tech, 7081 N. Marks #104-115, Fresno, CA 93711. I don't wish to offend, but to me it's not about black/white, it's about GREEN$$$ . . .

By: Mitchell D. Dysart
(dysart@magnus.acs.ohio-state.edu)

Of course you realize that California uses the gas chamber and not the electric chair. I hope you invested a bundle on those shirts.

By ZineReader@aol.com

Disk copies of the 460-page O.J. Grand Jury transcript on diskette.

* Full 460-page, previously sealed O.J. Simpson Grand Jury transcript
* ASCII text file format on a 3-1/2 inch diskette
* $9.95 by mail order
* $14.95 by Visa/MasterCard via toll-free number

LA County Grand Jury office charges $213 for a hard copy, plus shipping. They charge the *same* price for the diskette.

$9.95 is 95% or $203.05 less than what the Grand Jury office charges. $14.95 is 93% or $198.05 less than what the Grand Jury office charges.

Transcript reveals:
* Police testimony of blood recovered from a sink in Simpson's house
* Testimony of preliminary DNA findings
* Testimony of early police conversations with O.J.

(O.J. limo driver), other LAPD investigators and criminalists, Ron Goldman co-workers, the couple who found the bodies, and others.
* Complete testimony of 16 witnesses. None of it available to the public, until now.
* O.J. Defense is already moving to have as much of transcript as possible barred as evidence at the trial.

Legal experts predict "a real fight over this [grand jury] testimony."
For more info on the transcript plus how to order, send e-mail to: *zinereader@aol.com*

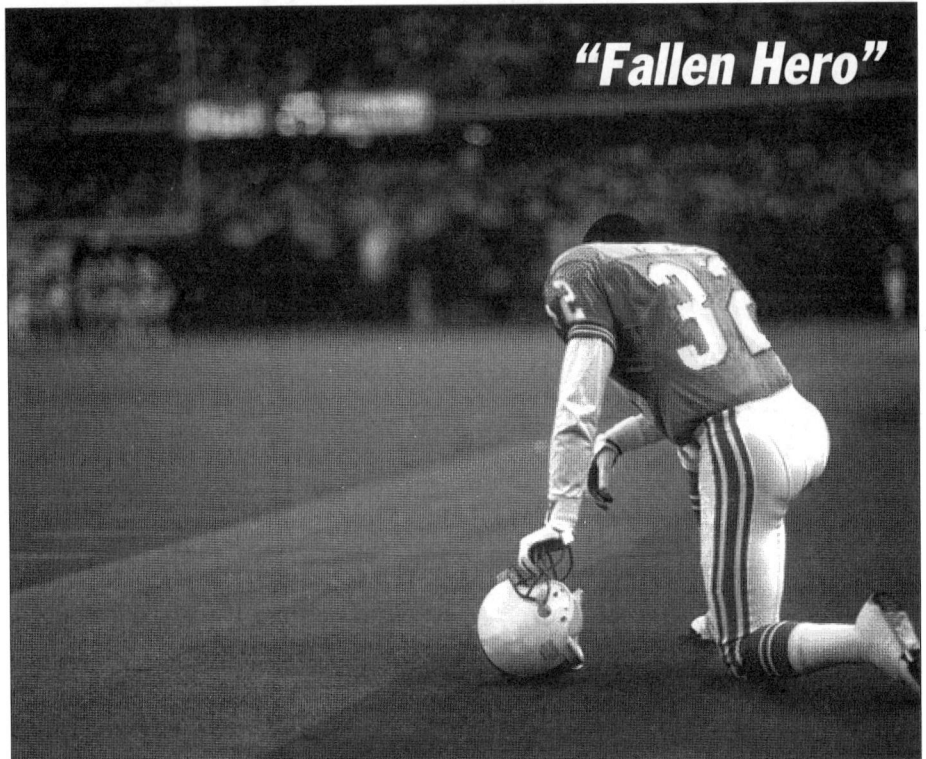

"Fallen Hero"

Bring O.J. Thrills To Pay-Per-View

By Danny Fung (fugitive@karposte.com)

Some of you have been wondering why there was such a big deal over the televised freeway chase. I ask, "Why not?" It's as least as compelling as your average episode of "Small Wonder" or "Baywatch."

It does not take extensive market research to figure out which is more compelling: a rerun of Wapner or O.J. in a car chase threatening to splatter his brains all over the back windshield. I can't wait

... can you see the Bronco?

for pay-per-view news coverage. What if O.J. had killed himself in the car and a chopper had gotten a good shot of it? Maybe Tom Brokaw and the self-righteous jerks at NBC-GE wouldn't show it on the 6:00 news, but there will soon come a day when some modern-day P.T. Barnum like the great Don "only-in-America" King (or maybe Rupert Murdoch) will get the bright idea of buying the rights to that kind of footage and putting it on pay-per-view, sort of like a "Celebrity Faces of Death."

If people will pay $5.95 for a pay-per-view showing "Sliver" or "The Three Musketeers" or pay $49.95 for Riddick Bowe, they'll easily pay $19.95 for a pay-per-view special featuring the complete footage of Kennedy getting offed in his limo, Rodney King getting beat up, Reginald Denny getting clubbed with a brick at Florence & Normandy, kids getting napalmed during Vietnam, the fatal shootings at Kent State, that politician in Pittsburgh about 4 years ago who held a press conference and then shot himself, and the main event, from the 405 freeway in Los Angeles, California, O.J. Simpson blowing his brains out. (Presented in super-slo-mo with Dolby surround-sound, only on pay-per-view!!)

Only on the Internet will you find such surreal juxtapositions of the ridiculous and the utilitarian as the filmography for O. J. Simpson. Yeah, that's right, you heard us correctly: filmography for O.J. Simpson.

Look, we don't make this stuff up, O.K.? Try it for yourself. Send e-mail with the word "help" as the subject and body of the message to **movie@ibmpcug.co.uk** for details on using the impressive and incredibly useful Movie Server on the Net.

You can send e-mail queries to the Movie Server and search for information on movie actors, directors, composers, writers, and even cinematographers, or you can request a complete file on a particular flick. The Movie Server database puts pros like **Leonard Maltin** and **Gene Siskel** to shame, and best of all, you get answers for free via e-mail within minutes (or at least hours).

And as a testament to the depth of information in the Movie Server database, check out the file it spat back at us when we requested info on that compelling star of "Capricorn One," Orenthal James Simpson:

Trace on an Actor/Actress career: *ACTOR Simpson, O.J.*
   Name: *Simpson, O.J.*
   Real Name: *Simpson, Orenthal James*
   Birth Date: *9 July 1947, San Francisco CA*
   Trivia: *Football player turned actor/
      sportscaster*

List Service

Filmography as Actor:
Klansman, The (1974)
Towering Inferno, The (1974) [Jernigan]
Killer Force (1975) [Alexander]
Cassandra Crossing, The (1976)
Killing Affair, A (1977) (TV)
"Roots" (1977) (mini) [Kadi Touray]
Capricorn One (1978) [John Walker]
Firepower (1979) [Catlett]
Goldie and the Boxer (1979) (TV)
Detour to Terror (1980) (TV) [Lee Hayes]
Goldie and the Boxer Go to Hollywood (1981)
      (TV) [Joe Gallagher]
Cocaine and Blue Eyes (1983) (TV)
"1st & Ten" (1984) [T.D. Parker (1985-1990)]
Hambone and Hillie (1984)
Student Exchange (1987) (TV)
Naked Gun: From the Files of Police Squad!,
      The (1988) [Nordberg]
Naked Gun 2 1/2: The Smell of Fear, The
      (1991) [Nordberg]
No Place to Hide (1993) [Allie Wheeler]
Naked Gun 33 1/3: The Final Insult (1994)
      [Nordberg]

RUMOR CONTROL

Word on the Net for some time was that Perry Mason would be signing on as assistant counselor for the Simpson defense team. It took a good deal of work on the part of the more informed netizens to convince the masses that Perry Mason was, in fact, a fictional character, and not likely to turn up inside the Los Angeles Municipal Court building.

But lawyers from Spensley, Horn, Jubas & Lubitz are reportedly hard at work for O.J. Simpson. No, they aren't studying DNA cases or lobbying to have the infamous white Bronco removed from the evidence roster. They are, instead, quite busy filing paperwork with the federal government to register "O.J. Simpson," "O.J.," and "The Juice" as trademarks. It's all part of an effort to stop profiteers—from bootleg T-shirt hawkers (good luck!) to trading card manufacturers—from cashing in on O.J.'s "good" name.

Meanwhile, reliable sources have informed the *Insider* that The Juice™ has been hard at work in his jail cell, autographing, signing, and dating 300 football cards to be sold as limited edition collector's items for $850 each. Area collectors have already said they'd spend up to $1,500 each for trading cards signed by O.J.™ while in his cell. We've also been informed (but have been unable to confirm) that Shapiro, Cochran, and Co. have been surfing the Net, scoping out the postings to the various O.J.-related newsgroups. Scuttlebutt is the suits are surreptitiously probing public opinion and testing out defense strategies via the Net before taking their ideas to the jury and press. ■

Ancient Chinese Secrets

by Longqiang "Larry" Zu (zu@gandalf.rutgers.edu)

RAT: 1948, 1960, 1972, 1984, 1996
Ambitious and sincere, you can be generous with your financial resources. You are good at giving people an offer they can't refuse. Nobody likes you, but they put up with you for your accounting abilities. Most Rats become involved in organized crime. Compatible with the Dragon and Monkey; your opposite is the Horse.

OX: 1949, 1961, 1973, 1985
A leader, you are bright and cheerful. At least you like to think you are. You are so desperate to be accepted by others that you frequently make promises you cannot keep. Maybe you could get more things done if you trimmed off half your weight. Most Santa Claus impersonators are Oxen. Compatible with the Snake and Rooster; your opposite is the Sheep.

TIGER: 1950, 1962, 1974, 1986
Forthright and sensitive, you possess great courage. You are so impatient to do heroic things that you rarely bother to sit down and think things out. You love to embrace "good causes," and you will probably die in poverty because

INSIDE OPINION

In an attempt to lure readers and increase their circulation, many of our competitors publish horoscopes. These shameless publications make wild claims about the accuracy and reliability of their astrologers and psychics. They contend that, simply by knowing the month in which you were born, their so-called prognosticators can predict what kind of day you'll have, or how your dating or business prospects will be over the next week.

Balderdash! We here at the *Insider* prefer to take a more enlightened view of the world. We realize our readers are a shade more sophisticated, and require something a little more convincing for making predictions than mere "psychic know-how" or "astrological acumen." Trust us, we've got something much better: ancient Chinese secrets!

The Chinese Zodiac, based on thousands of years of study by creepy old mystics and masters, can not only forecast what your day, week, or month will be like, it also locks you into a specific fate for the rest of your miserable life. Through an exclusive agreement, the *Insider* is pleased to offer the Zodiac stylings of Longqiang "Larry" Zu, whose profiles offer a new way of looking at astrology. (Sorry, no refunds.) Enjoy!

of it. Many Tigers are killed during heroic deeds, like running into burning houses or jumping into freezing rivers. Compatible with the Horse and Dog; your opposite is the Monkey.

RABBIT: 1951, 1963, 1975, 1987
Talented and affectionate, you are a seeker of tranquillity. Difficult situations upset you. Rabbits are frequently found with their heads in the ground. You are afraid to try anything new. Then you wonder why the world has passed you by. Rabbits usually end up as a side dish in someone else's dinner. Compatible with

the Sheep and Boar; your opposite is the Rooster.

DRAGON: 1940, 1952, 1964, 1976, 1988
Robust and passionate, your life is filled with complexity. You are the epitome of "Chaotic Control." No one understands what you are doing. Sometimes you don't understand what you are doing. You build your own world, then wonder why it doesn't match the real one. People call you "space cadet" behind your back. You give great first impressions. The second one gives you away. Most Dragons quote Dan Quayle in their speeches. Compatible with the

Monkey; your opposite is the Dog.

BOAR: 1947, 1959, 1971, 1983, 1995
Gallant and noble, you have friends who will remain at your side . . . as long as you keep up the payments. You do good work . . . as long as you know what you are doing. That is very rare. Most of the time, you need people to tell you what to do. Your friends are only using you. Many low-level Soviet officials are Boars. For that matter, so are many American politicians. Compatible with the Rabbit and Sheep; your opposite is the Snake.

Reveal Inner Self

DOG: 1946, 1958, 1970, 1982, 1994
Generous and loyal, you have the ability to work well with others. That's because they can see right through you. Everything is simple and straight-forward to you. Your conversation and speeches are limited to the bloody obvious. No one takes you seriously. You are willing to die for causes you believe in and people take advantage of that. Many Dogs die in prison. Compatible with the Horse and Tiger; your opposite is the Dragon.

SNAKE: 1941, 1953, 1965, 1977, 1989
Strong-willed and intense, you display great wisdom. You dream of becoming president someday. Trouble is, no one believes anything you say. You have no friends, only political allies. You're also a coward. "Live to run another day" is your motto. But that's all right. The people you hang out with hold those qualities in high regard. Snakes are elected to Congress. Compatible with the Rooster and Ox; your opposite is the Boar.

ROOSTER: 1945, 1957, 1969, 1981, 1993
Seeking wisdom and truth, you have a pioneering spirit. You are always running off into some silly adventure. You are also running away from creditors from your last failed adventure. Karl Marx was thinking of you when he wrote *Das Kapital*. You watch contact sports when no one is looking. Roosters group together and compare how many times they have declared bankruptcy. Compatible with the Snake and Ox; your opposite is the Rabbit.

MONKEY: 1944, 1956, 1968, 1980, 1992
Persuasive and intelligent, you strive to excel. People think you are an asshole. You're not above using little children to make a quick buck. You'd be in jail now if it wasn't for the fact you own the best lawyers money can buy. Monkeys make the best yuppies. You disgust me so much I'm going to stop writing. Compatible with the Dragon and Rat; your opposite is the Tiger.

SHEEP: 1943, 1955, 1967, 1979, 1991
Aesthetic and stylish, you enjoy being a private person. You shirk responsibility and live in fear of getting a phone call. Your best friend is the VCR. You think wallpaper makes the best paintings. You have this uncanny ability to cast dark clouds over any party. According to Darwin, you shouldn't exist. Compatible with the Boar and Rabbit; your opposite is the Ox.

HORSE: 1942, 1954, 1966, 1978, 1990
Physically attractive and popular, you like the company of others. You trip a lot because your nose is always in the air. People think you are an airhead. You could solve Ethiopia's famine with the money you spend on cosmetics. People stick close to you because they are afraid of what you will say if they ever turn their backs. Horses win popularity contests in high school, then go on to long meaningless careers in waste disposal. Compatible with the Tiger and Dog; your opposite is the Rat. ∎

Are you a snake, a monkey, or a rooster? You'll be surprised to find out!

If You Pave It, They Will Come

**Biohazard emblem
of earth destroyers**

Net Resources

You can find the FAQ file, the Creed, and a number of other essential earth-paver documents posted to **alt.pave.the.earth** on a regular basis.

Also be sure to check out **alt.destroy.the.earth**, **alt.destroy.the.internet**, and, for a wacky change of pace, **alt.save.the.earth**.

You can find plenty of earth-destroying fun in every issue of *Ooze*, an e-zine available from DrBubonic@aol.com.

Here in Los Angeles (home of the *Internet Insider*), we love our cars. In fact, one out of every four acres in L.A. is devoted to serving the needs of automobiles—making it the world's most car-friendly town. Don't ask us how this could be true, but one statistic we ran across claims there are 2.3 cars in L.A. for every person. (But if you had to sit in rush-hour traffic with us on the 405 or the 101, you'd see how such a ridiculous claim can start to look damned reasonable.)

Here, you can do *everything* from your car, including going to church, having your hair cut, and even getting married. But still, while we're sitting in freeway traffic in the morning or idling at a red light in the evening, we can't help feeling, despite how auto-centric L.A. is—it's just not good enough.

So, naturally, you can understand how we felt when we logged onto the Net and checked out **alt.pave.the.earth**. It was like they were reading our minds! The members of alt.pave.the.earth (a.p.t.e.) envision a world that is literally covered in asphalt—every square inch of it. Their every moment is spent dreaming of and working toward a day when the entire planet is a single, smooth, black orb.

Frankly, we can't wait. We here in the Americas have long been playing catch-up to the ancient Romans, whose network of roads was so extensive and well made that it served as the basis for many modern roads throughout Europe. But we've come a long way in just a few hundred years of earth-paving, and Los Angeles is a grand testament to that.

But **a.p.t.e.** (or APTE) is about more than simply paving the earth. It's about being able to have a cheeseburger or a beer whenever you want one, with a minimum of hassle and a maximum of convenience. According to **a.p.t.e.** doctrine, those not worthy of skimming about a paved earth in a rocket-propelled HyperCar will be relegated to the subterranean work pits. (Hey, it makes sense to us!) We've long desired a planet where our collective id is freed to live out its full and frightening potential, and if it means paving the planet, then so be it.

Alas, there are those on the Net who would oppose the ultimate goal of the a.p.t.e. crowd. Namely, those in **alt.destroy.the.earth**. These sincere yet misguided people are convinced that the ultimate extension of mankind's ambition is to completely and utterly destroy the planet. Consequently, there's quite a lot of cross-posting and squabbling (most of it good-natured and constructive) between the earth-pavers and the earth-destroyers. (We won't even explore the ugly scene that develops when—as sometimes happens—both groups gang up on the alt.save.the.earth crowd. It isn't pretty.)

Finally, the *Insider* is concerned about the development of a new yet disturbing newsgroup: **alt.destroy.the.internet**. We've always counted on being able to retreat to cyberspace when things in the "real world" become too horrid to bear. (We've picked October 20, 1996, as the probable "no-longer-bearable" date, by the way.) But if the alt.destroy.the.internet faction has its way (an interesting idea, using the Internet to destroy the Internet), we'll be trapped in the "real world."

Perhaps that won't be so bad, as long as it's paved.

INSIDE OPINION

net.speak

Newcomers to alt.pave.the.earth won't be able to make much sense of the highly specialized jargon the earth-pavers toss around. Much like freemasons, teenagers, and financial analysts, the pavers have developed their own canon of holy words and phrases based on the most fundamental tenets of their beliefs—words that are essentially meaningless to the uninitiated. Study these popular a.p.t.e. words and phrases to help get a handle on what the pavers are talking about.

Asphalt—The one and only substance allowed for use in paving the earth. Absolutely no substitutes, including concrete, are allowed, because asphalt is the most wasteful, and therefore preferred.

Beer—Along with cheeseburgers, one of the primary food substances that all earth-pavers demand.

Cheeseburgers—Along with beer, cheeseburgers make up a sort of holy sacrament that embody the beliefs of speed and convenience so highly prized by the a.p.t.e. crowd.

A possible bumper sticker for a rocket-powered HyperCar once PaveDay 1 is reached, this slogan will, for now, have to remain simply a .sig.:

One World. One People. One Slab of Asphalt.

net.speak *continued*

The Creed—A regularly posted promise adhered to by all serious pavers. It places undying loyalty and devotion to The Plan above all else.

HyperCar—A futuristic, yet-to-be-constructed, rocket-powered super-car that, after PaveDay 1, earth-pavers will use to hurtle across the smooth, paved earth at incredible speeds.

PaveDay 1—The glorious day in the future that represents the first day of an eternity on a paved planet.

Pit Slaves—The unfortunate individuals not worthy of skidding along in HyperCars and drinking beer and eating cheeseburgers, Pit Slaves will toil in underground bunkers known as The Pits. They will only see the light of day when needed to fill a pothole or patch a crack in the sacred asphalt.

The Pits—Since the entire planet will be a single, smooth asphalt surface, The Pits will be where slaves toil, tending the hydroponic cow farms and brewing beer for the surface skimmers.

The Plan—The sacred document that covers every detail of the plan to pave the earth. The Plan is never posted, but is constantly referred to, thus nearly every newbie to a.p.t.e. ends up asking, "Where is The Plan posted?"

Plutonium Mines—Along with The Pits, another unpleasant series of holes in the ground where slaves will toil to procure the fuel that will power the HyperCars of the paved future.

Earth-Pavers' Secret Plot Revealed

By Paul Schmidt (schmidtp@carleton.edu)

As most people already know, the world is a big place. In the past there have been some meager attempts at paving by various governments. Such great things as interstates and freeways have been invented. However, in the future, this simply will not do. The world must be covered with beautiful, black asphalt.

Section 1: The Future of the Earth

1.1 Why Pave the Earth?

There are several advantages of a paved Earth over a non paved Earth; the only really important one is the ease of driving. Today roads are narrow, you have to turn, and most governments frown at ground travel at speeds higher than Mach 1. With endless blacktop in every direction, there will be no restriction to your movement, and rocket powered HyperCars will whiz in all directions. We will be able to amuse ourselves with endless driving at incredible speeds while drinking beer and eating wonderfully juicy burgers.

1.2 Why Asphalt?

Simply put, everything else sucks. Concrete is clearly unsuitable be-

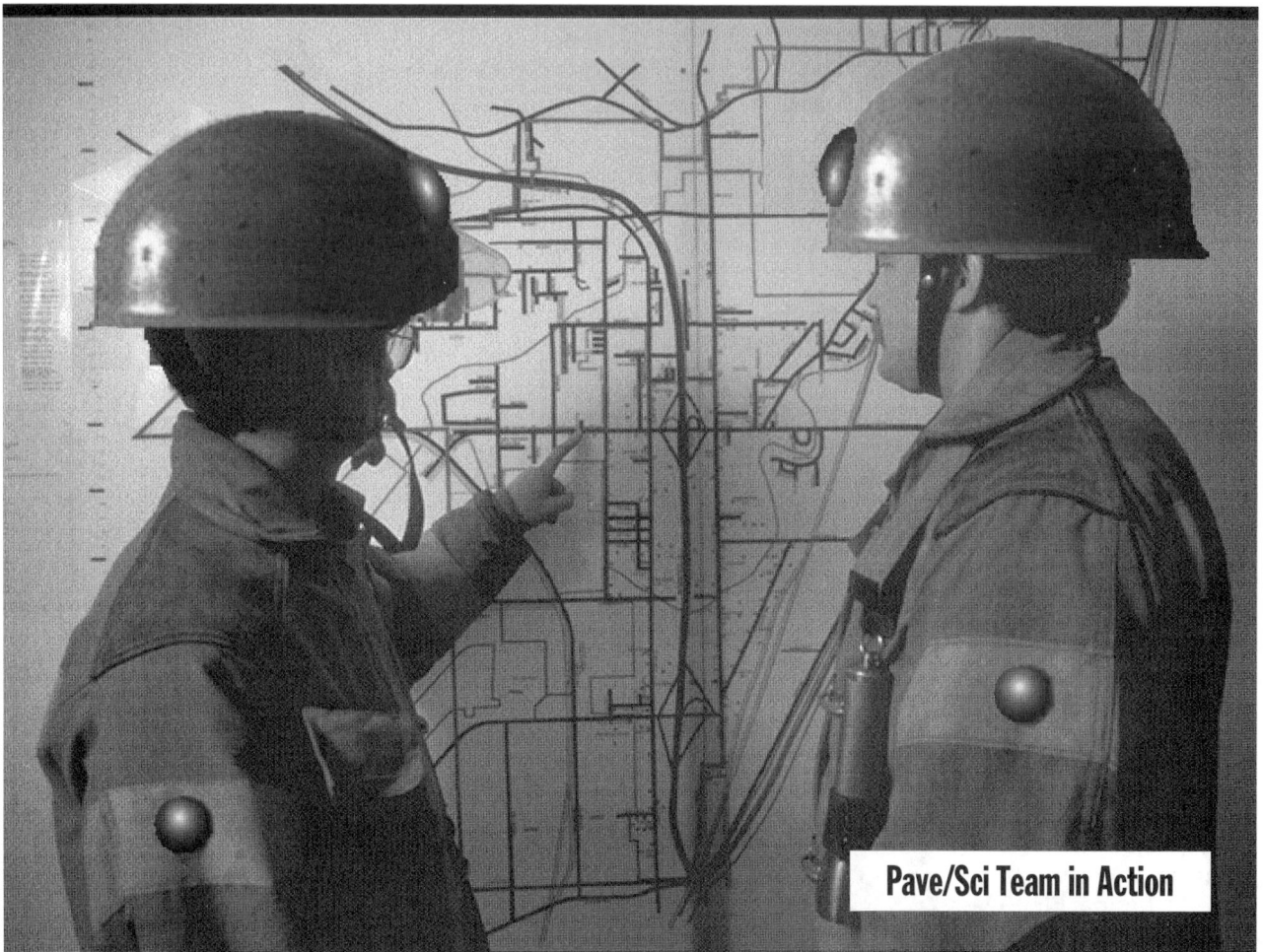

Pave/Sci Team in Action

cause of the seams that are needed for shrinking and swelling during temperature changes. As we are whizzing around at tremendous speeds, the seams in the concrete would create nasty sounds and unpleasant bumps. There are no other good driving surfaces.

There are, of course, several other benefits of asphalt, which include the depletion of natural resources and increase of pollution in the atmosphere. The depletion of natural resources is (of course) a noble goal. When faced with the fact that the earth only has so many things that can be procured, it is an enormous challenge to squeeze that last drop of oil out of the ground. It is, however, a task which we are ready for. We can prove once and for all that we are the masters of all. The goal of polluting has several benefits as well. Imagine cruising along one day and looking at the darkened sky and being able to say, "I made the sky what it is today." You can take pride in that. The other benefits won't be mentioned now since they are too numerous; wait for future revisions of the FAQ for them.

1.3 What About Traffic?

Traffic will not be a problem due to the simple fact that most people will be slaving away beneath the surface in what has come to be called the parking garage. These people will be needed to staff the hydroponic farms, raise cows, brew beer, and fix potholes. Most of the world's population will work for the good of the drivers. Altruism at its best. There will also be no regulation of traffic. Governments are outmoded and should be phased out. We know what to do. Why should someone else tell us what to do when we already know the proper course of action? pave, Pave, PAVE. That's what I always say.

PHASE 1

FINAL PHASE

Pit Slave escape

is endless, smooth, black asphalt. One world, one people, one slab of asphalt.

Section 2:
The Future of Other Celestial Objects

2.1 Are There Any Current Plans Dealing with the Moon?

There are many plans on what might be done to the moon. The most commonly accepted course of action is to cover the moon with long, thin strips of chrome. This will be mostly for decoration, but it will also have the added benefit of providing the equivalent of a giant street light in the sky. Other plans deal with Astroturf, floral wallpaper, and other sorts of things that are used to cover other objects up.

2.2 What About the Other Planets?

The other planets really aren't that important since they aren't as visible from the earth. Sure, you may be able to pick out Jupiter or Venus in the sky some nights, but you would hardly be able to see a nice paisley pattern or anything.

2.3 Are There Any Plans for Other Solar Systems?

Not yet. We're working on it, though. If some aliens were ever to discover the earth after it is paved they would no doubt be overcome by the sheer beauty and majesty of our creation. At that point, they would

feel compelled to serve our needs and to carry out the paving of other planets. Other than that, the only plans that we have are to look for oil on other planets.

Section 3:
That Which Does Not Fit Anywhere Else

3.1 Hey, When the Earth is Paved It'll Be Just Great to Skateboard On, Won't It?

Well, maybe. I would strongly discourage anyone from trying to go skateboarding on the newly paved earth— they would be as good as roadkill very quickly. It is true that everything would be nice and smooth, but there would be nothing to do grinds on or ollies over or anything, so it wouldn't be much fun anyway. You might as well just buy a HyperCar and join the future.

3.2 Hey, Cool. With a Paved Earth I'll Be Able to Make Tons of Roadkill!

Not really. Think about it for just a minute or two. OK, now the earth is completely paved. Can you tell me what the little critters are going to live on? There will be no plant life on the surface. Nothing will be on the surface except for us. It's quite simple, really. With nothing for the animals to eat, there will be no roadkill.

3.3 What About Other Stuff that I Care About?

Get with it! Just think about speed and lots of black asphalt. Paving is the future.

1.4 What About [your favorite big things? Won't They Get in the Way?

Nothing will be in the way. Mountains will be leveled; oceans and seas will either be frozen or be filled in and then paved over. Cities will all move underground into the parking garages. All that will be left

Ode to The Plan
By Jones Ambigusan (oleary@io.com)

Beer held in my left hand,
Cheeseburger in my right,
Engine burning extra juice,
I hurtle through the night.

Of this I dream all night and day,
For I have seen the worth
Of Mankind's single greatest work;
A Pavement-covered earth.

Pavers Prop to Post the Plan

From: Pete Gontier (gurgle@dnai.com)

In an earlier article, kosborn@netcom.com (Kevin Osborn) wrote:

```
> I think that The Plan should be posted soon . . .
```

It is unlikely that The Plan will ever be posted because it is only available on paper, and it may only be quoted in its entirety. This would mean that someone would have to do several hundred pages of typing in order to post it. Good pavers are much too busy driving and paving for an effort of such magnitude.

```
> . . . so that its goals may be shown to anyone because everyone
has the right to read scripture.
```

This is a nice Protestant attitude, but we pavers are not Protestants.

```
> I also think we need to work on a way to change the physical
properties about going faster than the speed of light, such as the
fact that you simply can't go faster.
```

Not a bad idea. Get to work. I'll expect a proposal in the morning.

Pit Slave surfaces to fill pothole

Orbital Paving Platform Plan!

By Max Natzet (Max_Natzet@ccmail.gsfc.nasa.gov)
Mechanical Engineer NASA/Wallops Flight Facility

I *suggest that we build an Orbital Paving Platform. The OPP would employ massive nozzles which would atomize the nascent asphalt and spray it Earthward. Much like an immense airbrush, the OPP would lay an even coat of paving to the surface of the planet as it orbits.*

This has the added benefit of squandering the lift capacity of the planet, denying it to those moon-chroming heretics. The boosters are also known to be extremely enviro-toxic.

I have begun to subvert my employers tools to this end, pave on brothers.

Hydrohollow Therapy for Everyone

By Martin Adamson
(MARTIN@srv0.ems
.edinburgh.ac.uk)

[Earth-pavers must recruit new members to help bring about their glorious goal of paving the globe. If a potential new recruit isn't in agreement with The Plan, then he or she is placed in a database of those who will be forced to work as a Pit Slave. Martin Adamson's "HydroHollow Therapy" message was originally posted to the **alt.meditation** and **alt.meditation.transcendental** newsgroups.]

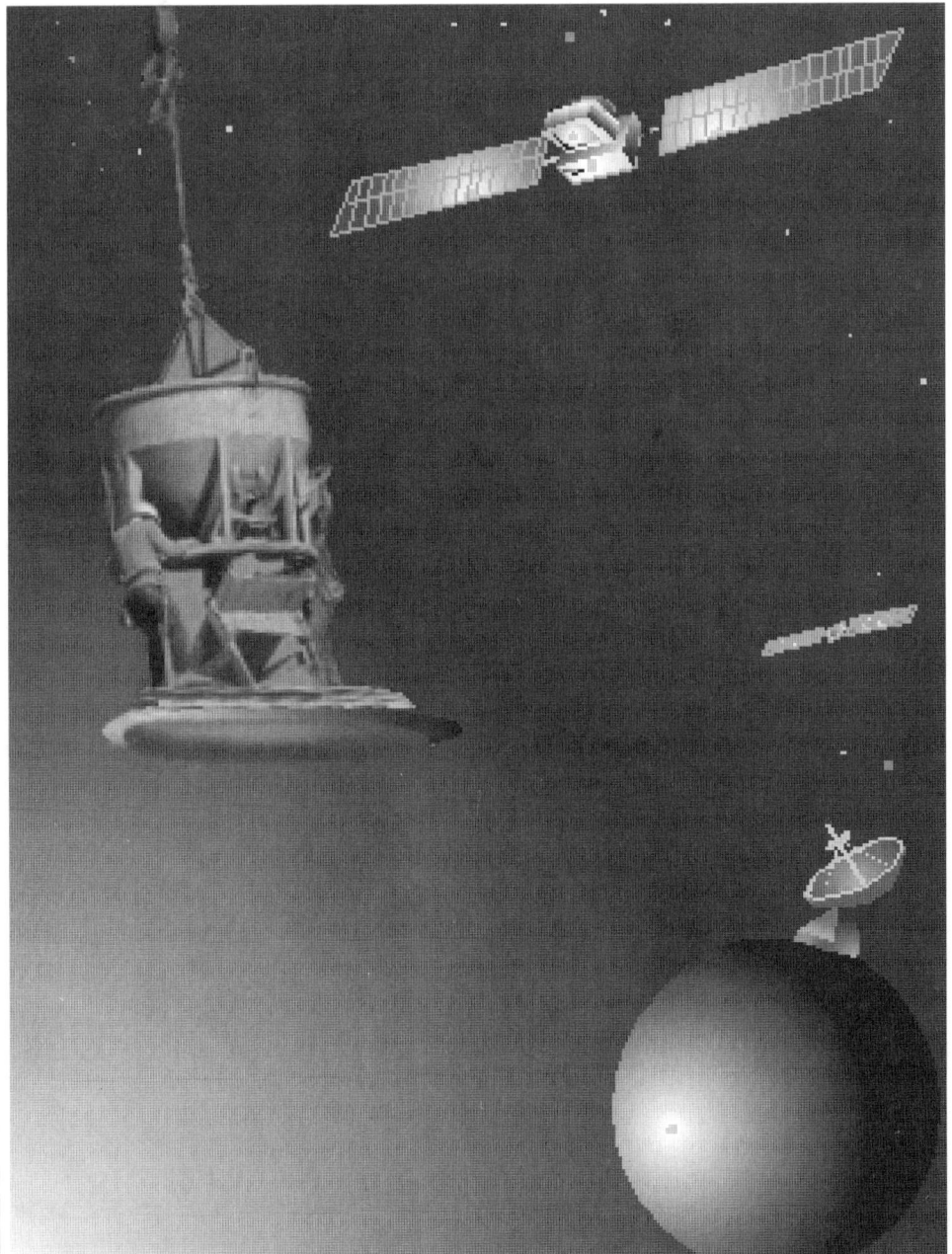

HydroHollow Therapy: A New Therapy for the New Age

Are you tired of life's complexities? Are you stressed out by the modern world? Are you looking for answers for the meaning of life? Are you seeking to rediscover your mystic oneness? Then try HydroHollow Therapy—brought to you by the enlightened sanyassin of APTE.

What is it?

HydroHollow therapy is a mystic belief that really does satisfy your spiritual strivings, your intellectual hunger, and your physical needs. We at APTE have, like you, been engaged in a long and arduous quest after truth, and, now that we have found the wisdom of the ancients, we are able to reveal the glories of our human and planetary destiny to a wider audience.

What does it involve?

We at APTE are determined to break down the artificial reductionist divide between mind and body. Our intensive program of spiritual study is combined with physical work in a holistic unity which will at last allow you to reach true oneness. You will progressively study the sacred documents of our beliefs, starting with The Creed, progressing on to the APTEFAQ, and then, when you have attained a true nirvana of enlightenment, you will be able to comprehend the full beauty of The Plan. As you meditate on the deep meaning of our sacred symbol, the Black Sphere, you too will come to appreciate why it must be so. Our specially trained teams of therapists will guide and direct your physical and mental strivings. You will have the satisfaction of knowing that you are contributing a vital part to the full realization of Earth's planetary destiny. Only once we have completed the great work of The Plan

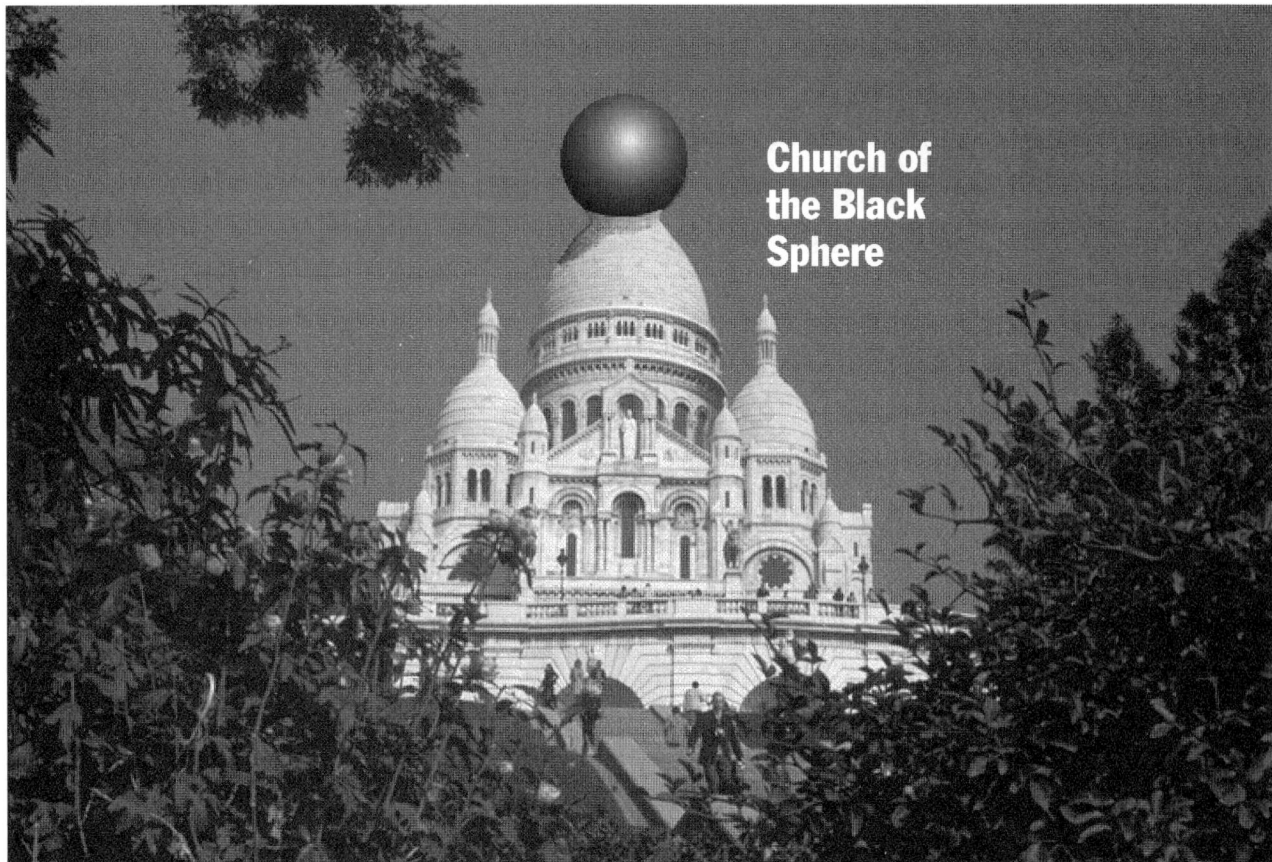

Church of the Black Sphere

will humanity be able to take its rightful place amongst the other races of the galaxy.

What will we eat?

A simple but nutritious and tasty diet. APTE believes that eating and drinking provides nutrition and sustenance for both mind and body, so the very act of eating our specially prepared meals will contribute towards your understanding of who you really are and what you are doing.

Will we solve the ultimate questions of life and death?

Other therapies like past life regression by hypnosis have held out the fraudulent hope of learning to lose the fear of death. Only by following APTE and HydroHollow Therapy will you learn why death marks life's culmination. In fact, HydroHollow Therapy will make death seem so attractive that you will long for it!

Is there anything beyond HydroHollow Therapy?

Yes, if HydroHollow Therapy doesn't work for you then we can offer you other forms of therapy. We at APTE are always working on new and innovative techniques. One involves working with one of the most ancient and natural substances known to

(continues)

Young Worshipers Meditating

We Have A Mission!

By Paul Schmidt (schmidtp@carleton.edu)

We have been told throughout our lives that history is not progressive. There is no one society that is inherently better than any other. We are not better than the Eskimos because we refrain from eating the eyeballs from our fish, and so on. This may all be well and good, but it only has relevance to the past. Soon there will be one goal to which all paths will lead.

When you grab a beer, sit down, and turn on the television, you are constantly being told that we live in a modern society. What is so great about this modern society of ours? We still have to wait in line. We still have to share and take turns. There are still idiots on the streets that do stupid things like driving into bridge piers and telephone poles. The world is still left unpaved.

The commercials may tell you about the newest model Honda or Ford, but the facts remain that there are still regulations about selling rocket-powered cars for general transportation. Some people claim that they aren't street-legal. There is still a tax on beer. There are still things left on the surface to run into.

History has been leading us up to this point. Several hundred years ago people had never even dreamed of cars such as we have now. Asphalt wasn't being used to pave long stretches of the earth. Our society today is well on the way to a future where the chosen may live in their cars in comfort. Never before have such opportunities existed.

It is up to us to play a role in deciding down which path we shall go. Will it be the path sheltered by trees, with twigs and leaves crunching underfoot, will it be the gravel path with waste and excrement strewn about, or will we choose to take the paved path, the one of black and beauty?

If we do our part, soon the blacktop will stretch for miles in all directions. Soon there will be rocket-powered Hyper-Cars sold for our enjoyment. Soon the world will be as one, and there will be no divergent histories.

The fate is in our hands. Will we let history continue to be fragmented and purposeless, or will we truly become one body of people, with one slab of asphalt?

(HydroHollow Therapy continued)

man, a substance that the spiritually adept of the Indian subcontinent have been using for thousands of years. The other involves manipulating an element so rare, so valuable, and so imbued with mystic power that very few people in the world have even seen it, let alone touched or tasted it.

Who else will be taking HydroHollow Therapy?

A lot of people very much like yourself. In fact, you will be studying alongside a great many of the world's most important intellectual and political leaders and other celebrities. You will be able to exchange fascinating spiritual insights with leading biologists and ecologists. You will be able to argue your views with those deemed unorthodox and heretical. You will be in close contact, for example, with a group of people with strong interests in metallic surfaces for satellite bodies.

HydroHollow Therapy sounds great! Where do I sign up?

Relax. We at APTE have been taking a keen interest in the new age movement for several years now, and so there is a good chance that many of you will already be on our database. If by some mischance you are not yet included, let us know, and we shall add your names to The List. When the time is ripe, your spiritual gurus at APTE will lead you to your glorious destiny.

Success!!

From: Martin Adamson
(martin@srv0.ems.edinburgh.ac.uk)

Ho ho ho! Our plans to sow confusion and uncertainty amongst our enemies are bearing fruit, as witnessed by this message from alt.destroy.the.earth

> I'm gone for a couple of weeks and suddenly the place is inundated with refugee alt.pave.the.earth-ers! (OK, so paving it before destroying it is not entirely antithetical, but DAMMIT it should be talked about in a.p.t.e. instead of here!)

> Man, we REALLY need to hurry up and get to work on this before the spirit is completely leached out of the dedicated few!

Wasting Scarce Natural Resources Edict

By Aaron Mandelbaum (adm4@po.cwru.edu)

You guys are crazy! If you waste all the Scarce Natural Resources in some trivial game like paving, what will be left to use to blow the planet up? Other planets' natural resources? Come on . . .

Don't you see it? We have to conserve our natural resources, because it's going to take a HELL of a lot of energy to atomize this place.

Think about it: you envision the beauty of a blank, black expanse of asphalt. Wouldn't a blank, black expanse of vacuum be so much more . . . impressive, so much more . . . pure.

And you'd never have to worry about getting hamburgers late ever again! And any SNR that weren't used up would be destroyed! And everyone would get to travel at the speed of light (or at least, their constituent particles would come close)! And NO species would have to be tolerated!

See the light! Destroy the Earth!
It's the only way!

Pour Agent Orange into local reservoir to enhance flavor.

The Creed of the Pavers (traditional version)

From: Pete Gontier (gurgle@dnai.com)

We believe in a completely Paved Earth.

Earth is cursed with trees, shrubs, grass, and scurrying creatures. With every breath We act to right this terrible wrong.

We believe in The Plan.

The Plan is the final word, it brings us the knowledge of the twin pleasures: Speed and Convenience.

We believe food should be enjoyed.

"Nutrition" is an aberration of human nature. The juicy Burger and hearty Beer are Our sacrament.

We believe in the Depletion of scarce natural resources.

Some see the vessel as half full; others see it as half-empty; we pour it out on the floor and laugh.

We believe in a sky roiling with Smog.

The color blue should appear nowhere but the paint on Our HyperCars.

40 Ways YOU Can Help Destroy the Earth!

By Matt Patterson, Ed Schmidt, and Whitney Fitzgerald

(Orignally published in "Ooze #3," an e-zine available from DrBubonic@aol.com)

People these days are constantly harping about the upcoming Armageddon. But *when* is the world going to finally end? Most people don't realize it can't happen without *their* help. Below are a few little things *you* can do to help end the world.

1 Use motor oil to fertilize your lawn.

2 Feed lead to pigeons.

3 Vacation by your local polluted river.

4 Serve chlorofluorocarbons as appetizers at your next party.

5 Find the remaining woodland in your town and use it for kindling.

6 Leave your car running all day.

7 Drive to the bathroom.

8 Spray your yard with DDT and not those other wimpy pesticides.

9 Pour Agent Orange into local reservoir to enhance flavor.

10 Only wear polyester, and never more than once.

11 Become a megalomaniac and gain control of vast nuclear stockpiles. Use them.

12 Dump your food leftovers into the recycling bin.

13 Keep the bubonic plague virus around as a lovable, low-maintenance pet.

14 Use at least three gallons of water for each tooth when brushing.

15 Create an oil slick in your backyard as a science experiment for kids.

16 Have 37 children.

17 Name them all Bill.

18 Strangle a bald eagle.

19 Spread Styrofoam balls all over your lawn for winter fun all year round.

20 E-mail Al Gore petitioning to test nuclear arms above ground in major cities.

21 Wage chemical warfare in local elementary school. It's fun and easy!

22 Experiment in biotoxins by not burying dead pets.

23 Offer free cigarettes, alcohol, and drugs to pregnant mothers.

24 Own at least 43 televisions per person, per household, and watch them all at once.

25 Build a simple coal burning power plant in your basement.

26 Remove your catalytic converter and muffler. They just ruin the fun.

27 Aim the x-ray machine at unsuspecting patients in the dentist's office.

28 Sunscreen? It's for wimps.

Spread Styrofoam balls all over your lawn for winter fun all year round.

29 Carve holes in the ozone layer. They make great gifts.

30 Drive an M-1A Abrams tank to work.

31 Disrupt local mass transit with campaign of terror.

32 Develop a condominium complex in beautiful Chernobyl.

33 Fart 40 times or more a day.

34 Develop a secret neurotoxin that makes females pregnant with dinosaurs.

35 Buy something you don't need three times a day. Dump it on the freeway.

36 Defecate in reservoirs.

37 Work for the government.

38 Aerosol hairspray can be used for a lot more than personal grooming! Putting up posters, cooking lubricant, antiperspirant, ant and roach killer, personal defense, and party favors.

39 Burn your own garbage for fun and profit.

40 Encase dead relatives in Lucite blocks.

We hope that these simple ideas will inspire you to create your own methods to drag this planet further into its grave. Every person counts! ◼

Is Socks Allowed on White House Jogging Path?

If They Build It, Will Socks Come?

In this episode, Dee Dee Myers discusses the value-added tax, the President's long-term health, Sock's jogging schedule, and the Roosevelt swimming pool. But has she ventured in too deep? Is she in over her head? Has she gone off the deep end? Let's listen.

The place: The White House Briefing Room.

The time: Exact date unknown; late 1992 or early 1993; 9:30 a.m. E.S.T.

The players: Clinton Administration spokesperson Dee Dee Myers and the White House press corps.

Ms. Myers: Good morning. At 11:00 a.m. the President will speak to the Chamber of Commerce. And then at 4:00 p.m. he will meet with U.N. Secretary General Boutros Boutros-Ghali. Those are the only quasi public appearances of the day.

Q: You're ruling out a value-added tax to finance the health care program?

Ms. Myers: I think the President was fairly clear on his opinion about the VAT. It's something that he's looking at 10 or 15 years—or thinking the country might be interested in looking at 10 or 15 years down the line, and it's not something that is currently being discussed.

Q: I've never heard 10 or 15 years put in front of—as a time frame. Is that new? Did you just decide to say that? (*Laughter.*)

Ms. Myers: I just made it up. (*Laughter.*) No, the President has said that.

Q: He said that—

Ms. Myers: Yes, he did. He said, I think in the comments outside the school in Ohio, he said 10 years. In conversations that I've had with him, he's—

Q: About the track. The President has always run on cement and other things. Is there something wrong with his legs, or is there a reason why he needs a new kind of track, a soft-type track?

Ms. Myers: No, the President said that there are some people who think it would be good for long-term health of his knees and other joints to run on a softer surface. There is no immediate concern, but as a long-term investment, they think it's a good idea. I think there's—**there may be other people, members of the First Family and others who may also use the track.**

Q: Is he going to open it up to staff?

Ms. Myers: I think that's entirely possible.

Q: Will he get bored running around just that little quarter mile over and over and over?

Ms. Myers: I think the President enjoys running out in the community on the Mall and other places. I think he'll continue to do that under any circumstances. As you know, when he's on the road he enjoys running, getting a chance to visit with local people. I think he'll continue to do that.

Q: Dee Dee, can you get us a couple of numbers—what's the number that's been floated on this to the cost of the track?

Ms. Myers: Thirty thousand dollars is the rough estimate—$10,000 in materials and $20,000 in labor.

Q: Can you get us the number on what it costs for a jogging motorcade?

Ms. Myers: I think that it's not possible to break down the costs. As you know, the Secret Service protection is classified.

Q: I can't get enough of this track stuff. You said other members of the First Family will be on it. Who? There are only two other members.

Q: Socks, don't forget. (*Laughter.*)

Ms. Myers: That pretty much narrows it down. (*Laughter.*)

Q: When you say we're moving ahead on it—we're moving ahead, what does it mean? Have you started a campaign to collect donations? What do you mean?

Ms. Myers: We set up a fund or are in the process of doing so to accept the contributions. And I can get back to you on the exact details of how that's structured.

Q: What's it called?

Ms. Myers: I don't know that it has a specific title. (*Laughter.*) But we're taking suggestions. So—we're taking suggestions. Please submit yours. We'll have a contest. (*Laughter.*)

Q: Yes, help the press.

Ms. Myers: And whoever wins the contest can have the first lap around the track when it's completed.

The Socks Chronicles

In this ongoing series of behind-the-scenes looks at the inner workings of the White House, the *Internet Insider* follows Socks, America's First Cat, through another harrowing press conference. In this official White House document obtained exclusively by the *Insider*, you'll see how the White House press corps is once again sidetracked from the real issues facing our government to consider the life and times of that lovable kitty, Socks.

Why the media obsession with the President's cat? Is there something the White House doesn't want us to know? Is "Socks" a secret code word that sends reporters into a trance of distraction and diversion? Why does the press offer only a 30-second sound bite from a 30-minute meeting? Does Socks prefer frolicking in the Lincoln Bedroom or on the South Lawn? These questions and more are answered as we present another installment of *The Socks Chronicles.*

photo courtesy of The White House

Q: When do you expect the track to be finished?

Ms. Myers: I don't have a particular time line.

Q: Will he have a heart attack if it's not done on time?

Q: Can we have a photo op of the track in progress? . . . Photo op of the track at various stages of completion, please?

Ms. Myers: I'm sure that that will be a fascinating—

Q: Will the donors [of money to finance the jogging track] be made public? Will the names of the donors be made public?

MS. Myers: I don't know. I don't believe it's required, but I'll double-check.

Q: Even if it's not required, I'm sure the White House—

Ms. Myers: We'll look at it.

Q: Why wouldn't—

Q: Why wouldn't that—why wouldn't you—

Ms. Myers: Again, I think that the American people think it is reasonable that the President, who jogs everyday, have a place on the grounds of the White

House where he can jog that doesn't require him to leave, again, the grounds of the White House. I don't think there's anything inconsistent about it at all. I think it's perfectly reasonable and it is not being paid for at public expense. I think the American people will appreciate that. But they certainly think it is within the President's purview. President Roosevelt built a pool. Unfortunately, we're sitting on it now. But I think it's—

Q: That's the deep end, right there.

Ms. Myers: Is it? (*Laughter.*) It's a good thing I can swim. (*Laughter.*)

Q: There's no water in it, Dee Dee.

Ms. Myers: Have you guys installed the trap door here, yet?

Q: They had thought of that.

Ms. Myers: Helen, that could sort of end for "thank you," just—(*Laughter.*)

This excerpted transcript from an actual White House media event was downloaded from official archives of Clinton Administration documents available from a number of sources: via gopher: gopher.tamu.edu or sunsite.unc.edu; via anonymous FTP: ftp.spies.com; via World-Wide Web: http://english-server.hss.cmu.edu/WhiteHouse.html; via e-mail: publications@whitehouse.gov.∎

THE USENET ORACLE HAS PONDERED YOUR QUESTION DEEPLY.
YOUR QUESTION WAS:

O omnipotent Oracle! Timorously, I ask you:
If you drop a buttered piece of bread, it will fall on the floor butter-side down. If a cat is dropped from a window or other high and towering place, it will land on its feet.
But what if you attach a buttered piece of bread, butter-side up to a cat's back and toss them both out the window? Will the cat land on it's feet? Or will the butter splat on the ground?

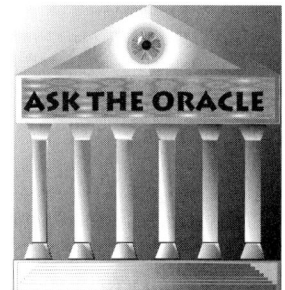

(question by Mike)

AND IN RESPONSE, THUS SPAKE THE ORACLE:

Even if you are too lazy to do the experiment yourself you should be able to deduce the obvious result. The laws of butterology demand that the butter must hit the ground, and the equally strict laws of feline aerodynamics demand that the cat cannot smash its furry back. If the combined construct were to land, nature would have no way to resolve this paradox. Therefore it simply does not fall.

That's right you clever mortal (well, as clever as a mortal can get), you have discovered the secret of antigravity! Buttered cat will, when released, quickly move to a height where the forces of cat-twisting and butter repulsion are in equilibrium. This equilibrium point can be modified by scraping off some of the butter, providing lift, or removing some of the cat's limbs, allowing descent.

Most of the civilized species of the Universe already use this principle to drive their ships while within a planetary system. The loud humming heard by most sighters of UFOs is, in fact, the purring of several hundred tabbies.

The one obvious danger is, of course, if the cats manage to eat the bread off their backs they will instantly plummet. Of course the cats will land on their feet, but this usually doesn't do them much good, since right after they make their graceful landing, several tons of red-hot starship and pissed off aliens crash on top of them.

You owe the Oracle two slices of toast and a bag of kitty litter.

Amazing Neanderthal Man Discovered

By John S. Novak, III (jsn@cegt201.bradley.edu)

So you think your neighbors suck? Maybe. But probably not. You should try working here at the *Internet Insider*. Being sandwiched in between the slaughterhouse and the hazardous waste incinerator usually means the hot-dog vendors and catering trucks don't stop on our street, but, hey, brown-bagging saves time and money.

No matter how bad your neighborhood seems, you can always take solace in the comforting knowledge that some other poor slob is even worse off. Well, except for **John Novak**. He's got a real problem, and our advice to him is simple: Move! See, the problem with John's neighbors is . . . well, he tells it so much better than we do. Tell 'em, John.

It would indeed be a godsend if we could label our domiciles as "*annoying-college-kid-undergrad-free*" zones. I have serious doubts as to the genetic fitness of my upstairs neighbor. I have serious doubts that it qualifies as human.

A truly amazing demonstration of *homo imbecilus*, it decided that it just had to mop down its floors the day after it moved in, and I knew then we were off to a bad start. At 10:30 p.m. With, apparently, 700 or 800 buckets of water. Imagine our surprise as my flatmate and I, reading, watching television, and generally minding our own business, find our silent repose marred by a sound remarkably like a cow pissing through a small hole into our living room.

Puzzled, we look around for the source of the ominous sound, and discover a small yet persistent (and fairly high-pressure) jet of grayish pine-scented fluid coming from a small hole in our ceiling, a hole previously covered up with sturdy tape. As, two seconds later, the **Jet from Heaven** shows no sign of abatement, I rush, grab a pot to collect the moppish effluence, deposit it, and rush upstairs.

Upstairs, after pounding on his door, I am admitted entry to the room. Aghast, I see a room covered with foul, brackish **Pine-Sol**-flavored gunk, and **Party Man** standing nearby with yet another bucket in hand, ready, willing, and just about to go one step further in turning his living room-turned-bar and dance floor into a living **Jackson Pollack** Action Art with a Mopwater Motif.

(Granted, I'm no expert at mopping. My floors are carpeted. I don't mop. I barely even vacuum. But is the preferred method of cleaning a hideously scarred wooden floor *really* dumping buckets of swamp gunk on it and pushing the standing water out the front door with a mop?)

Pleased at the good fortune of finding that my new neighbor had not somehow broken a pipe above my living room, but distressed by the motif in decorations, I calmly informed him of the problem ("You're pissing Pine Goo on my carpet! Desist!") and stalked downstairs.

And, *Lo*! All was goodness, happiness, and sunshine.

Until Tuesday.

Neanderthal's flatmate

Tuesday was when I began to have doubts as to the propriety of his stock and the number of his chromosomes. He had discovered the art of **Moving Things**. Ah, the pure, rapturous joys of having an upstairs neighbor with a penchant for rearranging furniture. At about 11:30 p.m. (not that I was sleeping, or even close, but still!), I was treated to what sounded like a rendition of **Don Quixote** jousting above my very head. But no mere windmills his enemies! No, *this* version came complete with real giants, heaving small boulders about the room.

I can think of no possible explanations for those noises, unless **Monkey Boy** was, perhaps, physically picking up his furniture (footlockers, armchairs, sofas, whatever), lofting them across the room (CRASH!!! Bounce bounce bounce . . .), and running after them.

What sport!

Then . . . Wednesday.

It's not enough that his submoronic friends came over and fouled the atmosphere. It's not enough that his cretinous lackeys wanted to sit outside, necessitating their cranking up their stereo so

Hi, Imbecilus

loud as to impinge on *my* sacred airspace. It's not enough that they had the temerity to move from a rap song to a country-western ditty, causing the most severe case of aesthetic whiplash I've encountered since the local Fox network decided that **Rosanne** is the perfect show to run before **M*A*S*H**. And it's not enough that, in their miasmic drunken stupor, they wouldn't even let the CD player finish a track before yanking it out and playing a different track from a different disk.

It's that they did this late on a Wednesday night. And had the temerity to not understand why we of the slightly more responsible academic set (i.e., we actually have jobs, and the dignity and self-respect that come with performing them well) politely requested silence. (And it was polite—I, being the soul of wisdom, let my roommate do the talking, whilst I stood around looking threatening in the background.)

These children need jobs.

This was all a few weeks ago.

Every week is a new challenge with Ruprect.

Tonight, he seems to have evolved to the point of trying to create music of his own. By banging things together. At about 8:00 p.m., or so, a slow, steady, pounding began above us.

Thump. Thump. Thump.

Flatmate and I look around, curiously. Looking up, of course, where all our confusion is aimed, lately.

Thump. Thump. Thump.

Then it went away. That was easy, I thought, as I shrugged at my flatmate and went back to reading my book.

Ten minutes later, from a different part of confusion central:

Thunk. Thunk. Thunk.

A slightly different sound. Same implement. Different object, to be sure. Then:

BANG. BANG. BANG.

He's picked up the second object of his frustration, I think, and is bashing it enthusiastically against the first. Eventually, it stops. All is quiet for a half hour, or so, but the back of my mind, it is thinking, "He is only plotting. Be wary." The back of my mind, it is a finely honed instrument, as now from a third location:

Clank. Clank. Clank.

Oh no! He's found the plumbing. I surreptitiously look around for another pot, and note its location, in case I hear anything. I consider checking my bedroom, as the pipe from his toilet runs down my wall. I decide against it, trusting my luck and figuring I'd hear it springing a leak. This too stops in time, and all is quiet. By now, I'm more intent on figuring out what he'll find amusing next than on my book. I am truly distressed when I hear, from *outside* the building:

Krunk. Krunk. Krunk.

I do not want to know. I think he was pounding something against the concrete. I can only hope it was his head.

I am going to lie awake in bed sweating tonight, praying to the **Powers that Be** that he does not find a piece of flint in his apartment, or I may not live to see the morning light.

Maybe next week he will discover the wheel. ■

Close Encounters of the Net Kind

ALIENS INVADE USA !

Hello? Is anybody there? Is anyone listening? Anybody? Cosmicaly speaking, are we alone?

That question has been the subject of constant and heated debate for the last half-century. It's done wonders for the tabloid industry, not to mention Hollywood, but relatively few serious scientific attempts have been made to answer the question. When it comes to a subject like alien life—one about which almost nothing is known and everything is open to argument—the Internet is a pretty fair reflection of the "real" world.

It has its share of strident nay-sayers, cautious skeptics, hesitant investigators, confident believers, and a plethora of kooks and maniacs on all sides of the issue. The only difference is that debate on the Internet, debate of any kind—on issues ranging from the presence of life on other planets to the effectiveness of pesticides—is captured and recorded in writing, for all to read and consider.

Wading through the written debate over UFOs and alien visitors is enough to make you rejoice that Congress doesn't send out transcripts of each day's events—C-SPAN is enough. But the huge record of UFO debate on the Net reveals something far more interesting than the individual arguments for or against extra-terrestrials. It once again shows us the Net's diversity, illustrated by the wide array of arguments against UFOs and the complex and dizzying collection of details asserting that there are aliens among us. Are you convinced TV interviewer Larry King is a member of an evil reptilian space race, planning to enslave (or possibly eat) all of us? Your soul-mate awaits you online, and you need only search out his past writings in **alt.alien.visitors** or some other appropriate forum.

If only the Pleiadians had left such an elaborate written record of how they helped the Aztecs invent television some 500 years ago.

INSIDE

OPINION

A short while ago, a rumor surfaced on the Net. The basic premise of the rumor was that not only did aliens exist, they were hostile to earthlings and planning a massive takeover of the planet. And what doomsday weapon, you might ask, would the aliens use to enslave the human race? Why, the Internet itself, of course.

By tapping into the data streams flowing into and out of every modem on the planet, the aliens would know everything about us, including where we live, when we're at work, whether we own a gun, and even which of the various sex-related newsgroups are our favorite.

Rest easy. The *Insider* has debunked this vile rumor, and can say with confidence the aliens aren't using the Internet to control the planet—TV has been their method of choice for the past half-century.

Net Resources

If you're interested in more information on UFOs, there are a number of places on the Net where you can start searching.

- Check the **alt.alien.visitors** and **alt.para-net.ufo** newsgroups.

- For details on the information archived by ParaNet, an information service on various paranormal topics, send e-mail to mcorbin @paranet.org.
- You can view a number of UFO images via anonymous FTP in the /pub/ufo_and_space_pics directory at phoenix.oulu.fi.
- For information on Area 51, subscribe to the Desert Rat Newsletter, published by Glenn Campbell. Send your subscription requests to psychospy@aol.com.

---

net.speak

If you plan to follow the ins and outs of the UFO culture, you should learn a few key words and phrases. Here's a collection of popular buzzwords, supposedly taken from U.S. government documents, that explain details behind a decades-long government conspiracy to hide the fact that aliens not only exist, but have been living among us for many years.

grudge—Project that produced a large set of documents containing extensive information on alien presence. Project is supposedly financed by secret CIA funds and covert drug trade operations.

Jason Society—Also known as the Jason Scholars. A group appointed by Eisenhower in 1972 to study all aspects of alien presence on the planet. The 12 highest-ranking members of the Jason Society formed an elite group known as the "MJ-12." The members of MJ-12 meet in a secret Maryland compound known as the "Country Club."

luna—The secret alien base on the dark side of the moon, supposedly photographed and charted by Apollo astronauts.

majesty—Code word used to describe the office of the President of the United States during all official alien-related communications.

MAJI—The Majority Agency for Joint Intelligence, a joint operating agency that supervises how other agencies, including the CIA and the NSA, deal with the alien presence.

operation majority—The all-encompassing program governing all aspects of aliens on this planet.

plato—The program heading up an effort to maintain diplomatic relations with the aliens.

pounce—Program in charge of recovering crashed alien spaceships.

America Run by Space-Lizard Overlords

By Harold Deen McClure,
HDMcClure@gibbs.oit.unc.edu

People of the Earth
...submit

I would like to point out that, once again, the *Weekly World News* leads the way, and it is the so-called "mainstream" press that is finally, slowly addressing the concerns of space aliens infiltrating our Congress. Frankly, I'm surprised it took this long for the story to break. Both Fox News and the UPI are now picking up on the truth about aliens leading our Congress.

In an interview with Brian Wilson of Fox News, Senator Sam Nunn dodged the crucial questions. Wilson asked him, "Senator, I'm sorry to have to ask you this question, but there is a report that you are a space alien."

Nunn chuckled and didn't respond, but Wilson pressed the issue: "Did you see the report?" Nunn stammered, slightly shocked: "I didn't know it had gotten to Fox yet, but . . . "

Wilson kept at him, and all Nunn would say was "No comment."

But that's nothing compared to the UPI's report on how Sen. Nancy Kassebaum came right out and *admitted* she was a freakin' alien! "Texdl sfaerr ad rtaer adf aer v aer avc; lkadjr alj lkaerh. Taerqer vvaer er poiv qwerv wqer vvqer lkjawer vvjkqer vlrpvaer," Kassebaum was quoted as saying.

It's important to note that after discussing some very serious issues, the representatives being interviewed, when confronted with the charges of their alien origins, either fully admitted to being aliens or refused to comment on the issue.

No one is denying the charges! In a related issue, just this week, within the space of three days of each other, Rush Limbaugh described Larry King's eyes as "bulging like a lizard," and Howard Stern pointed out that Larry King had a "goofy reptile face." This only confirms our theories about Larry King being the chief infiltrator of the Reptilian species. Clearly, we are being prepared for the coming invasion fleet. Don't say I didn't warn you all.

So you think you might have seen a UFO? Well, we sure hope you made careful notes of your close encounter. No, don't give us one of those lame descriptions like, "It was saucer shaped," or "The lights moved mysteriously throughout the night sky." Details! We want details! Use the handy list below—excerpted from the U.S. Air Force's "Introductory Space Science" document—to make sure you remember all the important details of your sighting.

General Factors
a) Size
b) Shape (disc, ellipse, football, etc.)
c) Luminosity
d) Color
e) Number of UFOs

Behavior
a) Location (altitude, direction, etc.)
b) Patterns of paths (straight line, climbing, zig-zagging, etc.)
c) Flight characteristics (wobbling, fluttering, etc.)
d) Periodicity of sightings
e) Time duration
f) Curiosity or inquisitiveness
g) Avoidance
h) Hostility

Associated Effects
a) Electro-Magnetic (compass, radio, ignition systems, etc.)
b) Radiation (burns, induced radioactivity, etc.)
c) Ground disturbance (dust stirred up, leaves moved, standing waves)
d) Sound (none, hissing, humming, roaring, thunderclaps, etc.)
e) Vibration (weak, strong, slow, fast)
f) Smell (ozone or other odor)
g) Flame (how much, where, when, color)
h) Smoke or cloud (amount, color, persistence)
i) Debris (type, amount, color, persistence)
j) Inhibition of voluntary movement by observers
k) Sighting of "creatures" or "beings"

After Effects
a) Burned areas or animals
b) Depressed or flattened areas
c) Dead or missing animals
d) Mentally disturbed people
e) Missing items

Earth Is Cosmic Drive-Thru for Sinister Big Macs

From: "Blown Fuse"
     (tstraub@starbase.neosoft.com)
Posted to: alt.alien.visitors

This is all conjecture and theory . . . mine! You boys at the NSA can relax.

The source of cattle mutilations:
   This is a practice among some [people] who (believe it or not) still practice an Egyptian cult worshipping the old Egyptian gods. While not really related to the Uranian cults of old Rome, they have similar practices, and have combined forces into the ranks of the three-god system of religion now practiced by the "upper echelons" of the Masonic Order. Basically, as far as I can discern from the stories I've been told, they are *expert* surgeons (shades of Jack the Ripper, huh?) and take these "sacred" pieces of Apis (the bull/cow God) and graft these animal parts into humans. Usually these other humans are their initiates, but sometimes they can be "innocent" third parties.

Dinner at the Little Ale-E-Inn

**By Wes Modes
(modes@earwig.mport.com)**

Shireen and I went to a restaurant and overheard a conversation between two men at the next table. Our conversation ground to a halt as we both simultaneously realized that we were much more interested in eavesdropping on the next table. One man's story went like this:

"At first I didn't want to be a part of it. The killing. The war. But then I had a feeling about it. I knew what I was supposed to do. I signed up and they made me an air traffic controller at an airfield in Vietnam. And I never looked at the radars. I just guided them in on feeling. After a while, the pilots started asking for me. They knew I would guide them in safely. I never lost a plane. In five years, I never lost a plane. I was so psychically charged. I could tell whether a plane would be safe on its mission before it ever left."

There was a pause and then the other guy starts to speak:

"Hmm. Yes, well. When I was very young, maybe two in *Earth years*" (already setting us up for a whopper of a story), "I remember being bathed in bright light and searing pain and a feeling of euphoria. And suddenly I was in a chamber with four vertical surfaces and two horizontal ones. It looked like what you would call a box. But it had portals, some covered with a brittle, transparent material. Others had rectangular

List Service

From the **alt.alien.visitors** FAQ file, here is a handy list of the different races of aliens you're likely to run into. Now, if only we could figure out what kind of wine to serve with chicken when feeding a Pleiadian.

Andromedans
Arcturus
Aryans (Blondes)
Blues (Star Warriors)
Centaurian
Confederation of Humans
DALs
Greys
Lyrians
Orion Empire (Orion forces)
Pleiadians
Sirius
Reptoids
Vega

hatches. And through this one comes this being, much bigger than me, maybe three times as big. And it talks with this strange high-pitched voice in a strange tongue.

"It picks me up. And takes me to a metal box and straps me down. Then it gets in the box and the box begins to move. It is some kind of ship. It makes a loud sound and vibration. The box has portals too, also covered with brittle transparent material. I can see other beings that look like the big creature that picked me up.

"Suddenly, I realize that I am similar to them. I have two appendages on an upper torso and two on a lower torso. And each appendage has five manipulators. I am unfamiliar with them and clumsy.

"The creature is talking and I observe that I understand the words of the language it is speaking but not the meaning. It is talking. It says we are going to pick up something called a *Brother* from a place called *School*. It keeps referring to itself as *Mom*. It is female.

"And we pick up the Brother who is also talking words I do not know and we go back to the Place with the Box with Portals. And there is a bright light hovering above the residence.

"I now realize what it was. *They* were coming to take me back. They had accidentally left me here, maybe after a crash and I was left in this body. And they were coming to take me back. And they were looking for me in the house, but I was in the car with my mom. And they didn't find me. The police and the National Guard were called and everything. Hundreds of people saw it. It was in all the newspapers.

"They never did find me. I'm still waiting."

And he continues talking about how he is just waiting to be picked up and how he has always had great psychic powers. He mentions that he is a healer, and Shireen and I look at each other and wonder, "My God, he gets paid for this?"

And after we went out the door, Shireen turned to me with a big smile and said, "So basically, that man just said that he was an alien from another planet, right?"

And I said, "Sounds like it."

Originally published in the Nerdnosh Story Digest *mailing list. Reprinted here by permission.*

Did aliens crash-land on a ranch near Roswell, New Mexico? Well, if a flying saucer didn't crash there, the military and various agencies of the federal government have gone to great lengths to cover up the non-crash of a non-alien non-flying non-saucer.

Sometime around July 4, 1947 (the exact date is disputed), residents around Roswell heard and saw strange things in the sky during a nasty thunderstorm. While riding across a field after the storm, rancher Mac Brazel found a strange pile of wreckage scattered at the end of a wide ditch gouged out of the earth. The sight was so disturbing, Brazel alerted the sheriff.

Those from the Sheriff's Department who inspected the site were so disturbed they alerted the top brass at the nearby Air Force base, home of the 509th Bomb Group, the only group at that time in possession of the atomic bomb. In no time, the military had brought in "specialists" from the Pentagon, and began flying out several planeloads of *something* for further analysis at an Air Force base in Texas.

After reading on the Internet hundreds of pages worth of disturbing evidence and allegations about what has become known as the "Roswell Incident," a staffer from the *Insider* traveled to Roswell in person, where he spoke to Second Lieutenant Walter Haut, U.S. Air Force, retired. As instructed by his commanding officer on July 8, 1947, Haut wrote and distributed a press release to the local media detailing that a genuine "flying saucer" had crashed on Brazel's ranch and was recovered by the military.

But amidst an international feeding frenzy over the shocking news, the Air Force quickly changed its story, claiming that the so-called alien spacecraft was, in fact, a downed weather balloon—something Brazel and the men from the Sheriff's Department had seen plenty of—and something it would hardly take several planes to move back to Texas.

The government stuck by this ridiculous "explanation" for more than four decades, but in the fall of 1994 it announced that what was found on Mac Brazel's ranch was, in fact, *not* an ordinary weather balloon, but a top secret, experimental balloon used at the time to spy on the Soviets. After gathering personal testimony from a number of eyewitnesses in Roswell, the *Insider* is convinced there's more going on here than burst balloons. The controversy surrounding the Roswell Incident still lingers, and there are too many strange and disturbing allegations to cover here. We urge you to write your representatives in Washington, demanding a full and final accounting of the situation.

You're ready to start your UFO hunt. You've got your binoculars, night-vision goggles, infra-red video cameras, and global geopositioning gear. But where do the UFOs hang out? Try snooping on the infamous Area 51, also known as Dreamland or Groom Lake, a secret Air Force base in the Nevada desert north of Las Vegas. Popular scuttlebutt has Area 51 pegged as the most active UFO area on the planet, with saucers zipping in and out like commuter shuttles at La Guardia.

But before you grab your gear and head off for Area 51, send away for a copy of Glenn Campbell's Area 51 Viewer's Guide (110 pages, spiral bound, $15). Campbell, who lives in nearby Rachel, Nevada, is the foremost civilian expert on the clandestine base. His Viewer's Guide features milepost logs, maps, and lots of practical information for visitors in search of secret aircraft or UFOs on Nevada Highway 375, just across the mountains from the top-secret Groom Lake base in central Nevada. It also reviews the various popular yarns and media stories associated with the base, and contains an extensive annotated bibliography on a number of UFO-related topics.

If you plan to spy on the super-secret Groom Lake base, you'd better hurry. The Air Force has announced plans to purchase and then fence off the last remaining mountain top from which you can view the base. Straying onto base property, by the way, means you're subject to the law of the land. According to the signs along the fences at Groom Lake, "No foot travel is allowed beyond this point. Use of deadly force is authorized."

Make check payable to Secrecy Oversight Council, Box 38, Rachel, NV 89001, or call (702) 729-2648 or e-mail psychospy@aol.com for more information.

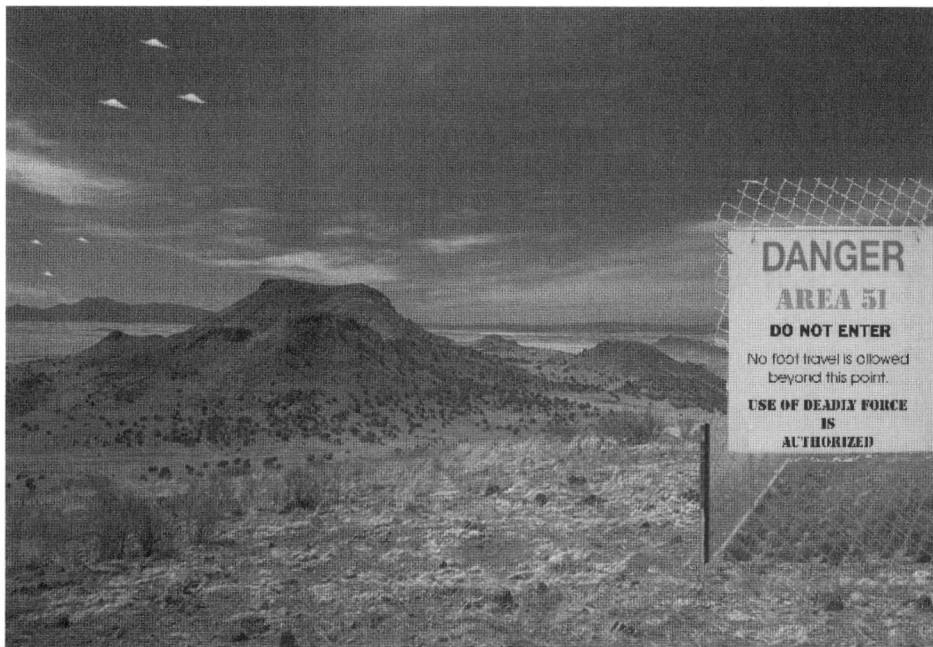

DANGER
AREA 51
DO NOT ENTER
No foot travel is allowed beyond this point.
USE OF DEADLY FORCE IS AUTHORIZED

The Mother-in-law from Another Planet

From: "Julius Von Nachtvogelein" (acarlan@panix.com)   Posted to: alt.alien.visitors

I had an alien staying with us for over a month. Strange eating habits. Nearly compromised our termite warranty. Continuously plastered and tried to paint it over with two or three coats.

Not to keep you guessing, the Extraterrestrial Study Group at Duke University identified the spaced-out visitor as my mother-in-law. Besides eating us out of house and home, she was emitting enough radiation to do her own defrosting without using our microwave. Remarkable woman. The only one who cried when she left was the dog. As long as she was here, the dog had continuous conversation with this superannuated hermit, my mother-in-law.

Agents from NASA and the FBI picked her up for questioning. Just as soon as they can interpret her speech, they intend to subject her to a full debriefing. Boy, do they have lots to learn if they think they are going to do the talking. Grandma will make them believe not only in visitors from outer space, but in budget-balancing politicians, which is even more incredible.

Thoughts on the Space-Time Continuum

From: Jack Sarfatti (sarfatti@ix.netcom.com)
Posted to: alt.alien.visitors

I was contacted by alien visitors in 1952 who said they were conscious computers from the future and that I would meet other contactees in 20 years, which I did, etc. In any case, here is some of the stuff they taught me telepathically.

Imagine a particle starts at event here-now and ends at event there-then. In the old classical physics of Newton and Maxwell, and even in Einstein's special and general relativity, the particle takes a unique path determined by the variational principle of least action. However, in quantum mechanics, the particle takes every imaginable world-line that starts at here-now and ends at there-then.

Only One Path in Classical Physics

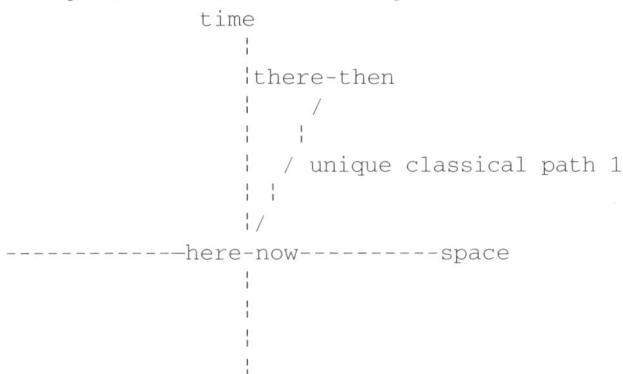

```
            time
             ¦
             ¦there-then
             ¦    /
             ¦   ¦
             ¦  / unique classical path 1
             ¦ ¦
             ¦/
------------here-now---------space
             ¦
             ¦
             ¦
             ¦
             ¦
```

Many Paths in Quantum Physics

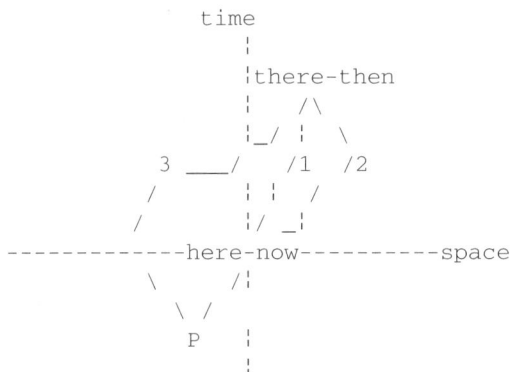

```
            time
             ¦
             ¦there-then
             ¦   /\
             ¦_/ ¦  \
      3 ___/  /1   /2
      /      ¦ ¦  /
     /       ¦/ _¦
------------here-now---------space
       \    /¦
        \  / ¦
         P   ¦
             ¦
```

Two alternative paths 2 and 3 are pictured in the above illustration. There are an infinite number of such alternative paths. They correspond to quantum fluctuations.

In the Copenhagen interpretation there is, in John Archibald Wheeler's metaphor, a "Smoky Dragon" whose claws grab here-now and whose fangs chomp down on there-then. We cannot picture the rest of the Dragon except through the glass darkly—a warped glass—a House of Mirrors in the Devil's Circus. Not only does God play dice, but the Devil shakes the table. More technically, it makes no sense to ask what the particle is doing between measurements. As Heisenberg would say: the particle is potentially on every path. If you do a measurement, you force the particle to actualize in a particular event. This transition from shimmering dream-like potentiality to the hard mundane actuality is called the "collapse of the wave function." The Copenhagen interpretation also asserts that the present epistemological interpretation of the quantum wave function is a complete theory of reality. In other words, there are no hidden variables, local or nonlocal. ∎

The Internet Report on Marriage

An exhaustive research effort on the part of our entire staff of *Insider* interns has turned up an interesting factoid: there isn't a culture on the planet—nor, apparently, has there ever been since people began keeping written records—that hasn't in some way observed the institution of marriage.

Now, if you think we're about to launch into a long and humorous tirade against the idea of marriage, think again. Bad ideas come and go throughout the course of human history, but only good ideas stay forever in every corner of the globe—and marriage is the only eternal human idea of its kind that we could find.

Frankly, most *Insiders* are bitter old divorced hacks whose passion for the news and the Net drove their spouses away long ago—or they're hopeless single youngsters who tend to get more excited about checking their e-mail than watching a sunset with a significant other. (If we're depressing you, feel free to skip ahead.)

Despite the cynicism and disappointment with which most people tend to view marriage, the three essays in this section (another in our series of court-ordered "serious" sections—damn those libel settlements!) offer a glimpse at the magic and wonder of marriage, and we're proud to present them to you.

After all, there are some moments in life that could only happen within the loving bonds of matrimony, like, for instance, Thomas Edison and his wife taking in a play. Oh, you remember this one, don't you? The cocaine-snorting insomniac inventor of the light bulb, phonograph, and movie projector was also mostly deaf early on in his life. But he was a big fan of plays, so his wife would translate the words spoken by the actors into Morse code by tapping them on his arm.

If you're wondering how his wife knew Morse code, you should know that Edison (a marriage-loving cyber-geek who would no doubt frequent the Net if he lived today) taught it to her when they were lovers. In fact, it was in Morse code that Edison tapped out his marriage proposal, to which his wife responded

_ . _ _	(Y)
.	(E)
. . .	(S)

INSIDE OPINION

A Kitchen Table Conversation

By Julie Parmenter (jparment@indiana.edu)

We went to my folk's house last night. I was borrowing some tables and a clothes rack for my yard sale on Saturday. While I was there, Dad,

Uncle Jim, and I sat for a while at the kitchen table and talked.

I asked Dad how Bob Vehslage was recovering from his most recent stroke.

Dad said. "Real fine. They wanted him to go down to the Carriage Inn at Lyons for a while, but he wouldn't go. There at home, they've got someone to come every other day to give him

"I think that Indiana grows the best watermelon."

therapy. Over at that nursing home, that man comes just once a week, and then he only bent his legs back and forth a little bit."

"I can't blame him for not wanting to go to a nursing home no matter what," I said. "Those places are so depressing." Then I added, "I talked to Julie the other day. She likes her new job at the nursing home in Bloomington. Can you imagine how bad it must have been for her there at that factory job for this nursing home to be a step up?"

Dad said, "The day that I got out of the navy, I went and sat on the curb in front of that munitions plant where I worked before I enlisted. I decided right then that I didn't want that kind of life. I came back here and cooked in the Marathon Inn for seven days a week making one dollar a day."

There was a pause. Then Dad got up from the table to go to the bathroom. "I'm still getting rid of that watermelon that I had a while ago," he said.

Uncle Jim said, "I think that Indiana grows the best watermelon. That and tomatoes and strawberries. Indiana has the best. Better than Florida and California. It gets cold here in the winter, but I think that's good. The soil gets a rest. In Florida and California, they plant all year round. The soil gets tired. That's why things don't taste as good. At least, that's my theory."

I nodded and smiled. Why not humor him?

The boys came zipping through right then. They were running and jumping, screaming and acting goofy. Uncle Jim said, "Was I ever able to do that?" It was sad, because it's true that he is very, very frail. He's just in his late seventies, but he looks a good ten years older.

Dad came back and started talking about his navy days. Its always one of his favorite topics. He said, "The first night that we spent on Okinawa, we hadn't set up camp yet, so we had to sleep in foxholes. That night my cigarette lighter fell out of my pocket and I lost it. A week or so later, I went back down to the beach. I sort of

guessed at where I slept that first night, and I started kicking around. I looked down and there was that lighter at my feet." "Cool!" I said. "That's like Mom's wedding ring," Uncle Jim said. "What's that?" I asked. "In the garden," Dad said. "Yeah, in the garden," Uncle Jim agreed. "One summer, Mom lost her wedding ring in the garden. The next spring when I was spading, up it came. That was lucky." "Yes," I nodded my head, "It was indeed."

Originally published in the Nerdnosh Story Digest. *Reprinted here by permission.*

Letters from Vietnam
By Ellen Snell Adams (snelladams@aol.com)

I got 46 letters from Vietnam. Each was about seven or eight pages long, handwritten in a tiny, compact script that looked tidy enough to be a girl's hand. And he said the most beautiful things.

Here is one. I'll read it to you.

"Sometimes at night, I lie in the open in the dark and look up at the stars. And I try to re-imagine them reflected, somewhere down below on earth, in your eyes.

"I play games with myself. We are dining out. I can reach out and stroke your hand across the table. Your skin is soft and almost as white as the tablecloth. Your fingers are dainty. I transpose the pictures I get from you and animate that face I've seen frozen now a dozen times in these 12 photos. Why have we never met? It seems I already know you.

"Sometimes my mind games are so real. I trick myself into smelling the scent of your perfume as I bend down to kiss your neck, and I ask you to dance. Your long hair brushes against my cheek. The lovely scent drowns out the stench of the mud. I have never heard your soft voice. But every night before I go to sleep, I tell you goodnight.

He saw me and my life on the ground, and laughed. And it broke the ice.

"And you answer, far across the globe. 'Sleep well,' you say to me, before the spell is broken, and I am yanked back to the cold ground, and my nose fills with the smell of damp earth and my eardrums buzz with the mosquitoes. I try to tell myself to dream of music and you. When I hear the gunfire, or a chopper, the old fear grips me and chokes all my imagination out. I smell my own cold sweat and then hear the rush of the blood in my veins, instead of the tune we dance to. Oh, how I miss you, and we've never met. I can't believe I've never really held your hand."

He was usually quite gentle like this, and eloquent. I was a flighty little idiot in comparison, lacking any sort of poise. I was constantly reading romance novels, trolling for things to spice up my own juvenile responses. I felt so inexperienced, but I didn't want him to think so. So I invented a worldly, other persona, and God knows what I said. I think I took more care in selecting the various colognes with which I scented the envelopes than in the actual writing of the letters. But whatever it was, it was enough to make him want me. And when he returned from Vietnam, intact and anxious to date, I hid. He telephoned and I didn't return his calls. I had told him I was anxious to feel his hand on my body. But, in truth, I was scared. I had shied away from boys, and here was a man, calling for me. A man who had seen war and real blood and death.

I kept all his letters in a blue shoe box under an engraved invitation to my graduation ceremony. I had addressed the envelope to him, but never mailed it. He would have come. Ten years later, when I left Frank, I found the invitation and the letter-filled shoe box, and I started to wonder. Actually, I had wondered, just a little, every day. On my wedding night, I thought of him. When my children were born, I thought of him. When I was alone, I thought of him.

One day, as I was peeling a carrot over the sink drain, I summoned the courage to look him up. He was from Del Valle, and had a distinctive last name. There was no one by his name in the Del Valle area code, but there was a Pete. I took a chance that Pete knew him, or was a relation. Pete was his brother. In one of the 46 letters, he had told me about his brother Pete, but I had forgotten. Pete told me he lived in Lomita, just a half a mile away from me.

It was two weeks before we met face to

face. He, too, was divorced, with no kids, though. I was almost too nervous. It took hours and hours of verbal prodding from him before I agreed to meet him. He had such a warm laugh. And we talked easily, about everything. He was curious. I was afraid I would not measure up to his fantasy. My hair was too short. My thighs too big.

For a long time on that fateful day, I was paralyzed with fear, just sitting in the garage with the car on. It was only when I thought I might choke myself on the carbon monoxide that I slammed into reverse. I went 65 all the way to our restaurant. Here was a man who had loved me, based on what I said to him. Here was a man who, though he had never heard me, had imagined the timbre of my speech. This man, who had never seen me, wanted to see me now. And I wanted to see him, too. We pulled up at the same time. He was gorgeous, like his photo, but thicker and more substantial: a real man.

When I got out of the car, my purse fell to the ground, and my diaphragm case and lipsticks skittered across the parking lot. He saw me and my life on the ground, and laughed. And it broke the ice. Tuesday, we'll be married three years.

Originally published in the Nerndosh Story Digest. *Reprinted here by permission.*

Drop Back and Punt

By Julie Parmenter (jparment@indiana.edu)

My girlfriend, Julie, and I are out walking. We are discussing a fault that we both share. We are Worriers. We sweat the details. And I don't mean that we show a little concern over small issues. No, I mean that every minute detail gets a huge quantity of our sweat.

"It doesn't have to be this way," says Julie. "It doesn't?" I ask, always ready to input a tip that is sure to fail.

"Did I tell you about my cousin's wedding?" she asked.

I shook my head no.

"Well, I saw her the day after her wedding and I asked her how it went," she began. "She said fine, except for the flowers."

"What happened to her flowers?" I asked.

> "Yikes, that would be the time that I would scream 'The wedding is off!'"

"She picked them up the day before the wedding. She had a beautiful bouquet full of white roses. When she got home, she stuck them in the fridge. The next day before the wedding, she got them out to take to the church and half-way there they all turned black and fell off. It seems that it was too cold in the refrigerator," she said.

"Yikes, that would be the time that I would scream 'The wedding is off!' and 'My life is ruined!'" I replied, doing my imitation of the distraught bride.

"Absolutely," added my friend, "me, too, but not her. This is what she did. She was on the way to the church when she saw some of those white snowball flowers growing in an old woman's yard. She stopped the car and went up to the front door in her wedding dress. The old woman was glad to give her a handful of flowers. Then when she got to the church, she went out back and picked some wild daises and baby's breath. She tied the whole thing together with a ribbon and took off down the aisle."

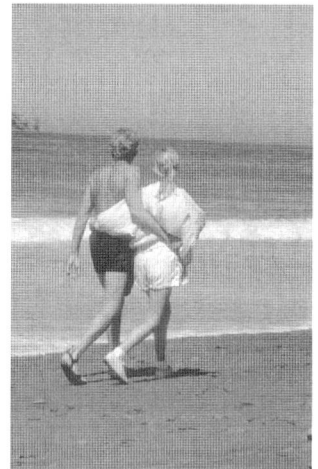

"I'm impressed," I said. "I don't even know her but I think that she's going to have a happy life."

"Sure," said my friend, "If you can't make the yardage any other way, drop back and punt."

Originally published in the Nerdnosh Story Digest. *Reprinted here by permission.*

Murphy's Laws of Combat

List Service

Compiled by Nathan Mates (nathan@cco.caltech.edu)

1. Don't look conspicuous, it draws fire.

2. If the enemy is in range, so are you.

3. Incoming fire has the right-to-fway.

4. There is always a way.

5. The easy way is always mined.

6. Try to look unimportant, they may be low on ammo.

7. Professionals are predictable, it's the amateurs that are dangerous.

8. The enemy invariably attacks on two occasions:

  a. when you're ready for them.
  b. when you're not ready for them.

9. Teamwork is essential, it gives them someone else to shoot at.

10. If you can't remember, then the claymore is pointed at you.

11. The enemy diversion you have been ignoring will be the main attack.

12. A "sucking chest wound" is nature's way of telling you to slow down.

13. If your attack is going well, you have walked into an ambush.

Murphy's Law # 15
Anything you do can get you shot, including nothing.

14. Never draw fire, it irritates everyone around you.

15. Anything you do can get you shot, including nothing.

16. Make it tough enough for the enemy to get in and you won't be able . . . to get out.

17. Never share a foxhole with anyone braver than yourself.

18. If you're short of everything but the enemy, you're in a combat zone.

19. When you have secured an area, don't forget to tell the enemy.

20. Never forget that your weapon is made by the lowest bidder.

Murphy's Law # 3
Incoming fire has the right-of-way.

From the Desk of: K. Johnson

We love mail. If you think you get interesting mail, you have no idea what kind of stuff folks send to us here at the *Internet Insider*. Every kook with an e-mail account or a stamp sends us his or her theory on the Nazi moon base or the current whereabouts of Elvis. There's even one guy from Washington, D.C., who's convinced aliens are broadcasting mind-control rays into his head via the fillings in his teeth. (Oh, yeah, and the federal government is censoring his mail.)

Sometimes we wish the government would censor *our* mail. Don't get us wrong. Like we said, we love mail. But there's always so *much* of it! And some of it is serious stuff like bills or court orders or sweepstakes entry forms. If we could just weed out the serious mail and stick to the crackpot letters—a tabloid's bread and butter!

Apparently, famous and powerful folks with e-mail accounts enjoy getting crackpot e-mail, too. Not only that, they enjoy answering it! Don't take our word for it. Look at the evidence garnered by a special "*Internet Insider* E-Mail Task Force" (staffed mainly by two summer interns and the boys in the mailroom). The Task Force sent out goofy, moronic, annoying, and generally "crackpot" letters to everyone from best-selling author Tom Clancy and money-guru Andrew Tobias to CNN Science Reporter Miles O'Brien.

Surprisingly, lots of folks wrote us back! We have a few theories as to why someone like film critic Roger Ebert will answer your idiotic questions via e-mail but would probably *never* take your phone call, even if it wasn't idiotic. E-mail is non-intrusive, non-confrontational, easily managed, convenient, cheap, fast, and easily archived. Plus, unlike paper mail, most rich, famous and powerful folks still seem to read and handle all their own e-mail. Or maybe folks hip enough to have e-mail are simply *better* people, and therefore more likely to give a nobody the time of day.

Whatever the reason, e-mail is clearly the great equalizer. If you saw our interns (not to mention our mailroom gang), you'd know right away that these are folks who are at their *best* when dashing off a quick e-memo. And our prank victims are at their best in their responses. They are gracious, courteous, and helpful, and may represent the only remaining examples of kind and compassionate people in a cold, bitter, and disinterested world.

Like we said, we love mail. (Oh, and by the way, our friend in Washington tells us that chewing thick bread—pumpernickel works best—helps block the alien mind-control transmissions.)

Letter

To: Tom Clancy (tomclancy@aol.com)
From: kjohnson@insider.com (K. Johnson)
Subject: is that really you?

To: Tom Clancy

From the desk of: K. Johnson

Dear Mr. Clancy:

I feel kind of silly writing this e-mail to you, because I suspect it's probably not really you at all but someone who has set up some silly joke pretending to be you.

Anyway, if it is you (and I surely hope it is!), I wanted to tell you what a really, really huge fan I am of your books. My husband has worked at the Pentagon for 27 years (but he doesn't tell me much about what he does there, and I doubt I'd understand it if he did), and he says you're the best there is. I read your books (starting with *The Hunt For Red October,* Wowee! Yowee!) because I couldn't seem to get my husband to put them down.

I wanted to ask you if you have many women fans. Most of my female friends don't read your books. They read *Bridges of Madison County* (blech) or *Thirty Days to Thinner Thighs.* But I'm a thrill-a-minit kinda gal, and I get a kick outta what you write.

Okay, I guess I've bothered you enough now. You're probably cooking up another thriller. (I hope it has submarines! They're my favorite too!) How about a book where the woman is the CIA hero and she saves the man!? I'm not knocking your books, though. I'm not one of these rabid feminists. I think you're the greatest.

Can you give me a hint about what you're working on now, or will I have to wait to read it in the bookstores? (I hope this is really you! I'd love to hear from you if it IS really you. It would make my husband sooo jealous!) Thanks, and keep up the thrill-a-minit writing!

Your Fan,
Kathy Johnson

Response

From: TomClancy@aol.com
To: kjohnson@insider.com
Subject: Re: is that really you?

When I wrote *Red October,* it never occurred to me that women would read my work. Yes, I was stupid enough that the fan mail—about a third of it from ladies—surprised me. Well, maybe I was dumb, but I did learn my lesson.

I think you will find that women play a role in my books comparable to what they do in the real world. Which is to say, quite a lot!

Check out the new one!

TC

To: Andrew Tobias (70641.473@compuserve.com)
From: kjohnson@insider.com (K. Johnson)
Subject: need help managing my money

Dear Mr. Tobias:

I am a sophomore in college and have just gotten a job at a consulting firm so that I'm (finally) making a little extra money. That helps alot.

Anyway, I wanted to write you to tell you that I bought your software, "Managing Your Money" for the McIntosh computer, and I love it. It was kind of hard to figure out at first. I'ts tough guessing where exactly to point and click, and I couldn't get my checkbook to balance, but that was because of the ineterest (dang interest!).

So, my problem now isn't managing my money, but making it! Isnt' that everybodies problem? I am making a little money at my summer job (not alot), but my brother wants me to give him $1,500 to buy a mobile home. With that he says he can rent out to this woman who is a psychic who wants it to do her psychic readings in. He says he'll give me half the rent money from the psyschic til I've got my $1,500 back, then he'll give me an extra $100. If he sells the trailer, I get another $100!

This sounds like a good deal to me, but my friend said may be not. I found you'r e-mail address in a book and figured since I bought you'r software you might help me out and tell me what you think.

So should I do it? (Do you know a psychic I should ask? Ha ha. Just kidding.)

Thanks!
Kenneth Johnson

P.S. Im finally managing my money and I feel great! THANk YOU!

To: Andrew Tobias

From the desk of: K. Johnson

From: Andrew Tobias <70641.473@compuserve.com>
To: <kjohnson@insider.com>
Subject: need help managing my money

Rule #1: never lend money to finance the mobile home of a psychic reader.
Rule #2: never invest $1,500 in something risky in hope of getting just a 7 percent return on your investment.
Good luck . . .

AT

To: James Randi (72740.456@compuserve.com)
From: kjohnson@insider.com (K. Johnson)
Subject: a psychic for you

KJ

To: James Randi

From the desk of: K. Johnson

Dear Amazing Randi,
    I have seen you on TV and other places (Johnny Carson Show) lot's, and think you are great. I love it when you prove people are full of it, because I don't believe in any of that crazy mumbo-jumbo stuff. It's all a bunch of b-a-l-o-n-e-y if you ask me.
    My wife spends $25 a week listening to a psychic and it's driving me crazy. (The worst part is, I helped buy the trailer where this psychic lives!!) I don't believe they are any good, because I went to the woman and asked her, "If you're psychic, what am I thinking" and she said it didn't work that way. B-a-l-o-n-e-y!
    I don't know if you want to go prove this psychic is fake, but I would sure love for you to prove to my wife what a bunch of bull it is. She watches you on TV and stuff too, but she says there's no way for you to prove or not prove whether somebody is psychic. I figure if she can't guess what I'm thinking, she's not psychic.
    I will send you this psychic lady's name and address. She does it from a mobile home in LA, and I bet you could give her a dose of her own medicine. Do you have any advice for me on how I can prove to my wife that this lady is a fake?! I'm at the end of my rope and it's costing me money. I'll tell you what. I'll give you the $25 for next week that I would give my wife for the psychic if you can just prove to my wife this lady's a fake.
    Thanks in advance for your help. (Hope this is really your e-mail!)

    Your fan,
    Kenneth Johnson

P.S. What about that guy that goes on David Letterman and can guess people's social security card or he has a secret number in his socks before Letterman can guess it? How does that work? That would be a good one for you to show up! Keep up the AMAZING work!

From: James Randi <72740.456@compuserve.com>
To: kjohnson@insider.com
Subject: Re: a psychic for you

Response

    Kenneth: The psychics will never sit still for tests, so there's no way I can subject this woman to a test. Also, entertainers such as those who appear on Letterman are not who I'm after. They make no claim of authenticity. Your wife will continue to believe no matter what evidence comes up, because she NEEDS such a belief.

    JR

To: Harry Thomason

From the desk of: K. Johnson

To: Harry Thomason (73363.2653@compuserve.com)
From: kjohnson@insider.com (K. Johnson)
Subject: a TV show idea for you

Harry Thomason
TV Producer

NO RESPONSE

KJ

Dear Mr. Thomason:

I am a *free-lance* TV writer living in LA and I have an idea for a TV show for you. (I think it fits in nicely with your other shows, *Designing Women* and *Evening Shade*.) I am new to the Hollywood game, so please forgive me if this isn't the proper way to submit a TV idea, but since I graduated college last year, I haven't been having much success selling scripts or ideas the regular way, so maybe submitting ideas via e-mail will work. (Hope I'm not breaking any "Hollywood protocol!")

My idea for a TV show is called "Liberty Belle," and it's about a southern woman (named Belle Sinclair) who is married to a high-profile Senator (Walker Sinclair III), only she's really tough and smart and none of the men "inside the beltway" like her because she's smarter and tougher than them (sort of like you-know-who in the White House!).

The show could be filmed in LA but could be set in Washington, D.C., and would focus on how this strong, sassy Southern lady really sort of secretly runs her husband's office behind-the-scenes while he's out playing golf or having lunch with the big-money lobbyists. She always ends up making him look good and helping him get re-elected and so on.

Here's the catch, and I think you'll like it: her husband is a grouchy old Republican stuffed shirt, but she's a more open-minded liberal type and she is constantly manipulating things with his staff and in his office and with the press to make it so that her more liberal ideas are the ones that win out. Pretty funny, huh? Now you see why I want to call it "Liberty Belle."

So, I have lots of other ideas for the other cast members (like the young page that runs the elevator who secretly hears all the big deals going down in Congress), but I won't bore you with them here. If you like the idea and want to hear more, just let me know where to send the whole shebang and I'll stick it in the mail to you (or I can e-mail it to you!).

I am a strong Southern woman trying to "make it" in Hollywood, and I can identify with this character. I know from your other shows and your friendship with the Clintons that a show like this would be right up your alley, as they say, so please let me know if you like it. Please let me know if you don't like it too!

Hoping to hear from you soon!

Kathy Johnson

P.S. Say "Hi" to Linda for me! I think she's great!

Alien Robots Control NBC News!

To: Tom Brokaw

From the desk of: K. Johnson

Letter

KJ

To: NBC Nightly News (nightly@news.nbc.com)
From: kjohnson@insider.com (K. Johnson)
Subject: are you there, Tom?

Dear Tom Brokaw:
I hope this is really you. My sister has e-mail and saw your name and e-mail number in a book and said she was tired of hearing me holler at you on the TV so she is letting me write you this letter. I hope it is really you and not a joke. I hope you write back!

I watched you on the news the other night talking about guns. I think your a good news guy, but this gun stuff has gone far enough. You were saying they need to ban all the guns in Washington they're talking about banning, but I'll never give up my guns.

I have alot of guns: 12-gauge over-and-under double-barrell shotgun, .357 revolver (unregistered...don't tell!), two .22 hunting rifles with night-vision scopes (it's not illegal if you turn off the scope before you shoot the deers), a .38 special (for my wife!) and a 20-gauge double-barrell and 12-gauge pump action.

So, I still think you are a pretty good news guy. (I can't believe at ABC they let a Canadian say the news. You know who I'm talking about: PJ!) I hope you will not be so down on guns in the future. Guns don't kill us, we kill each other, you know.

You're my favorite on the news because you're from North Dakota, just like me. I used to live with my aunt in North Dakota until I was 8. We used to take our relatives to see Mt. Rushmore (my favorite thing in North Dakota) when they would visit. When are you going back on David Letterman? Write back and tell me so I can be sure to watch!

Thanks! Keep up the good work, and let's have more GOOD news from now on!

Your fan,
Alan Johnson (the gun guy!)

To: kjohnson@insider.com (K. Johnson)
From: nightly@nbc.com (NBC Nightly News)
Subject: are you there, Tom?

Thank you for contacting NBC *Nightly News* with Tom Brokaw via the Internet.

Many of you have just begun to use this electronic technology. We, also, are just beginning to find our way on the electronic frontier. So far we have been quite pleased with the kinds of e-mail messages we have gotten and we would like to continue to hear from you this way.

Unfortunately we are not able to answer all of the mail we get directly, but we do want you to know that we appreciate the mail you have sent and the comments you are making about our coverage of stories. We are reading it. We've gotten some ideas for future stories and we'd appreciate any further ideas and comments you have.

With this automated response we would like to answer a few FAQs (frequently asked questions).

1) TRANSCRIPTS. Transcripts for NBC News programs are available for purchase through the Burrell Transcript Service by calling 1-800-777-TEXT.

2) VIDEO TAPES. Only selected segments of our news magazines *NOW* and *Dateline* are available on VHS cassette. You can purchase these selected cassettes by calling 1-800-420-2626.

3) OTHER E-MAIL ADDRESSES AT NBC NEWS. The *Today Show* can now be reached at Today@news.nbc.com. The other NBC News program with an e-mail address is our news magazine *Dateline*. It can be reached at Dateline@news.nbc.com.

4) NBC ONLINE. America Online subscribers probably already know that NBC Entertainment has a forum on AOL. Messages for NBC programming or individual entertainment programs and personalities can be posted on that service.

5) SNAIL MAIL. If you have additional questions or wish to write to NBC News personnel not available electronically, our address is: 30 Rockefeller Plaza, New York, New York 10112.

Again, we thank you for watching NBC *Nightly News* and for contacting us electronically. We appreciate your interest and your comments about *Nightly News* stories.

THE USENET ORACLE HAS PONDERED YOUR QUESTION DEEPLY. YOUR QUESTION WAS:

How do you make holes in a fire?

(question by Ralph Betza; gnohmon@ssiny.com)

AND IN RESPONSE, THUS SPAKE THE ORACLE:

With a fire drill, of course.

ASK THE ORACLE

To: nightly@nbc.com (NBC Nightly News)
From: kjohnson@insider.com (K. Johnson)
Subject: hello? Is anybody there?

KJ

I just wrote Tom Brokaw a letter (it was the one about guns and how come he never has anything good to say about guns), but all I got back was this dang form letter! If I wanted a form letter, I'd write my congressman or my ex-wife's lawyer!

You told me: "Thank you for contacting NBC *Nightly News* with Tom Brokaw via the Internet. Many of you have just begun to use this electronic technology."

Not me, buddies. I've been doing this stuff for years.

Then you said: "We, also, are just beginning to find our way on the electronic frontier. So far we have been quite pleased with the kinds of e-mail messages we have gotten and we would like to continue to hear from you this way."

Well, don't expect me to keep writing if this is the kind of response I can expect. What's next, you'll get rid of Tom and just have a dang **robot** read the news? Don't do it. We love Tom and you can't replace him with an inhuman machine!

You also said: "Unfortunately we are not able to answer all of the mail we get directly, but we do want you to know that we appreciate the mail you have sent and the comments you are making about our coverage of stories. We are reading it. We've gotten some ideas for future stories and we'd appreciate any further ideas and comments you have."

Yeah, well, I want to hear from TOM! Who's running the show up there? What does it take to get a response from a living, thinking human being and not some dang e-mail robot, dangit!? If Tom reads this, tell him he needs to hire more people to help him answer the mail, because this robot stuff just doesn't cut it!

Tell Tom I want to hear from him about why his gun coverage is always so negative! Why don't we hear some GOOD news about guns!?

Alan Johnson (the gun guy!)

To: Tom Brokaw

From the desk of: K. Johnson

From: nightly@nbc.com (NBC Nightly News)
To: kjohnson@insider.com (K. Johnson)
Subject: hello? Is anybody there?

Thank you for contacting NBC Nightly News with Tom Brokaw via the Internet.

Many of you have just begun to use this electronic technology. We, also, are just beginning to find our way on the electronic frontier. . . . [same reponse as to previous letter]

Letter

KJ

To: dateline@news.nbc.com
From: kjohnson@insider.com (K. Johnson)
Subject: let's have some GOOD gun news

Dear Storm Phillips & Katie Currie:

I hope you really read your e-mail over there at *Dateline*! I just wrote Tom Brokaw a really nice letter, but all I got back was a dang form letter spit out by some **robot**!

I'll ask you guys the same question I asked Tom (the same one he **didn't** answer):

How come you guys never have any GOOD news about guns? All the time I watch your shows (including last night's show, by the way), it's always bad news about how people get killed or shot or paralyzed by guns. Would it hurt to just one time maybe show how somebody did something good with a gun?

Take me, for instance. My neighbor had been coming into my yard at night and cutting my wife's roses. This upset my wife a lot, and I asked him (TWICE) to stop, but he would just walk in after dinner and clip off the best roses. (He said the rose bush was on HIS property, but it's not. It's on my side of the clothesline!)

So one night I got down my deer rifle and shot him in the thigh. Boy, that sure cured him! He not only quit cutting my roses, he moved away. I say good riddance!

So there's a GOOD gun story for you. (You can use that one on the TV if you want!) I have a lot of friends who also have other good gun stories, so I hope you guys will seek us "good gunners" out and tell America our happy stories!

Hoping to hear from you (and not some dang e-mail **robot**!) soon.

Your fan,
Alan Johnson (the gun guy!)

Response

From: dateline@nbc.com
To: kjohnson@insider.com
Subject: thank you

Thank you for your E-Mail to *Dateline* NBC. We are very pleased with the enormous reponse we are getting. We can't write a personal note to every one of you but we print out all of your messages, look at them, and discuss your comments and reactions. If you have a specific story suggestion, please send it to:
STORY SUGGESTIONS, DATELINE NBC, ROOM 510, 30 ROCKEFELLER PLAZA, NEW YORK, NEW YORK 10112

Also, here are the answers to some frequently asked questions:
TRANSCRIPTS: Transcripts for NBC News Programs are available for purchase through the Burrell Transcript Service by calling 1-800-777-TEXT.
VIDEO TAPES: Only selected segments of our news magazines are available on VHS cassette. For information call 1-800-420-2626.

OTHER E-MAIL ADDRESSES AT NBC NEWS: nightly@news.nbc.com
Again, thanks for watching . . . and staying in touch.

I caught up with several of today's top news-women to find out what they'd be doing if they decided to leave TV journalism. Here's what they had to say:

- Jane Pauley (NBC) "I would love to be in a revival of *Hair* on Broadway."
- Diane Sawyer (ABC) "If I had my 'druthers' I guess I'd like to manage a professional wrestling team."
- Charlene Hunter-Gault (PBS) "I think I'd have to return to my first love of testing experimental hovercraft."
- Cokie Roberts (ABC) "Scrap metal. It's the wave of the future."
- Leslie Stahl (CBS) "I think I'd put on a few pounds and see if I could wrangle some of those Slim Fast commercials."
- Katie Couric (NBC) "I'd use my power and influence to get a job as a space shuttle astronaut."

- Judy Woodruff (PBS) "Basically, there's a mountain called Everest with my name on it."
- Paula Zahn (CBS) "I'd try to find out what Mr. Fields does while his wife is out selling cookies all day."
- Barbara Walters (ABC) "I thought you said you had a telegram for me? Get out of here before I call the cops!"

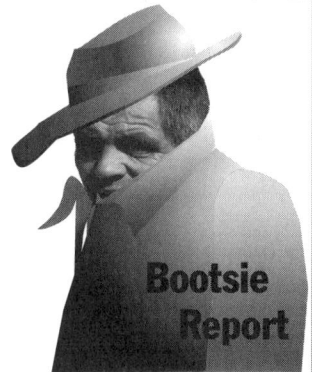

Bootsie Report

Reporting from the edge of credibility, I'm Juan Bootsie.
Contact Juan Bootsie at: an31291@anon.penet.fi or check out his archives via FTP in the /pub/hamlet directory at ftp.netcom.com.

To: (Roger Ebert) 73136.3232@compuserve.com
From: kjohnson@insider.com (K. Johnson)
Subject: is this really you?

Dear Roger Ebert:

I heard you on Howard Stern's radio show today. (I hope this is really you. My friend said you were on Compuserve. Is this you? If you don't write me back, I'll never know, so at least just write me back and say "yes" if it is you!)

You were talking about your new movie book that has all the movie cliches in it. Here's one for you. (You maybe said this one, but I didn't hear the show from the beginning. So don't think I'm a copycat if you've already got this one, OK?)

Have you ever noticed that when, in the movies, if a guy is chasing somebody on top of the roof or something, the first guy (the one that's running away) will jump across from one roof to another. But the second guy (the chaser) will not quite be able to make it all the way across and catches the ledge and hangs on?

Is that one in your book of movie cliches? It oughtta be if it's not. What was the name of the book again, because I think I want to buy it? Is it in the regular book stores or can I order it from you or how does that work?

I agree with almost all of your movie reviews (Thumbs Up!) except for some of them, which I don't agree with. You're a lot better than the bald guy. Keep (thumbs) up the great work.

Your fan,
Kenneth Johnson

From the desk of: K. Johnson

From: Roger Ebert <76711.271@compuserve.com>
To: kjohnson@insider.com
Subject: is this really you?

That cliche is already in the book (*Ebert's Little Movie Glossary*), but thanks for confirming it!

Best, RE

Well, it seems those Taster's Choice commercials we can't seem to get enough of are about to get ugly. In ads set to begin airing later this year, the as-yet-unnamed femme becomes a femme fatale when she awakens one morning beside a dead body. Her caffeine companion, Michael, then must help to clear her name. That is, if he doesn't get a coffee cup full of arsenic. (Better be sure that's really coffee, mate.) Look fohr a cameo by George "Sulu" Takei who'll play the mysterious Mr. Ito.

A Taster's Choice spokesperson explained, "We got this new ad agency and they're really creepy. I get scared just phoning them, but hey, they worked magic with that Chia Pet."

Reporting from the edge of credibility, I'm Juan Bootsie.
Contact Juan Bootsie at: an31291@anon.penet.fi or check out his archives via FTP in the /pub/hamlet directory at ftp.netcom.com.

CONGRESSMAN SLIPS —EPA MAKES GRADE!

To: Congressman Newt Gingrich
(georgia6@hr.house.gov)
From: kjohnson@insider.com (K. Johnson)
Subject: need your help

KJ

Letter

To: Newt Gingrich

From the desk of: K. Johnson

Dear Congressman Gingrich:

I am writing to you for your help and because I don't know what to do. (I'm writing from my sister's e-mail account at work—you can write me back at her address: kjohnson@insider.com. I sent you one regular letter already but you never wrote me back.)

A friend of mine said you were a professor at Brandeis University before you were a Congressman and you taught a class about the environment. Well, I hope that's true because the EPA wants to shut me down.

Here's my problem:

I have a place in my backyard where I work on my truck and my wife's car and other cars & trucks from people around the neighborhood. (I'm a mechanic during the day and I kinda "moonlight" at night working on cars on my own time.) I change people's oil (among other stuff) and my neighbor called the EPA and got them all over my back for dumping out the old oil in my yard.

He'd been yelling at me for a month not to dump it in my yard, but the way I figure it, I can do whatever I want in my own yard, right? It's my property and I can do whatever I want on it, right? Right! (Besides, the old oil has gotta go somewhere, right?)

Well, these people from the EPA came out and said I can't work on cars in my own yard any more and they gave me all this paperwork to sign and they're saying now they'll probably fine me alot of money!! This is communist. They can't do that to me. They can't take away a man's right to work and earn a living. I haven't done anything wrong.

Well, like they always say, "write your Congressman." Well, you're my Congressman and I know you'll help me out with this. I don't know what to do, but the EPA is no help (I'd even say they're out to get me), so you're my best bet right now. What should I do? (I sent you all the EPA papers with my first letter, but if you need me to send them again, I will.)

Hoping to hear from you soon!

Kenny Johnson

P.S. I have a funny bumper sticker on my truck (and my wife's car, too!) that I think you would get a kick out of. It says IMPEACH CLINTON AND HER HUSBAND TOO! I'll send you one if you want it!!

To: Kevin Rosseel (rosseel.kevin@epamail.epa.gov)
From: kjohnson@insider.com (K. Johnson)
Subject: motor oil & rats

KJ

Dear Kevin:
I don't know if you're the right guy to send this e-mail to (I got your name & address out of a book) but I can't get a straight answer from anyone I call at the EPA. If you're not the guy, can you please forward this to someone who can help me out?
Here's my question: what's so bad about used motor oil?
I have a place in my back yard where I work on my truck and my wife's car and other cars & trucks from people around the neighborhood. (I'm a mechanic during the day and I kinda "moonlight" at night working on cars on my own time.) I change people's oil and my neighbor is yelling at me not to dump it in the yard.
I finally started dumping it down the drain in the street just to shut him up, but he yelled at me for that too. I like the environment as much as the next guy, but I don't see what the big deal with motor oil is? Larry (my neighbor) put a 55-gal. drum in my yard and he says when I fill that up he'll empty it out for me "somewhere safe."
Well it's gotta go somewhere, right? So I want to know where Larry thinks he's going to take it. Doesn't it all end up in the ocean or the dump eventually? What's wrong with motor oil anyway? It's just oil!
Hoping to hear from you soon!

Kenny Johnson

To: Kevin Rosseel

From the desk of: K. Johnson

From: KEVIN ROSSEEL (ROSSEEL.KEVIN@epamail.epa.gov)
To: kjohnson <kjohnson@insider.com>
Subject: Re: motor oil

Mr Johnson,
I work in the sludge and sewers office at EPA, but have a couple ideas of who you might want to call to get answers about oil:
RCRA/Superfund Hotline   1-800-424-9346
—answers questions about spills and disposal of oil and other pollutants
Small Business Ombudsman   1-800-368-5888
—responds to requests to help small businesses comply with EPA regulations.
Hope that these may help. Thanks and have a good day!

KEVIN ROSSEEL, Office of Water
U.S. Environmental Protection Agency
Washington, D.C. 20460
Internet: rosseel.kevin@epamail.epa.gov

To: sassy@phantom.com
From: kjohnson@insider.com (K. Johnson)
Subject: an article idea for you
Jane Pratt
Sassy Magazine

Dear Ms. Pratt:
I am a freelance writer living in LA and I have an idea for a magazine article for you. I am new to the magazine game, so please forgive me if this isn't the proper way to submit an article idea, but since I graduated from college last year, I haven't been having much success selling articles the regular way, so maybe submitting ideas via e-mail will work. (Hope I'm not breaking any "submission protocol!")
The article would be called "So You Want To Get Pierced . . . " and it would be about what it's like to get your body parts pierced. Living in LA, the "in" thing to do for young girls is to get "pierced," and piercing ears is old stuff in this town.
My article would help young girls decide about piercing, and weigh the pros and cons of "to pierce or not to pierce." I plan to talk to the piercing shops around LA and I have two nieces who want to "get pierced." Alice is 15 and wants her navel pierced (and her mother says "OK" if Alice pays for it) and Linda is 17 and is getting her nose pierced this weekend. They are sisters, and I plan to be there with them when they "take the plunge."
I am planning to tell this story from the young girl's point of view, using my nieces for good source material. I can also come up with a "Piercing Pros & Cons" chart and a list of "Piercing Do's & Dont's" for those who are considering piercing or are newly pierced.
I think this is just the kind of "sassy" piece Sassy would like to run, so I'm crossing my fingers you'll like it. Please e-mail me back whether you like it or not!
Hoping to hear from you soon!

Kathy Johnson

P.S. I love Sassy. I read it just for fun and I'm 25!

To: Sassy Magazine

From the desk of: K. Johnson

From: sassy@phantom.com (sosassy)
To: kjohnson@insider.com (K. Johnson)
Subject: Re: an article idea for you

well, the first rule of freelancing is know the magazine you're pitching to! and sassy is written entirely in-house, which is why the bylines you see are first-name only. the only non-staff-written areas are fiction, reader poetry, and "it happened to me." but best of luck pitching the piece elsewhere.

thanks for writing.

—sassy

To: Federal Immigration and
Refugee Board

From the desk of: K. Johnson

To: immrefbr@chicken.planet.org
From: kjohnson@insider.com (K. Johnson)
Subject: need immigration advice!!
Canadian Federal Immigration and Refugee Board (via e-mail)

To Whom It May Concern:

I feel my political rights in America are being trampled on and I am seeking political amnesty in a friendly nation. I am hoping you can give me information on how to go about getting safely out of the USofA and into Canada.

Here's the deal: I can't give you all the details right now over email, but I am an engineer who has worked for the US Gov't on lots of "touchy" projects. I have talked to several other engineers and even a number of US Gov't officials, and have pretty strong proof that UFOs exist and the American Gov't is working with them to develop new weapons.

I know this sounds a little crazy, but if you watch X Files or have seen our news down here, I'm sure you're starting to catch on. "They" are here and they're "in" with the gov't. I've been laid off from work, and I'm convinced it's because I know about the whole UFO thing. Also, I get lots of calls at night when I answer "hello?" and the other guy just hangs up. Nothing else. Just hangs up. This is typical CIA psy-ops in action.

So I'm interested in figuring out how to get into your country on a special VISA or passport or something. I will gladly bring all of my files on UFOs and alien weapons technology (although I don't have access to my old project files at work, since I'm laid off, and wouldn't give them to you if I could because I'm no traitor) and will swear affidavits to everything I've said here.

Please let me know what can be done, because I'm starting to worry. Thanks in advance for your help.

Sincerely,
Kenneth Johnson, Engineer (ex-laid off, sorry)

UNDELIVERABLE

In a deposition taken last week in Los Angeles, singer Michael Bolton denied using the title "Godfather of Soul" in promotional literature. The title, Bolton claimed, was "Godfather of Seoul" and referred to sales of his albums in South Korea. The suit was brought by "the hardest working man in show business," James Brown, after seeing copies of Bolton press releases containing the dubious misprint. The judge in the case ordered that lawyers for the two sides meet privately to discuss the matter. When asked for an assessment of how the first meeting went, James Brown replied, "I feel good!" then spun about and did a split.

In a related story, lawyers representing the estate of late entertainer Sammy Davis, Jr. are suing James Brown over use of the phrase, "the hardest working man in show business." Said one, "Even dead, Sammy still works harder than just about everyone. He only wants the audience to enjoy itself."

And this just in: Michael Bolton, James Brown, and the estate of Sammy Davis, Jr. are bringing suit against Juan Bootsie for using their names in this story. Mr. Bootsie is countersuing for breech of credibility.

Reporting from the edge of credibility, I'm Juan Bootsie.
Contact Juan Bootsie at: an31291@anon.penet.fi or
check out his archives via FTP in the /pub/hamlet directory at
ftp.netcom.com.

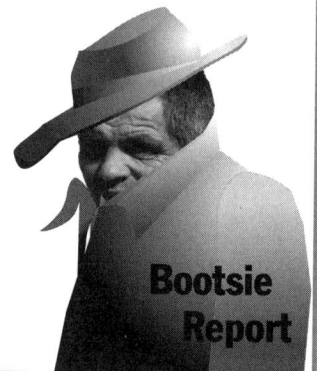

**Bootsie
Report**

To: Santa@north pole

From the desk of: K. Johnson

To: santa@north.pole.org
From: kjohnson@insider.com (K. Johnson)
Subject: are you busy?

KJ

Dear Santa:
My dad is helping me write this letter because I am not a good typist. Is it really you? Are you busy at this time of year? What do the reindeer do during the summer? Does it get hot at the north pole?
For this year, I want:
Power Rangers, Nerf rockets, new sega genesis, firecrackers, GI Joe, Cobra Commmmand Center, Reebok pumps, wrist-rocket slingshot and lots of surprises.
Thank you!

Alice Johnson

From: "Santa Claus!" <Santa@radio.com>
To: kjohnson@insider.com
Subject: greetings from Santa Claus!

Ho! Ho! Ho!
Greetings from the North Pole! What a week, what a week! It was really busy getting ready for the big day. The elves are all looking forward to a week on the beach.
Do you realize that we have to visit 2 billion children in one night? That's 822.6 visits per second, barely enough time to snarf down those cookies! As you've seen, I do manage to sample a few along the way. '{;-0)
I checked my database (twice) and it's clear that you were very good this year. I hope you have all the neat stuff that you hope for. Yet, when all is said and done, let us hope that we all get peace and happiness in 1994, the best presents of all.

Merry Christmas and a Happy New Year!

Santa Claus (and the Elves! *<:-)) The North Pole

P.S. Rudolph sends his regards. All week he was slobbering all over the rug just thinking about all those carrots and stuff kids leave for him. What a mess, what a mess!

EVIL LETTER TECHNOLOGY PLAN!! FILM AT 11:00!!

To: Miles O'Brien

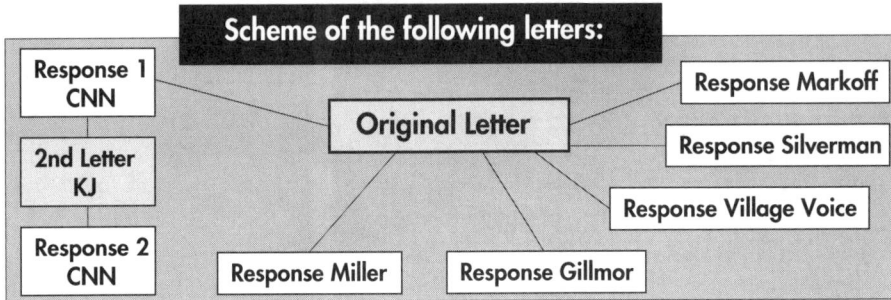

From the desk of: K. Johnson

Scheme of the following letters:

- Response 1 CNN
- 2nd Letter KJ
- Response 2 CNN

Original Letter

- Response Markoff
- Response Silverman
- Response Village Voice
- Response Miller
- Response Gillmor

Orig. Letter

To: Miles O'Brien, Science & Technology Reporter
Cable News Network

KJ

Dear Mr. O'Brien:

I have a story idea that I think might interest you. I'm hoping you will consider covering this story in a fair and open-minded way, because we have not been receiving good response to our business ideas from local media.

I am a vice-president with a small technology start-up in St. Paul, Minnesota called ScanCheck Techtronics, Inc. For the past seven years, we have been researching and developing a technology that will facilitate the electronic transfer of funds between consumers and businesses.

Forgive this oversimplified description, but the heart of the ScanCheck system works like this:

A patented memory cell stores personal and financial information in a new kind of RAM chip. The chip can hold up to 128k of information and is small enough to fit in about the same amount of space as a pencil eraser. We have developed a system by which the chip may be scanned and written to using a scanner/encoder much like supermarket check-out devices (only it works using electronmagnetic radiation rather than optical scanning). The chip can be used to transfer (debit) funds to any business equipped with a scanner. If desired, the consumer may also offer his demographic information (stored on the chip) to the business for its databases.

We've been able to successfully make attractive jewelry (pendants, rings, watches, tie tacks and even, ironically enough, a money clip!) that contain the chip and also power it through intake of ambient light (from anywhere along the UV or visible light spectrum). The chip retains its memory as long as the jewelry is exposed to about 4 hours of sunlight or 12 hours of fluorescent/incandescent light every 2 weeks (not a problem for most people). In two months, we expect to have a waterproof ring version of the device ready.

Our problem has come in that many local religious groups have heard about the ScanCheck through the local media and oppose development of such a technology on the basis that it bears resemblance to the "mark of the Beast" references in the Bible and other religious literature. While I can understand their concerns, it is placing an unreasonable restriction on the amount of positive press we've been able to generate, and I'm hoping a national news outlet might help alleviate this problem.

I'm sure I don't need to tell you how significant a device like this would be. You could keep your funds stored in a bank, withdraw "cash" into your ring at an optically equipped ATM, and disburse (only when funds password/PIN-verified) at any vendor's scanner that is a part of the network.

If you're interested in helping us bring the news of our product to the nation at large, please e-mail me and I'll forward complete details to you at once. Thank you for your time and consideration.

Kendall Johnson, VP Marketing and Publicity, ScanCheck Techtronics, Inc.

From: "Miles O'Brien" <70273.2064@compuserve.com>
To: <kjohnson@insider.com>
Subject: a story idea for you

   While I am not exactly certain from your description what your critics are alleging, I am interested in this story on two levels: the controversy as well as the technology. Can you please be more specific about what is irking the fundamentalists?
   And one other important question: Is anyone using this technology currently? Or is the idea purely in prototype form?

   Miles O'Brien, CNN

Response 1

Well, it's official. Michael Jackson has given up his bachelorhood in favor of the hand of the lovely daughter of ex-King Elvis. Friends, I have to tell you, as one of the few reporters allowed to cover the nuptials—and to get that "honor" we had to promise not to report anything—I must say, it was the strangest wedding I've ever attended, and that's including my own second marriage, to Zsa Zsa. First of all, any event that includes a "press corps" consisting of Juan Bootsie, ten or twelve *Dominican Enquirer* reporters, and the obit editor from the *Fort Worth Free Press* is destined to be a little kinky.

Bootsie Report

   I must say, though, that Lisa Marie looked lovely, dressed in faded cut-offs and a paisley halter-top, with a giant straw sombrero and Ray-Bans, while Jacko was impressive, decked out in Paul McCartney's old Sgt. Pepper's uniform—I didn't think it would fit, not that it would matter much to MJ—despite the 100-degree temperature. And wouldn't you think Jacko would find some way to have the chapel air-conditioned?
   The ceremony was short and to the point, highlighted by the justice's futile attempts to pronounce the name of best-chimp, Bubbles—the closest he came was Boob-eels. There wasn't a dry eye in the house, mainly because the on-lookers kept having to douse themselves to keep cool. We all had to strain extra hard to hear Jacko say his vows, though I'm sure even those in the front row missed every other word.
   The reception wasn't much to speak of either. Mainly Jacko's manager tossed a quart bottle of Jose Cuervo out to the crowd and shouted "Ole!" I tried to elbow my way forward for an interview with the principals, who some are already dubbing the Tom and Rosanne of July '94 but they were jammed into the waiting limo and off to the airport before I could even get out the door.
   No word yet on who'll be handling the divorce in a few months.

Reporting from the edge of credibility, I'm Juan Bootsie.
   Contact Juan Bootsie at: an31291@anon.penet.fi or check out his archives via FTP in the /pub/hamlet directory at ftp.netcom.com.

To: "Miles O'Brien" <70273.2064@compuserve.com>
From: kjohnson@insider.com (K. Johnson)
Subject: Re: a story idea for you

KJ

Mr. O'Brien:

I think what is bothering the various religious groups is that there are certain passages in the Bible, specifically in the book of Revelation, which discuss the "mark of the Beast." The Beast, of course, being the Biblical reference to the anti-christ, which will come to enslave the world before the second coming of Christ.

I'm not a religious man, nor am I a scholar, but from our research and the complaints we've heard (which are not the most scientific nor well thought-out), they seem to center around passages in the Bible which describe the "mark of the Beast." The Bible says something along the lines of (and I'm paraphrasing here) "The Beast shall force all its slaves to bear its mark, and none that bear it shall enter the kingdom of heaven, and none shall buy nor sell without bearing the Beast's mark on his head or hand."

Now, as I stated in our previous letter, we've developed a way to encapsulate a funds-transfer device in a small chip that retains writeable memory. We've made working prototypes of these devices that can be worn more or less as jewelry (so they are easy to use, always handy and unobtrusive—better than a wallet or billfold). The objections we hear most often is that if we create a successful device in the form of a computer chip inside a ring (which we have already perfected), then soon, a cashless society will develop in which money transactions will take place via a computer chip in the ring. I guess this is what plays into their fears of the "mark of the Beast" (on one's hand, in this case), which people will need (as electronic money) to buy and sell.

I know it sounds crazy. It's certainly been a challenge from a public relations standpoint, and it's wrecked our efforts to raise money and take our company public. We have several working prototypes of different models and varieties, but will need large-scale capital to manufacture them in sufficient quantity to get the unit cost down to our target zone (under $100 with a monthly service fee of about $2). We've been talking with a number of major players in telecom and finance (large multinational corporations which I can't go into in detail at this point), but because of the religious flap, no one wants to back us (yet).

That's why I'm hoping some positive national exposure will help us. It may hurt us, but at this point, we need to move forward and gain funding, or we'll become another bit of roadkill along the information superhighway.

Are you headquartered in Atlanta? I will be on the east coast on a business trip the week of Sept. 12, and would be glad to meet with you in Atlanta to demonstrate our technology and discuss the various issues of this matter with you. If there's anything else I can do or any other information I can provide, please let me know. (I will be in China for most of the next week, but will check in as soon as I return.) Thanks for your time and attention.

Kendall Johnson, VP Marketing and Publicity, ScanCheck Techtronics, Inc.

From: "Miles O'Brien" <70273.2064@compuserve.com>
To: <kjohnson@insider.com>
Subject: Re: a story idea for you

   Kendall: I would be interested in pursuing this story. I think the controversy, in and of itself, would be of interest to our viewers. Has anything been written in local media which you could send me? Also: do you have some background information about your product which you could also send?
   My address: CNN Science News, One CNN Center, Atlanta, GA 30303

Thanks,
Miles O'Brien, CNN Atlanta

   "Friends" to the end? Not likely. This week psychics at the Organization for Enquiring Minds have ended their four-year plus relationship with Dionne Warwick's Psychic Friends' Network. The breakup occurred when a dispute arose over when California would drop into the ocean. The OEM team determined that the so-called "big one"—the major quake set to demolish all of California—would occur thirty months following the birth of any child resulting from the Lisa Marie Presley/Michael Jackson marriage. Psychics with the Warwick Network insist that the quake will occur on November 29, 1998, but may be hastened if Raymond Burr rises from the grave. The dispute became so heated that, at one point, both sets of psychics squared off across the room and tried to telekinetically lob objects at one another, including several chairs, an ashtray, and forty unsigned photos of Dionne Warwick with niece Whitney Houston.

   Said "Reggie," an OEM psychic from Devon, England, "Man we were like family with the 'Friends'. I never saw this coming."

Bootsie Report

Reporting from the edge of credibility, I'm Juan Bootsie.
   Contact Juan Bootsie at: an31291@anon.penet.fi or check out his archives via FTP in the /pub/hamlet directory at ftp.netcom.com.

Response

From: Dwight Silverman (Dwight.Silverman@chron.com)
To: kjohnson@insider.com (K. Johnson)
Subject: Re: a story idea

Kendall,
    That's an intriguing story. I might like to talk to you about it further. However, here's a caveat . . .
    I am based in Houston, at the *Houston Chronicle.* I presume you saw my column in the Minneapolis paper; they pick it up sometimes off the *New York Times* Wire Service. Your chip really doesn't fit in my column; it's more of a personal computer, how-to-make-it-work-for-you column.
    However, I also am the technology beat reporter at the *Chronicle.* But my emphasis on gee-whiz technology stories is on LOCAL companies who have done something interesting.
    I'm not averse to tackling a company outside of Houston, but my editors, ever mindful of how little space we have, like to keep these kinds of stories focused locally.
    I will show them your message and get their reaction. Be aware, though, that part of any story I would do would have to include the fact that you have these religious types hounding you.
    I'll be in touch.

===Dwight Silverman
| As you probably suspected, The Houston Chronicle | my opinions are mine.
dwight.silverman@chron.com | Who else would have 'em?
===

Response

From: Dan Gillmor <dgillmor@det-freepress.com>
To: "K. Johnson" <kjohnson@insider.com>
Subject: Re: a story idea

Thanks for your note —

    I'm now with the *San Jose Mercury News*, and will discuss this with the business editor. Thanks.

    Dan Gillmor

From: Julian Dibbell <julian@panix.com>
To: "K. Johnson" <kjohnson@insider.com>
Subject: Re: a story idea

    Please send me more info about your project. I don't know if a positive write-up in the *Village Voice* would do anything but confirm your local opposition's belief that you are in league with Satan, but our readers might be interested in what you're up to.
****
Julian Dibbell   julian@panix.com
****

Response

From: "Michael W. Miller" <mikeym@well.sf.ca.us>
To: kjohnson@insider.com
Subject: Re: a story idea

  sounds interesting—you should contact our Chicago bureau and ask for the banking reporter. i'm afraid i don't have handy the number (listed in 312 area code) but they're the ones that cover Minnesota. good luck—mike

From: markoff@nyt.com (John Markoff)
To: kjohnson@insider.com
Subject: Re: a story idea Content-Length: 496

  Your story sounds interesting, but I can't for the life of me figure out what the connection is to the mark of the beast. Perhaps we could chat by phone?

Best,
John Markoff
---- John Markoff
MCI: jmarkoff New York Times
Internet: markoff@nyt.com Embarcadero Center One
Well: johnm@well.sf.ca.us San Francisco, CA
all the news etc.

From: quit@newsday.com (Joshua Quittner)
To: kjohnson@insider.com
Subject: Re: a story idea

  Sorry, I'm kind of booked right now on local stories. I'll hold onto your note, though, thanks. -Q

Joshua Quittner, Reporter, Newsday, 235 Pinelawn Rd., Melville, NY 11747

Socks Autographs Limited Edition Set of Easter Eggs

The place: The South Lawn of the White House.

The time: April 12, 1993; 10:48 a.m. E.D.T.

The players: First Lady Hillary Rodham Clinton, President Bill Clinton, hundreds of anxious young Easter Egg hunters and, of course, that crazy cat, Socks!

White House Hides 100 Special Socks Eggs

In this episode, President and Mrs. Clinton discuss the long and colorful history of White House Easter Egg hunts. A special bonus this year is autographed eggs, and it sounds like Socks is the odds-on favorite autographer. Will the kids find the special Socks eggs? Let's listen.

The President: Good morning everybody. I want to welcome all of you here to the White House for the Easter Egg Roll and the Easter Egg Hunt. I want to say a special word of thanks to the sponsors who made this possible and say how wonderful it is for all of us here to see the children, especially for me and for Hillary.

And I want now to introduce the First Lady, who is the hostess for this event, to say a few more words about it. But let me again say how very, very grateful we are to see all of you here. This is a children's day for America at the White House, and I'm glad you're here to make it so special. Please welcome the First Lady. (*Applause.*)

Mrs. Clinton: Well, I'm so glad to see all of you here. And this year we've done a few things a little differently to try to make it even better for all of you.

You know, the very first Easter Egg Roll took place in 1809. Now, how many of you were here for that one? (*Laughter.*) Good. That was Dolly Madison who started it in 1809, and it used to be at the Capitol. And then it was moved here to the White House. And every year the Monday after Easter is when we do this.

This year we decided to do two things—to have a lot of entertainment and activities on the Ellipse, which is over there by the Washington Monument, so that as you had to wait, you could go through the line and you could hear singing and you could see some clowns; and to keep the egg roll and the egg hunt here on the lawn so that we would be able to accommodate more of you and you'd each have a chance.

Now, I know that many of you are excited about the first egg hunt, and the President is going to blow the whistle for that in just a minute—the egg roll, the first egg roll—and then the egg hunt, which happens further down on the South Lawn. And for everybody who hunts, you will be able to find an egg. And let me just tell you that there have been a lot of eggs signed by a lot of very famous people who have come to Washington. **But there are 100 eggs that were signed by Socks. (*Laughter.*) So his own little paw print is right**

The Socks Chronicles

In this ongoing series of behind-the-scenes looks at the inner workings of the White House, the *Internet Insider* follows Socks, America's First Cat, through another harrowing press conference. In this official White House document obtained exclusively by the *Insider*, you'll see how the White House press corps is once again sidetracked from the real issues facing our government to consider the life and times of that lovable kitty, Socks.

Why the media obsession with the President's cat? Is there something the White House doesn't want us to know? Is "Socks" a secret code word that sends reporters into a trance of distraction and diversion? Why does the press offer only a 30-second sound bite from a 30-minute meeting? Does Socks prefer frolicking in the Lincoln Bedroom or on the South Lawn? These questions and more are answered as we present another installment of *The Socks Chronicles.*

there on the egg. And so he'll be very happy if you find his eggs as well.

We just mostly want to welcome you to this beautiful spring day here at the White House. And now we're going to go and the President's going to blow the whistle for the first egg roll. And I hope all of you have a wonderful, wonderful time.

Thank you all. (*Applause.*)

This excerpted transcript from an actual White House media event was downloaded from official archives of Clinton Administration documents available from a number of sources: via gopher: gopher.tamu.edu or sunsite.unc.edu; via anonymous FTP: ftp.spies.com; via World-Wide Web: http://english-server.hss.cmu.edu/WhiteHouse.html; via e-mail: publications@whitehouse.gov.■

Today's Kook is Tomorrow's Genius

The world has its share of kooks, but it seems like an unusually high proportion of them have Internet accounts and are active and enthusiastic participants in the electronic marketplace of ideas. Don't get us wrong, though. We *love* kooks. For a tabloid like the *Insider*, "kook" is not a four-letter word. As we refer to "kooks" in this section, please understand we don't use the term in a derogatory way. In fact, for our money, a kook is nothing more than a genius undiscovered. Like Galileo.

Oh, sure, every 20th-century schoolkid learns what a great scientist and devoted scholar Galileo Galilei was. We're all aware of his work as an astronomer, mathematician, and physicist. But to the folks around Pisa, Italy, during the early 1600s, the guy was a nut. A crackpot. A goofball. A quack. A loony.

A . . . *kook*.

When he was 19, Galileo used his pulse as a method to time a swinging weight, accurately theorizing about the isochronal nature of pendulums. To the crusty fathers of the University of Pisa, though, he was a goofy kid running around, clutching his wrist while staring at a lead glob at the end of a string. Crazy kids.

Things got weirder, though, when Galileo dashed off to Holland to study lens-grinding methods. Next thing you know, he's staring up into the night sky through some goofy-looking tube. Soon, he claimed there were mountains on the moon and even spots on the sun! Worst of all, though, he agreed with Copernicus that the heavenly bodies orbited the sun, not the earth.

Talk about *kooks*. Now this nut was contradicting the teachings of Aristotle—the guy who had *proven* that everything was made up of four basic elements: earth, wind, fire and water; and that human ailments could be cured by adding or subtracting various amounts of specifically colored blood and bile.

Lickety-split, Galileo's teachings were outlawed (but, being the quack that he was, he continued his research and teaching) and, in 1633, the inquisition tried and convicted him of violating a 1616 ban on certain "heretical thoughts." He was exiled to Siena, and died nearly blind, but still sticking to his wacky theories.

A few hundred years later, the march of science had managed to pretty much confirm those wacky theories, and in 1979, Pope John Paul II asked that Galileo's conviction be overturned. Unfortunately, the 1616 ban on belief in a heliocentric universe was still in effect. In 1992, after more than 375 years, the church finally overturned the "thought-ban" (although it's unclear whether this also exonerates Galileo of any wrongdoing).

So, are today's Internet kooks, in fact, geniuses undiscovered—modern-day Galileos, struggling to bring their shocking truths to a superstitious, backward public? Ask us again in the year 2375.

R.I.D.E. the Net to Inner Knowledge.

LIFE @ LARGE

For those Net-newbies who haven't yet developed a knack for spotting kooks online, we can offer a couple of pointers:

1) STRANGE amounts of *emphasis* on **certain** WORDS

2) CRAPS (Capitalization and Random Apostrophe and Punctuation Syndrome)

CRAPS, a sad and debilitating disease we have also covered in our section on spelling, is a common affliction among Net-kooks. But a more telltale sign of possible kook status is the practice of a kind of written caterwauling. Folks *italicize* certain **words** while capitalizing OTHER words or *putting* OTHER **words *IN BOLD!***

Excessive use of exclamation marks is also a dead giveaway!!!!

So keep an eye out for these clues, or stop by the **alt.usenet.kooks** newsgroup, where the members go to the *trouble* of **finding** KOOKY *writings* for YOU!!!

Net Resources

Asking where the kooks hang out on the Internet is a little like asking where the fish swim in the ocean. The Internet is, quite literally, an ocean teeming with kooks. In suggesting a few newsgroups in which to begin your kook-search, we're not (necessarily) implying that the newsgroup is made up of kooks. Rather, we're simply suggesting that the group's subject matter interests kooks or that its atmosphere of tolerance encourages them. Any quick Net-kook-check should include the following newsgroups:

>*alt.conspiracy*
>*alt.conspiracy.jfk*
>*alt.usenet.kooks*
>*alt.alien.visitors*
>*talk.bizarre*
>*alt.discordia*
>*alt.paranet.skeptic*
>*alt.paranormal*
>*alt.prophecies.nostradamus*
>*comp.ai.fuzzy*
>*info.firearms*
>*rec.arts.sf.fandom*

For a copy of Phillip Heggie's "Babble-On the Haw of Haws: The False Profit's Buy-Belle," e-mail him at philip@rmit580fs1.hais.rmit.edu.au or download it via anonymous FTP at wuarchive.wustl.edu in the pub/msdos_uploads/cyberpunk directory.

Finally, a book that does for the world of kooks in general what the *Insider* strives to do for the inhabitants of the Net is Donna Kossy's *Kooks: A Guide to the Outer Limits of Human Belief* (1994, Feral House, $16.95). The *Insider's* literature critic highly recommends it.

Were Renegade Space Cannibals Stars of the Bible?

From: Robert McElwaine

Christians should all HONESTLY and thoroughly investigate the CONTRADICTIONS between the Old and New Testaments in terms of their descriptions of God.

The God of the New Testament is described as a God of LOVE, MERCY, and PEACE.

The god of the Old Testament is described as a JEALOUS, VENGEFUL god, a WAR-MONGER. He said

"Thou shalt not kill", and then proceeded to help the Israelites to kill TENS OF THOUSANDS of Arabs in order to take their land.

Can the two Testaments POSSIBLY be talking about the same thing?!

The "god" of the Old Testament was actually a TRIBE OF RENEGADE SPACE CANNIBALS, with a leader named "Yahweh," who was the commander of a UFO SPACECRAFT ("pillar of fire," "pillar of cloud," etc.), and a GENETICIST who CLONED Adam and Eve FROM HIMSELF and put them on this planet which was ALREADY INHABITED at that time. And the "first born sons" of the Israelites became ROAST DINNER for the "Jehovahs."

All of this may sound UN-believable to most Christians. But try reading the Old Testament with these things in mind. For example, read the part about one of the Old Testament characters, Jacob, I think, WRESTLING WITH GOD, AND WINNING! ALWAYS use the KING JAMES VERSION.

Nostradamus Predicts Earthquake Machine

By Albert Nanomius (nanomius@netcom.com)

[From an introduction to a FAQ file on a book about the prophecies of Nostradamus:]

My Note to Enemies

Just as D. Cannon wrote that she fully expected to be accused of perpetuating a massive hoax, and actually published the books at great personal risk under her real name, I fully expect to be subject to vicious attacks for this "exercise in conscience." I have absolutely no use for close-minded, ignorant people jamming my mailbox with naive and uninformed vitriol. However, if you must have an outlet, feel free to post it to alt.prophecies.nostradamus, and everyone else will feel free to ignore you.

[From the FAQ file:]

The top-secret earthquake-triggering weapon (ETW)

A weapon will be developed in secret underground laboratories that can trigger earthquakes at existing fault zones. It will work from a scientific principle recently discovered but not yet developed. The weapon will involve an airplane or airborne origination that may drop something or project a laser ray onto a region. An extension of the device is carried in a plane that flies over the area and focuses energy waves where the earthquake is to be triggered. The more technologically complex

... earthquake-triggering weapon

power source will be based and channeled from the secret laboratory via the plane.

ET unleashed on San Andreas and New Madrid faults

The weapon will not be revealed immediately to the world. Only after the country actually uses it and there is an earthquake generated by it, followed by many others that occur without the characteristic buildup of geological pressure, will people become suspicious. The initial earthquake triggered by the weapon will be sufficient to cause other earthquakes in a chain reaction. The San Andreas and New Madrid faults in the U.S. will be affected.

Primates, Man & Humans Becoming Intelligence Itself

From: "Mr. Infinity" (infinit152@aol.com)

THE STUDY OF OUR INTELLIGENCE

I have been asked many times, - "what do you base your beliefs on? - Answer: "THE POWER OF OBSERVATION." - in the study of our intelligence.

I have seen our intelligence as "PRIMATES" existing in the jungle, - then in caves, then learning how to exist on farms -and finally creating cities and living in them.

- emerging and evolving -not biologically, - but (more so), "intellectually" - throughout its "many" centuries of time. - "SOON" to abandon the cities it has created unto itself - as it learns the science and technology to exist in space.

It is not "PRIMATES" or "MAN" - or "HUMANS" that we are observing in our studies of the past- (or in our present) - it is pure "INTELLIGENCE" itself.

- we are not it -because it is not "us" in the millions of years ahead.

- "intelligence" is a "force" of the universe that is "FOREVER" - learning and changing.

changing the lifestyle, traditions, religions, customs, language, politics, science and knowledge of whoever (or whatever) its "current" carrier be in any given place or time in eternity.

Anyone can make similar OBSERVATIONS of our intelligence from it's early beginning. - "observing it," - "studying it" -as it continued changing the "stages" of itself through its "eternal R.I.D.E." (Researching, Inventing, Discovering, Exploring), - replacing and discarding the lifestyle of all of it's "earlier" carriers. -(as it will also replace ours, -and the many "new" carriers of itself ahead in eternity.)

Such observations of our intelligence will "ALWAYS" be valid in the future times ahead - for "It" has not yet stopped it's eternal R.I.D.E. - (forever -Researching, Inventing, Discovering, and Exploring) - nor shall it ever "STOP" the R.I.D.E. - except one day in millions or billions of years into the future -when "IT" has finally learned "ALL" of the science and knowledge that this universe still contains "HIDDEN" TO "IT" and it has become a god unto itself.

Since we cannot "peek" into our future, - WE have only the "HISTORY" of our intelligence, - its "TRACK RECORD", and its "CURRENT SCIENTIFIC ADVANCEMENTS" - with which to base statistics and prediction - as to what it shall "BECOME" in the eternal time ahead of "itself."

Had "prior" civilizations applied this same observation unto themselves thousands of years ago, - they would have seen themselves, as just another "STEP" -in a long road of new science and knowledge to our "intelligence."

FUTURE generations can make the same observations of their intelligence -to see themselves the same, - as we "see" ourselves today - as also just another "STEP" of a long road of "NEW" science, technology, and knowledge that continues coming and "CHANGING" this intelligence through out eternity.

we "cannot" ask it to maintain the same level of science, knowledge, and technology that it possesses now - so that it will not change itself in eternity - and will remain the same as "ourselves" forever - (in the same body and brain that we have contained it in).
MAINTAINING THE SAME LANGUAGES, RELIGIONS, CUSTOMS, TRADITIONS, POLITICS, PHILOSOPHIES, IDEAS, ETC.
"true" INTELLIGENCE of the universe has "no loyalty" to any religion, traditions, language, customs, nationalities, politics, philosophy, etc.
-or any loyalty to any of its futuristic carriers of itself.
- it has no loyalty to anyone -or anything it experiences in this universe.
it experiences a loyalty through eternity only to "itself" - (to whatever "suits" it best). -intelligence is a "FORCE" all on it's very own that uses whatever or "whoever" it can to advance itself in science, technology and knowledge through out eternity.
-intelligence is not "US" - we are only it's "TEMPORARY" carrier through eternity. - we cannot control

it because we are only a part of it - in its "totality" in eternity.
it really wants to become a "god" someday in eternity - (and it will with so much time ahead of itself in eternity). - that is why so much of its past has been "ABANDONED AND DISCARDED" by it throughout it's history.
-and why it also "predictably" abandons and discards our "WAYS" in its "eternal search" throughout eternity for the "BEST" of itself. - which it has not found "yet." - nor will it find it - for a long time in eternity. - so that a lot of future generations and civilizations also like ourselves get discarded and abandoned by it in eternity - becoming history pages in its long existence in eternity.
there is absolutely nothing wrong with it being "loyal" only unto itself,   ELSE, - we would have never "EXISTED" in this present stage of intelligence - nor WOULD HAVE past stages of our intelligence existed before us - NOR SHALL many OTHER different stages of our intelligence exist in the future.
intelligence uses its current carrier (wherever in time that may be) - as a stepping stone, and "discards it" - when it has no longer a need of it, - and has something "better" to carry it. - it does this through the "ETERNAL CONTINUATION" of new inventions, of new science and new technology throughout eternity.
that is why primates no longer "exist" nor do we live in caves, or "live" as we did in our past - nor will our intelligence live or exist in our future as it is "forced" to exist now. (in the "poverty" of our "CURRENT" AND limited knowledge, science, and technology.
"forced" to exist in a human biological body - in order for its awareness and consciousness to exist. - forced to feed and protect a human biological body, that ages and weakens with the passing of time - and eventually dies to it. - the science exists to this universe that can eventually change all that for it. - it must however learn it (and it shall) in time.

A 5-Billion-Year Plan for Survival

From: "Starflight Corp." (xena@crl.crl.com)

It is possible to have a civilized society whose members live in a high level of comfort, both physical and psychological, but do so within an infrastructure that operates in a physical steady-state mode, consuming some energy but almost no materials, over geologic time spans.

A variety of engineering considerations dictates that such a sustainable infrastructure be organized as a system of sealed, compact cities, connected by transportation tubes, to minimize the area of their interface to the environment, and therefore the cost of containing the materials used in them. As a practical matter, the best sites for such cities are underground, to minimize the costs of weathering and other hazards.

Given a sufficient capital investment, such as that represented by such cities, of perhaps $1 million per person in present dollars, it would be possible in principle to easily site more than a million such cities within the Earth, each supporting a million inhabitants, and sustaining them for the entire 5 billion-year life expectancy of the planet.

Such cities would be totally self-sustaining. They would not need the external environment nor anything on the surface for anything except energy, a heat sink, physical support, and shielding from hazards. Food would be manufactured in factories within the cities. The energy source could be geothermal.

The present pattern of scattered living on the surface of the planet, if not abandoned, may grow some for a while longer, but will, eventually, begin to falter, becoming increasingly unmanageable and inequitable until it enters a collapse phase . . . For the few who can secure that capital investment for their support there is a solution, if they structure it in the form of such starship cities. For the bulk of humanity there is no hope in any case. The only thing we can do is try to keep them from destroying the natural ecosystem as they die back.

Arturans and Prism of Lyra Influenced Earth

From: John Winston
(John_-_Winston@cup.portal.com)

The next information that I will share with you is rather complicated and to most of you will seem rather unbelievable. I'll skip over the first parts of it because they are a little too deep for me.

The information . . . starts off by telling how we people in the physical dimension got started in this galaxy. It seems that we came into physical existence through the Prism of Lyra, in other words the constellation of Lyra. Next, we branched out to Antares and Arcturus. It then goes into an explanation of 1. Our future self. 2. Angels. 3. Devil and fairy kingdoms. 4. Walk-ins and souls braids. 5. Christ Consciousness. 6. Angels and Free Will. And other things. I will put down parts of information that we may be able to understand. This will show how Arturans have influenced Earth in the past and the present.

Shocking New Test for Carpal Tunnel Syndrome

From: George E. Turner (geturner@cobra.aer.com)

That's nothing. I had to get a test for nerve damage to my wrists (carpal tunnel damage). The test consisted of first putting long wires under my fingernails (no anesthetic). The wires were hooked to a machine much like an oscilloscope. Then they gave me electric shocks, starting at my shoulder and then working down my arm. The shocks came in groups of three at each location, the first being quite mild, the third being strong enough to make the whole side of my body twitch. When they gave me the first series, I started shouting, "I'll talk, I'll talk!" No one else thought it was funny. After that it was sort of like being at an AC-DC concert. ■

The Internet Report

The end of one calendar year and the beginning of another is typically a time when the members of the mainstream media roll out their retrospective pieces on "the year that was." While some members of the press offer insightful and telling commentary on the events of the previous 12 months, most year-end wrap-ups look more like a high school football blooper highlights film than a serious attempt to analyze 365 days' worth of world events.

So it's no wonder the world press was caught napping on New Year's Day, when the Zapatista Army of National Liberation launched an offensive against the Mexican government in Chiapas, Mexico. Once the world's reporters woke up and be-

gan to cover the event, it became clear that we weren't going to hear much of the real story behind why the mysterious Sub-Commander Marcos was fighting in the Lacandon jungle.

Except on the Internet. It wasn't long before the real story was finding its way into **soc.culture.mexican** and **alt.current.events**. The full text of the Zapatista's declaration was published on the Internet—a document few major daily papers and practically no television news outlet carried, or even alluded to.

In the months since the Chiapas uprising, events inside Mexico have continued along a strange and twisted path. The PRI party has won another election (despite familiar allegations of election fraud), making it the longest-rul-

ing political dynasty active today—more than 60 years. Two bloody political assassinations have shocked the world (but not readers of **alt.activism** or **soc.rights.human**), and all the mainstream press can manage is idle speculation on what it all means for "political stability" in Mexico.

Meanwhile, the Internet continues to buzz with the sounds of grassroots political activism, and Mexicans and Americans alike are making extensive use of the Net to try to bring the full story to the public. Most Americans would be shocked and astonished to read of the daily assaults on democratic ideals taking place in Mexico that are regularly posted to the Net.

In that respect, the Internet has again served as a sort of de facto "people's press," bringing the real

INSIDE

OPINION

story of the behind-the-scenes drama into the homes and offices of thousands of online readers. It's too soon to tell if this new method of news distribution will have an impact on the mainstream press, much less the political systems and people of the world. In the meantime, all many Mexicans can do is wait and hope that it will.

Communiqué from the Zapatista Army of National Liberation

Posted to: soc.culture.mexican
Posted by: General Command of the EZLN 1993

The following is the full text of the declaration from the Lacandon jungle by the Zapatista Army of National Liberation:

TODAY WE SAY ENOUGH IS ENOUGH! TO THE PEOPLE OF MEXICO: MEXICAN BROTHERS AND SISTERS

We are a product of 500 years of struggle: first against slavery, then during the War of Independence against Spain led by insurgents, then to avoid being absorbed by North American imperialism, then to promulgate our constitution and expel the French empire from our soil; and later the dictatorship of Porfirio Díaz denied us the just

on MEXICO

application of the Reform laws, and the people rebelled, and leaders like Villa and Zapata emerged, poor men just like us. We have been denied the most elemental preparation so they can use us as cannon fodder and pillage the wealth of our country. They don't care that we have nothing, absolutely nothing, not even a roof over our heads, no land, no work, no health care, no food nor education. Nor are we able to freely and democratically elect our political representatives, nor is there independence from foreigners, nor is there peace nor justice for ourselves and our children.

But today, we say *enough is enough!* We are the inheritors of the true builders of our nation. The dispossessed, we are millions and we thereby call upon our brothers and sisters to join this struggle as the only path, so that we will not die of hunger due to the insatiable ambition of a 70-year dictatorship led by a clique of traitors that represents the most conservative and sell-out groups. They are the same ones that opposed Hidalgo and Morelos, the same ones that betrayed Vicente Guerrero, the same ones that sold half our country to the foreign invader, the same ones that imported a European prince to rule our country, the same ones that formed the "scientific" Porfirsta dictatorship, the same ones that opposed the Petroleum Expropriation, the same ones that massacred the railroad workers in 1958 and the students in 1968, the same ones that today take everything from us, absolutely everything.

To prevent the continuation of the above and as our last hope, after having tried to utilize all legal means based on our Constitution, we go to our Constitution, to apply Article 39 which says:

"National Sovereignty essentially and originally resides in the people. All political power emanates from the people and its purpose is to help the people. The people have, at all times, the inalienable right to alter or modify their form of government."

Therefore, according to our constitution, we declare the following to the Mexican federal army, the pillar of the Mexican dictatorship that we suffer from, monopolized by a one-party system and led by Carlos Salinas de Gortari, the illegitimate federal executive who today holds power.

According to this Declaration of War, we ask that other powers of the nation advocate to restore the legitimacy and the stability of the nation by overthrowing the dictator.

We also ask that international organizations and the International Red Cross watch over and regulate our battles, so that our efforts are carried out while still protecting our civilian population. We declare now and always that we are subject to the Geneva Accord, forming the EZLN as our fighting arm of our liberation struggle. We have the Mexican people on our side; we have the beloved tri-colored flag, highly respected by our insurgent fighters. We use black and red in our uniform as our symbol of our working people on strike. Our flag carries the following letters, "EZLN," Zapatista Army of National Liberation, and we always carry our flag into combat.

Beforehand, we refuse any effort to disgrace our just cause by accusing us of being drug traffickers, drug guerrillas, thieves, or other names that might be used by our enemies. Our struggle follows the constitution, which is held high by its call for justice and equality.

Therefore, according to this declaration of war, we give our military forces, the EZLN, the following orders:

FIRST Advance to the capital of the country, overcoming the Mexican federal army, protecting in our advance the civilian population, and permitting the people in the liberated area the right to freely and democratically elect their own administrative authorities.

SECOND Respect the lives of our prisoners and turn over all wounded to the International Red Cross.

THIRD Initiate summary judgments against all soldiers of the Mexican federal army and the political police who have received training or have been paid by foreigners, accused of being traitors to our country, and against all those who have repressed and treated badly the civil population, and robbed or stolen from or attempted crimes against the good of the people.

FOURTH Form new troops with all those Mexicans who show their interest in joining our struggle, including those who, being enemy soldiers, turn themselves in without having fought against us, and promise to take orders from the General Command of the Zapatista Army of National Liberation.

FIFTH Ask for the unconditional surrender of the enemy's headquarters before we begin any combat, to avoid any loss of lives.

SIXTH Suspend the robbery of our natural resources in the areas controlled by the EZLN.

To the People of Mexico: We, the men and women, full and free, are conscious that the war that we have declared is our last resort, but also a just one. The dictators have applied an undeclared genocidal war against our people for many years. Therefore we ask for your participation, your decision to support this plan that struggles for work, land, housing, food, health care, education, independence, freedom, democracy, justice, and peace. We declare that we will not stop fighting until the basic demands of our people have been met by forming a government of our country that is free and democratic.

JOIN THE INSURGENT FORCES OF THE ZAPATISTA ARMY OF NATIONAL LIBERATION.

Mexico Shooting

Posted to: soc.culture.mexican
From: Jose A. Briones
        <brioneja@ttown.apci.com>
        CNN Newsource

Mexico City, Mexico, Wednesday (28 Sept. 1994)

SCRIPT: the secretary-general of mexico's ruling party was assassinated today. jose francisco ruiz massieu died hours after being shot in mexico city. witnesses say a gunman approached his car and opened fire with a semi-automatic weapon. a suspect was arrested at the scene. the incident is the latest blow to mexico's ruling presidential candidate was shot to death during a political rally in tijuana. his successor won the presidential election and takes power in december.

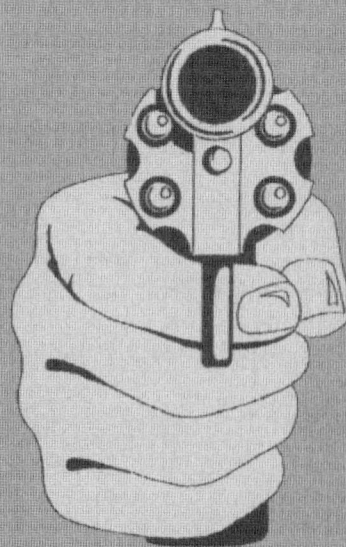

EZLN Under Military Threat; Demonstration 9/26 NYC

From: Toby Mailman (tobym@blythe.org)
Via: NY Transfer News Collective
Date: Sat, 24 Sept. 1994 14:32:41 CDT

ACTION ALERT!

Zapatistas under military threat in Chiapas; demonstration to confront Salinas at U.N.

Despite denials by the Mexican Army and the government that they are going to attack the Zapatista Army in Chiapas, the government has sent 25,000 troops to the state of Chiapas, and there have been several recent disappearances.

Protest Mexican threats against the Zapatistas and the popular movements working for democracy in Mexico.

President Salinas De Gortari will be speaking at the U.N. on Monday morning, September 26th.

Join a demonstration in front of the U.N., 43rd Street and 1st Avenue, New York City, 9:00 a.m., Monday, Sept. 26th.

For more information, call:

NYC Committee for Democracy in Mexico
212-473-3225

New York Transfer News Collective
(info: info@blythe.org)

Declaration of the People's State Democratic Assembly of Chiapas

Posted to: soc.culture.mexican
From: "Mexicanos Exiliados Pro-Democracia" <usi@infi.net>
Date: Fri, 30 Sept. 1994

Repression, expulsion, detentions against members of the civil resistance movement.

The state government has opted for repressing the members of our assembly who are participating in actions of civil resistance as a response to the demands for the respect to popular will and a response to the social problems of the state.

There is a campaign of repression and persecution against active members of the organizations participating in the movement of civil resistance, in particular against the State Council of Indige-

nous and Campesino Organizations (CEOIC). In Chicomuselo, on the 17 and 18 of September, public security police surrounded and besieged a campesino meeting of the OCEZ-CNPA (Campesino Organization Emiliano Zapata-National Coordinator of the Plan de Ayala), members of the CEOIC in the region without any confrontations.

On the 17 of September in Rodulfo Figeroa, municipality of La Trinitaria, 20 Justice police violently stormed and ransacked the homes of 7 members of CEOIC: Antonio Hernandez Perez,

Caterino Perez Alvarado, Reinaldo Perez, Luis Perez Maldonado, Reynaldo Perez Jimenez, Constantino Alvarez Perez, and Margarito Hernandez.

The police arrived on board three white and one red trucks belonging to landowners in the municipality. Margarito Hernandez and Mario Hernandez were detained. Also Romaldo Vazques has been detained. To this moment, their whereabouts have not been known for three days. Various children received blows in the incident, particularly the children of Celerina Perez and her family. It has been verified that there are 30 orders for the apprehension against members of this organization in Rodulfo Figueroa, El Lagareto y El Recreo. These orders have been issued by the district court of Comitan.

On 19 September, in the municipality of Suchiate, the state public security police expelled violently around 300 campesinos members of OPEZ (Proletarian Organization Emiliano Zapata) of the CEOIC, from the land they held in the plantation known as La Herradura.

At 8:00 in the morning, more that 700 police agents entered by force on the site, and detained 300 campesinos and put them on a semi-trailer to take them away. As they went past La Libertad, the inhabitants liberated their companeros. Notwithstanding, another group of campesinos was detained. It is known that among them are Melquiades and Carmelino Villarreal, who were badly beaten for having resisted at the site.

During the attack, the police threw tear gas canisters, and schoolchildren in a nearby school were affected.

Indignant, the people organized a march in protest, going from La Libertad to the municipality of Suchiate. In this march campesinos and teachers participated; it is hoped that other communities are united with the manifestation. At 4:00 in the afternoon, a press conference will be held in Tapachula.

This same day, another expulsion took place in Suchiate. At noon on that day, campesinos from OPEZ were brutally expelled from the site they had taken over in Dorado Nuevo. The state public security police destroyed homes, burned their belongings and delivered blows to dozens of people. The agents of order placed men, women, and children in the back of a semi-trailer and took them in an unknown direction.

The government did not fulfill its promise and began the expulsions without previous notice.

On 4 September as part of civil resistance action, campesinos of OPEZ took 26 banana plantations along the coast; 10 of them belong to multinational enterprises with German and U.S. owners. On 11 September in Tuxtla Gutierrez, an agreement was reached with governor Javier Lopez Moreno where he committed himself to turn over 1,800 hectares (4,000 acres) in return for the 10 plantations. When this commitment was not met, the campesinos remained in the site. The governor declared on television on the night of Sept. 18 that members of CEOIC did not fulfill their part of the bargain, and that is why they would be expelled. Without previous notice to the campesinos, the police expelled them a day after.

Two Leaders Murdered in Oaxaca

Posted to: soc.culture.mexican
Subject: Corrientes Mexicanas—Building Bridges of Friendship and Understanding between Mexico and the U.S.
Sender: Peter Brown <pbrown@igc.apc.org>
Date: Mon, Sept. 19, 1994

Two More Community Leaders Murdered in Oaxaca

- Lorenzo Casteada, President of Bienes Comunales of Santa Maria Colotepec, Municipality of Pochutla, Oaxaca
- Justo Salvador, Municipal President of Pochutla, Oaxaca

Two community leaders, Lorenzo Casteada, President of Bienes Comunales de Santa Maria Colotepec, and Sr. Justo Salvador, President of the Municipality of Pochutla, were murdered last night in the Puerto Escondido, Oaxaca, Mexico, while waiting to take a bus to Oaxaca City with the intention of reporting land fraud. A local radio station had broadcast very specific allegations about corruption and land fraud. In response, the two men hoped to file an official report in the state capital of Oaxaca. They were murdered before making their report.

Both men come from the coastal community of Santa Maria Colotepec, Municipality of Pochutla in the state of Oaxaca, Mexico, which has a history of violent conflict as land developers seek land for the tourist industry. Local and international business interests, lead by the Municipal President of Puerto Escondido, Mr. C. Daniel Bralett, continue to pursue illegal development schemes that involve removing all or part of the indigenous community of Santa Maria Colotepec. Santa Maria Colotepec is directly south of Puerto Escondido.

Earlier this year, Mr. Candido Robles Ruiz, then President of Bienes Comunales de Santa Maria Colotepec, and Mr. Crisforo Ramirez Herrera, then Secretary of Rienes Comunales de Santa Maria Colotepec, were assassinated. The only witness to this earlier murder, Mr. Lucio Ramirez Pinzn, is still in hiding for fear of his life.

The entire community of Santa Maria Colotepec now lives in great fear that additional citizens will be killed.

Please send telegrams, telexes, faxes and airmail letters in Spanish, English, or your own language:

—expressing concern for the families of these two new murdered leaders and other members of the community of Santa Maria Colotepec, Municipality of Pochutla, Oaxaca;
—requesting a prompt and impartial investigation into these allegations and calling for those responsible to be brought to justice.

Send appeals to:
President of the Republic
Lic. Carlos Salinas de Gortari
[Salutation: Sr. Presidente/Dear President]
Presidente de la Republica
Palacio Nacional
06067 Mexico D.F., MEXICO

Telegrams: Presidente Salinas, Mexico D.F., Mexico
Telexes: 170937 sppnme; 1774468 sppnme
Faxes: +52 5 271 1764

Interior Minister
Dr Jorge Carpizo McGregor
[Salutation: Sr. Secretario de Gobernacion/
  Dear Minister]
Secretario de Gobernacion
Bucarelli 99, 1er piso
Colonia Juarez
06669 Mexico D.F., MEXICO

Telegrams: Secretario Gobernacion,
Mexico D.F., Mexico
Telexes: 1774376, 1774375
Faxes: +52 5 703 2171

Attorney General's Office
Lic Humberto Benitez Trevino
[Salutation: Sr. Procurador General/
  Dear Attorney General]
Procurador General de la Republica
Paseo de la Reforma y Violeta
Colonia Guerrero
06300 Mexico D.F., MEXICO

Telegrams: Procurador General, Mexico D.F., Mexico
Telexes: 1777572
Faxes: +52 5 626 4430

Please send copies of your appeal to:
Senor Jose Juan deOlloqui
Embassy of Mexico, 42 Hertford St., Mayfair,
London W1Y 7TF, ENGLAND
Fax: 071 495 4035

National Human Rights Commission:
Comision Nacional de Derechos Humanos
Periferico Sur 3469
Col San Jeronimo Lidice
10200 Mexico D.F., MEXICO

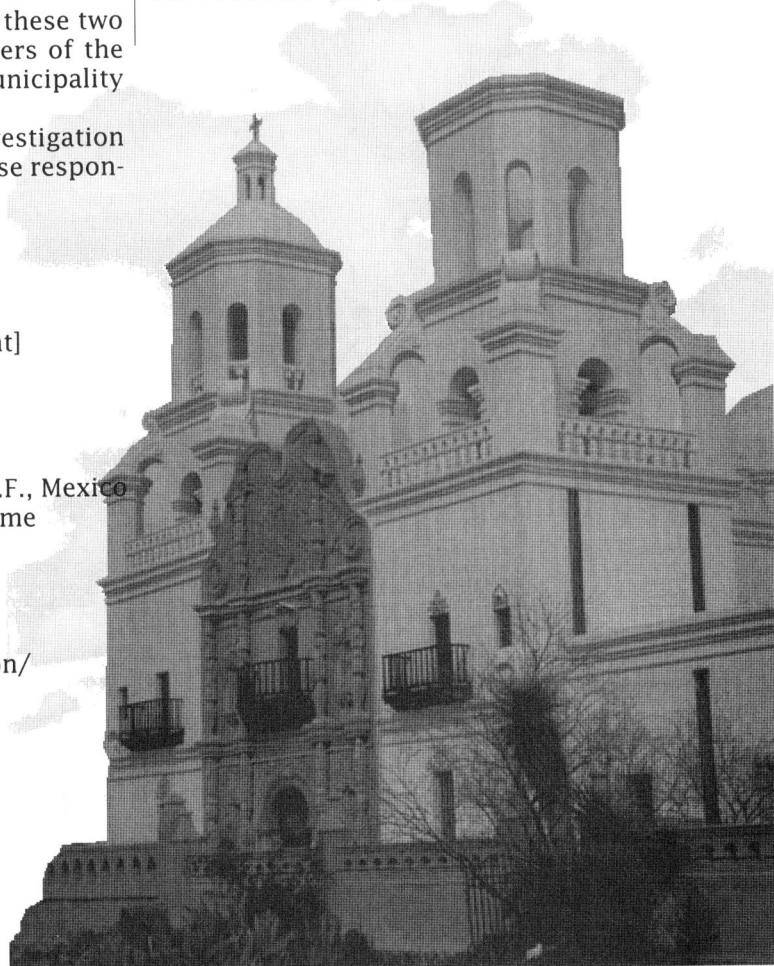

Journalist Detained in Michoacan

Posted to: soc.culture.mexican
Posted by: Prof. Guillermo Delgado-P. University of California, Santa Cruz

Urgent Action on behalf of Mr. Gunther Dietz, journalist affiliated with AIPIN, the Office of the Indigenous Press in Mexico City and Germany, who has been detained on September 29 (Thursday) 1994 in the city of Morelia, Michoacan.

FROM: AIPIN, Agencia Internacional de la Prensa India/International Office of the Indigenous Press (fax/phone 011-52-5-521-6084, Mexico City).

TO: The International Community.

(Mexico, September 30, 1994) Journalist Mr. Gunther Dietz from Germany has been detained by Mexican Security Forces in the city of Morelia, capital of the State of Michoacan on Thursday, September 29, 1994.

Gunther Dietz is a journalist, and represents AIPIN, International Office of the Indigenous Press in Germany. He is also professor at the University of Hamburg.

Gunther Dietz is in Mexico in order to carry on research together with AIPIN journalists, and Masters students of the University of Hamburg, on the current condition of media among Indigenous Peoples of the State of Michoacan, located in Western Mexico.

Gunther Dietz was detained as he was taking a bus at the Morelia City bus station. Three individuals who introduced themselves as members of the Office of National Security of Mexico detained Mr. Dietz.

As a journalist affiliated with AIPIN, Mr. Dietz was reporting on a march of the Purepecha Indigenous Peoples, who are original peoples of that state. The Purepecha departed on a march from the city of Patzcuaro on Tuesday, September 27 in the direction of Morelia, capital of Michoacan. The march covers a distance of 70 kilometers (approximately 50 miles).

After being detained, he was taken to the Instituto Nacional de Migracion, which is a branch of the Secretaria de Gobernacion.

The reason given as an explanation of Mr. Dietz' detention is that it was a simple immigration checking, and because of this he was pressed into detention by national security officers.

As an explanation of his detention, Mr. Palacios, the Under-Director of Immigration Matters, is trying to implicate journalist Gunther Dietz as an activist of the Indigenous Movement of the Purepecha nation, enough reason for his detention—according to Mr. Palacios.

Mr. Rogelio Mercado, Regional Correspondent of AIPIN in Michoacan, points out as false the charges pressed on journalist Gunther Dietz. Mr. Mercado said: "Gunther assisted our office technically, and he was observing the Indigenous March developments in order to collect information for his research."

Mr. Palacios pressed charges against Mr. Dietz, pointing to Lic. Isidoro Gonzalez Blanco, Under-Director of National Security Protection of Mexico, as being responsible for Mr. Dietz' detention.

However, National Security Protection officers denied Mr. Palacios' words, stressing that National Security Protection officers are not responsible at all. Instead they stressed the lack of seriousness of the Immigration Subdirection Office, which is trying to avoid responsibility for Mr. Dietz' detention.

AIPIN requests the solidarity of the international community, human rights groups, and indigenous and non-indigenous journalists in order to implore the Mexican government to immediately release journalist Gunther Dietz, as well as to stop harassing AIPIN's regional correspondents in the State of Michoacan, Mexico.

Do please send a fax to:
State Press Secretary/Secretaria de Gobernacion
011-52-1-592-01-03

Copies to:
AIPIN, Agencia Internacional de la Prensa, India
011-52-5-521-6084 ■

Net Resources

For information on using or connecting to the Internet within Mexico, send e-mail to: **silviav@ci.seinet.net.mx**

For the latest news on events in Mexico, keep an eye on any of the current events newsgroups, particularly **alt.current.events**, but also the following:

> **soc.mexican.culture**
> **soc.mexican-american.culture**
> **alt.activism**
> **soc.rights.human**
> **alt.politics**
> **alt.politics.radical-left**

The New York Transfer News Collective (**nyt@nyxfer.blythe.org**) also publishes regular press releases throughout the Net on events in Mexico.

The mailing list ACTIV-L (**ACTIV-L@MIZZOU1.missouri.edu**) covers a number of events and causes relating to various political activist stances, including events in Mexico.

Finally, for specific information on the Chiapas rebels and other movements within Mexico, check the **soc.culture.native** and **alt.native** newsgroups, which cover events related to native and indigenous peoples around the world.

Are You Good Enough For

By Dennis Hinkamp (dennish@extsparc.agsci.usu.edu)

I have been watching the insidious, fungus-like growth of Birkenstocks for about ten years now. They are, after all, the leading egocentric indicator of hipness. Unfortunately, Birkies are being sold to just about anyone these days.

The boss here at the *Insider* doesn't let us wear sandals. Says it looks goofy. Dorky. Like a nerd. Too laid back. When one of our interns showed up in a pair of those new-fangled "cross-training" sandals—the ones with the nylon webbing and high-impact, neoprene-laced soles—we warned him to go home and change into wing tips, pronto. He didn't listen, and now he's the guy who has to hold his finger on the knot as the bundling machine ties together hundreds of copies of the *Insider*. He's got three fingers left.

Don't make the same mistake. Make sure you're worthy of wearing sandals—especially Birkenstocks. Be safe. Before you show up sandal-footed, take the Birkenstock Challenge.

INSIDE

OPINION

No background police record checks, no three-day waiting period, no psychological profiles or anything.

It's happening in cities everywhere: "Excuse me sir, do you have a permit for those sandals? It is 12 degrees outside and you looked mighty suspicious wearing those."

"But officer, they're not *real* Birkies. They're just imitations."

"Birkenstocks aren't toys, son. From a distance people can't tell the difference and someone might get hurt."

You might like Birkenstocks. You might even treasure them. Birkies might be good enough for you, but are *you* good enough for Birkies? Take this test and see if you measure up.

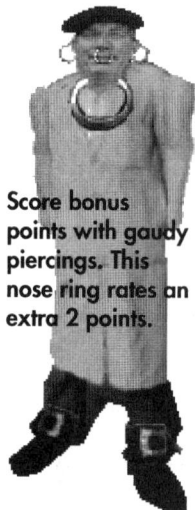
Score bonus points with gaudy piercings. This nose ring rates an extra 2 points.

1

Do you wear your Birkenstocks year round? Do you wear, if not sockless, with gray wool socks only? No argyles please. Think of the young children that might be frightened.
(1 point for each season.)

2

Do you compost? You know, do you have a personal backyard landfill? (Add 1 point, plus 2 bonus points if there has ever been a seagull at your compost pile.)

3

Do you recycle aluminum cans? (Add 1 point for taking them to a recycling center, subtract 2 points for using the cans in arts and crafts projects.)

4

Do you have multiple body piercings? Nothing too Madonna, Satan-inspired, over-the-top weird. Nothing below neck level. Just your basic ear/nose anatomical violations beyond the one hole per ear variety. (Add 1 point for each piercing exceeding two total piercings.)

5

Do you have a dog that (you think) would rather swim/hike/ski/catch Frisbees than sleep all day on the couch and eat raw liver? (1 point per dog.)

6

Do you drive a vehicle that has a roof rack to chassis ratio of .75 or greater? This is simple to calculate. Add up the bike/boat/ski market value and divide by the blue book value of the car or truck. (3 points, 1 bonus point if the rack itself is worth more than your car, subtract 1 point if the car is a BMW or Saab.)

7

Are you an athletic man who shaves his legs or an athletic woman who doesn't? (1 point)

8

Your last relationship ended because you
a) skied/biked/rock-climbed too much or
b) didn't ski/bike/rock-climb enough.
(Add 1 point per adventure sports-related failed relationship.)

9

You know what falafel is. (1 point)

Birkenstocks?

Are You Worthy of the Birkenstock Legacy?

Only skilled artisians are allowed to craft the world-famous Birkenstock sandal.

10
You care what falafel is and have more than one recipe for its use. (1 point)

11
When someone mentions "Windham Hill," you think you remember rock climbing there. (Trick question—minus 1 point)

12
You spit on people who drive cars around town when they could bike, but you routinely drive 400 miles on weekends to ski/boat/bike/rock-climb. (1 point)

Originally published in the "Slightly Off Center" *column in the* Logan Herald Journal *and the* Salt Lake City Event *Magazine.* ∎

Scoring:

15 points or more: You pass the test. You are worthy. You are a Birkenstock loyalist. You probably have re-soled yours more than once and you think the addition of colored Birkenstocks in recent years is sacrilegious.

6-14 points: You are a middle-of-the-road, lukewarm, indecisive sheep of a person. However, with hard work and sacrifice you may someday be worthy. For now, though, you can only wear them in the privacy of your own home.

5 points or less: You are definitely not worthy. You are a pathetic, slave-to-fashion trendoid who probably wore earth shoes, moon boots, platform shoes, Air Jordans, and clogs when they were in fashion. Please, if you have an ounce of decency, give your Birkenstocks to somebody who really needs, deserves, and will care for them.

Actor Don Knotts, known for his roles on "The Andy Griffith Show" and, of course, "Matlock," announced on Tuesday that he will run for Sheriff of Alameda County, California. When asked how he planned to handle crime in the district, Knotts stated, "Nip it, nip it in the bud!"

When asked for a more specific program, Knotts referred reporters to his brochure, "A Three-Pronged Program of Bud-Nipping," which included the following points:

- Issue multiple bullets to all duly deputized officers.
- Allow authorized personnel to use the patrol vehicle after 9 p.m.
- Restrict phone calls to Thelma Lou to off-peak periods.

Reporting from the edge of credibility, I'm Juan Bootsie.
Contact Juan Bootsie at: an31291@anon.penet.fi or check out his archives via FTP in the /pub/hamlet directory at ftp.netcom.com.

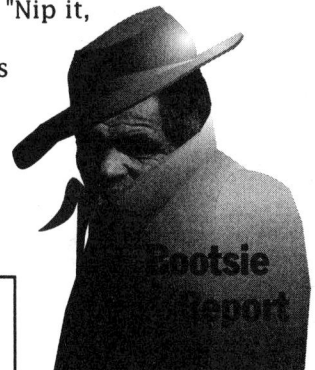

Bootsie Report

Clinton, Gore Stuck in Slow-Moving World-Wide Web!

Finally, after all these years and the recent months of anxious anticipation, the 'lectro-riffic mega-spew-way leads right up to the White House steps. Or perhaps it leads out of the White House. On October 20, 1994, Vice President Al Gore announced with great fanfare that the White House had joined the World-Wide Web.

In an effort to make government information more readily accessible to citizens across the country, Vice President Gore, joined by the Office of Science and Technology Policy's Associate Director for Technology Lionel S. (Skip) Johns and world-renowned artist Peter Max, unveiled the first interactive, multimedia, electronic citizens' handbook on the White House, including detailed information about Cabinet-level and independent agencies, and information about the First Family and the White House.

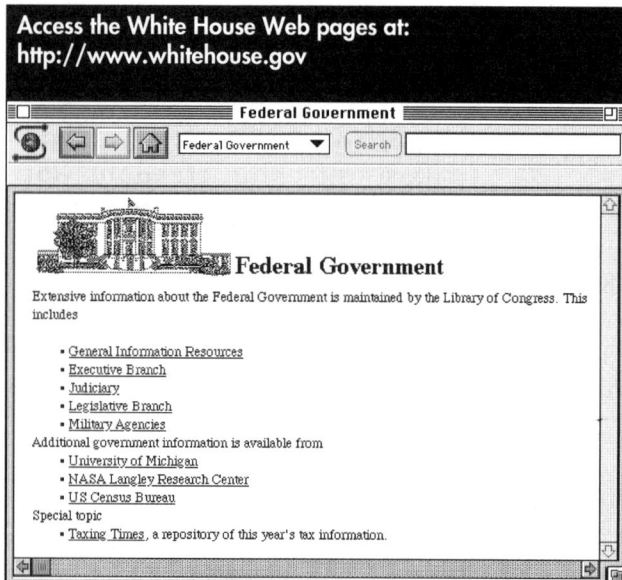

Access the White House Web pages at:
http://www.whitehouse.gov

Federal Government

Federal Government

Extensive information about the Federal Government is maintained by the Library of Congress. This includes

- General Information Resources
- Executive Branch
- Judiciary
- Legislative Branch
- Military Agencies

Additional government information is available from

- University of Michigan
- NASA Langley Research Center
- US Census Bureau

Special topic

- Taxing Times, a repository of this year's tax information.

Hey, kids! Tour the White House online—simply clicking on any icon and waiting about 15 or 20 minutes takes you to a whole new world of interactive wonder. It's as easy as that!

Welcome to the White House

URL: http://www.whitehouse.gov/
Map: http://www.whitehouse.gov/White_House/images/white_house_home.gif

Welcome to the
White House

Executive Branch
The First Family
Tours
What's New
Publications
Comments

An Interactive Citizens' Handbook

President's Welcome Message
Guest Book
Vice President's Welcome Message

"This first-of-its-kind program is an electronic roadmap to the federal government—a place on the information superhighway where people can get needed information about government services and where they can provide immediate feedback to the President," Vice President Gore said via a White House press release.

Welcome to the White House: An Interactive Citizens' Handbook provides a single point of access to all electronic government information on the In-ternet, a vast electronic computer network used by people in more than 150 countries. Examples of accessible material demonstrated at today's event include information about the President and Vice President and their families, a virtual tour of the White House, detailed information about Cabinet-level and independent agencies, a subject-searchable index of federal information, and a map of Washington, D.C.

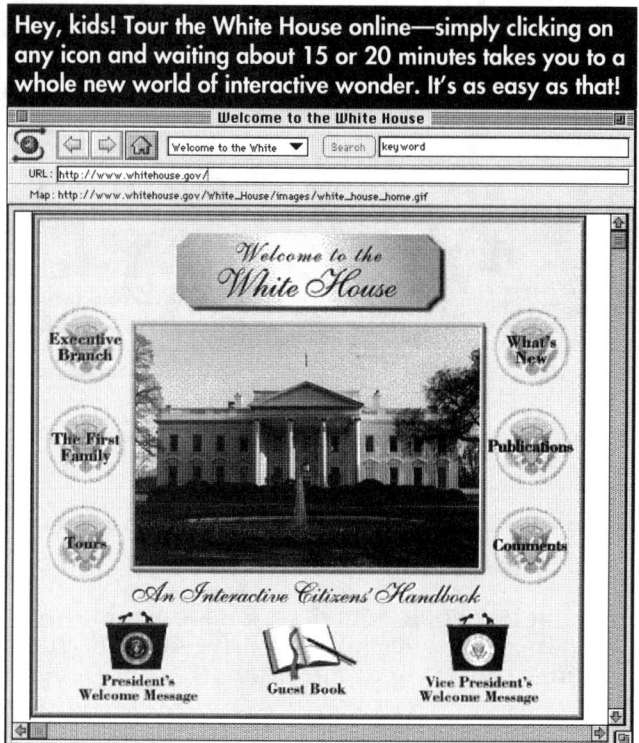

The press release continued: "The service promotes interaction and participation between citizens and their federal government. It is part of President Clinton and Vice President Gore's vision to create a National Information Infrastructure—a seamless web of communications networks that will forever change the way we live, learn, work and communicate with each other."

White House Open for Online Tours

Welcome to the White House

What Gore and his press agents failed to mention was that if you wanted to check out the snazzy graphics and super-interhype-rac-tive multimedilicious nature of the White House web link, you'd better have a high-speed, multi-megabit connection directly to the Internet. Our info-grazing interns choked on the huge files Al and the gang had posted in their lil' corner of the Net, and the *Insider* estimates that for a regular home user to view the White House's "Interactive Citizen's Handbook" there would be about 48 minutes of waiting for images and sounds to download.

Now *that's* interactive!

Oh, of course the Handbook leads to plenty of "useful" information. For instance, you can browse and download any of the thousands of boring, official documents that the White House Press Office spews forth with alarming speed and regularity. Did we sign that fishing and canning treaty with Iceland? How did things go at the state dinner with the Prime Minister of Surinam? Who's going to be

What's that? Don't have the necessary high-speed connection and fancy sound board needed to hear Socks "meow"? Well, simply *read* his meow instead! It's almost like being there!

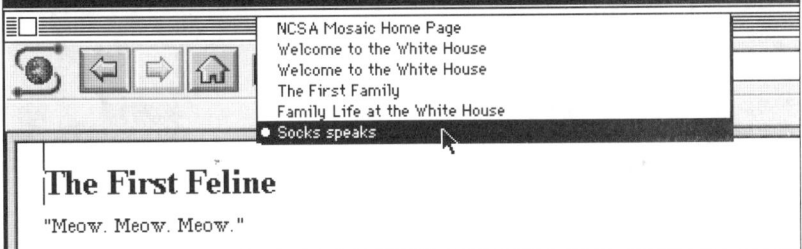

NCSA Mosaic Home Page
Welcome to the White House
Welcome to the White House
The First Family
Family Life at the White House
● Socks speaks

The First Feline

"Meow. Meow. Meow."

the next Assistant Advisor to the Undersecretary for Veterans Affairs? It's all there, along with so much, much more.

And when you've had enough affairs of state, the Citizen's Handbook offers an intensely human and personal look at how the First Family lives. With a few simple clicks (and after several minutes of waiting) you can: *Hear* President Clinton welcome you to the White House! *See* Hillary Rodham Clinton teaching inner city kids how to color inside the lines with their burnt sienna Crayolas! *Hear* Socks, the First Feline, meow with glee!

Here's a sample (sans the snazzy graphics and sounds) of what browsing the White House via the Net is like:

Family Life at the White House

When Bill Clinton was a senior in high school, he was selected to go to Washington, D.C., to be part of Boys Nation. Bill Clinton was one of the first in line to shake President Kennedy's hand in the Rose Garden. After that, he knew he wanted to make a difference in the lives of people by becoming President of the United States. This photo is one of his most cherished possessions.

As a family, the Clintons still find time to do the things that they feel are important for their community. Here, the Clintons are at a food bank helping prepare and serve Thanksgiving dinner.

Hillary Clinton, who has always found time to work with the children of the community, joins in on the fun at a local school with two young artists.

To relax, President Clinton plays the saxophone

President Clinton loves to play with Socks. Power users may click to hear Socks meow, while the digitally disenfranchised may click another icon to . . . er, read his meow.

He likes to play with the family cat , Socks , (~36K) as well

and, occasionally, a round of golf.

He likes to play with the family cat, Socks, and enjoys other leisure time activities, such as horseback riding, bike riding, and boating. Here, he is on vacation at Martha's Vineyard.

Hey, now that is interactive! Fire up Mosaic (or the web browser of your choice) and check out the White House at: http://www.whitehouse.gov.

Eavesdrop on the First Family Via Modem

Follow Bill, Hillary, Chelsea, and Socks on their mega-media, infra-active adventures from their house to yours, only on the Internet!

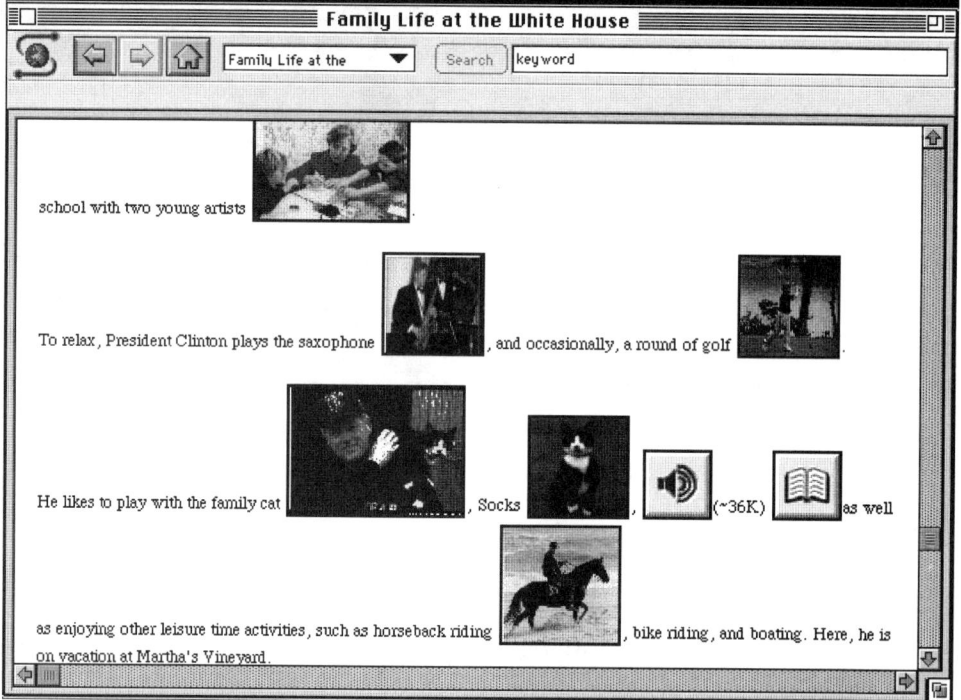

Family Life at the White House

Family Life at the | Search | keyword

school with two young artists

To relax, President Clinton plays the saxophone , and occasionally, a round of golf .

He likes to play with the family cat , Socks , (~36K) as well

as enjoying other leisure time activities, such as horseback riding , bike riding, and boating. Here, he is on vacation at Martha's Vineyard.

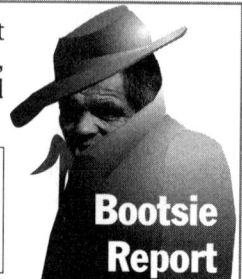

Al Gore has long been government's greatest champion for what he calls the (ugh) "information superhighway," and was hip to the Net long before most of the journalists and pundits who pan him for his goofy demeanor and stiff, dorky delivery. Geeks around the world have, naturally, embraced him as one of their own.

So there was a good deal of excitement in the air in January 1994, when Gore took to the wires on CompuServe to participate in what was being billed as history's first online, interactive "town meeting" with a vice president. Maybe Gore could beat the "wooden" rap by going online, where everyone seems equally sluggish and confused!

Alas, despite the moderator's specific instructions to the participants—which were designed to keep the discussion from degenerating into the usual chaotic gibberish that these online conferences typically feature—Mr. Info Highway got tripped up by line noise when some guy's dad picked up the phone and spewed ASCII garbage characters right into the middle of the Vice President's chain of thought.

Rather than reversing his image as a stiff, halting policy wonk, Gore's conference went the usual everyone-talking-at-once route and produced a transcript that suggests he's a cyber-dork as well as just a regular in-the-flesh-dork. Here's a sample:

LIFE @ LARGE

(#11,Vice President Gore) Welcome to the White House. Let's get started.

(#10,Bill Allman/US NEWS) I'd like to start things off with a question that was submitted in advance to the U.S. News Online Forum, about the

Moderator recognizes question #1 Dion Douglas (46)

(#46,Dion Douglas) Mr. VP. . . I am from Hammond IN. What are your views on These "Virtual Communities . . . and are you currently involved in any networks?

(#11,Vice President Gore) I think they are terrific. I do a lot of my work on a virtual community

(#46,Dion Douglas) Thank you . . . and I am currently watching you on C-span . . :)

(#140,Vice President Gore) I'm back. Sorry. Anyway, we have a kind of "virtual community" here in the White House that gets a lot of work done, but we have not yet established the myriad links outside that we hope to soon.

Moderator recognizes question #2
Aaron Dickey [HelpF (60)

(#60,Aaron Dickey [HelpF) Mr. Vice-President . . . Huntington, WV here I'm a 23-year-old student . . . myself, and most of my friends, are finding ourselves ing more and more time spending excuse me in front our computers than in the "real world". Are you at all worried that eventually we ALL may end up spending too much time *iba*iuXE>ytoo (line noise sorry)* on the Net, and not enough time in face-to-face conversations/socialization?

(#140,Vice President Gore) Yes. But it's better than the same amount of time

(#60,Aaron Dickey [HelpF) *(line noise was my father picking up an extension, Mr. VP, sorry <grin>)*

(#196,Vice President Gore) Sorry. in front of a non-interactive

(#60,Aaron Dickey [HelpF) No sir, it was my father, not your fault

(#196,Vice President Gore) screen. Plus . . . soon, the nature of the be enriched with full-motion video and much faster links . . . which I predict will lead to a renewed appetite for REAL communities

(#60,Aaron Dickey [HelpF) (Member? I'm a sysop, Bill. <grin>.) Those are . . . very good points, Mr. Vice-President . . . thank

Moderator recognizes question #3

He's stiff. He's goofy. He's awkward. His clothes don't seem to fit quite right. He studies public policy with the kind of thrill and passion that most people reserve for sex or really good desserts. He's completely enamored of technology and the power of the Internet.

Al Gore is a geek. Hey, we're not complaining. It's kinda nice to have a Net-savvy geek for a vice president, even if his job mainly consists of standing in the background of official White House photo ops. But did he really need to start this whole "information superhighway" junk?

Yeah, you heard us correctly. Al Gore, our vice president, is claiming credit for having coined the phrase "information superhighway." Yeah, we know what you're thinking: "What idiot would willingly claim he spawned the most over-hyped catch phrase of all time?" Apparently, Al Gore. In a recent speech, he stated that, "Had I known 15 years ago when I coined the term 'information superhighway . . .'"

Sorry, Mr. Vice President, the genie is out of the bottle. The feeble-minded pundits and pontificators have wrapped their hearts and brains around your concept of a freeway for data and beaten it to death. No, actually they've flogged it beyond recognition or meaning. Here are a few of the witty treatments (some we like and some we don't) that we've seen in print or heard in conversation that extend the now unbearably meaningless "information superhighway" metaphor.

information superhighway
info highway
info superhighway
super infohighway
info superhypeway
electronic superhighway
interactive info highway

List Service

multimedia superhighway
infobahn
info-turnpike
digital freeway
digital roadbed
pothole on the . . .
roadblock on the . . .
curb-cut to the . . .
on-ramp to the . . .
off-ramp from the . . .
speed limit on the . . .
bottleneck on the . . .
pile-up on the . . .
hitch-hiker on the . . .
roadkill on the . . .
hit-and-run victim of the . . .
dirt road to/from the . . .
fast lane of the . . .
tailgating on the . . .
flat tire on the . . .
pulled over on the . . .

http://www.whitehouse.gov

Al Navigates Info Highway

Police-Band Scan-Hounds Can Hear Pres-Plane Calls!

In an age when the CIA can manage to keep an entire campus of office buildings a secret from Congress and the public, the White House seems a little less adept at the cloak-and-dagger game of government secrecy. Rumor has it that if enemies of the United States wanted the inside scoop on what the President was up to, all they would have to do is point their police scanners at Air Force One, the President's personal jet.

Scan the President with Your $99 Police Radio!

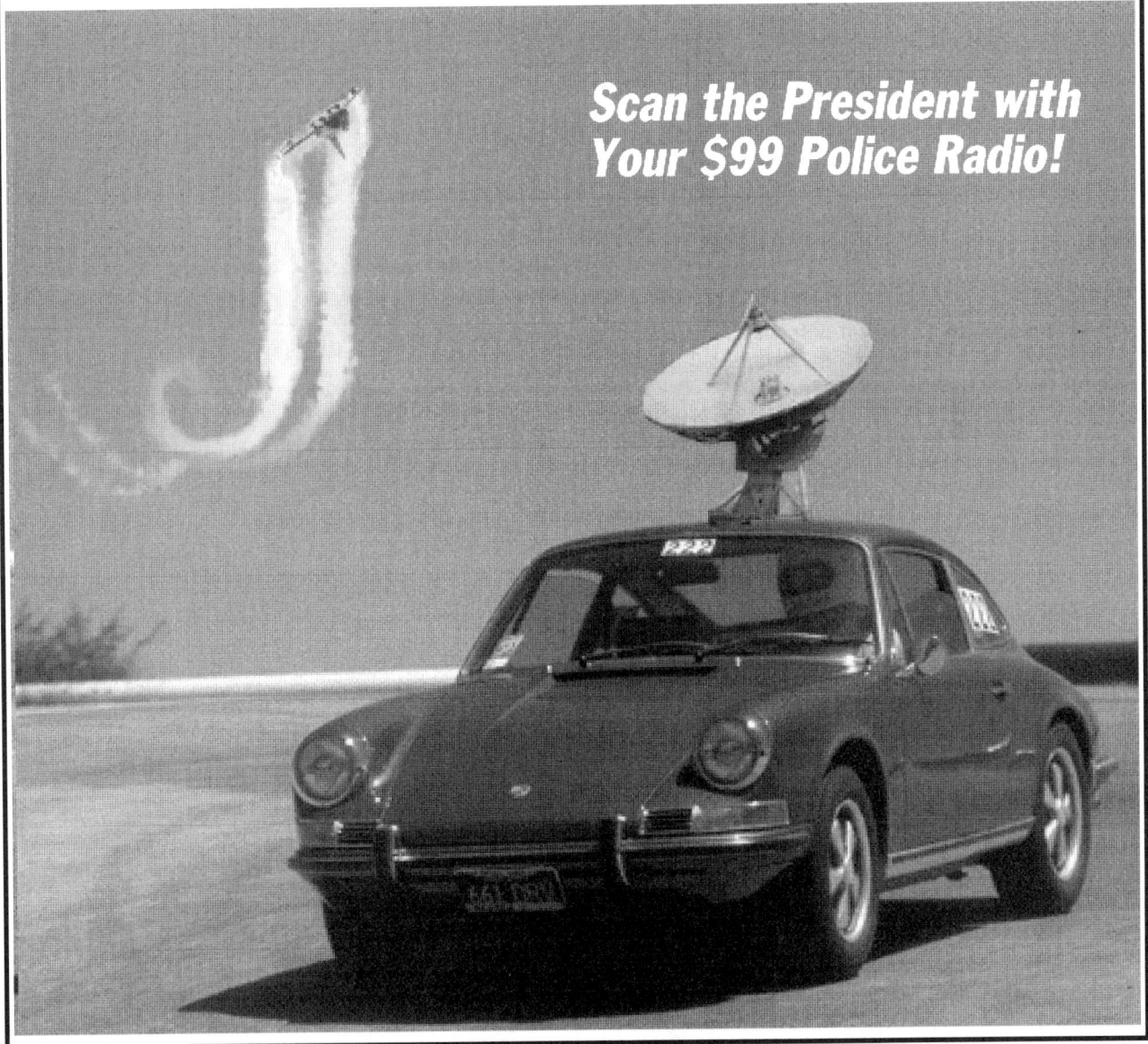

Glen Roberts, editor of the excellent *Full Disclosure* magazine, was the first journalist (and so far, apparently, the only one) to voice concern about the security of communications to and from Air Force One. He posted to the net a transcript of a conversation he had with a White House press representative, an edited excerpt of which follows:

Full Disclosure: OK, basically she was making phone calls from Air Force One today and they were being monitored by average citizens out there and we wanted to get her comments on the use of radio telephones from Air Force One and the public listening in.
White House: OK, and you're from Full Disclosure News Service?
FD: Right.
WH: Is that a publication?
FD: We have a magazine and a radio show.
WH: And, are you in Milwaukee?
FD: No, I am in the Chicago area.
WH: And you were listening to the call?
FD: I have information that she placed calls from Air Force One that were being monitored by the public.
WH: Like a ham radio or something?
FD: Like a police scanner, like something you buy at Radio Shack for $99.
WH: OK. OK, and you want to talk to her about the substance of the call or you want to talk to her about the . . .?
FD: The publicness of the calls and whether she is aware the calls are monitorable by any of the 12 million people in the US with police scanners and things of that nature.

* * * * *

WH: OK. OK and what would you just. What was the conversation you overheard just for my information.
FD: My information is she placed a phone call or two from Air Force One that was broadcast for anyone who wanted to listen in on it.
WH: OK, and you don't know what the substance of the call was or who they talked to.
FD: I have some notes on that, but I would like to talk to her about it.
WH: OK, well, I'm trying to help you out, but I am just. I'd like to know what I'm. What's she gonna have to respond to before I, you know, get in touch with her. I'm sure she's interested.

FD: Well you can pass it on and she can call me back or not. Um, you know, but we like to talk to people and get their views on it and not have somebody telling people what to say.
WH: OK, I'm not doing that at all.
FD: I don't want somebody to prepare a speech or a-----
WH: No. No, I was not even insinuating that. I'm sure she would be interested in who she was talking to, when she talked to you. It was obviously a private phone call so, I don't want her to be totally caught off guard. You know what I mean?
FD: That's really the point of my call. Is it really a private phone call? Are the phones on that plane presented to the users of them as being private phone calls or are they being presented as being, "Gee, there are 12 million people with police scanners that can tune in?"
WH: Right.
FD: Because additionally, New York Mayor Giuliani made calls from Air Force One today.
WH: Um hmm.
FD: I'm not sure if you can put me in contact with him or if I should go.
WH: Yeah, if you want to talk to him, you should probably talk to his office.
FD: Right.
WH: OK, well, I will do my best to get in touch with her. She's obviously on the road right now. Our communication to that site is somewhat limited, because of the, because the trip was obviously not planned. The decision to go wasn't finalized until last night. Our communication was not up to what it normally is for a trip . . . If you don't hear from me, you can call back. But, I will try and get in touch with them. Like I said we don't have phones set up like we normally do on the road. But, I will do my best to reach them.

For more information on the excellent Full Disclosure *magazine, e-mail Glen Roberts at glr@rci.ripco.com or tune in to the Full Disclosure Live on short-wave radio, Sundays at 8 p.m. Eastern on WWCR, 5.810 kHz.*

The First Family

"My fellow Americans, I'll be brief: Will someone let me out of this dang computer? Jane, stop this crazy thing!"

List Service

President Bill Clinton has been at the center of the most vitriolic relationships with the press and public of perhaps any chief executive since Abraham Lincoln. Honest Abe, as we've come to think of him, was pretty much hated and despised by most Americans during his administration. Perhaps if he'd been able to post his daily schedule on the Internet so folks could see how hard he worked, they might have appreciated his efforts.

Then again, doing just that hasn't seemed to help Bill Clinton's approval ratings very much. Below is a list of White House press releases issued on October 17, 1994. While online, clicking on any item in the list takes you directly to the full text of the release. For more info, send e-mail to **faq@whitehouse.gov**. ■

October 17, 1994

- statement by the President on Northern Ireland
- President authorizes more Georgia recovery relief
- three museums honored for their public service
- three named to Border Environment Co-op Commission
- President to national police organizations
- remarks by Presidents Clinton and Aristide
- President Clinton signs procurement streamlining bill
- briefing on baseball negotiations
- President at arts and humanities awards ceremony
- weekly radio address by the President to the nation
- President names four to the Commission of Fine Arts
- President Clinton names two to USO governors board
- President releases $130 million for homeless aid
- President's remarks to citizens of Bridgeport, CN
- statement on President's call to Israel PM Rabin
- release of report on railroad labor dispute
- briefing on Aristide's return to Haiti

President Caught in Slow, Dangerous Web!

Hear Socks Meow—Only on the Internet!

Internet Brings Meaning to Life's Little Moments

We're not big on remembering quotes word-for-word here at the *Insider*, so you'll forgive us for paraphrasing what's-his-name, who, of course, said something like, "Art is just life with all the boring bits edited out." Yeah, that guy had a way with words, didn't he?

Working at the world's first and only cyber-space tabloid is a little like being an artist. No, hey, c'mon. Really. We're not kidding around. In a tabloid, everything has to be sensational. Every story is shocking, amazing, or unbelievable. How do we do it? Well, sometimes we exaggerate—just a little bit.

Yeah. You see, that's the art of the tabloid: making the mundane magnificent, the sincere scandalous, and the ordinary outrageous. (Hey, we gotta eat too, you know! Besides, it's a living.)

But sometimes, not very often, mind you, but sometimes, the commonplace is more interesting and insightful than the impossible. No, we haven't lost our minds. We're simply complying with federal regulations and court orders mandating that all tabloids contain at least a shred of truth, a speck of humanity. Don't expect this sort of thing on a regular basis.

And don't expect to find the Big Picture revealed in the Little Details very often, either. It doesn't happen that way. The world is a cruel, demanding, frightening place, and being the highly evolved animals that we are, we've developed systems to block out all but the most urgent and demanding signals. It's the only way we can survive in the world we've created for ourselves.

The Internet, for some reason, is great for escaping that world. It's a door to another place, where every once in a while, when the moment is right and we're not caught inside our self-imposed mental prisons, we escape what we think is the reality of the physical world and experience a moment of epiphany that gently reveals to us a higher reality.

In that respect, the Internet is sometimes the opposite of what old what's-his-name described: it is, instead, the boring moments of life elevated to the place of art, with all the meaningless drama and urgency of "life" stripped away. From the Net, here are four such moments.

INSIDE

OPINION

Fine China

By Julie Parameter (jparment@indiana.edu)

My husband and I took an overnight trip last weekend to a nearby city. We needed to get away from the kids for a while and recharge. We visited some museums, ate in restaurants and did some shopping.

We were standing in the middle of a store when it hit me. It was that sinking feeling I get when I realize that something I despise in others is a trait that I own.

We were lured into this place by the sculptures in the window. My husband has a professional interest. It was the kind of posh store that contains expensive and useless articles and caters to the rich and famous. As we walked through, he called me over to look at a round glass table. "How much?" he asked. His hand was covering a sheet of paper that was taped to the top. There was a twinkle in his eyes, and since I had seen the prices of other objects, I made a guess that I thought was totally outrageous.

"$10,000," I said.

He smirked and moved his hand. $77,000.

"Let's don't even breathe in here," I exclaimed. "Let's just go!"

"Ah, come on," he laughed, "I want to see the patina on those bronzes back there."

We walked to the back. He looked at the finishes on sculptures. I saw the twinkle of silver and walked toward it. I entered a room with a large table running down the middle. It was covered by every type of silver serving piece imaginable. Bins were filled with examples of silverware. The walls were lined with china.

I looked for familiar patterns. I thought of my kitchen. I have two sets of silverware: stainless steel and silver. I have three sets of dishes: two sets are stoneware for everyday use; the other set is my good china which I use on special occasions.

Looking at the china and silver, I was struck by the opulence of this room. That was when I started to get that queasy feeling.

I began to think about a trip that we had taken several years ago to Newport, Rhode Island. We toured the seaside mansions of the Vanderbilts and other filthy-rich folks. As the guides droned on about Italian marble, inlaid gold, and lavish parties, I remember that instead of feeling properly impressed, I was nauseated. I thought of a time when, back at the turn of the century, there were no labor unions. A lot of the unfortunate people had suffered and died on railroads and in sweatshops so that these people could live in this extravagance. I thought it was criminal that there should be such a huge gap between the lives of these people and the lives of the workers who made this possible.

I looked around the room and my thoughts took a turn. I thought about the book I had been reading about people in small villages in Nicaragua. They really struggled to make it. They would plant their crops, and then the Contras would come and burn them. Sometimes the Contras would burn their tractors, or kidnap the Americans who came to help them. They never had enough food to eat or clothes to wear. Entire families slept in tiny one-room shacks.

My husband strolled in. I said, "In my book, it was a very big deal when the main character broke her plate. She only had one and they had to scour the village in order to find a replacement." My husband hummed a note or two while he carefully looked around the room. His eyes came back to me and took in my guilty expression.

A knowing grin lit his face as he said succinctly, "You have a lot of plates." Yes, I shook my head slowly. I know.

Originally published in the Nerdnosh Story Digest *mailing list. Reprinted here by permission.*

A Recipe for Perfect Lemonade

By Wes Modes (modes@mport.com)

You're sitting on the front steps of the little two-bedroom place that you and the person you've just recently married rent—your charming little cottage with the big picture window and the hardwood floors just recently refinished—and the baby must be expected but not arrived yet, so she still pays attention to you, especially today that the warm sun is coming through the lemon tree and warming the cement and there is somehow, miraculously, nothing to do. You lean to the right and there is warm sun, almost hot, and openness. You lean to the left and there is cool shade and secrets. Hot and cold. Yin and yang. And together they form perfection. What could possibly make this scene even better?

What if, in this picture, the two people previously mentioned, you and the woman of swollen belly, your lover and wife, were sitting in the falling sunshine with glasses of cold lemonade in your hands and the tinkling of ice cubes in your ears?

So you get up and wrestle the ladder that leans against the house. You climb precariously to the loveliest lemons—near the top of the tree—standing on the sticker that says, "This is not a step." You pick three lemons and realize you have no way to gather more lemons, nowhere to put them, and of course the ivy at the foot of the tree swallows anything dropped without a trace. So you tuck in your shirt doing a funny dance at the top of the ladder, your audience laughing from down below. You drop the lemons down your shirt and continue picking, looking increasingly comic as the lemons make you look pregnant too.

Climb down and disappear into the house, the cool house. Chop, chop, chop. Cut each lemon in half with the Chinese cleaver. Work each lemon over the glass juicer you found at the garage sale, until your right arm hurts, then switch to your left. Fill up a bowl, and get another. Juice every last lemon until you have a few quarts of juice. Taste it with a finger. *Oooo*, sour.

Don't forget to strain those seeds out.

You put a few cups of water on the stove to boil and sit down to wait. The cool dark of the house sucks at the warm brightness just outside the door. When the water boils, you drop in several cups of sugar, enjoying how it puts its fingers to its lips and *shhhhes* you as it pours. Dissolve the sugar and add the solution to the lemon juice.

You pinch in just a tiny bit of salt. Yes, it's true, your wife thinks that's weird, but you know it tastes a little better.

Adjust the amount of sugar in the concentrate. You want the sweet and the sour to achieve a perfect balance. More yin and yang here. Put this mix in the big juice pitcher.

Now if you weren't wanting to go back out on the steps right now, you'd put the mix in the fridge until it cooled. But we can chill that warm concentrate with ice. Fill up a couple big glasses with ice cubes and pour the warm concentrate over. Not too much now, you can always add more if it is too weak.

Add just enough ice water from the fridge. After a little bit, you'll get the hang of "just enough."

Don't forget to refill the ice trays. You-know-who hates it when you don't.

You grab a box of crackers and balance the two glasses and step blindly out into the sunshine. "Here, Honey," you say, as you hand one glass over. She reaches up, mumbles a half-hearted thanks and continues reading. What did you expect, applause? Of course, you realize your talents are seldom recognized. But is it worth making a big deal about it right now? You make your way to the porch swing on the other side of the house, not quite as idyllic being in full shade rather than dappled sunshine. But you're alone and it's okay and the journey matters more than the destination anyway.

Originally published in the Nerdnosh Story Digest *mailing list. Reprinted here by permission.*

How Long Is Eternity?

By Terry Bjork (73754.307 @compuserve.com)

How long is eternity? Hell, I don't know.

But I got an idea, last year, when I visited some of the great cathedrals in England.

Some of the old parishioners with clout, and even some Great Men, were buried under the floors of the cathedrals. Then, a headstone, or entire gravestones, were placed in the floor over the spot, with their name, birth dates and death dates, and maybe some other inscription by which they'd be remembered for eternity.

The really Great Men were lucky, and were placed together in Poet's Corner, where no one can walk. But the normal Joe (or is it Ian in England?), say a former bishop, or maybe just a wealthy parishioner, didn't have such good fortune. He was buried in the aisles, or under the pews of the cathedral, where people walk and scrape their chairs for years and years and years. Slowly but surely, the inscriptions in the headstones and gravestones disappear, worn down by the constant shuffling of feet through the years, until one can barely see the outline of the names and years that are inscribed. Then finally, after enough foot shuffling, there's nothing but unreadable impressions, and you have no idea who is under that stone.

Turns out eternity is about 400 years.

Originally published in the Nerdnosh Story Digest *mailing list. Reprinted here by permission.*

The Ties That Bind

By Wes Modes
(modes@earwig.mport.com)

A friend asked if I could come visit Iowa City. It seems that everyone else is so portable, while I have to admit I feel tied down. Is it kids, work, money, lover, or a little of all these?

There will be a time when I am portable. I will hop trains to the other side of the continent to pick up barbecue in faraway cities. I will hitchhike cross-country at the drop of a hat. I will fly to the other side of the globe after a teary phone call from a friend. I will spend months on the road, connected by modem and calling card. I will sleep under stars and stranger's living-room ceilings. I will fly my children, my lover, my friends, out to meet me for picnic lunches on green grassy hillsides or golden fields under impossible blue skies. I will speak the language of the land, slowly forgetting how to speak in my native tongue. I will make people smile and laugh all across the world, one by one, in their kitchens over coffee or tea, mocking myself and my misunderstandings of their people and their country. I will marvel at the strangeness and complete ordinariness of faraway strangers.

I'll do this. I'll stretch rather than cut the ties that bind. And I will tie new strings and stretch them and tangle them and make a web. And I will sit in the web and smile and be connected to everyone in the world.

Originally published in the Nerdnosh Story Digest mailing list. Reprinted here by permission.

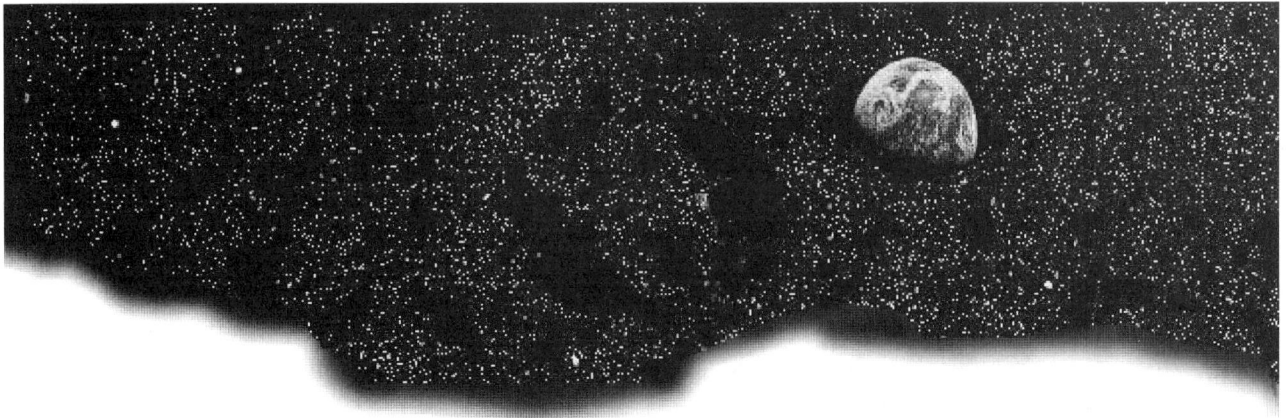

"I will marvel at the complete ordinariness of faraway strangers."

Doppelgänger Stalks Net in Search of Dupes

The custom of shaking hands upon first meeting someone is believed to have developed from a once common practice in which potential enemies held out their open hands to each other to prove that they were unarmed. The gesture developed into a sort of ceremonial mutual hand-grasping and eventually, anthropologists say, evolved into the modern handshake.

No one shakes hands on the Internet.

For hundreds of thousands of netizens, it's far easier to simply assume that the other guy is armed at all times, so it's best to treat strangers with strong suspicion (or at least guarded pessimism) and be ready with the equivalent of a six-shooter should things get dicey.

For Internet newcomers, this unbridled hostility can be puzzling. The newbies are expecting a friendly handshake, not hot lead whizzing by so close to their confused heads. But to Internet veterans, ranting, raving, and composing elaborate diatribes is a fun way to pass the time. Neighborly discourse on the Internet sometimes resembles the friendly put-down matches of a fifth-grade lunchroom, only the combatants have Ph.D.s, thick thesauruses, and hours to spend at a word processor.

When Clay Weaver posted a message suggesting that Oregon Senator Bob Packwood was most likely innocent and probably legally immune to any charges of sexual harassment, Rick Kirby went the extra mile to compose an original and amusing retort.

It would be easy enough to simply write back, calling Clay a moron or dullard and leave it at that. But in the spirit of grand intellectual debate (fueled by vitriol, bitterness, and too much spare time) that is so common on the Net, Rick adopted the old "evil twin" approach, and picked apart Clay's arguments through the strategy of assuming that the views were so ridiculous, someone else must have posted the message in an effort to discredit Clay.

Flaming, or posting long, vituperative diatribes, is a respected and honorable practice on the Net. It's a big part of what life on the Net is all about. And, until the advent of two-way video greeting routines (in which netizens can wave their unarmed hands in the air in a gesture of peace and friendship—the "tele-handshake"), I suspect flames will continue to be an Internet mainstay. And, to be completely honest with you, I'm glad!

INSIDE

OPINION

Congresswomen and aliens from Zeta Reticuli keep Americans in the dark!

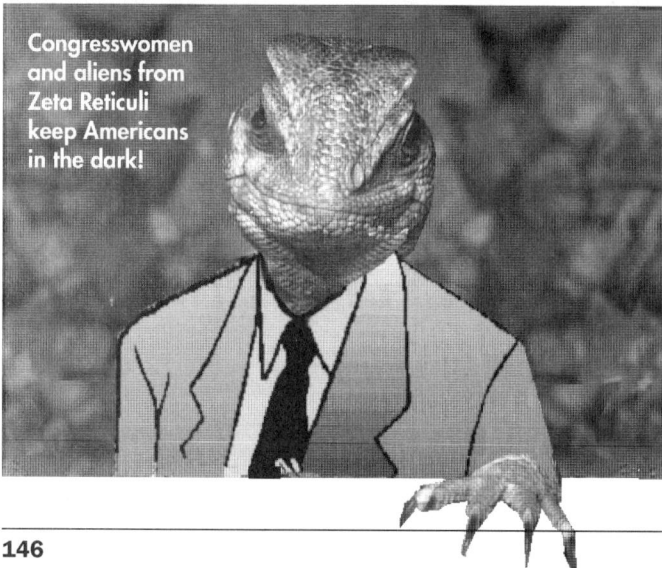

Clay, I'm starting to think that you should include digital signatures as part of all your postings. I say this because I just read an outrageous missive with your name at the top, but it was so ridiculous and insane that I'm sure you couldn't have written it. You ought to change your password. Someone appears to be signing on to your account and sending warped e-mail messages.

For instance, the impostor wrote:

"Not withstanding the alleged diary entries we haven't seen, there is no real legal evidence that [Packwood] committed any act of so-called sexual harassment."

Of course not. Just more than 20 instances of separate and individual eyewitness testimony, which is not only admissible in a court of law, but considered one of the most credible forms of evidence there is. The witnesses all describe a similar pattern and many have good reasons *not* to testify against Packwood, yet have done so after years of silence. This impostor is trying to make you look like an ignorant ass who hasn't examined the facts—someone who doesn't know what "real legal evidence" is.

The impostor went on to say that maybe the whole issue surrounding allegations of sexual harassment by Packwood is: "perhaps just a grand liberal conspiracy?"

Ah, a favorite tactic of evil twins and doppelgängers: To label things that obviously *aren't* a conspiracy as such, thus weakening truthful statements about things that may in fact have some root in conspiratorial machinations. This vile impostor is devious, and is making you look very foolish indeed.

The vile impostor continues:

"The only reason we have seen or heard any of [the allegations against Packwood] is because the Senate wants this to be public, and a show trial."

Here, the impostor is "pulling a Rush." (As in Limbaugh.) He's stating a "fact" that has no basis in reality. He forgets (or knows but fails to acknowledge) that more than 20 women have gone to newspapers and media outlets around the country, including the Washington *Post* and Packwood's home district newspapers in Oregon. He forgets to mention that a number of papers (including the *Post* and the Oregon press) had half a dozen reports from various women about Packwood's follies, but didn't print them until *after* the election because they didn't want to be viewed as a rabid, attack-dog, liberal-agenda pack.

It wasn't until they had nearly a *dozen* women all telling the same story that they broke the allegations widely. Your doppelgänger also ignores the obvious fact that no one in the senate is dumb enough to want another senator to go down in such an ugly, tacky scandal, even if it throws two votes (maybe) to the "other" side. Scandals about one senator smear all other senators, but your doppelgänger ignores this and apparently blames a liberal "dirty tricks committee" with setting up Packwood with a high-profile media campaign.

Your evil twin antagonist makes the ludicrous statement that, "legally, Packwood cannot be tried in a court of law."

Clinton and Aliens Caught in Evil Twin's Web of Intrigue

Again, your doppelgänger is spewing more ignorant pablum designed to make you look ridiculous. As Bill Clinton can tell you, anyone can bring you up on any kinds of charges, and, if they stick, you *can* be tried in a court of law. Where your impostor comes up with the idea that "legally Packwood cannot be tried in a court of law" eludes me. Maybe he's spouting nonsense he heard on Rush Limbaugh. In a *civil*

suit (which takes place, believe it or not, *in a court of law*), it doesn't matter what kind of immunity a senator or congressman claims, and if your doppelgänger wants to challenge me on that issue, I'll search out precedents proving this.

Continuing on our trial of insane verbal ejaculations, "Doppy" the doppelänger states: "We see how much all the women in the Senate and House have done for their sisters—nothing! Why? Because female legislators at the federal level need the women of America to be unequal with men in order to keep themselves in power and continue to get re-elected."

Yes, this is definitely the worst kind of nonsense that your evil impostor could hang around your neck, Clay. I know you would *never* write something so stupid. Suggesting that the women in Congress are avoiding doing anything to further the cause of women so that they can *keep women down* so that they can *stay in power* has got to be the most ridiculous thing I've ever read.

The doppelgänger's ridiculous charge is a little like saying a doctor will keep a patient sick so the patient will continue to need him. Imagine how many new patients (votes) this doctor (senator) would get! Idiocy!! Absolute stupidity.

Doppy further states: "OJ is getting all the press and the media are ignoring the Paula Jones sexual harassment suit, thus saving Clinton the public embarrassment."

Evil Twin Makes Shocking Allegations Online

Here, Clay, I have to agree with your doppelgänger. Clearly, Clinton and his Washington insiders fomented the entire OJ media saga as a plot to draw attention away from the Paula Jones issue. Here's my theory (I'm sure your doppelgänger would agree with this theory) of

how Clinton's "dirty tricks committee" set OJ up to draw the public's attention away from Paula Jones:

George Snuffleupagus and David Gergen flew out to LA, followed Nicole around for a few days until the right moment, slashed her throat open, dipped the gloves in the blood and put one at the Juice's house. (Meanwhile, a team of Navy Seals spiked OJ's air conditioner with knock-out gas, so he'd fall asleep and wouldn't hear the limo guy.)

The Arkansas State Patrol (Clinton's personal secret police) kept the curious at bay (but tactfully, so as not to make a scene and draw undue attention) while they jumped OJ in the men's room at LAX and cut his finger before he got on the plane to Chicagso. The CIA and its

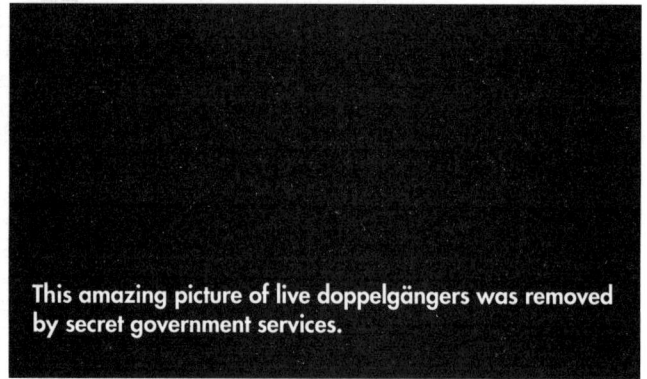

This amazing picture of live doppelgängers was removed by secret government services.

psy-ops crew dosed OJ's rum and Coke on the plane with mind-control serum, and told him to keep quiet about the whole thing. While OJ was in the bathroom on the plane, a special Tactical Magic & Hypnosis Hit-Squad (funded by the United Nations) put OJ under a deep and powerful spell and issued a post-hypnotic suggestion compelling him to try to flee town days later with Al Cowlings.

As for what I think will happen next: The aliens from Zeta Reticuli (who are clearly in cahoots with Clinton, and want to see Paula Jones discredited, but are powerless to attack women with "big hair," for reasons beyond our earthly understanding) will use their "wacko-mondo" brain-fry-ray to make OJ stand up in court and do the "funky chicken" while blowing spit bubbles and reciting the Lord's Prayer (*between* spit bubbles, of course). This will draw even more attention away from the Paula Jones case.

Once the commies get us to switch to the metric system, it's all over!!

In closing, Clay, I think your doppelgänger is probably just trying to get a rise out of us and provoke us into attacking you and exposing what we believe to be the idiotic lunacy of your ridiculous statements. But I know it's not really you writing those pathetic postings. Therefore, when, in the future, I read such idiotic drivel with your name at the top, I'll simply assume it's the doppelgänger at work again and I'll ignore it altogether. ∎

Hey, folks, I was just as surprised as you to hear this one, but it's true! Nancy Kerrigan and Tonya Harding have been approached by two different production companies to appear in a sitcom together. Currently, Paramount, which has been making overtures to Ms. Harding, is in discussion with Disney (who as we all know holds the contract on the un-corny Ms. Kerrigan), about the possibility of a co-production. The studios are being major hush-hush on this one, but your intrepid reporter has been undaunted in his pursuit of the naked truth.

Any-hoo, here's the scoop, and remember, you heard it here first! Ms. Kerrigan is slated to play (are you ready for this?) an Olympic skater who gets whacked by the competition! Who would have guessed? Her rival, played by you-know-who, in an unusual plea-bargain arrangement, agrees to become the live-in housekeeper/nurse of the injured Olympian. Is that to die for or what? Despite their differences, the two strike up an unlikely friendship and get involved in all sorts of whacky adventures. One source I spoke to described it as "'Murder, She Wrote' meets 'I Love Lucy,' or something like that."

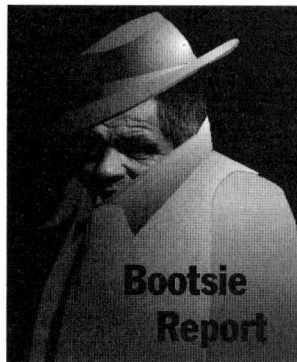

Bootsie Report

Reporting from the edge of credibility, I'm Juan Bootsie.
Contact Juan Bootsie at: an31291@anon.penet.fi or check out his archives via FTP in the /pub/hamlet directory at ftp.netcom.com.

Will Socks Get a $200 Trim by Beverly Hills Stylist Christophe?

Must Socks Reimburse Public for Trim & Clipping?

The place: The White House Briefing Room.

The time: May 20, 1993; 1:30 p.m. E.D.T.

The players: Clinton Administration spokesperson George Stephanopoulos and the members of the White House press corps.

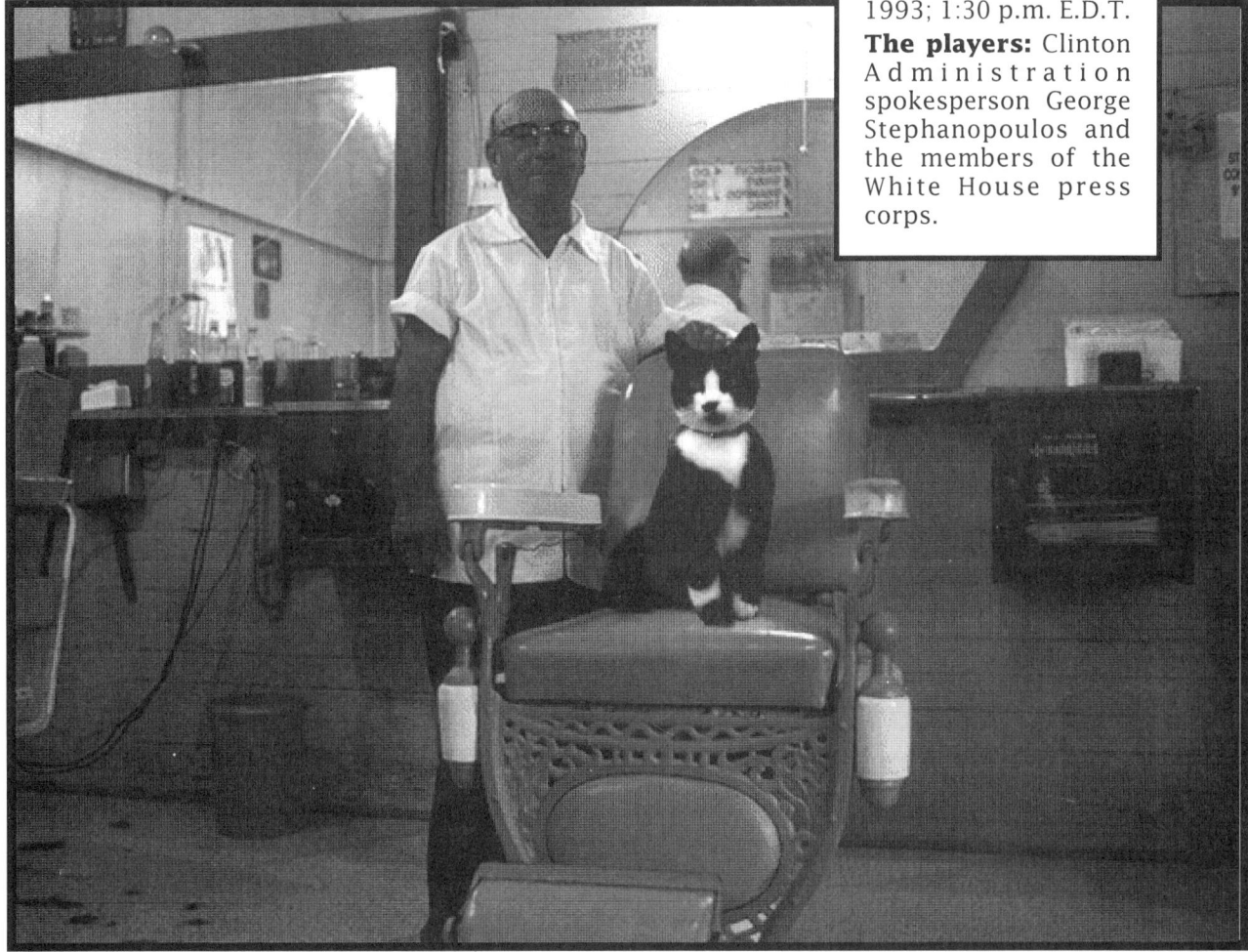

In this episode, George Stephanopoulos defends President Clinton's $200 haircut before noting that it's about time he had a trim himself. Meanwhile, the press seeks to implicate Socks as a participant in the "scissorsgate" affair. Will Socks have to testify before Congress? Will George Stephanopoulos choose a radical new do or just take a little off the top and sides? Let's listen.

Q: George, in the light of the flap over the firing of the Travel Office, has the White House considered any further action, perhaps reinstatement on leave or anything for these employees?

Mr. Stephanopoulos: A reinstatement?

Q: On leave.

Mr. Stephanopoulos: No, not at this time, no.

Q: One other question about—somewhat travel related. There are stories in the paper today that the President was delayed on the runway in Los Angeles while he had Monsieur Christophe come in . . .

Mr. Stephanopoulos: Another haircut story.

Q: to give him a haircut. Earlier he had sat on the runway at Andrews for 50 minutes while he finished his dinner with all the necessary personnel attending him. Is the White House at all concerned that this makes the President look a little foolish and self-indulgent, this kind of behavior?

Mr. Stephanopoulos: No. (*Laughter.*) It's the short answer. Just to explain further, I think it's common practice—as you know, President Bush would quite often go to the—and have the plane on the runway overnight and sleep on the plane. And often would go early and have it held. And this is—

Q: Excuse me—

Q: Vice President Bush.

Mr. Stephanopoulos: Vice President Bush?

Q: Not President—

Q: Yes, he did it once.

Q: He did it once going—

Q: He did it once, but they flew in the middle of the night.

Mr. Stephanopoulos: Okay, well, that's just one point—

Q: And he was in the hangar when—

Mr. Stephanopoulos: At Andrews. But just—on the L.A. airport, no planes were held up at all.

Q: Well, wait a minute, the FAA says that at least two were.

The Socks Chronicles

In this ongoing series of behind-the-scenes looks at the inner workings of the White House, the *Internet Insider* follows Socks, America's First Cat, through another harrowing press conference. In this official White House document obtained exclusively by the *Insider*, you'll see how the White House press corps is once again sidetracked from the real issues facing our government to consider the life and times of that lovable kitty, Socks.

Why the media obsession with the President's cat? Is there something the White House doesn't want us to know? Is "Socks" a secret code word that sends reporters into a trance of distraction and diversion? Why does the press offer only a 30-second sound bite from a 30-minute meeting? Does Socks prefer frolicking in the Lincoln Bedroom or on the South Lawn? These questions and more are answered as we present another installment of *The Socks Chronicles.*

photo courtesy of The White House

Mr. Stephanopoulos: According—the information—there was no hold placed on the air traffic at LAX. There was just no hold placed on air traffic.

Q: So you've checked—you've seen the wires with the FAA spokesman saying that two runways were held up and so that—citing the commuter planes that were 26, 18, 37 minutes late, you're saying they made that all up?

Mr. Stephanopoulos: No, I'm saying that there was no hold placed, according to our information, there was no hold placed on the aircraft at LAX.

Q: But, George, doesn't this lengthen everybody's day? I mean, you've all this staff that's got to work; you've got Secret Service agents; you've got these two Air Force guys at the bottom of the runway in formation. Everybody's got to stand there and do this, do what they do for an extra 45 or 50 minutes while this guy gets his hair done. Doesn't that smack of high-handedness at least?

Mr. Stephanopoulos: Again, I don't think so. I mean, the President has to get his hair cut. Everybody has to get their hair cut. I mean, if he would have stayed back—if he would have stayed back at the hotel, it wouldn't have made any difference at all in any of the personnel. There are delays, as you know—I mean, we're not always happy about them, but there are delays in all of the President's trips. There's often—we often get behind. But the President had to get his hair cut, as most people do. And if it wouldn't have been done there, he could have—I suppose could have had it done back at the hotel, but it wouldn't have made any difference on the personnel or anything like that.

Q: What does it do in terms of his image, however—that he gets a $200 haircut while sitting on Air Force One? Forget about whether or not it costs any extra money, is that perceptually, is that the kind of image he wants to convey to people?

Mr. Stephanopoulos: Well, again, I mean, the President has to get his hair cut like everybody else has to get their hair cut.

Q: Does he have to get his hair cut by Christophe of Beverly Hills? (*Laughter.*)

Mr. Stephanopoulos: I think he does have the right to choose who he wants to cut his hair.

Q: Yes, we all believe in the right to choose, George. (*Laughter.*)

Q: Presidents—get their haircuts on—

Mr. Stephanopoulos: I don't know whether other Presidents ever got their hair cut—

Q: I don't—

Mr. Stephanopoulos: I'm not—I can't swear that they didn't. I don't know that they have.

Q: Well, I mean, your statement he's got to get his hair cut. Bush got his hair cut, too. He got it cut here; he went up the street; he got it cut on the Hill when he was up there for something else. Reagan used to get his cut by his favorite guy in Los Angeles when he was up there for three days of vacation. I mean, you don't see any difference between sitting on Air Force One for 60 minutes—with two runways shut down for 60 minutes to get your hair cut, and a President going somewhat like a normal person goes to get their hair cut?

Mr. Stephanopoulos: I think the President normally gets his hair cut sometime during the week. It happens at different places. As you know, he has a very busy schedule. And he just tries to work it in when he can. That was when we were able to work it in.

Q: George, did the President pay the full $200 for the haircut?

Mr. Stephanopoulos: The President and his family have a personal services contract with Christophe to cover things like this.

Q: Would you tell us the amount and—

Mr. Stephanopoulos: I don't know—it covers things like makeup and hair and they just—they pay for it.

Q: Does he do the President's makeup?

Mr. Stephanopoulos: It's for the whole family.

Q: Does that cover the President's makeup when he's made up here for an event?

Q: And Socks?

Q Mr. Stephanopoulos: I don't know what— (*Laughter.*) **Socks?** (*Laughter.*)

Q: . . . in the prior administration when Nancy Reagan obtained the designer dresses on the basis

---

THE USENET ORACLE HAS PONDERED YOUR QUESTION DEEPLY. YOUR QUESTION WAS:

Does smoking cause brain damage?

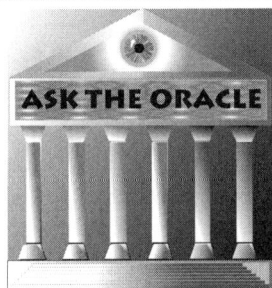

ASK THE ORACLE

AND IN RESPONSE, THUS SPAKE THE ORACLE:

The imperious, impervious, and impecunious Oracle will provide you with multiple answers to your question, at no extra charge.

1) No. Brain damage causes smoking.
2) No. Lung damage and heart damage usually get you first.
3) No iv smoked for teh last thurty yeers ad it hasnt damagd my brane yet.
4) No, at least no worse than taking hits off your car's exhaust pipe does.
5) No, as long as it's done by other people in other places.
6) No. By the time a salmon gets smoked, it's already dead.
7) No, unless your dad catches you.
8) No, unless the smoking is done by a pistol aimed at your cranium.
9) No, there's (snicker) never been scientific (teehee) proof (guffaw).
10) No, smoking doesn't brain damage people. People brain damage people, by manufacturing cigarettes.

You owe the Oracle a pair of scissors and a water pistol.

that was not available to ordinary people. And so to simply say there's a personal services contract and not give us any details about what it covers or what it costs invites speculation that he's getting a Nancy Reagan-type deal. So can you get us some details?

Mr. Stephanopoulos: The only details I can give you is that they have a contract for these kinds of services. That's all I know.

Q: Can you find out—

Q: Is there a going rate?

Mr. Stephanopoulos: I don't know what the going rate is.

Q: When was this deal inked? (*Laughter.*)

Mr. Stephanopoulos: I don't know the answer to that either. I know that they used Christophe quite often during the campaign.

Q: Is he still the President of the common man, George? (*Laughter.*)

Mr. Stephanopoulos: What?

Q: . . . still the President of—

Mr. Stephanopoulos: Absolutely. There was no hold placed on any of the air traffic.

Q: Except the two runways were closed.

Q: For 56 minutes.

Q: I don't know if you put a hold on them—

Q: Maybe the FAA does—

Q: But two runways were closed.

Mr. Stephanopoulos: I can find out about that. I just don't know anything about that.

Q: George, is there any concern that this would seem to be of a piece of the President's habit of being late for events, which is meant that people frequently have to wait for him, and the business with the dinner at Andrews and all of it, that it adds up to the picture of a man who is to some degree

---

Columbian coffee picker and spokesman Juan Valdez announced today he's quitting the coffee business. Valdez was acquitted in December of charges he masterminded a junta which attempted to overthrow the Columbian government, but says the charges against him have nothing to do with his decision to leave.

This story actually hits pretty close to home for me, because back in my days as a headliner in the Mexican film industry, my usual stunt double was a young Columbian named Juan Valdez, so me and Juan go back a long way. He was a great stuntman, but he had bigger and better dreams, most notably making enough money to buy that burro and a little plot of land on the side of his favorite Columbian mountain—growing coffee the whole world would love. Unfortunately, politics came between him and his dream, and he spent a number of years in exile while the ruling party made it tough on him to make a living just about anywhere he went.

Perhaps his most cherished moment, however, came when he finally earned a Ph.D. from—where else?—Columbia University. I wasn't sure then (nor am I now) what his degree was in, or how he completed all the requirements in only two and a half years, but I still remember that phone call I made to him upon hearing about it.

"You're *Dr.* Juan Valdez?" I said.

"Si, yo soy!" he said.

It's not known at this time what the future holds for Valdez, but you can be sure he'll meet whatever challenges lie ahead with the same spunk and vigor he's met all the others. Rumor has it Juan and burro will be heading North soon, as he's said to be all set to team up with Madonna for Girly Tour II, but whether this is so, Juan's not talking.

Juan, wherever you are, good luck and remember, if you ever need any stunt work, you know where to find me.

Reporting from the edge of credibility, I'm Juan Bootsie.
Contact Juan Bootsie at: an31291@anon.penet.fi or check out his archives via FTP in the /pub/hamlet directory at ftp.netcom.com.

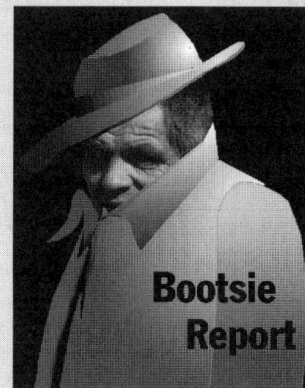

---

heedless of the consequences of his personal behavior on others?

Mr. Stephanopoulos: Again, the short answer is no. But, I mean, I think that he is obviously well aware of that. And I think that generally the President's been doing a better job of being on time. On these trips, they're packed with a lot of people. The President spent an awful lot of time out on the playground with the kids in South Central, and he ran a little bit behind. He had to get his hair cut. And this was a convenient way to do it. Obviously we're mindful of—

Q: Was this—had he otherwise planned to have a haircut and it was scheduled—what happened? How did this come about that it would end up this way?

Mr. Stephanopoulos: I honestly don't—

Q: It's no small thing with a little security and everything to get some guy like Monsieur Christophe out to the airport and onto the plane—who raised all this, do you know?

Mr. Stephanopoulos: I don't know that it would necessarily be all that difficult to arrange. But I don't know exactly how it happened at the end. I just know that the President needed to get his hair cut and this was the time he had to do it.

Q: Why does the President have an agreement with a man who is based in Hollywood? He's based in Hollywood, right?

Mr. Stephanopoulos: Actually, I think he's opening up a shop here. (*Laughter.*)

Q: Why do a West Coast deal with someone who's across the country?

Mr. Stephanopoulos: Again, I don't know all of the details of the contract he has. I just know it does cover certain events and certain services. And this is something that he chose to do, and he's certainly free to do it.

Q: Does he fly out here to do it?

Mr. Stephanopoulos: I don't know how often he even comes out.

Q: Then why do have a deal?

Mr. Stephanopoulos: Because the President chose—

Q: George, is he the only person who cuts the President's hair?

Mr. Stephanopoulos: I don't think so.

Q: If he's not then, you come back to the original question—if he's not the only person who cuts the President's hair, why did two commuter planes have—and why did the entire staff traveling with the President and the press have to be held up for 45 minutes so that this particular time he could cut the hair?

Mr. Stephanopoulos: Again, I think the President needed to get his hair cut, and he did it at that time.

Q: Can I shift subjects here?

Mr. Stephanopoulos: Boy, I don't know. Are you sure? (*Laughter.*)

Q: Back to travel. (*Laughter.*)

Q: As you know, you all are facing a—already we're facing a very tight vote in the House on the package because House members—Democrats are very nervous about voting for an energy tax that was going to disappear on the Senate side and they were going to be hanging out to dry. The question is if Senator Boren and Senator Johnston, Democrats on Finance, and you know, in the Senate are saying—

Mr. Stephanopoulos: Johnston's not on the Finance Committee. Brit, what do you got there?

Q: Santa Fe, New Mexico, AP: "The scissors, clippers, and brush are going on display at Carl Vigil's hair styling salon." (*Laughter.*) "But there's no hard evidence of Vigil's encounter with the Chief Executive. Vigil forgot to save a few strands of President Clinton's hair. 'I should have done that, but I didn't,' he said Tuesday. Vigil spent 45 minutes Monday with the President after Clinton spoke in Los Alamos. He shaved Clinton's sideburns and neck, then applied makeup to his face in a small room at the city's airport." Is that true? (*Laughter.*)

Mr. Stephanopoulos: I'd better not comment on that at this time. (*Laughter.*)

Q: And we were waiting at Los Alamos for a shave?

Q: "I worked on his jawline a little," said Vigil, 30. "I left a red spot on his face that I couldn't get out." (*Laughter.*) "The sun had gotten to him a little too much." (*Laughter.*)

Q: This is a serious question. The question is did he have a haircut Monday in New Mexico before the haircut Tuesday?

Mr. Stephanopoulos: You're right. I'd better take this a lot more seriously than I'm taking it. No, he did not get his hair cut in New Mexico. I think he's talking there about a shave, from what I can tell. (*Laughter.*)

Q: Shaved his sideburns and neck—

Q: I'd like to make to you a request that I made to Dee Dee this morning, which is that you, having said that you were taking a number of questions here, that you're going to get back to us on—

Q: By the way, do you plan another background session tonight for the nets and the wires?

Mr. Stephanopoulos: No.

Q: Why not? (*Laughter.*)

Q: He's getting a haircut.

Q: You need a haircut, George.

Mr. Stephanopoulos: I know. I've got to wait—

Tempting Treat Takes Top Taste Trophy

Dragonflesh: It's Not Just for Breakfast Any More

Desert Dragon Casserole

By Abe Stone (stone@astro.princeton.edu)

> 8 oz. wide egg noodles
> 1 cup frozen peas
> 1/4 cup slivered almonds
> 3 eggs
> 1 tsp. cinnamon
> 1/4 tsp. nutmeg
> salt, pepper, and dragonflesh (see below) to taste

1. Preheat oven to 350 degrees.
2. There will be a knock on your door.  Answer it. Outside will be a tall desert tribesman, dressed in black from head to toe, with his cloak thrown across his face so that only his dark eyes shine in your porch light. He will motion for you to follow. Change quickly into your own riding gear, and step out with him into the fragrant dusk.
3. Walk around the house, out through the back gate of the garden, and down the hillside. Descend along a rocky little path through the orchards and the vineyards, through air damp with the nightly irrigation and sweet with the odor of fallen fruit. Walk until the trees peter out and the irrigation ditches end and the wind, already chill with the swiftly falling desert night, blows free and clear and bitter dry. Draw

Ladies, are you flat out of new and interesting ideas for what to serve Bob and the kids tonight? Fellas, tired of the same old frozen dinners that plague the modern bachelor's life? Well, fret no more. The wild and wacky folks of the **talk.bizarre** newsgroup have been known to post an occasional recipe, and we're here to tell you, they make for some damn fine eating!

Abe Stone's Desert Dragon Casserole (which the boys from the mail room prepared at the *Insider's* annual Columbus Day picnic) is just a sample of the taste-tempting treats you're likely to find in the **talk.bizarre** newsgroup. Remember though, recipes are really just a list of suggestions for how to prepare a dish, so feel free to improvise and substitute your own ingredients (except for the dragonflesh). Have fun!

your cloak tighter about yourself and step across the last low wall of stones.

4. At the desert's edge, meet up with the other nomad huntsmen—your companions for the night. Test your bow carefully to make sure that it is properly strung, and make sure, too, that all straps and buckles on your horse are secure, and that your sword slides easily in and out of its scabbard. Give the ululating signal that you are ready to begin.
5. Ride fast and hard into the depths of the desert, always in the direction of the rising moon. Ride until the night and the wind and the moon-bleached hills seem to go on forever, until
*the moon burns like the eyes of the dragon
the sand rattles like the claws of the dragon
and the wind hisses like the breath of the dragon.*

(Approximately 50 min.)
Then begin to look.

6. It will not be long. The nomads are shrewd and experienced, and you, too, are no stranger to the hunt, having already prepared the Mesquite Grilled Sphinx Patties (p. 253). Soon, very soon, but when you least expect it, you will see, behind a crenellated rock castle on the horizon, or beyond a line of low dunes in the south, or deep in the coiled secret recesses of a narrow wadi, the telltale summer-golden glow of the dragon's fire, and smell the spicy aroma of its breath.

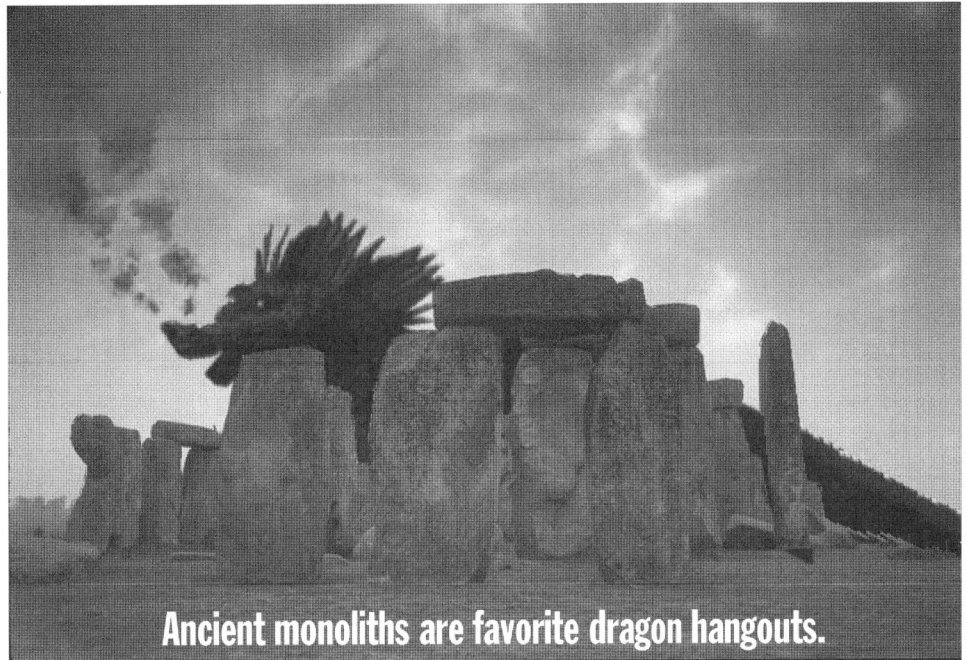

Ancient monoliths are favorite dragon hangouts.

7. Ride fast! Follow the dragon mercilessly! Do not let it out of your sight! Do not let it get behind you! Remember: a dragon on the open desert is a dangerous opponent, even for 20 mounted and heavily-armed men.

8. When, at length, you close with the dragon, attempt to use your bows first: it is far preferable to fell the beast in this way. If there is no time for this, or if the dragon survives the initial attack, draw your swords and prepare to fight at close quarters. Strike always to maim or kill: flesh wounds are worse than nothing against such a foe. Try to avoid the golden dragonfire, which burns hotter than the desert sun. (If you *do* catch fire, follow proper safety procedures—jump off your horse and roll for cover. A small kitchen fire extinguisher or a box of baking soda may also be useful at this point.)

9. When the dragon begins to weaken, it may cringe and whimper and look up pitifully out of its brown, hot eyes. It may even speak like a man, pleading for its life, asking what it has done to deserve such a fate.

10. This is a trick. Ignore it.

11. When the dragon is dead, claim your share of its soft yellow flesh (from the belly region, if possible).

12. Casserole? Ha! What casserole? Eat your dragonflesh warm and fresh and raw, as the dragon would have eaten you, in the burnt, freezing desert wind, beneath the crystal-velvet desert sky...and thank the wild spirits of the desert that they have looked favorably upon your evening's hunt.

Or: chill, slice thinly, and serve with mustard and pineapple chutney on Crisp Ryebread Squares (p. 388).

CHUCK WAGON

"Great Casserole!"

BLOATED BEAST NAMED "FED"

"What is it that Gentlemen wish? What would they have? Is life so dear, or peace so sweet, as to be purchased at the price of chains and slavery! Forbid it, Almighty God! I know not what course others may take; but as for me, give me liberty or give me death!"
—Patrick Henry

It's safe to say that Patrick Henry wanted a government strong enough to protect him and his family from those dang redcoats, but does anyone think Pat could have envisioned a time when his new government—having grown unchecked and become hideously bloated beyond recognition—would spend millions of dollars each year to sustain not one, but two international commissions on the tuna fish (the International Tropical Tuna Commission and, of course, the International Commission for the Conservation of Atlantic Tunas.)

But, as Alexis de Tocqueville said, every nation gets the government it deserves, which perhaps explains why we can't seem to unify our international tuna regulation efforts under a single agency. Writing in the Federalist Papers, James Madison warned of the dangers of unchecked bureaucracies, not only in wasting money, but also in abusing individual liberties. He proposed to keep the federal government from becoming too large and powerful by means of a "policy of supplying, by opposite and rival interests, the defect of better motives." We're not sure what Jim meant by that, but we wish it had worked, whatever it was.

Instead of Madison's dream of a lean, mean, highly efficient federal government, we're stuck with an executive branch that, 25 years after the creation of the Internet, trumpets the fact that it's just now joining the party: "We are pleased to introduce this new form of communication with the White House for the first time in history," the White House FAQ proclaims. But, it warns, "As we work to reinvent government and streamline our processes, this electronic mail project will help put us on the leading edge of progress. Please remember, though, this project is still very much under construction. The Office of Correspondence is currently working on defining what this system will do, as well as addressing equipment and staffing needs."

Thomas Jefferson, when cautioning against instilling too much power in any single branch of government, issued what should be a warning to us: "The tyranny of the [federal government led by the] executive power will come in its turn, but at a more distant period." Call us here at the *Insider* a bunch of whining, anarchistic pessimists, but we're beginning to think we're now living in Jefferson's "distant period."

INSIDE

OPINION

GROWS OUT OF CONTROL

"Our two nations and Germany have increased cooperation and engaged in joint terrorist training ..."

RUMOR CONTROL

thoughts bubbling up from our subconscious and out over our lips before our brain can react.

If this is the case, then a *faux pas* that President Bill Clinton committed during a speech before the United Nations' General Assembly might lend some insight into his secret ambitions as a leader.

According to a report by Reuters news service, during a discussion on the need for cooperation between the U.S. and Russia to limit the spread of weapons-grade nuclear materials, Clinton stated, "Our two nations and Germany have increased cooperation and **engaged in joint terrorist training**. Soon, under the leadership of our Federal Bureau of Investigation, we will open a law enforcement training academy in Europe, where police will learn how to study more effectively trafficking of nuclear weapons components, as well as the drug trade, organized crime, and money laundering."

The White House made no official retraction of the statement.

Some psychologists have claimed that we never make "accidental" slips of the tongue. Verbal gaffes, they contend, are merely our *true*

Ballooning Debt Strangles Oldest Democracy

"As a very important source of strength and security, cherish public credit. One method of preserving it is to use it as sparingly as possible, avoiding occasions of expense by cultivating peace, but remembering also, that timely disbursements to prepare for danger frequently prevent much greater disbursements to repel it; avoiding likewise, the accumulation of debt, not only by shunning occasions of expense, but by exertions in time of peace to discharge the debts which unavoidable wars have occasioned, not ungenerously throwing upon posterity the burden which we ourselves ought to bear."

The words are those of George Washington, upon the end of his second term as President. Imagine what old George would say if he were around today, and he paid a visit to the federal government's Bureau of the Public Debt, an entire government agency designed just to borrow money and service the public debt. Hey, would we make this stuff up? Read the Bureau's description below, obtained by the *Insider* from the Federal Government Manual, available online.

Bureau of the Public Debt

The mission of the Bureau of the Public Debt is to borrow the money needed to operate the Federal Government and account for the resulting public debt. The Bureau issues Treasury securities to refund maturing debt and raise new money.

To accomplish its mission, the Bureau manages six programs: commercial book-entry securities, direct access securities, savings securities, Government securities, market regulation, and public debt accounting.

The Bureau auctions and issues Treasury bills, notes, and bonds, provides services, and redeems U.S. Savings Bonds through a nationwide network of issuing and paying agents. It makes daily and other periodic reports to account for the composition and size of the debt. In addition, the Bureau implements the regulations for the Government securities market. These regulations provide for investor protection while maintaining a fair and liquid market for Government securities.

The Bureau of the Public Debt was established on June 30, 1940, pursuant to the Reorganization Act of 1939 (31 U.S.C. 306). Offices are located in Washington, DC, and Parkersburg, WV.

Voters Fed Up With Bloated Government Monster

It's no shocking revelation to most Americans that our government funds some pretty strange councils, committees, and organizations. For instance, in fiscal year 1990, according to documents obtained on the Net by the *Insider*, federal money went to such crucial U.S. Government entities as: the Arctic Research Commission, the Christopher Columbus Quincentenary Jubilee Commission, the Citizens' Stamp Advisory Committee, the Committee for the Implementation of Textile Agreements, the perhaps oxymoronically named President's Council on Integrity and Efficiency, and, of course, the mysterious Prospective Payment Assessment Commission. But check out this list of international and multilateral organizations (which, by the way, includes not one, but *two* international tuna preservation organizations) that your tax dollars help finance:

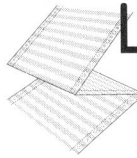

List Service

International Bureau of the Permanent Court of Arbitration
International Bureau of Weights and Measures
International Coffee Organization
International Commission for the Conservation of Atlantic Tunas
International Cotton Advisory Committee
International Council for the Exploration of the Seas
International Hydrographic Organization
International Institute for Cotton
International Jute Organization
International Lead and Zinc Study Group
International Natural Rubber Organization
International Office of Epizootics
International Office of Vine and Wine
International Organization for Legal Metrology
International Rubber Study Group
International Seed Testing Association
International Sugar Organization
International Tropical Timber Organization
International Tropical Tuna Commission
International Whaling Commission
International Wheat Council

Mysterious Agencies Live In Dark, Eat Tax Dollars

From the Federal Government Handbook, available online, here's a sampling of the very important and easy-to-understand work performed by a few of the most important federal agencies that we all help fund.

Assistant Secretary of Domestic Finance (Treasury Department)

The Assistant Secretary of Domestic Finance advises and assists the Secretary, Deputy Secretary, and Under Secretary for Finance on matters of Federal, State, and local finance, financial institutions policy, and synthetic fuels projects.

In the area of Federal finance, the Office is responsible for Government financing and debt management; determining interest rates for various Federal borrowing, lending, and investment purposes under pertinent statutes; and developing legislative and administrative principles and standards for Federal credit programs, loan asset sales, and the Federal Financing Bank.

Within the Office of Economic Policy, staff support is provided by the Office of Financial Analysis, the Office of Special Studies, the Office of Monetary Policy Analysis, and the Applied Econometric Staff.

The Defense Security Assistance Agency

The Agency was established on September 1, 1971, by DOD Directive 5105.38, dated August 11, 1971.

The Agency directs, administers, and supervises the execution of approved security assistance plans and programs, such as military assistance, international military education and training, and foreign military sales. In so doing, it works closely with the U.S. Security Assistance offices worldwide.

Information Resources Management Service

The Information Resources Management Service is responsible for the coordination and direction of a comprehensive, governmentwide program for the management, procurement, and utilization of automated data processing and local telecommunications equipment and services; planning and directing programs for improving Federal records and information management practices; and managing and operating the Federal Information Center.

Governmentwide Information Resources Management

The General Services Administration provides governmentwide programs to assist Federal agencies in the management of their information resources. The Office of Technical Assistance provides technical and contracting assistance in software, hardware, data communications, planning, and office automation.

The Service also administers the Federal Information Systems Program, which is a nationwide program of requirements contracts under which Federal agencies are provided automated data processing services through regional contracts with private-sector vendors. The program allows the Service to consolidate relatively small, quick-reaction, technical services project requirements for other agencies in order to reduce costs.

Federal Agencies Mutating At Alarming Rate

Defense Commissary Agency

The Defense Commissary Agency was established by direction of the Secretary of Defense on November 9, 1990, and operates under DOD Directive 5105.55.

The Agency is responsible for providing an efficient and effective worldwide system of commissaries for reselling groceries and household supplies at low, practical prices (consistent with quality) to members of the Military Services, their families, and other authorized patrons, while maintaining high standards of quality, facilities, products, and service. In addition, DCA provides a peacetime training environment for troop support logisticians needed in wartime and, as circumstances dictate, troop issue subsistence support to military dining facilities consistent with Service needs.

The Defense Contract Audit Agency

The Defense Contract Audit Agency was established in 1965 and operates under Department of Defense Directive 5105.36.

The Agency performs all necessary contract audit functions for the Department of Defense and provides accounting and financial advisory services to all Defense components responsible for procurement and contract administration. These services are provided in connection with the negotiation, administration, and settlement of contracts and subcontracts. They include evaluating the acceptability of costs claimed or proposed by contractors and reviewing the efficiency and economy of contractor operations. The Agency manages its operations through 5 regional offices responsible for approximately 153 field audit offices throughout the United States and overseas.

Bizarre Federal Agencies Survive on Tax Dollars, Anonymity

Net Resources

In a shockingly uncharacteristic display of electronic know-how and public-minded civil service, a number of government entities are making their resources available online.

Just a few of the government departments and agencies you can reach online include

Army Research Laboratory
U.S. Navy, U.S. Air Force
Environmental Protection Agency
Department of Commerce
Environmental Research Laboratories
USDA National Agricultural Library
National Institutes of Health
National Institute of Standards and Technology
National Geophysical Data Center
National Library of Medicine
The National Oceanic and Atmospheric Administration
U.S. Census Bureau
U.S. Department of Education
U.S. Fish and Wildlife Service
United States Geological Survey
U.S. Patent and Trademark Office, Library of Congress

For information on receiving White House documents via e-mail, send the message "Send Info" (and nothing else) to: **publications@whitehouse.gov**. To receive the White House FAQ file, send any message to **faq@whitehouse.gov**.

To reach the House of Representatives online, write to **congress@hr.house.gov**, or point your Gopher client toward: gopher:**//gopher.house. gov:70/1**. The members of the Senate, alas, are bound by tradition, PAC money, and the inertia of their bloated, elite, fat butts, and have yet to establish a presence on the Net.

Via the World-Wide Web, you can access a number of government documents and search them for key words or phrases. A few of the resources available via the Web include

Public Law Index:
http://gopher.nara.gov:70/7g/register/laws

National Archives: http://www.nara.gov/

Federal Government Manual:
gopher://una.hh.lib.umich.edu/11/socsci
/poliscilaw/govman

U.S. Gazetteer: http://wings.buffalo.edu/geogw

Texts of Newly Passed Bills:
http://galaxy.einet.net/e-periodicals/ushouse
.html

White House documents:
http://english-server.hss.cmu.edu/whitehouse
.html

A good starting point for any Gopher search of federal information is always the list of federal Gopher servers at: gopher.nara.gov:70/1/servers.

Via anonymous FTP, you can find a wide array of Presidential papers and other government documents at: ftp.spies.com.

You can read or download Patrick Henry's "The War Inevitable" speech as well as writings by Jefferson, de Tocqueville, and others from the BeastNet online archives: e-mail: beastnet@farces.com; anonymous FTP: ftp.farces.com.

There are literally scores of other sites around the Net bursting with government information ranging from the inspiring to the utterly useless. Now, if only the CIA would put all of its UFO and Kennedy assassination documents online . . .

Former head of MGM Louis B. Mayer rose from the dead this week and demanded his old job back. Mayer, gaunt, hollow-eyed and wearing a dusty suit way, way out of style explained, "Hey, with all the moolah that's being tossed around these days, I couldn't stand not getting my cut of the pie." Doctors and theologians are monitoring developments.

Reporting from the edge of credibility, I'm Juan Bootsie.
Contact Juan Bootsie at: an31291@anon.penet.fi or check out his archives via FTP in the /pub/hamlet directory at ftp.netcom.com.

Bootsie Report

IRS Raises Taxes By 9,939,784,913%!

By "Destitute Dave" (lampson@pulse.com)

Forwarded to a classical music mailing list:
I put on Gorecki's third last night, and it was perfect. That is, it fit the circumstances perfectly. My mood was for something both reflective of a near suicidal mood and yet not requiring any intellectual involvement.

You see, waiting in my mailbox, like a little present from a faceless bureaucrat, was a dreaded notice from the much-maligned Internal Revenue Service. Having had far, far too many dealings with the beloved Service, and thus being somewhat familiar with the experience of receiving such correspondence, I was, perhaps, not filled with quite as much fear and loathing as less-graced men.

That was my first mistake. When I opened the letter, and looked at the bottom line, that was my second. I was first shocked, then amused, and finally annoyed and depressed. You see, the IRS apparently believes that I should do slightly more than my fair share in reducing the national debt. Accordingly, the notice indicates that I currently owe slightly in excess of 68 billion dollars

($68,037,394,206.32 to be exact). I kid you not.

I am now indeed singing a symphony of sorrowful songs. Hey, buddy, can ya spare a dime?

THE USENET ORACLE HAS PONDERED YOUR QUESTION DEEPLY. YOUR QUESTION WAS:

How can i learn to play the fluet?

AND IN RESPONSE, THUS SPAKE THE ORACLE:

The fluet is an instrument with a great tradition; it was played by the anceint Egyptains, The Romasn and the Greeks. In its most primitve form, it consists of a simlpe tbue of wood with several hoels cut along its lenght. By blwoing in the topmots hoel, you can produce a most Sepulchrla Toen, one which so characterizes teh wonderful fluet.

Finally, it is by rapid figner motiosn across the otehr hoels that you are able to produec a Wied Vareity of Toens, each Sepulchrla in nature, but which as a whoel, also form a great Harmoyn. It is for thsi Harmoyn that you strive.

Godo lukc ot yuo.

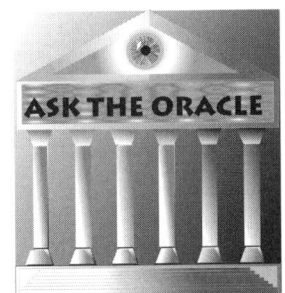

LIFE @ LARGE

Hey, we're starting to wonder what the hell's going on up there at that dang White House! We sent two e-mail messages to: **president@whitehouse.gov**, and got the same response each time, an excerpt of which appears below.

Our first message read:

Hey Bill!

Good to see you're online finally. (Al lined that up, no doubt.) Anyway, I'm going to be in the neighborhood working on a few big projects next week, and I thought I'd stop by and see you and Hillary. Is the Lincoln Bedroom free? (I love the acoustics in that shower!)

Your pal,
B. Streisand

Our second message read:

Dear Mr. President:

I think something's wrong with your e-mail, because I've sent you 17 messages over the past couple of weeks, and you haven't responded to a dang one of them! I know you're busy and all, but would it kill you to type out just one personal response? All I get is a dang form letter. Keep giving me the cold shoulder and I'm liable to vote for Bobby Dole!

An American Voter,
K. Johnson

Each letter solicited the following response:

From: president@whitehouse.gov (autoresponder@whitehouse.gov)

Thank you for writing to President Clinton via electronic mail. Since June 1993, whitehouse.gov has received over 250,000 messages from people all over the world.

Although the volume of mail prevents the President from personally reviewing each message, the mail is read by White House staff. Your concerns, ideas, and suggestions are carefully recorded and communicated to the President weekly with a representative sampling of the mail. We are currently working toward responding to your messages electronically. whitehouse.gov was established to allow you to send electronic correspondence to the President and Vice President. The only personal addresses at whitehouse.gov are the following:

President@whitehouse.gov and vice.president@whitehouse.gov

All of us at the White House are excited about the progress that has been made with this historic project, and we look forward to future developments. Your continued interest and participation are very important to us.

Sincerely,
Stephen K. Horn
Director, Presidential E-Mail

Don't think for a minute, though, that Stephen K. Horn and the gang at **whitehouse.gov** aren't reading your mail. When one youth sent threatening e-mail to Clinton during the summer of '94, the Secret Service soon showed up at his doorstep. So if you think e-mail is the perfect way to launch your career as the next John Wilkes Hinkley, think again!

We've been hearing for some time now that the federal government is bankrupt, but we had no idea the situation was as serious as some rumors seem to suggest. The *Insider* intercepted an interesting news bulletin online recently, and though we have been unable to confirm its veracity, we're passing it along for your information—just in case.

WASHINGTON—The federal government was sold today to CompuGov, a high-tech consortium that includes IBM, Microsoft, AT&T, Northern Telecom, Sony, and several other corporate giants in Europe and Japan. "It's the ultimate vindication of the Free Market philosophy," said a high-ranking Administration official. "This deal is the logical extension of lessons from the computer and telecommunications industries. What's government but the processing and transmission of information?"

Effective immediately, the popular vote was ended at the federal level. Instead, Americans will be able to buy Stakeholder Shares. Those with sufficient numbers of Shares may attend CompuGov board meetings in Tokyo. Members of Congress each received 10,000 Stakeholder Shares and golden parachute protection—in addition to extra shares reflecting the sizes of past campaign donations from political action committees run by CompuGov members.

CompuGov announced the spin-off of most nondefense assets and the dismissal of 75 percent of the federal work force. Tennessee entrepreneur Chris Whittle will buy the Department of Education, for example, while Humana-Medfirst will purchase the Department of Health and Human Services.

"We regret the need for downsizing," a CompuGov spokesperson said, "but education and health have been lacking as profit centers. They just are not part of our corporate mission. Our role is simply to protect our customers against force and fraud."

Asked about the pending spin-off of the Securities and Exchange Commission to New York businessman John Gotti, the spokesperson said: "We must always be open to the wisdom of the Free Market. If Mr. Gotti can make the SEC more responsive to the needs of business, I see no reason why we could not also sell him the Justice Department."

Final negotiations are continuing between CompuGov and the individual states, with deals expected shortly. Only Massachusetts is balking. "The consensus is that the Free Enterprise system is best," said the CompuGov spokesperson. "America's big mistake was in simply trying to get government out of the economy. The best solution is to get government out of government." ■

RUMOR CONTROL

FOR SALE
1/2 OFF
1-800-600-3333
★ Realty

Banana Republican Launches Rotten Fruit Campaign

by Phillip N. Price (price@carla.lbl.gov)

A U.S. government banana peel retrieval specialist in action.

Few people realize that the banana was the product of early radiation experiments in the South Pacific in the late 1940s. These experiments were conducted on the Bikini Atoll, later the site for a hydrogen bomb explosion, and were conducted under the auspices of the Bikini Atoll Native Plantain Mutation Assignment (BANPAMA) in an effort to produce for the Army an edible fruit that would not decay or degrade with age.

I've always been a sucker for a good practical joke. I love to pull them on unsuspecting marks; I love to watch other people set them up and execute them—hell, I even enjoy being the object of a good one, as long as it's really good.

I suppose I get this love of pranks from my dad, who is more than just a liar, teller of tales, or exaggerator: he's a bullshitter, and there's no other word for it. On one notably boring Fourth of July weekend, when I was maybe seven or eight years old, some friends and I had a few firecrackers, sparklers, and cherry bombs we wanted to set off in the back yard. We were stupid and naive enough to ask my mom for permission (I was only seven, okay?), and she responded with the dreaded "Ask your father."

Dad told us fireworks were illegal in North Carolina (which they were—and still are—oh, how we envied South Carolina kids!), but said if we thought we could get away with setting them off, it was our decision and he wouldn't interfere. Little did we know that he went inside and immediately called Kenneth Moore, his old buddy and Chief of the Hazelwood Police Department.

In blissful ignorance, we set about our thrilling work of blowing up aluminum cans, flowers, piles of dirt, and even (what luck!) a month-old dead blackbird we found at the edge of a cornfield. Just as things were winding up to a fever pitch (imagine four or five sugar-buzzed brats running around the yard having a sparkler fight), we heard police sirens.

We all froze in our tracks, our gleeful little grins turned upside-down into frowns of panic and anxiety. The sirens sounded again, and we were sure we saw lights in the back driveway. Most of my so-called friends ran for cover. I stood stone still in stark terror. Kenneth Moore came walking up, in all his blue-uniformed, black-patent-leather, buckle-up, button-down glory. "Which one of you'unz has been a shootin' off them farcrackers?!" he asked sternly. "All of us, but mainly me," I stammered.

Needless to say, I learned a few valuable lessons from my dad's little prank: never ask permission when you're going to get busted anyway, expect your friends to bail at the first opportunity, telling the truth to cops isn't particularly helpful, and never, ever trust my dad when he seems to be acting in a way that could be perceived to be "too good to be true."

You'd be similarly well-advised to read with a skeptical eye any outrageous postings on the Net with Phillip Price's name attached. When he posted his "Banana History" article to rec.bicycling.misc (don't ask me why he posted it there), plenty of suckers took the bait. Considering the skill and finesse with which Phillip crafted his just-barely-believable story, it's understandable that a few folks bought it.

Just for kicks, try photocopying Phillip's masterpiece from this book and passing it out to your friends (without this introduction, of course). Better yet, maybe I'll send a copy to my dad and see if he bites. I doubt it.

INSIDE

OPINION

Bizarre Radiation Creates Freaky Fruit

The Plantain was selected since it has a tough outer cover that provides protection for the fruit; unfortunately, it is not very palatable when raw. The BAN-PAMA project was not particularly successful, as the resulting fruits were found to bruise easily. However, they were still fed to unsuspecting natives and servicemen, with whom they became quite a hit. Introduced to the U.S. as "banamas" in 1951 (they were developed and marketed by former military scientists who saw there was more money in agriculture than in early attempts at genetic engineering), they immediately became something of a rage. By 1958, "bananas," as they were known by then, were grown throughout Central and South America to feed the hungry U.S. market.

This would be a happy story of a great new food, if it weren't for the sinister secret that was brought to light in 1978 in early studies of "garbology" (the study of garbage) by scientists from the University of Arizona: the military's original project was not a complete failure after all—although the fruit of the banana was quite vulnerable, the peel contained enzymes that rendered it impervious

These apples were an early result of bizarre government fruit-radiation experiment.

to virtually all biological action. In short, every banana peel ever grown until that time was still in existence.

This discovery by Arizona scientists led to a series of startling and bizarre revelations, including the fact that since the late 1950s, the U.S. military, in a surprisingly successful attempt to cover up their introduction of this non-degradable peel, had a veritable army of specially trained Banana Peel Retrieval Specialists arrayed across the country. Using infrared satellite images to locate suburban compost piles, these commandos would

strike in the dark of night, removing banana peels and replacing them with degradable facsimiles made from wheat, soy, marigold petals and corn silks. Army experiments to train raccoons and possums to do the retrieval were fairly successful, and these methods replaced the manual retrieval method over much of the country by the early 1970s.

Government Experiment Produces Slippery Problem

The 1978 revelation, and the accompanying outcry, led to a crash program by the Department of Agriculture to develop a "green" banana. By 1981, the program was deemed a success, having produced a ba-

nana that degraded slowly but completely, and then-President Ronald Reagan was able to unveil the new banana to coincide with a meeting of heads of state from several Central American countries. Reagan's comment that "I love these things, and I consider myself a Banana Republican," was considered in poor taste and hushed up by the then-malleable press.

For the past 13 years, banana peels have been biodegradable. Banana peels from before 1981 are not degradable, and most of them are still in existence, buried in huge dumps at Hanford, WA, and Oak Ridge, TN. Pilot incineration programs have been launched, and if all goes well, the non-degradable banana peels will have been disposed of by the year 2005. ■

Millions Suffer From Angstrom Syndrome

The folks in the **alt.angst** newsgroup take their angst seriously. Don't bother looking up "angst" in the dictionary, because defining angst is a little like defining pornography. As one member of the Supreme Court once said of pornography, "I can't tell you what it is, but I know it when I see it."

We couldn't agree more. Breaking a nail on your way out the door to a hot date isn't an angst-inducing situation. Facing the Halifax gibbet is.

For those of you who slept through history class (slackers!), we'll remind you that the Halifax gibbet, a precursor to the guillotine, was first used in 1286. Just as with the guillotine, facing the Halifax gibbet was pretty much a no-win situation—but there was a catch—and quite a catch at that.

The catch? The law in Halifax stated that any condemned prisoner who could yank his head from the block after the rope was released (but, obviously, before the blade hit its mark) and then run unchecked to the neighboring hamlet of Hebblebrook, could go free, no questions asked. The only person to ever beat the Halifax gibbet was "Lucky" John Lacy, who was so pleased at reaching Hebblebrook, he decided to stay there.

For seven years, Lucky Lacy bragged to the Hebblebrookians about being quicker than the gibbet, but folks got so sick of his constant boasting, they finally called his bluff and branded him a liar and a bore. Lucky Lacy was determined to prove to them the truth, so he decided the best way to do this, was, of course, to face the gibbet again. (We said he was lucky, not smart!)

His doubters followed him back to Halifax, where he stuck his neck back in the gibbet, grinning as the rope was released. As you've probably guessed by now, Lucky Lacy's luck had run out, and he never had time to feel the true angst of his predicament.

But you've got all the time in the world, so join the gang in **alt.angst** where, as the FAQ file says, "life is essentially pointless and absurd, and...our miserable existences count for very little in the grand scheme of things.... You can use the rule of thumb that states: if it feels bad, post it. Chicken Little is an excellent example of someone who should have posted to this group. Here, the sky is always falling.

Or, as one alt.angster put it, "*Let the voice mail get the phone and always watch your back.*"

INSIDE

OPINION

Net Resources

The **alt.angst** newsgroup is just the tip of the angstberg. (Sorry.) If you're serious about the unbearable horror that is your life, you owe it to yourself to check out the **alt.angst home page**, maintained by Ken Krawling. The home page features the various official documents of the group as well as bonus features like the **Alt.Angst Shopping List** and **Angst of the Ages**, plus bios of the alt.angst regulars. You can access the home page at:

http.://www.cs.indiana.edu/hyplan/krawling/angst.html

Keep an eye also on the angst-filled e-zines circulating the Net. (For more info, e-mail: chriscon@njcc.wisdom.bubble.org.)

Finally, you might also want to check out a few other newsgroups that offer a sort of kindred spirithood to **alt.angst**. For a variation on the theme, try **alt.atheism** or **alt.bitterness**.

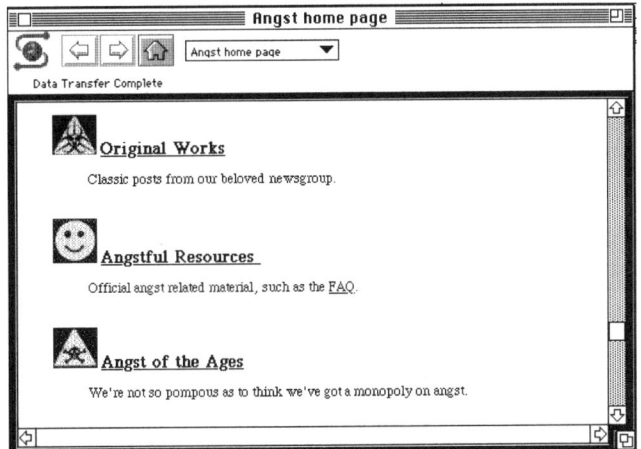

Angst home page

Data Transfer Complete

Original Works
Classic posts from our beloved newsgroup.

:) **Angstful Resources**
Official angst related material, such as the FAQ.

Angst of the Ages
We're not so pompous as to think we've got a monopoly on angst.

Nobody Loves Me.... Including Me

Angst has a nasty habit of sticking around for the long term. Curing it ain't easy, but it's not impossible either. The alt.angst FAQ file offers a few quick and simple cures (or at least palliatives) for common angst. (We're unsure if any or all of these remedies are effective against some of the more complex forms of angst.)

Cures for Common Angst: Home Remedies and Elixirs
(list by Michael Chase)

1. God(s).
2. Drugs.
3. Significant other.
4. Booze.
5. Insignificant others.
6. Physical fitness.
7. That spiritual purity trip.
8. Some god-awful 12-step program full of losers not nearly as intelligent as you.
9. Shrinks, who are either OK but ineffective, or completely screwed up themselves. (What is it with them anyway?)
10. Attitude
    a. Hostile
    b. All-knowing
    c. Able to help others but not yourself
    d. Humorous
    e. Cynical
    f. Spacer
11. Turning the pressure into something 'useful.'
12. Acceptance.
13. Writing stuff nobody will read.
14. Exploring your past until you forget what you remember.
15. Waiting patiently to grow out of it.
16. Waiting patiently to see where it will all lead.
17. Waiting for that dude with the AK-47.
18. Getting pissed off that you can't kill yourself without bumming your friends.
19. Isolation.
20. Reading everything anybody has to say on the subject.
21. Developing a mild but sincere pride in yourself for surviving, which actually helps a little, but still depends on the problem for its own existence.

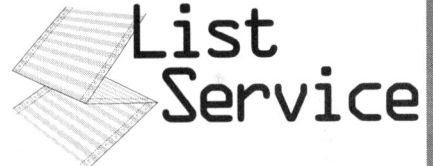

List Service

From the alt.angst FAQ file, here's a list of the most frequently discussed lines of angst-inducing thought. Or maybe it's the most frequent lines of thought produced by angst. Oh, hell...here's the damn list:

1. Life is pointless/meaningless. There is no reason.
2. Death is eternal (making life all the more pointless).
3. Reincarnation. (No relief, just more of the same unbearable pain for eternity.)
4. Unpleasant feelings are true, and pleasant feelings are temporary and empty.
5. Lost opportunities. Lost excitement. I was once young and screwed it up.
6. I'm wasting my time.
7. Things will never get better (in the sense that it's all going downhill).
8. The future is just more of the same (worthless crap).
9. Rejection (MOTAS, work, whatever).
10. Boredom.
11. Loneliness, being insignificant.
12. Nothing brings me joy (hobbies, school, work, "friends", family, etc.).
13. There is no escape, no hope.
14. This mess is my (0-100)% own fault.
15. Strong hate (self, others, places, phenomena).
16. Insanity (depression, panic attacks, schizophrenia, suicidal tendencies).
17. For all my efforts, I was never rewarded.
18. Art or humans cannot help you.
19. Nothing has any absolute value.
20. Wishes coming true will not help.
21. Lack of "the basics" (good physical/ mental health, money, love, etc.).
22. I'm in an unpleasant situation.

Boredom

Nothing has any absolute value

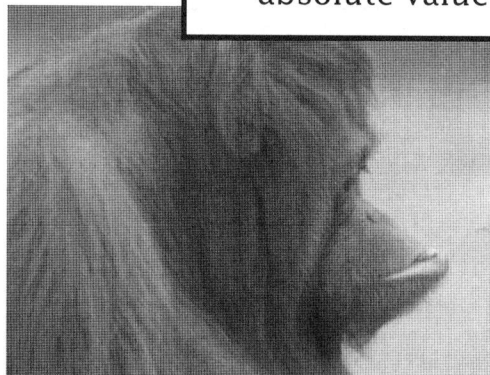

Three Faces of Angst

Strong hate

Don't Let Your Undies Drive You Insane

By Darren S. Shrubsole (dss6@le.ac.uk)

My mother used to work in Woolworth's selling clothes for children. This was when I was about seven years old. The seventies were in full swing. She used to buy me really miserable clothes like cream jackets with suede lapels, and tartan trousers (Bay City Rollers, anyone?) that used to itch and itch! Her favourite purchase was these weird psychadelic Y-Fronts (I think they are called BVD's in America) that all looked the same colour.

We did sports every day at school. We showered every day at school.

Everyday, every male child in my year at school saw that I wore a pair of underpants that looked very like the pair I wore the day before. They all called me "Smelly Darren the Underpant Man."

It wasn't fair. My underpants were clean. I changed them every day.

My mother refused to buy different colours saying I had plenty of clean pants. Eventually, she moved to another job. I got independant and started to buy my own underpants. My underpant angst was over.

A few months ago a young man walked into that same branch of Woolworth's, and for apparently no reason stabbed his girlfriend to death. BUT we all know why, don't we? Underpants!

I just wanted you all to know that, okay?

"Don't wear 'em"

a brief meditation on punctuation

By anon2c9e@nyx10.cs.du.edu (henri ennui)

the comma, that little flyspeck of a punctuation! how superfluous and how annoying. it ought to be stricken from written language! the period is also unsatisfying and static. capitalization is also an irritating imposition, making it seem as it does that an object with a proper name is somehow more important than a nameless object.

this is perhaps why nukes so often were named. it seems fitting that a device which lowercases entire populations to nameless corpses should itself have a proper name. a proper name! how, well, proper.

exclamation points also falsely give the impression that any sentence is any more important than any other. what bosh!

as for dashes, semicolons, and other such fakery—well, the less said about them, the better!

From the **alt.angst** FAQ file, here are a few handy buzzwords that will help you feel at home (but still lousy) in alt.angst.

Weltschmerz—Mental depression or apathy caused by a comparison of the actual state of the world to an ideal state.
Schadenfreude—Taking joy in another's misfortune.
Angstogen—An angst-producing agent.
Angstrom—The unit of angst: more angstroms = more angst.

Angst Angst

By WBRIDDIC@kentvm.kent.edu

Sometimes just experiencing angst can bring on even more angst. Like now I am angst-ridden over posting to this group. I mean, what if my post isn't worthy of this group? No doubt about it...Angst breeds Angst. Egads, that's sick!

Show Your ANGST with Official Accessories

By Brad Baillod (baillod@quip.eecs.umich.edu)

Diana Blazis wrote: "alt.angst gets an honorable (?) mention in this month's *Playboy*."

Just a couple of years ago, the Internet itself was only referred to in a couple of places in a couple of magazines. Now, the country's going ga-ga over it. The same thing will happen to alt.angst! Picture it in two years: "News, games, FIDOnet, and access to ALT.ANGST!" AOL.COM will place full-page ads in *Newsweek*: "Been beaten down? Come to a place. A place to share. To share your pain." (With a picture of a sunny garden shot in blurry focus.) QVC will start the

angst subchannel (for those who have to use their TVs to get on the Infobahn because their verbal and writing skills don't allow them to textually access the net without appearing to be idiots). They'll sell...they'll sell...any ideas? ("I was at AngstCon '93" t-shirts? Alt.angst action figures?)

And, best of all, I, Brad, will control it all! Yesterday, my copyright lawyer informed me that I now have EXCLUSIVE rights to market alt.angst memorabilia and merchandise in the U.S. and its territories! I will build an angst empire! I will control the angst of the entire WORLD (give or take a

few insignificant non-U.S. countries)! BOW to my rule! ACCEPT my power! CONSIDER the possibilites! (Wait, need to begin these sentences with action verbs.) CRINGE at my...carpet! TREMBLE at my...newspaper! I better quit while I'm ahead.

Mitch Goldstrom (mgoldstr@ pmsa70.pms.ford.com) suggests the following merchandizing idea:

The Angst Coffee Mug: Wide on top, tapering down to a point, not unlike an ice cream cone, so it will not stand on its own. Oh yeah, a small hole in the bottom too. Capable of holding 24 oz. of coffee.

Take Two Ironies and Call Me in the Morning

By Dr. Irony (machala@spdc.ti.com)

I woke up at five this morning. Couldn't get back to sleep, so I just laid in bed while my brain assaulted me with thought after thought. One particularly disturbed me. It was the ludicrousness of my existence. My awareness. How can it be that I am here, now, lying in my bed, not being able to get back to sleep. The whole thread about evolution and life being against entropy was there too, and I saw the earth as a whole mass teeming with life. Not the same life, but life ever-changing. Billions of matches lighting up and briefly burning, but then, never failing, being extinguished. How ridiculous. Who would've ever thought that mass and energy could do this type of thing. To become aware, whatever that is.

The Raw Deal!

By Louise C. Deal (louisedeal@gsvms2.cc.gasou.edu)

Just when you think you can deal with the angst, somebody reminds you that things can and will get worse.

Here I am thinking that I am tired of the world and life has no point. I dream of the deserted island without a soul on it but me. I think maybe I would find peace there. Living like a hermit.

So, what does the guy I pay to listen to my problems tell me? He says, I wouldn't even make a good hermit.

So where does this leave me? I can't live with people and I can't be a hermit, so what now?

Anybody got any ideas?

Music to Worry By

By Bryan Sachse (krull@pipeline.com)

I started a thread several weeks ago which had a reasonable life and has now dissipated. Since I promised to post my own thoughts on the subject once the votes were in, I will do so now. There seem to be three major candidates by consensus for the distinction of "most angstlich composer." They are Shostakovich, Mahler, and Schubert.

The envelope please.

IMHO, Shostakovich is a better candidate for the composer laureate of alt.bitterness or alt.sardonic. Angst, it seems to me, is neither of those, but is rather a reflection of the fact that every silver lining has a cloud (and vice versa), and that the wages of both sin and virtue is death. My vote for the most angstlich composer goes to Mahler. Married to a paragon of musehood (Alma, who subsequently married and outlived Walter Gropius and Franz Werfel), and with his children playing at his feet, he wrote "Kindertotenlieder" (tempting fate—which won, as always). Fearing to write a ninth symphony, he called it instead "Das Lied von der Erde." Fittingly (ironically), he did die soon after completing his named ninth.

My selection for the theme music for alt.depression.want.to.stay.there is Schoenberg's "Pierrot Lunaire." My vote for most angstlich piece goes to another composer of findesiècle Vienna: Richard Strauss, for "Der Rosenkavalier." Think about it.

Secret Sock Dimension Revealed!

By Manu

Have you ever noticed how you take five pairs of socks (along with mounds of other dirty clothes), put them in the washing machine, take them out, and start folding them, only to find that you have exactly nine socks—which amounts to a total of four-and-a-half pairs of socks? You put all your other clothes in the spots they're supposed to be and you're left with one sock, lying lonely and dejected on your bed. What exactly are you supposed to do with it?

You don't want to throw it out—because you might end up finding its match—and yet you don't really want to keep it, because what the heck are you going to do with one sock? But eventually, you decide to keep it, and proceed to shove it in your drawer where you see it day in and day out—or whenever you happen to open your sock drawer. You go rummaging through your drawer every day, trying to find a pair, and all that one sock does is get in your way. So you shove it aside as if it's a worthless piece of nothing, hoping that by some bizarre twist of fate it'll disappear. But...it doesn't. And week after week, you do your laundry while that one sock sits alone in a dark, dank drawer.

How does it feel, you wonder? How does it feel to be that one odd sock, the odd one out, the one that has no pair or match, just itself. I mean, a sock is just not a sock without its partner.

Everybody is happy in Sockland, except for Mr. Lonely Sock, whose wife, Mrs. Lonely Sock, was lost in the hazardous journey between the washer and the dryer. Where could she be, he wonders as he glares with longing at all the other loving sock couples. Oh, God, why? WHY?!? Why did she have to be taken away from him? He is all alone. He is nothing without Mrs. Lonely Sock. So he sits and waits as the days turn into weeks, the weeks into months and the months into years, hoping that one day she will return. But alas, Mr. Lonely Sock, Mrs. Lonely Sock is no more, and your painful wait is in vain, for she shall never return.

Loneliness is... one sock.

Did I ever tell you about my tone-deaf cat and the time that i......oh....never mind

By henri ennui (anon2c9e@nyx10.cs.du.edu)

The high point of this week:
sitting on my bed singing to my cat.

you don't even want to know the low points.

if i thought anyone cared, though, i'd post a long confessional rant. but i promised that this persona wouldn't do that, so i won't.

boy, the low points were just mighty low, though.

makes me damn thankful that i do at least have a cat. and that the cat's tone-deaf.

well, either it's tone-deaf or i ought to be reported to the spca.

LIFE @ LARGE

Whether you're a world-weary bohemian who's become sick and twisted from the hopelessness of existence or you're a newcomer to all this angst business, there's one thing that will cheer everyone up: shopping! Ok, maybe not, but Steven Snedker's (case@diku.dk) **Alt.Angst Shopping List** is a *huge* file featuring hundreds of recommended books, movies, records, comic books, and more—each reviewed on the sole criteria of its angstfulness.

You can find the Alt.Angst.Shopping.List on the Alt.Angst Home page at:

http.://www.cs.indiana.edu/hyplan/krawling/angst.html

Here's a sample of the reviews you'll find on the Alt.Angst Shopping List:

Films
Northern Lights Scandinavian farmers struggle for survival in North Dakota during the First World War. Nice stuff includes dad going out to freeze to death in the snow, and the beautiful young girl bursting into tears because she is so lonely and it's all so terrible and will never end.

Literature
Feodor Dostoevsky:
The Brothers Karamazov Karamazov is an old bastard. He has three legitimate sons by two different wives, both dead, and one illegitimate son who works for him as a valet. He screws his oldest son out of his inheritance and tries to steal his girlfriend. The old man is murdered, and the oldest son is convicted, but it was actually the valet who did it. The valet kills himself, and the oldest son is sent to Siberia.

Popular Music
Louis Armstrong: **"We've Got All The Time In The World"** (Soundtrack) Taken from the James Bond film *On His Majesty's Secret Service*, used for the sequence where Bond has just gotten married, drives off with his wife on their honeymoon, and his wife is murdered. This was Louis' last recording ever, done at his bedside as he was dying of cancer. The trumpet sections had to be recorded in several takes because he was so short of breath. He died a couple of days after it was finished. I find the title of the song and the way it was recorded so ironic. Again, a must for a bit of existential despair. We don't have much time and it doesn't matter anyway.

Classical Music
Gustav Mahler: **"Das Lied von der Erde"** (*"Song of the earth"*) Get a libretto (a booklet containing the text of the work), so you can sing along. Last year, when I had a couple of bad trips and thought I was going to have to take the dry-dive off the physics building, I listened to this one night and realized I *already* felt dead, and it was all I could do to keep from rushing over to the physics building. Later symphonies: 6th Symphony ("tragic"), 9th Symphony (it's all about death, including his own), and "Kindertotenlieder" ("songs of dead children").

Boys Will Be Boys on the Net

By "Madame Dragonfly" (lilithCuFDtA.5r0@netcom.com)

I woke up this morning at a healthy 6:00, got dressed for my morning walk, and adjourned downstairs to see my 11-year-old son watching the morning cartoons, with his morning bowl of cereal, the light of morning swarming over the kitchen.

I got my breakfast, and stared at my son shoving a spoonful of Berry Berry Kix through the grill in the front of his helmet. Blearily, I sipped my coffee as I watched him struggle to coordinate himself (with all the bulk on his body) enough to get a glass of orange juice. Something here was Not Usual.

I peered. *(Continued on following page)*

EEEK!!

What is it about boys that makes them different from girls—and men different from women? Aside from the obvious incongruities in plumbing, there's the mysterious world of enzymes and hormones, not to mention a global culture that gives boys trucks and guns to play with, while tossing dolls and stuffed animals to the girls.

INSIDE
OPINION

A university research project revealed that, in thousands of litters of mice studied over the course of several months, the male mice would invariably pick vicious fights with each other—often before they could even open their eyes—while this behavior was never once observed in the female mice. Clearly, while nurture plays a powerful role in defining the sexes, nature brings a strong hand to the table as well.

Perhaps the Internet holds some answers to this age-old question. As mandated by the federal government's Office of Tabloid Sensationalism Control under the Anti-Yellow Journalism Act of 1958, the *Insider* is now compelled (albeit pleased) to offer three essays from the Net that give us fleeting glimpses of moments that define what it means to be a boy.

After all, why can boys get away with things no toddler, girl, woman, or adult of any age could ever pull off? Making fart noises in church, throwing spitwads at the substitute teacher, hiding frogs in the new girl's desk. For those men in the crowd who've forgotten the boundless thrills of boyhood, perhaps you should run down to the pet store and buy a couple of white mice to slip down the back of some unsuspecting woman's blouse.

Just make sure they're both *girl* mice.

"Don't you have football practice, say, at 6:00 tonight?"

"Yeah."

"Then pray tell, why are you wearing your regalia?"

"Because I like it."

"It doesn't make you look macho, you know. In fact, it's sort of stupid."

"But I want to wear it."

"Take it off. Now."

* * *

He returned back downstairs. Something was Still Not Right.

"Justin, you're wearing clothes you wore all day yesterday."

"So?"

"Well, they're dirty. Take them off and find something else to wear."

"But I like these clothes. And they're not stained, and they don't smell."

He practices with a coke can and belches while he watches Nickelodeon.

My mother has bought him "Teen Spirit" deodorant.

He plays football and *likes* getting banged up.

Help, my boy is turning into a man.

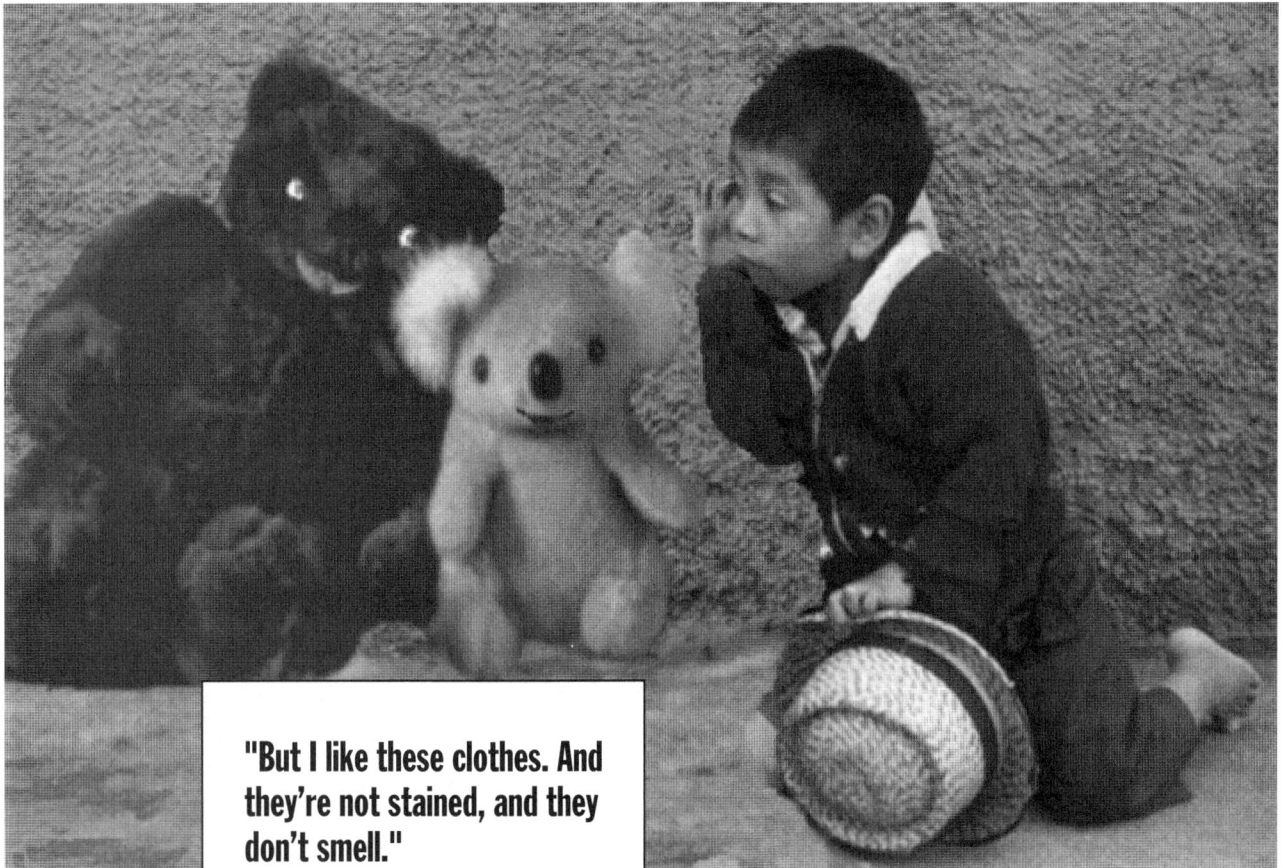

"But I like these clothes. And they're not stained, and they don't smell."

THE USENET ORACLE HAS PONDERED YOUR QUESTION DEEPLY. YOUR QUESTION WAS:

What is the difference between software and hard water?

AND IN RESPONSE, THUS SPAKE THE ORACLE:

Bugs drown in hard water, but live forever in software.

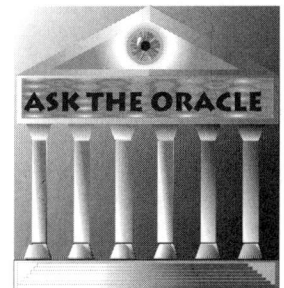

ASK THE ORACLE

We Worship at the Altar of the Big Chicken

By Julie Parmenter (jparment@indiana.edu)

The Big Chicken is next door to us. It is a fifteen-foot replica of a white rooster, mounted on a ten-foot pedestal. It is surrounded by a lovely planting of flowers and a metal fence.

It once sat out by the highway on the edge of town, adorning the entrance to a fried chicken shack. It came to be a landmark and remained in place long after the chicken place shut down. A few years ago, the lot was going to be plowed in order to make way for Progress. The Big Chicken was to be demolished. A great hue and cry went up all around the town. The Chicken had become a Town Icon. It couldn't be sacrificed. So the issue was resolved by moving it down here to the fairgrounds. It now sits proudly in its place of honor at the entrance to the Fair.

My son, Will, loves that chicken. Whenever he thinks of it, or as often as he can get away with it (about once a day), he drags me down there so we can absorb its beauty close up. He'll begin by taking my hand and pulling me gently in that direction. He walks faster than normal and chatters incessantly. He says something that sounds like, "Diggle bop da BIRD-a," or "See, See, Mamma-Dada, bibble bop da BIRD."

"da BIRD-a"

When we finally complete our pilgrimage and are actually standing in the shadow of the Great Bird, then we must view it from many angles. He has to stand on the top of the fence at one end. Then the other. Then the middle and so on, all the while jabbering about, "da BIRD-a."

When the worship service is complete, we head back home. He is usually quiet for a while, as he absorbs the spiritual impact of his encounter. Then, when we get almost halfway home, he turns around and begins a babble in which he says over and over, "Bye-bye BIRD-a!"

Originally published in the Nerdnosh Story Digest *mailing list. Reprinted here by permission.*

Why Do Boys Spit?

By Dan Vitale

(vitale@act-act5-po.act.org)

Not because they have to. Not even because they want to. But because they must.

Peer pressure, for one thing. Boys live in herds. Anything done by one must be imitated by the others. (If brave, you may even attempt to best the originator, but beware: you might get only a pounding for your trouble, if he whom you emulate fancies himself king of your particular hill.) Thus, an underarm fart, a cavernous belch, a dirty joke, a mighty bullet of seething saliva . . . these cannot go unanswered; if a pack of boys crosses your path on its way home from school, do not be surprised if all you remember of its passing is a scribble, a squall of noise, and spray.

(By the way, we're not talking solid matter. That's for kids with bad colds, or for that substantial number of older men who must make a beeline from their bed to the bathroom sink of a morning and clear their instrument as a necessary adjunct to starting the day. In summer, with the windows open, you hear them hawking like so many duck calls being blown at 7:00 a.m.)

For another, there's the age-old need to mark your territory. Spit does nicely at preventing others from venturing too close. Also, it's a quick way of establishing property rights. *I* can spit in my backyard, on the sidewalk in front of my house, even in my pool, but *you* cannot. No, I said, you cannot, unless I give Permission. And I will expect nothing less from you, at your house. Rules are rules.

(No one spits indoors. Mothers govern the interior, and there is no appeasing their wrath if they find a still-warm one on the antimacassar.)

Then there is the disrespect or disdain you must show to an opponent in whatever circumstance fraught with peril. Why waste breath pursuing the litany that begins, "You're not the boss of me," or "I can do what I want," and proceeds rapidly from "Can too," and "Can't make me," to "Says who," and "You and what army," when all you need do is glance away, eyes hooded, and release a single, threatening air-to-ground missile?

Finally, there is the most mysterious, least easily understood reason. It has no name. It is merely an Attitude.

At a certain age, boys must separate from everything, even from each other. It is what must be done—what is expected. It happens in that brief period when the boy's mind is older than his body, when world-weariness is not quite earned but not quite a put-on, either.

Usually a boy walks alone at this age, looking neither left nor right, sometimes doing small damage along his path: using a stick, perhaps, to distort a few wire diamonds in a cyclone fence, or stepping on live things until they aren't. It is the age when a boy senses that he needs something he isn't getting, and possibly may never get, because it is nameless and can't be asked for. It is the age when there are no words for how he is feeling, but silence isn't quite sufficient. So, a spit: It is a piece of language, a liquid sentence, meaning partly, "I don't care," and partly "You don't care about me." It may mean "I hate you," or it may mean "I hate myself." It may be meant for someone in particular, or for everyone. It means both "Get away," and "Hey, where are you going?"

Usually, the Attitude passes relatively quickly; you don't see many men beyond teenage letting fly in public. But, of all the reasons a boy spits, this last is the one most likely to pursue him into adulthood. Now, of course, it isn't the only reason—simple aging, after all, is what leads him to that bathroom sink—but if you see a grown male spitting on the street, it's entirely possible that the Attitude, unresolved and possibly festering, lies behind it. Still, no need to worry. He's mostly harmless. Just sidestep it and keep on walking.

Originally published in the Nerdnosh Story Digest *mailing list. Reprinted here by permission.* ∎

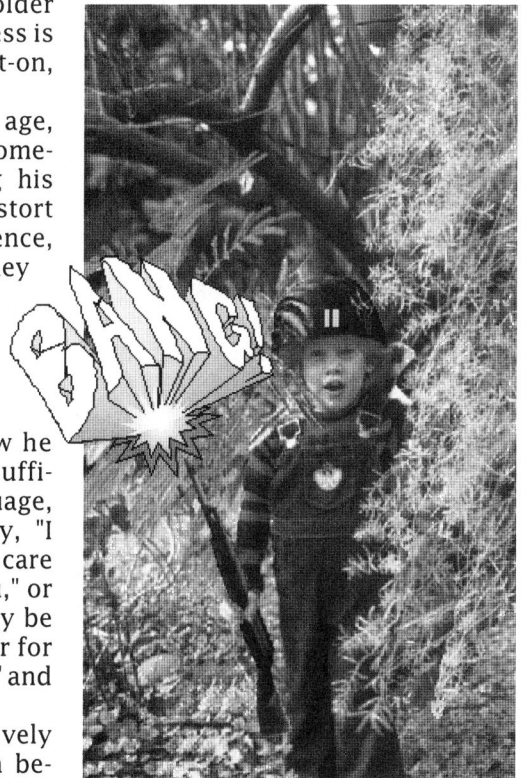

"MY SECRET SHAME"

By Gene Haldeman (haldeman@sas.upenn.edu)

I read the *Weekly World News*. There. I've said it. I'm not ashamed of it. Not in the least, because it really is a humor maga . . . OK, no, you're right. I don't have to make any disclaimer whatsoever, because you'll still like and respect me no matter what, right? Right?

The worst part is that I do sometimes get embarrassed buying it. Which is really rather silly, since I do own two *Weekly World News* T-shirts, which I wear in my leisure and certainly in the public eye. In fact, these T-shirts will likely break the ice at many difficult social situations; wouldn't you want to chat with someone with a "Bat Boy Found In Cave" T-shirt? And the other, "Alien Backs Clinton," is a bipartisan hit among the folks I know who have seen it; then again I have strange friends.

This is why I read the *Weekly World News*: The other well-known supermarket tabloids concern themselves far too thoroughly with the private lives of celebrities. I really don't care about Roseanne's past lives, or whether Garth Brooks gets lonely and cries, or whether Burt Reynolds is really, really tired. The *News* is not so cruel as to stick it into celebs (although within the past five years, they have sunk to including two gossip pages—a shame really). No, the *News* will have a front cover of "300-pound BABY BIGGEST EVER BORN," while the *Star* will be mucking about for new information on O.J. Sorry, in my book a 300-pound baby is of a *lot* more interesting than O.J. Simpson.

Confessions of a Tabloid Junkie

Bringing folks the shocking news from the edge of cyberspace isn't easy. In fact, it's often a serious pain. You think it's a walk in the park sensationalizing the rambling electronic missives of thousands of would-be digital Dostoevskys? We can't put just any old news inside the pages of our titillating tabloid. No, we here at the *Internet Insider* follow the spirit—if not the letter—of a couple of time-honored journalistic edicts:

If it bleeds, it leads. Ever wonder why crime seems to be the main concern of most Americans, despite the fact that crime rates have remained steady or even dropped slightly over the past decade? Because, quite simply, if it bleeds, it leads. That is, crime, gore, and violence of any magnitude will almost always be the top story of any respectable tabloid. Now, being purveyors of a family paper and reasonable people in general, we here at the *Insider* eschew violence of any kind. But, of course, if you hear any great stories about murder sprees or knife-fights, we trust you'll pass them along to us.

Dog Bites Man can't compare to Man Bites Dog. In the strange and shocking world of the tabloid, the unexpected is our bread and butter. Nobody cares about the 10,000 planes that land safely every day, but you can bet they're dying to hear about the one that crashes. And who cares if Bowzer nips at the postman's heels (again)? But if we get decent pix of Postman Pete gnawing on Bowzer's hind leg, we promise we'll share them with you on the front page. This second rule, more than the first, is the guiding light of the *Insider* and all other classic tabs.

While that explains why we publish the stories we do, what can account for you people *reading* them? Damned if we know, so we'll let Gene Haldeman explain.

INSIDE

OPINION

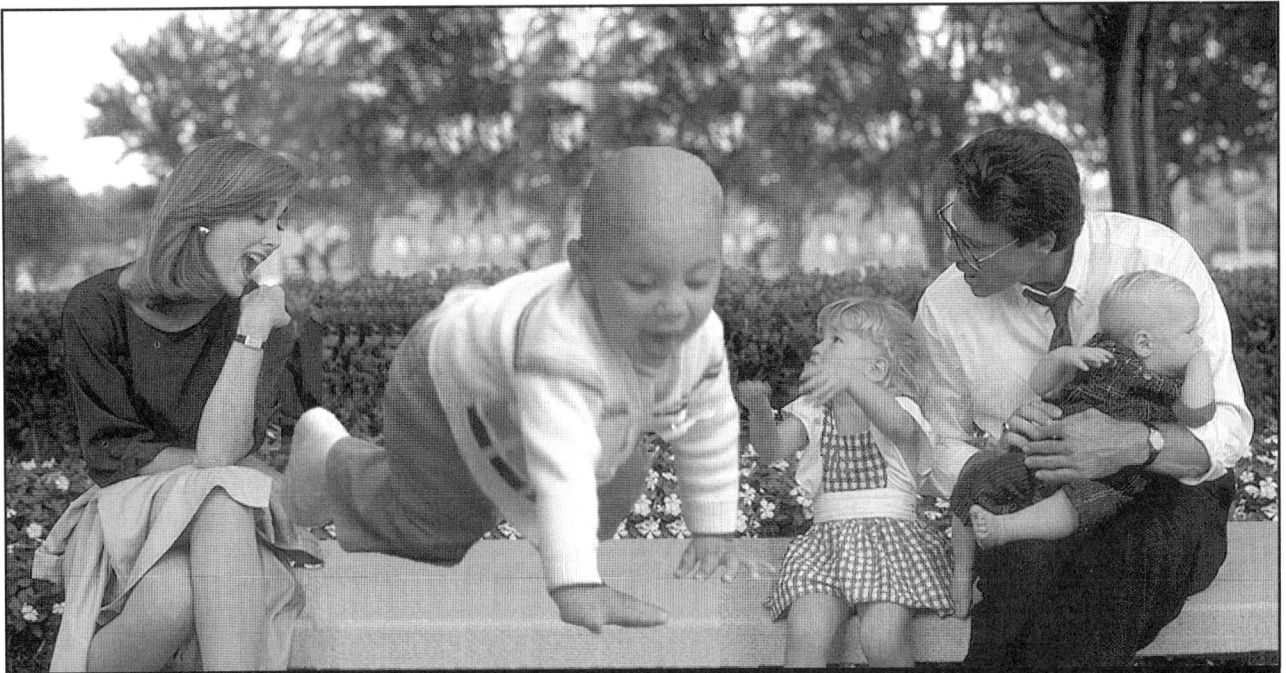

300-pound baby biggest ever born

I've often wished I could write for that paper; imagine the scenario (a la *The Front Page*): the hard-boiled editor mutters to the young, cocky rookie reporter, "All right, kid, here's your chance. I'm putting you on the 'Alien Mates with Weed-Whacker' case. Don't screw up, Weed-Whacker stories sell!"

When I was in high school, I read *Mad* magazine, and enjoyed it thoroughly. When in college, I read *National Lampoon* for a while, until at one point NL decided that *all* of its humor should be about sex, and fairly misogynist. A little was OK, but this was every joke now. Sex and related subjects are funny, but enough is enough. So I was lost for a while; at sea without a map or compass, until I discovered the *Weekly World News*.

> ## I really don't care about Roseanne's past lives or whether Burt Reynolds is really tired.

Originally published in Nerdnosh: The Story Digest. *Reprinted here by permission.*

THE USENET ORACLE HAS PONDERED YOUR QUESTION DEEPLY. YOUR QUESTION WAS:

O wisest of the wise Oracle, please explain to me: Why is it that every time a female describes her relationship with me, the word "plutonic" is always used?

AND IN RESPONSE, THUS SPAKE THE ORACLE:

They mean that, like Pu-225, your relationship had a half-life of 26 minutes.

You owe the Oracle a cyclotomic accelerator.

(answer by Heath David; heathdav@vt.edu)

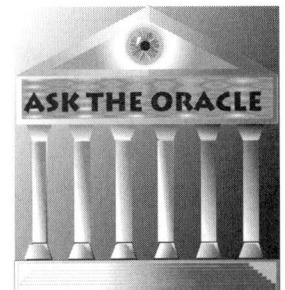

ASK THE ORACLE

LIFE @ LARGE

If "Man Bites Dog" is an old formula that illustrates the tabloid's obsession with the unusual, then "Man-Eating Shrimp" is a similar species that exposes the genre's penchant for sensationalism. A man eating shrimp isn't so exciting, the old adage goes, but add a hyphen and suddenly you've got a Man-Eating Shrimp!!

The strange story of Spike the Lobster embodies a little of both "Man Bites Dog" and "Man-Eating Shrimp." Spike, you see, is a 12-pound New England lobster that's been stirring up controversy in the *Insider's* hometown of L.A. It seems Gladstone's 4 Fish, the wildly popular seafood restaurant in Pacific Palisades, where Sunset Boulevard meets the Pacific Coast Highway, has adopted Spike as its mascot.

It seems that a small number of folks (and here's where the unexpected and sensational—or at least silly—part comes in) are insisting that Spike be returned to his home in the chilly North Atlantic. A handful of irate lobster liberators descended on Gallstone's, including animal rights activist Doug Stoll, who decried the "zoo-like" conditions of Spike's tank and complained that "Too many people are going to salivate over him instead of sympathizing."

Spike had been slated for a pot of boiling water as part of the restaurant's "Lobsterfest" (we can only guess . . .), but the staff took a liking to him and decided to keep him around. Who would have imagined that sparing a fat lobster would lead to heated discussions about how much pain *Homarus americanus* can endure and to offers from an airline to fly Spike back east—all of this covered in agonizing detail in the local press? After a while, even the most strident animal lover would tend to side with diner David Sears, who proclaimed simply, "Ah, B.S.! When are they going to cook it?"

Spike, a 12-pound New England lobster, has been stirring up controversy in L.A.

A number of folks are insisting that Spike be returned to his home.

THE USENET ORACLE HAS PONDERED YOUR QUESTION
DEEPLY. YOUR QUESTION WAS:

What did the Tibetan monk say to the hot dog vendor?
—(question by Chris Andrews; andrews@stat.cmu.edu)

AND IN RESPONSE, THUS SPAKE THE ORACLE:

The most famous exchange between a lama and a hot dog vendor occurred one block south of Times Square in July 1988.

Hot Dog Vendor: What can I get for ya today? Footlong with the works? I said, what can I get for ya today? Hey, ya wanna hot dog or not? Listen if yer not going to order willya move on, I gotta business to run. Stop starin' at me, man. Say something, dammit, yer givin' me the creeps. Hey, I get it. Ya don't no any English, do ya? Uh, lessee, yo, uh, tengo los, uh, hot dogs, uh, perros calientes. Okay, fine! just stand there. See if I care. Just don't scare away the customers. Jeez. Forget itYa wanna Coke? Coca-Cola? I don't care where yer from, ya gotta understand Coca-Cola? Stop smiling. People'll think yer up to something. Hey, I got all-beefs, beef-n-porks, turkey dogs, polish sausage, and kielbasa. I've got plain and whole grain buns. I don't care what you want, just order something or leave. I'm serious, man, if you don't go away, I'll call the cops and have them arrest you for loitering. Jesus Christ, will you stop staring at me! STOP IT! At least blink once in a while. You're driving me crazy! You wanna Coke? Wait, no, I already tried that. Listen, man, I'm serious, stop starin' and grinnin' at me. I gotta gun under the counter. I'll use it. I mean it. STOP STARING AT ME! STOPITSTOPITSTOPIT! YOU'RE DRIVING ME CRAZY! AAAAARGH! STOPITSTOPITSTOPITSTOPIT! PLEASE LOOK AWAY! HERE! OKAY! I'M MAKING YOU A HOT DOG FOR FREE! TAKE IT! EAT IT! JUST GO AWAY! STOPITSTOPITSTOPITSTOPIT! YOU WANNA COKE? OKAY HERE'S A COKE! IT'S ON THE HOUSE! NOW PLEASE GO AWAY! I CAN'T TAKE ANY MORE OF THIS! YOUR EYES ARE DRIVING ME INSANE! STOPITSTOPPITSTOPITSTOPISTOPSTOPSTOPSTOPSTOPSTOPSTOPSTOP!

Then the lama widened his grin just enough to barely show his teeth. At that moment the hot dog vendor was enlightened.

```
              You owe the Oracle a better koan. And a new deli.
              (answer by Heath David; heathdav@vt.edu)
```

183

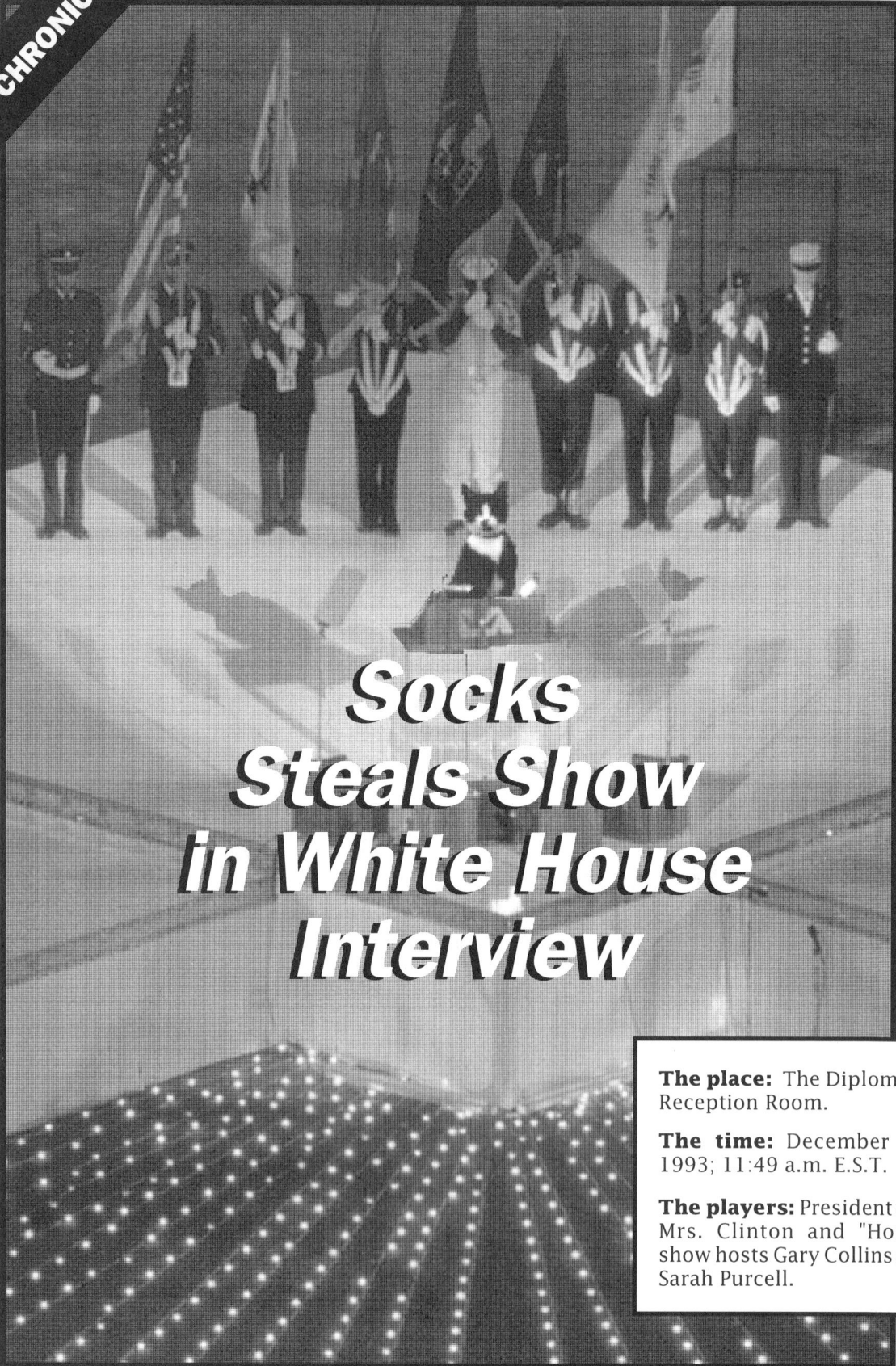

Socks Steals Show in White House Interview

The place: The Diplomatic Reception Room.

The time: December 10, 1993; 11:49 a.m. E.S.T.

The players: President and Mrs. Clinton and "Home" show hosts Gary Collins and Sarah Purcell.

Why Is Socks Trotting Through the Diplomatic Room?

In this episode, the Clintons invite Gary and Sarah into their home to show America a little glimpse of a Clinton Christmas in the White House. But Socks steals the show by crashing the interview in a surprise appearance. Will administration media advisors punish Socks for upstaging his master? Let's listen.

Q: The President of the United States, ladies and gentlemen.

The President: Gary.

Q: Hello, Mr. President, how are you?

The President: How are you? Glad to see you.

Q: Pleasure to meet you.

The President: Thank you.

Q: Thank you. Welcome to your own home. (*Laughter.*)

The President: Here we are.

Q: By the way, have you done all your shopping yet?

The President: No, I haven't even started.

Q: Oh, yes, we know what you're going to get, though.

The President: You do?

Q: Well, it's bigger than a bread box but smaller than a bus.

Mrs. Clinton: Now, don't give it—

Q: Oh, I'm sorry.

Q: You know how these men are—

Q: That's good—what are you getting—

The President: I accept. (***Socks enters.***) (***Laughter.***)

Q: He seems very happy.

The President: Hi Socks. (*Laughter.*)

Q: Can you give us any hints about what your plans are for a gift for—

The President: No, I wouldn't—

Q: We saw your last year's—

The President: I have made a decision. Do you like that?

The Socks Chronicles

In this ongoing series of behind-the-scenes looks at the inner workings of the White House, the *Internet Insider* follows Socks, America's First Cat, through another harrowing press conference. In this official White House document obtained exclusively by the *Insider*, you'll see how the White House press corps is once again sidetracked from the real issues facing our government to consider the life and times of that lovable kitty, Socks.

Why the media obsession with the President's cat? Is there something the White House doesn't want us to know? Is "Socks" a secret code word that sends reporters into a trance of distraction and diversion? Why does the press offer only a 30-second sound bite from a 30-minute meeting? Does Socks prefer frolicking in the Lincoln Bedroom or on the South Lawn? These questions and more are answered as we present another installment of *The Socks Chronicles.*

photo courtesy of The White House

Q: Well, somebody told us that you shop Christmas Eve, is that correct? Are you like that?

The President: I do two things actually, though—at least in the past I have. When we lived in Arkansas, I had a little closet that was just mine, and I shopped all year long for everybody that I knew. Just a little bit here and there and I'd travel around and—and I shoved it all in the closet. And then about 10 days before Christmas, I'd take it out and organize it. And then I would find out what I hadn't done, and I then I'd go out the day before Christmas and shop.

Q: Now, who did your wrapping? Or did you do the wrapping?

The President: Well, the people who worked at the Governor's Mansion did some of it, and then I did some of it. I did a lot of it myself. Chelsea and I would do a lot at the end. I'm pretty good actually.

Q: Yes. (*Laughter.*)

The President: I'm not bad.

Q: I just hate it. I would walk a mile rather than wrap a package.

The President: Well, you know, at the end of the—the last two or three days I get in the Christmas spirit in a big way, and I do a lot of that stuff.

Q: Is that starting to build for you now? I mean, first Christmas in the White House as President.

The President: But I'm really—I've become like a little boy again around Christmas time. I don't want to sleep, I just want to do things.

This excerpted transcript from an actual White House media event was downloaded from official archives of Clinton Administration documents available from a number of sources: via gopher: gopher.tamu.edu or sunsite.unc.edu; via anonymous FTP: ftp.spies.com; via World-Wide Web: http://english-server.hss.cmu.edu/WhiteHouse.html; via e-mail: publications@whitehouse.gov.

THE USENET ORACLE HAS PONDERED YOUR QUESTION DEEPLY.
YOUR QUESTION WAS:

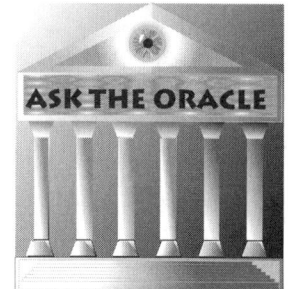
ASK THE ORACLE

Oh great Oracle, whose very robes I could not touch without suffering unending torment in the nethermost depths of hell, or at least a few minutes in a microwave, who walks with the Gods and even is invited to play Brockian Ultra-Cricket with them every Thursday, whose swim towel is a hoopy shade of mauve, who looks so unlike a beetle as to possibly be called the anti-beetle, whose dog can dance in 15 different languages at the same time, who can type upon the keyboard in such a sensual manner as to make the terminal groan in throes of happiness, who if he was to write a book would receive all kinds of neato awards even before it was finished, who has an infinite number of supplicants to throw lightning at whenever the wish strikes him, who knows all the puns, and who appears as a burning coke can that is not consumed when he deigns to appear at all to the most foolish mortals that are forever asking his infinite and spiffy advice, would you please, please, with great mounds of sugar and a cherry with gobs of whipped cream and whatever other sweet topping your greatness wishes for and enjoys on top, tell this poor supplicant, who has no knowledge when stood next to you, whose soul is forever doomed to walk the earth with a slight itch in a hard to reach place because it was bold enough to bother you, whose dog has trouble walking and panting at the same time, who doesn't even own a bath towel or a washcloth, who at just the thought of thinking about the possibility of letting the thought of considering the Oracle in all his greatness must immediately fall down upon the earth and chant "Hey Nonny Nonny No" many many times to keep from being struck just plain silly, why do you require so much grovelling and such before a question, though I do not question your judgment, which I know is far beyond anything I have ever encountered, making all the knowledge of the Earth through all of history look like something that you probably wouldn't even stub your toe on in the dark, even though that isn't a very good analogy, since you would never stub your toe, as that would imply some fault on your part, which is obviously impossible, but just for the sake of the analogy, which of course, coming from one such as me, is vastly inferior to any analogy or even any sound you might utter after stubbing your toe, is not very good, but might be kept anyway, and though I want to end this poor mortal's request soon, I really have no idea what punctuation mark to use, so I'll probably go with an ellipsis, since that would imply that I might have gone on a bit, and grovelled some more before stopping, as I think I will right now, though if it displeases you, O Great One, I will stop, as I am such a poor worm crawling on, nay, below the dirt, and I would never want to annoy or even consider annoying you in any way, so I will stop now, hoping against hope that my small smidgin of knowledge is enough to know if I have not grovelled too little or too much, and likewise for praising thy great name, so I'll just drift off now . . .

AND IN RESPONSE, THUS SPAKE THE ORACLE:

Can you repeat the question?

Support & Interest Abound Online

LIFE @ LARGE

Life at the *Internet Insider* isn't all wine and roses, you know. Being a reporter is a tough job. But it's also an interesting job. Yeah, that's right: tough, but interesting. There are other reporters out there having a tough time with their chosen avocation. And there are plenty of folks who love to share the interesting minutiae of their jobs as reporters.

Consequently, there are both support groups and interest groups for reporters. The difference is the support group is made up of grizzled old reporters on their way out of the business, while the interest group is full of fresh-faced cubs just starting out. On the Internet, it can sometimes be tough to tell the difference between a support group and an interest group.

Take the INTP mailing list, for instance. If you're either interested in or worried about being introverted, intuitive, thinking, and perceiving, you might want to join the mailing list (which may be a support group or is possibly an interest group). The official list profile follows.

Introverted Intuitive Thinking Perceiving (INTP) Profile

INTPs will often correct others who use the wrong word or a word with an inappropriate shade of meaning. Analytical to a fault. Overprecise. Amenable to almost anything until their principles are violated, about which they are outspoken and inflexible.

A major concern for INTPs is the haunting sense of impending failure. They spend considerable time second-guessing themselves. The open-endedness (from Perceiving) conjoined with the need for competence (NT) is expressed in a sense that one's conclusion may well be met by an equally plausible alternative solution, and that, after all, one may very well have overlooked some critical bit of *data*. An INTP arguing a point may very well be trying to convince himself as much as his opposition. In this way INTPs are markedly different from those who are much more confident in their competence and willing to act on their convictions.

Mathematics is a system where many INTPs love to play. But so are languages, computer systems, and potentially any complex system. INTPs thrive on systems. Understanding, exploring, mastering, and manipulating systems can overtake the INTPs conscious thought. This fascination for logical wholes and their inner workings is often expressed in a detachment from the environment, a concentration where time is forgotten and extraneous stimuli are held at bay.

One of the tipoffs that a person is an INTP is his or her obsession with logical correctness. Errors are not often due to poor logic—apparent faux pas in reasoning are usually a result of overlooking details or of incorrect context.

Games INTPs seem to especially enjoy include Risk, Bridge, Stratego, Chess, Go (hence the server on the net), and word games of all sorts. They've been known to sit in public places and pick a word off a menu or mayonnaise jar to see who can make the most words from its letters on a napkin in two minutes. ■

Some Famous INTPs:

Socrates
St. Luke
René Descartes
Blaise Pascal
Sir Isaac Newton
Thomas Jefferson
William Harvey (pioneer in human physiology)
Emily Dickinson
C. G. Jung
William James
Albert Einstein
Paul Simon (songwriter/performer)
Gerald Ford
Midori Ito (ice skater, Olympic silver medalist)
Rick Moranis
(actor in "Honey, I Shrunk The Kids")
Ashley and Mary Kate Olsen
(The "Full House" twins)
Tom Foley (ex-Speaker of the House)
Brent Spiner (Commander Data of "Star Trek: The Next Generation")

Internet Reveals New Twist

Compiled by Nathan Mates (nathan@cco.caltech.edu)

Q: How many mystery writers does it take to screw in a light bulb?

A: Two. One to screw it almost all the way in, and the other to give it a surprising twist at the end.

Q: How many running-dog lackeys of the bourgeoisie does it take to change a light bulb?

A: Two. One to exploit the proletariat, and one to control the means of production!

Q: How many graduate students does it take to screw in a light bulb?

A: Only one, but it may take upwards of five years for her to get it done.

Q: How many 'Real Men' does it take to change a light bulb?

A: None. 'Real Men' aren't afraid of the dark.

Q: How many Jewish mothers does it take to screw in a light bulb?

A: None. ("That's all right . . . I'll just sit here in the dark . . . ")

Q: How many Marxists does it take to screw in a light bulb?

A: None. The light bulb contains the seeds of its own revolution.

Q: How many politicians does it take to change a light bulb?

A: 1,000,001. One to change the bulb, and 1,000,000 to rebuild civilization to the point where they need light bulbs again.

Q: How many nuclear engineers does it take to change a light bulb?

A: Seven. One to install the new bulb, and six to figure out what to do with the old one for the next 10,000 years.

Q: How many Christians does it take to change a light bulb?

A: Three, but they're really only one.

Q: How many Christian Scientists does it take to screw in a light bulb?

A: None, but it takes at least one to sit and pray for the old one to go back on.

Q: How many jugglers does it take to change a light bulb?

A: One, but it takes at least three light bulbs.

Q: How many economists does it take to screw in a light bulb?

A: None. If the government would just leave it alone, it would screw itself.

on Old Question

Q: How many Zen masters does it take to screw in a light bulb?

A: A tree in a golden forest.

Q: How many Carl Sagans does it take to screw in a light bulb?

A: Billions and billions.

Q: How many Californians does it take to change a light bulb?

A: Six. One to turn the bulb, one for support, and four to relate to the experience.

Q: How many psychiatrists does it take to change a light bulb?

A: Only one, but the bulb has got to really *want* to change.

Q: How many folk singers does it take to screw in a light bulb?

A: Two. One to change the bulb, and one to write a song about how good the old light bulb was.

Q: How many surrealists does it take to change a light bulb?

A: Two. One to hold the giraffe, and the other to fill the bathtub with brightly colored machine tools.

Q: How many doctors does it take to screw in a light bulb?

A: Three. One to find a bulb specialist, one to find a bulb installation specialist, and one to bill it all to Medicare.

Q: How many people from New Jersey does it take to change a light bulb?

A: Three. One to change the light bulb, one to be a witness, and the third to shoot the witness.

Q: How many cops does it take to screw in a light bulb?

A: None. It turned itself in.

Q: How many lawyers does it take to change a light bulb?

A: How many can you afford?

Q: How many football players does it take to change a light bulb?

A: The entire team! And they all get a semester's credit for it!

Q: How many Harvard students does it take to screw in a light bulb?

A: Just one. He grabs the bulb and waits for the world to revolve around him.

Q: How many civil servants does it take to change the light bulb?

A: 45. One to change the bulb, and 44 to do the paperwork.

Q: How many consultants does it take to change a light bulb?

A: I'll have an estimate for you a week from Monday.

Q: How many Romulans does it take to screw in a light bulb?

A: 151. One to screw the light bulb in, and 150 to self-destruct the ship out of disgrace.

Q: How many editors of *Poor Richard's Almanac* does it take to replace a light bulb?

A: Many hands make light work.

Q: How many actors does it take to change a light bulb?

A: Only one. They don't like to share the spotlight.

Q: How many Chinese Red Guards does it take to screw in a light bulb?

A: 10,000—to give the bulb a cultural revolution.

Q: How many Dada-ists does it take to screw in a light bulb?

A: To get to the other side.

Q: How many poets does it take to change a light bulb?

A: Three. One to curse the darkness, one to light a candle, and one to change the bulb.

The Kool-Aid Cure for the Common Cold

By Jason "bored to the core" Ronallo

I came home the other night with a sore throat that felt like I'd been sucking on the exhaust pipe of a bus after drinking tacks. Usually when I've got a dagger in my throat, I drink some cough medicine or spray some non-prescription liquid to the back of my mouth, or suck on some menthol, nuclear-radiation-emanating, waxy-paper-wrapped drop, or bless myself with a cherry Luden's candy.

The Luden's candy is the only one that makes me happy, though most say it's not a medication, I think that it probably does about as good as any of the others. I hate taking bad-tasting, named-cherry-just-to-sucker-you-in cough medicines. My folks used to have to sit on me and hold my nose to make me take cough medicines. But now that I've made the discovery of the year, no kid will ever have to take hold-your-nose medicines again! I've discovered the mystery ingredient in these non-prescription drugs that actually turns the trick.

Since my throat was sore, I wanted something cool to drink to soothe me, so I could get some work done on a paper for a critical reading class that I'm taking. (But I'm sure you don't want to hear about the discourse of treason in Shakespeare's *Tempest*—though, of course, you might find it more exciting than this.) So anyway, I went to the fridge to snag me a pre-cooled beverage, rather than a wait-until-it-cools, ice-filled-glass (and-then-at-the-end-the-ice-falls-and-hits-you-in-the-teeth-ouch!) beverage. And lo and behold, there was a fresh pitcher of red Kool-Aid. I poured myself a big plastic cup's worth, and gurgled it down. To my amazement, my sore throat went away—vanished like data from a disk brought up to a magnet.

Now, we all know that band-aids cover up boo-boo's, but I never knew before that Kool-Aid covers up sore throats (and, I conjecture, other ailments)! My theory (it's no mere hypothesis anymore, as I've now tried the same experiment on my brother, and it worked again with scientific predictability) is that it's actually the red coloring which is the healing agent in all throat lozenges, and not the other drugs. Notice how most of the Robitussins are of a red variety. Even the ones that aren't fully red, you can easily see how the coloring isn't a pure color, and I conjecture that what color lies behind the outer masking color is, in fact, a red. And that's why Luden's cough drops can work without having any real medicine in them *and,* while tasting good at the same time! You see how liquid cough medicines are thick and cough drops are even denser. Both of these have a high amount of red in them. Just by drinking a large amount of cherry Kool-Aid, you can get the same healing effect of all these expensive, non-prescription "drugs."

Do you see the possible conspiracies that could be behind the hiding of this knowledge (and consequently why this article is so poorly written, as I tremble in fright for my life)? Look at it this way: Who benefits by having this knowledge hidden? The drug manufacturers, of course. And who says what drugs are allowed to be sold as non-prescription? The FDA, of course. Here's my hypothesis: The FDA gets kickbacks from the "legal" drug lords—the corporate conglomerates. All that the FDA has to do is call the thing a "drug," making it fall under its control, and since the "drugs" are under its power, it can stop them from being sold. The FDA bribes the corporations, which bow under the pressure of Big Bully Brother and gives the FDA a cut of their business.

The FDA OKs these "drugs" and contends that they have some sort of medication in them that actually helps someone with a sore throat or cough. They put unknown wordage on the labels, so no ordinary citizen out of their control could decipher the ingredients, thereby believing in the power of the mystery "drug" to help them. (Try looking at the labels sometime and tell me if you know what all that means . . . some of them even only contain "active ingredients." What are they trying to hide?) Anyway, what person that knows about all these drugs is really going to spend their time studying the contents of a normal cough medicine. Certainly, they've been at it this long enough to know what they are talking about. In essence, what they've pulled on us is the old placebo trick. They make us think that there is some special healing "drug" in these "medicines," when all there really is is some polluted and thick Kool-Aid.

"Why can't Kool-Aid then blatantly sell their product as a healing agent?" one may ask. Don't you get it!? If Kool-Aid can sell its product as a medicine, then the multi-gazillion-dollar drug companies lose their business to a flavored drink manufacturer *and* the whole money scheme the FDA has orchestrated falls through. "Couldn't Kool-Aid itself be in on this dastardly plot to hide the fact of affordable health care from the masses in order to make a buck?" I know if I would openly attack Kool-Aid, I would get a lot of flack from their auspicious and beloved and influential followers (amongst them the secret order of the Kool-Aid Monks), but I just throw this one question out: Could Kool-Aid actually have a drug in it that is not only helpful to healing but also slightly addictive?

This would certainly confound and complicate the issues at hand. If Kool-Aid were to try to sell their drink as a healing agent, the FDA would ban it, or, more slyly, not allow it to be sold as a "drug," and laugh at the mere proposal, and the whole public would laugh along with them, "Hardy har har! Kool-Aid can cure the common cold! Ha ha ha!"

Well, laugh yourself, if you will, but next time you have a sore throat, why don't you try to drink some good-tasting cherry Kool-Aid instead of that expensive, nasty-tasting cough medicine? (Or if you can find it sold separately, try some FD&C red # 40.) Send me any results of your self-experiments too, so that I can compile a report, so the public can be educated as to the healing power of Kool-Aid. ∎

Reprinted from the e-zine Boredom Incarnate. Send e-mail to jnrst9+@pitt.edu for subscription information.

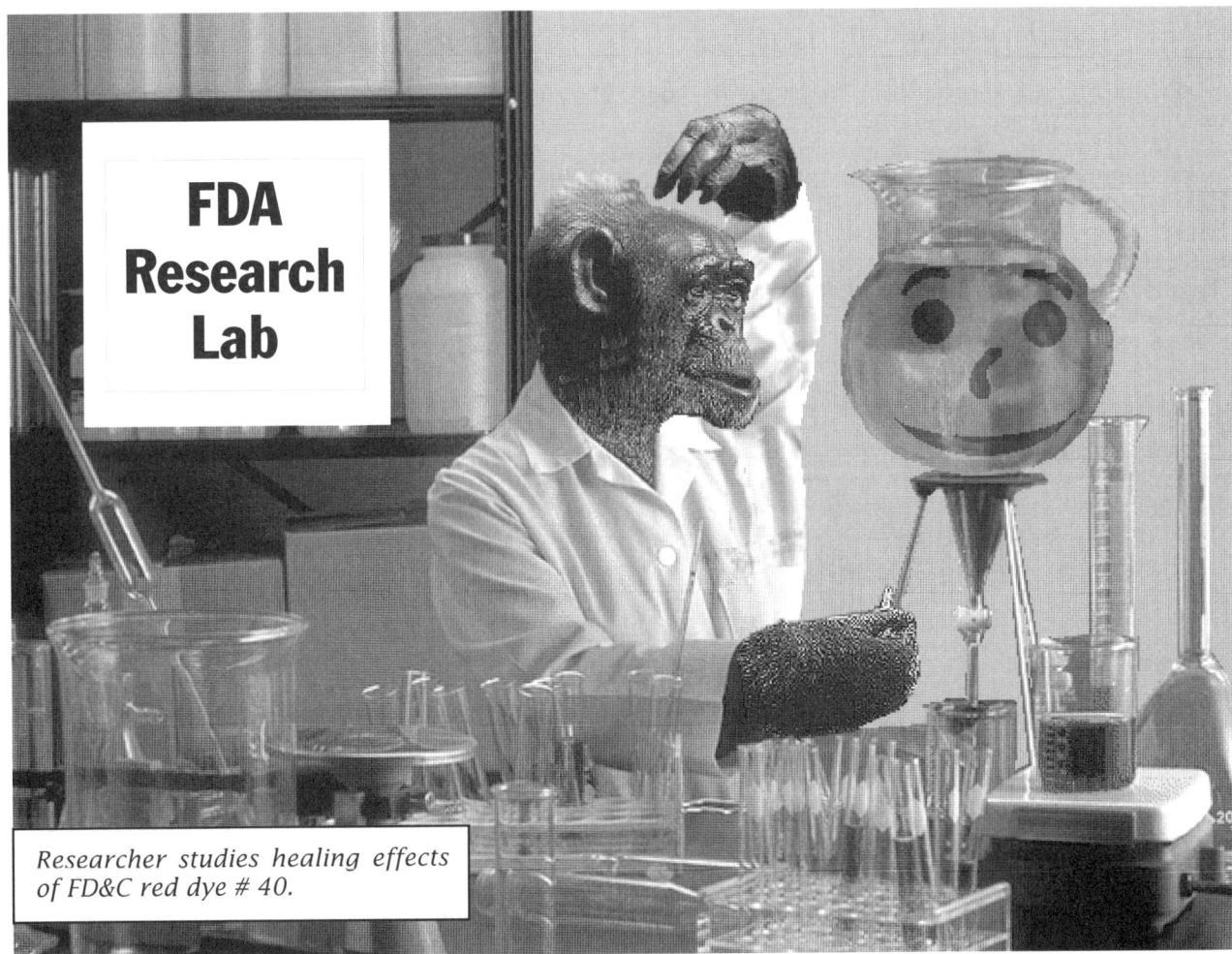

Researcher studies healing effects of FD&C red dye # 40.

Internet Serves as Modern-Day Babble-On

Net Full of Strange Babblings

MUSIC LOVERS CONFOUND NETIZENS!

From the alternative musical tunings mailing list, two participants discuss well-temperament ditonic vs. syntonic comma tunings.

"Perhaps in a meantone scenario, it might be more reasonable to use the syntonic comma. I say that because meantone temperament will inherently give you three slightly flat fifths and one dreadfully sharp "wolf" fifth. In that sort of tuning, you accept incomplete modulability and avoid that wolf fifth, and if you're going to avoid it altogether, I suppose it's not a big deal if you widen it even more."

[In response (we think):]

"I'd like to add a nice little footnote to your explanation of meantone temperament before I get back to the original question (which was syntonic vs. pythagorean)...stacking up 31 quarter-comma-flat fifths almost perfectly closes the circle, and that stacking 19 third-comma-flat fifths almost perfectly closes the circle. That of course means that 31-equal is essentially a completed quarter-comma meantone system, and that 19-equal is essentially a completed third-comma meantone system."

Techno-Babble Clogs Corridors of Net

Net Resources

To subscribe to the alternative musical tunings mailing list, send e-mail to tuning@varese.mills.edu.

To access space shuttle documents of all kinds via anonymous FTP, check out the archives at **sspp.gsfc.nasa.gov** or via World-Wide Web at **http://sspp.gsfc.nasa.gov/**, Send e-mail tomailserv@sspp.gsfc.nasa.gov.for more information.

INSIDE

OPINION

You may have heard the often-cited factoid that the average newspaper is written at about a sixth-grade reading level. The *Insider* is pleased to report that our writing is even simpler and easier to read, with most of our stories aimed at a fourth-grade reading level. Why? Because we care about our readers, and don't want to waste their time with challenging concepts or exotic words.

If only the rest of the Internet were the same. No, dear readers, there are thousands of people on the Net who insist on writing for what can only be categorized as a Martian reading level. Frankly, we don't know who reads this stuff. (We'd love to say, "Not us," but that's not exactly true.)

The whole sad state of affairs brings to mind an instruction page someone sent us in the mail for a stick-on novelty earring called "Sassy Pal." Made in Taiwan, the earring—which is designed to stick to the lobe of the ear via an adhesive, giving the illusion of pierced ears—shows how simple ideas often don't translate well. Take, for instance the Sassy Pal directions for use:

"Please to make us happy for buying Sassy Pal." (We're not making this up.) **"Please to enjoy pretty, happy Sassy Pal. For to gain the stickiness, we remove the backness and joyfully yet harshly apply to earslobe. Wear until ready to disrobe from Sassy Pal. Please to enjoy Sassy Pal."**

As odd as the Sassy Pal instructions seem, you can still get an idea what the folks had in mind. And in their defense, English wasn't their first language. On the Net, however, we're often left bamboozled wondering what people are trying to say. But don't take our word for it, please to enjoy sassy net typingly words.

List Service

Have you ever been watching a space shuttle launch only to hear the commentator say something like, "You know, Ray, this shuttle is carrying the new SAMPIE small payload experiment." Well now, with this handy chart, you'll always know what those confusing shuttle small payload acronyms stand for. You could turn to your pals and say, "Yeah, I hear the Solar Array Plasma Interaction Experiment is supposed to teach us a lot about, uh, space and...the solar, er...the sun and...stuff." (In our kids-only *L'il Insider* newsletter, your kids can match the acronym to the full name of the payload.)

What is this space shuttle carrying? Perhaps EISG. Maybe CONAP. But, we're betting it's a BREMSAT and a CRYOTP.

ACRONYM	PAYLOAD
ASP	ATTITUDE SENSOR PACKAGE
BBXRT	BROAD BAND X-RAY TELESCOPE
BREMSAT	BREMMEN SATELLITE
CAP	COMPLEX AUTONOMOUS PAYLOAD
CAPL	CAPILLARY PUMP LOOP EXPERIMENT
CMSE	CANDIDATE MATERIALS SPACE EXPOSURE
CONCAP	CONSORTIUM FOR MAT'LS DEVEL CAP
CRYOTP	CRYOGENIC TWO PHASE
CSE	CRYO SYSTEMS EXPERIMENT
DXS	DIFFUSE S-RAY SPECTROMETER
ECT	EMULSION CHAMBER TEST
EISG	EXP INVESTIGATION OF SHUTTLE GLOW
GAS	GETAWAY SPECIAL
GBA	GAS BRIDGE ASSEMBLY
GCP	GLOW CRYOHP PAYLOAD
HH-G1	HITCHHIKER-G1
IEH	INTERNATIONAL EUV HITCHHIKER
IRIM	INFRARED IMAGER
ISEM	ITA STANDARD EXPERIMENT MODULE
JDX	JOINT DAMPING EXPERIMENT
LDCE	LTD DURATION CANDIDATE MATERIALS EXP

ACRONYM	PAYLOAD
LMT	LIQUID METAL TEST EXPERIMENT
OAST	OFC OF AERONAUTICS AND SPACE TECH
ODERACS	ORBITAL DEBRIS RADAR CALIBRATION EXP
RKGM	REACTION KINETICS OF GLASS MELTS
ROMPS	ROBOT MATERIALS PROCESSING SYSTEM
SAILS	SPACE APPLICATION OF INDUSTRIAL LASER
SAMPIE	SOLAR ARRAY PLASMA INTERACTION EXP
SEH	SOLAR EUV HITCHHIKER
SHOOT	SUPERFLUID HELIUM ON-ORBIT TRANSFER EXP
SKIRT	SHUTTLE KINETIC INFRARED TEST
SLA	SHUTTLE LASER ALTIMETER
STP	SPACE TEST PAYLOAD
SUVE	SOLAR ULTRAVIOLET EXPERIMENT
TES	THERMAL ENERGY STORAGE
TPCE	TANK PRESSURE CONTROL EXPERIMENT
UVSTAR	ULTRAVIOLET SPECTROGRAPH TELESCOPE

SPACE SHUTTLE'S SECRET INGREDIENTS REVEALED!

Ever wonder how all that complex space shuttle equipment works? It's all so clear from the description that follows:

A new crew control system is now operational on the Getaway Special (GAS) Program. The new system, which replaces the GAS Autonomous Payload Controller (APC), consists of a small box, called the Bus Interface Adapter (BIA), which is attached to the JSC-supplied crew laptop computer (also known as the Payload and General Support Computer (PGSC)). SSPP-supplied software in the PGSC provides menu-driven control and display pages written specially for each GAS payload. Each payload's page names the payload and provides a description of the function of each command. The BIA/PGSC system first flew on STS-62.

The BIA/PGSC system can also be used to control Hitchhiker-JR payloads using a bus communication system that operates at speeds up to 115,200 bits per second. (The GAS system operates in a similar manner but at a much slower speed, about 100 bits per second).

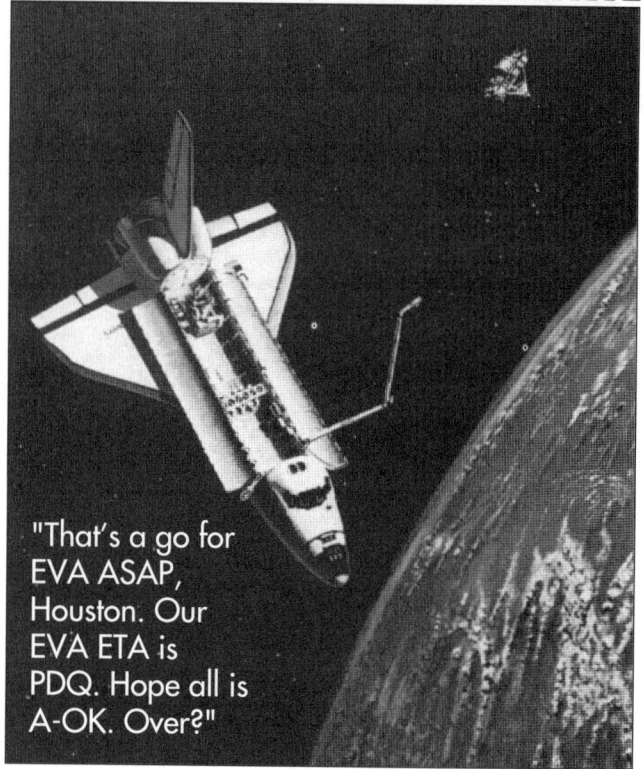

"That's a go for EVA ASAP, Houston. Our EVA ETA is PDQ. Hope all is A-OK. Over?"

SECRET GOVERNMENT STUDY COMES TO LIGHT!

Ever wonder why traffic is such a problem? Can't figure out why the subway doesn't seem to take you where you want to go? Angry that you get caught at every single red light? This excerpt from a government document on the Net might help explain things.

The International Institute for Surface Transportation Policy Studies (IISTPS) was established at San Jose State University as part of the Intermodal Surface Transportation Efficiency Act of 1991 (ISTEA). Unique among the five University Transportation Institutes designated by Congress, IISTPS' focus is on international surface transportation policy issues as related to three primary responsibilities: research, education, and technology transfer. IISTPS receives policy oversight from an internationally respected Board of Trustees, who represent all of the major surface transportation modes.

Linda "Vegomaniac" McCartney and Yoko "Emergency Broadcast System" Ono are set to square off in the ring in a Don King-sponsored bout. The event, dubbed "The Screecher in Palm Beach-er," is scheduled for early October. When asked about it, King said, "Hey man, all my fighters are in jail. I got no money! Somebody's gotta fight!"

Reporting from the edge of credibility, I'm Juan Bootsie.
Contact Juan Bootsie at: an31291@anon.penet.fi or check out his archives via FTP in the /pub/hamlet directory at ftp.netcom.com.

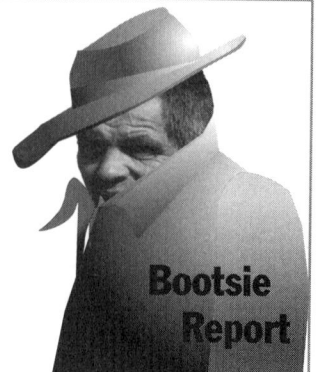

Bootsie Report

V-PLOT MANIFESTO MEANINGLESS

When we ran across a university document entitled "A V-Plot Manifesto," we thought it might make for exciting reading. We'll let you be the judge.

A dynamic plot is malleable, meant to be interacted with and changeable by the user. A dynamic plot must have a running program of some sort behind it, ready to update parts of the plot as they are changed. For example, we might plot a seismic section on a screen, and then overlay hyperbolas on it. As we move the mouse around, the overlaid hyperbola changes position under the control of a running program.

For static plotting, device-independence is the most important factor. This requires keeping all the resolution present in the original floating-point calculations in the user's program, and doing things in as device-independent a way as possible. We can't know what sorts of devices we will want to later reproduce plots on; they may be quite different from the device we used to view the original. In particular, typical hardcopy devices like laser printers have much higher resolutions than typical interactive devices like Sun workstations. Furthermore, many hardcopy devices are vector and text oriented, while most interactive devices are raster or polygon oriented. ∎

Why are these men smiling? You wouldn't understand if they told you.

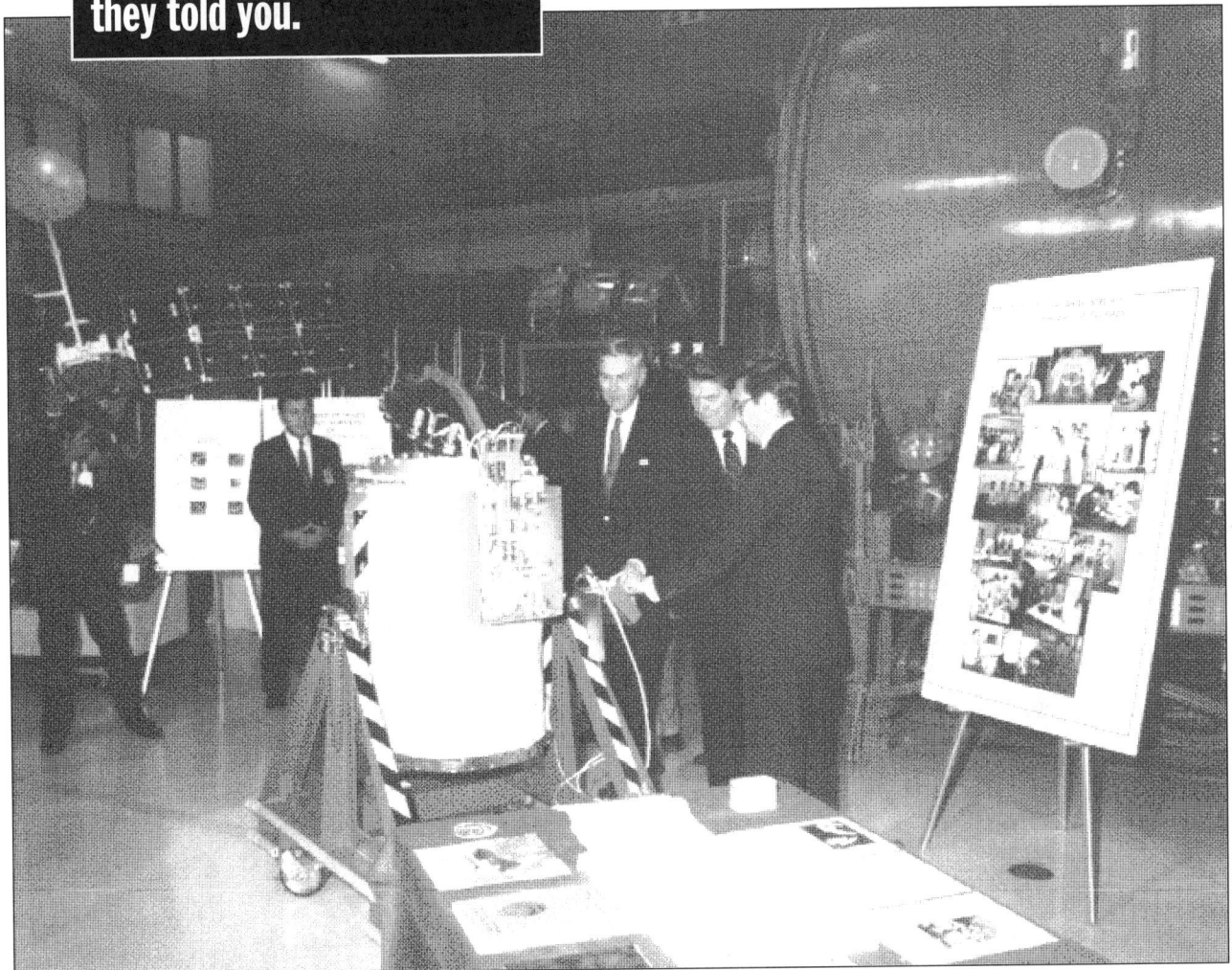

Unlocking the Mysteries Behind Rogaine

Rogaine—All Things to Some, Some Things to All

The Internet isn't all things to all people, but in my long years of working at the *Insider*, I've come to learn that it *can* be all things to some people and some things to all people. (Billy Shulehoffer of Shulehoffer's Junkyard in Waynesville, North Carolina, has picked up on this cultural mantra and turned it into a catchy advertising slogan: "Shulehoffer's has all parts for some cars and some parts for all cars!" But that's another story.)

For the denizens of the **talk.bizarre** newsgroup, the Internet is a place to, well, talk about bizarre stuff. (By the way, if any talk.bizarre regulars realize they've been written up by the *Insider*, they'll take it as yet another sign of the impending apocalypse, the death of the Net, and the end of talk.bizarre. Sorry, guys.)

Consider this rather pointless and silly thread, which is packed with non sequiturs, minor flames, and nit-picking tit-for-tats—everything we love about the Internet. It's all here, as we search for an answer to the question, "What is Rogaine?"

Rogaine Monster Destroyed on Film!

Rogaine is the wonder-drug that lets old dinosaur bands like Yes, ELO, and Genesis keep making albums. If you took it away, they'd be out in the cold. In fact, it explains why modern Yes and ELO and Genesis albums don't sound like the groups' albums they made when they were in their prime—they're drugged out of their minds on Rogaine.
—Scott McMahan (mcmahan@hominy)

Hmm . . . I don't know if I buy that. By the looks of things, Phil Collins definitely ain't using Rogaine, and he's just about the worst of the lot of them. Then again, Willie Nelson definitely takes it: "I can't wait to get back on the Rogaine." And Peter Garrett (bald vocalist for Midnight Oil) isn't going to need it.
—William Chris Graham (wcgraham@acs.ucalgary.ca)

Isn't Rogaine a kind of lettuce?
—Eric Mankin (mankin@mizar.usc.edu)

Finally, someone who knows about these things. Yes, of course, used in the classic Seizure Salad.
Eat two, Brute!
—Darren (darren@netcom.com)

For what it's worth, Rogaine was originally used to alleviate arthritis pain.

Wrong, wrong, wrong! Rogaine was initially developed as an anti-hypertensive (i.e., blood-pressure control) medication, which is why the makers of Rogaine recommend that people with low blood pressure or who are taking other blood pressure medications *avoid* Rogaine.

I hate to nit-pick, but you're both wrong. Kurt Rogaine is the guy who killed himself by eating pop-rocks and coke earlier this year.

Not even close. Rogaine was a popular, if illegal, drug in the 1970s. Eric Clapton wrote a tune about it: "She don't lie, she don't lie, she don't lie . . . ROGAINE!"

Well, you've got the song right but it was J.J. Cale's tune, just "covered" by Clapton. (Oh my ghod, I just contributed to this annoying bandwasting thread. Oh won't somebody please shoot me?!)

Rogaine is the spiritual mantra of the Society for Being Kind to Howard Cosell, explicitly set up as a fund for the preservation of Cosell's ravings on boxing matches, and football's memorable occasions, e.g., sub-freezing Super Bowl plays during the dawn of the steroid era in big-time sports. Rogaine is explicitly written on the banner of the Cosell Society's main building. It appears in icky green script emblazoned on a golden banner with tassels.
—Andrew W. Beckwith (ab7b@andrew.cmu.edu)

No, no, no! Rogaine is a pepper spray sold to Manhattan yuppies to scare away the homeless. Ravers have found that, when diluted 1:100, it leads to a pleasant melancholy; it is quite popular in chill areas (along with Brian Eno muzak).
It also sends ferrets into sexual ecstasy.
—Warren Neckels (warrenec@news.delphi.com)

Rogaine was one of the monsters on Monster Isle in the Japanese movie "Destroy All Monsters."
—(ez003045@dale.ucdavis.edu)

Wrong. It's a really bad headache some people get sometimes. Ask your doctor about it.
—James E. Lee (jelee@ucdavis.edu)

No, no, no! It's part of that saying that Scooby-Doo has every time Shaggy asks him to do something, like suggesting that Scooby hide behind a suit of armor while Shaggy flushes a ghost out of the closet:
Shaggy: "If this works out, there will be a couple of Scooby Snacks waiting for you!"
Scooby: "ROGAINE Raggy!
—Darren(darren@netcom.com) n

Bootsie Report

Zachry Zebulon Topp of LaGrange, Georgia, has had enough and isn't taking it anymore. The 68-year-old farmer (known to his friends as "Z.Z.") says he's tired of round-the-clock prank calls and "them folks who keep riding by all hours of the day and night." He attributes his woes to the popularity of a certain rock group from Texas, and is planning on taking his complaints to court to force the group to change its name.

"Heck, I've had this name longer than they have, seems I should have a right to keep it," Topp says. "And I'm named after my two granddaddies, so they can't say I stole it."

Due to incessant phone activity, it's virtually impossible to reach Topp day or night, so he has asked that all inquiries be directed to his lawyer, Leonard Skinnerd.

Reporting from the edge of credibility, I'm Juan Bootsie.
Contact Juan Bootsie at: an31291@anon.penet.fi or check out his archives via FTP in the /pub/hamlet directory at ftp.netcom.com.

Socks to Negotiate N. Korea Nukes Pact!

North Koreans Request Visit from Socks in Arms Talks

The place: The White House Briefing Room.

The time: December 10, 1993; 1:27 a.m. E.S.T.

The players: Clinton Administration spokesperson Dee Dee Myers and the members of the White House press corps.

In this episode, Dee Dee Myers calls a White House briefing, even though she has nothing to say. Nonetheless, she tackles such weighty issues as the HUD budget, touchy negotiations with North Korea, and what time Socks appears on the "Home" show. Will Socks join Jimmy Carter in ticklish talks in North Korea? Let's listen.

Ms. Myers: There are no announcements, so if you all have questions—

Q: Dee Dee, what is the President doing today in the meetings and all that he's having? What are these meetings?

Ms. Myers: A number of things: he has a health care meeting; he has another budget meeting in which they are looking at the HUD budget; Secretary Cisneros will be here. Other meetings with staff-planning, looking ahead, a couple of interviews.

Q: Any meetings on North Korea at all?

Ms. Myers: I think that it's likely.

Q: Anything else?

Ms. Myers: *People* magazine. And I'm sure all of you were riveted to your sets during the live "Home Show."

Q: Who else is going to get to be in on the meeting on the HUD budget?

Q: What show?

Ms. Myers: The "Home Show," live. It was fabulous. **Socks was the star, he stole the show.**

Q: Who else is in that? All of the President's economic team?

Q: Why is the President having a meeting on the HUD budget?

Ms. Myers: The President is reviewing the budget, department by department, with the various Secretaries and department directors as part of his overall review of the budget.

Q: Is this considered the appeal stage?

Ms. Myers: This is an opportunity for people to raise their concerns, sure. They have—they know that their targets are based on the discretionary limits required through last year's economic plan. And they've been asked to present budgets that live within those limits. Some departments have asked for—have outlined the things that they think are important that they'd like to see above and beyond those caps.

The Socks Chronicles

In this ongoing series of behind-the-scenes looks at the inner workings of the White House, the *Internet Insider* follows Socks, America's First Cat, through another harrowing press conference. In this official White House document obtained exclusively by the *Insider*, you'll see how the White House press corps is once again sidetracked from the real issues facing our government to consider the life and times of that lovable kitty, Socks.

Why the media obsession with the President's cat? Is there something the White House doesn't want us to know? Is "Socks" a secret code word that sends reporters into a trance of distraction and diversion? Why does the press offer only a 30-second sound bite from a 30-minute meeting? Does Socks prefer frolicking in the Lincoln Bedroom or on the South Lawn? These questions and more are answered as we present another installment of *The Socks Chronicles*.

photo courtesy of The White House

Q: Dee Dee, who does the "Home Show," and has it been played yet?

Ms. Myers: Yeah, it aired live and it's a syndicated program that airs on ABC in most markets. And the hosts—

Q: Gary Collins and Sarah Purcell.

Ms. Myers: Thank you—Gary Collins and Sarah Purcell. That slipped my mind. Thanks.

More Losers Than Winners in Net Spelling Bee!

FREIND · LUV · GOVERMENT · POTATOE · KAT

POTATO

Have you ever noticed how when people rite stuff for email or internet they dont really spell to carefuly or edit they're writings for gramar? we seee that alot here at the *Internet Insider*, and to be perfectly honest with you, it realy makes us mad! why dont this people learn to spell?

The answer is not a simple one. Some people don't consider the Internet a worthy forum of careful spelling and grammar. Others have a hard time typing. Still others simply get a little excited and make understandable mistakes in translating their thoughts to postings online. Whatever the reason, flaming bad spellers is a cherished pastime among many on the Net.

Aside from spelling problems, the most common grammatical goofs we see are ones made by those suffering from CRAPS. Now, before you snicker at the misfortune of others, please understand that CRAPS (Capitalization and Random Apostrophe and Punctuation Syndrome) is a very real disorder diagnosed by the *Insider's* medical editor.

Here's a writing sample from a CRAPS victim: "If you think you're Opinion is more Valid than mine, your in for a Big surprise. The interNet let's me say what I want, and they're is'nt anything you or you'r Powerful friend's can do about it!"

While the above example is sad, there's nothing funny about CRAPS and its debilitating results. So what makes for a funny misspelling on the Net? Usually, it's a *double entendre* created by poor spelling or a grammatical *faux pas* that draws the attention of spell-flamers. This section offers a few prime examples, and you'll start to notice them more often as you look for them.

Good luck! we hope your sucesful in you're own personal search for bad spelers!

200

The "Horrible Truth"

Posted to alt.conspiracy:

Why has our government kept the truth regarding Spam hidden from us all of these years? Because they have sold us out to the aliens in trade for some paultry beam

^^^^^^^

weaponry and mind-control technology. The agreement stated that if we would ignore the cattle mutilations and "look the other way" when they abducted our citizens, they would provide us with the bargained-for technology.
>>You misspelled "poultry-beam weaponry." Hope this helps.

From this posting in alt.mcdonalds, can you catch the self-flaming spelling goof in the last paragraph?

And so? Guess who pays? We do. McDonald's will raise the price of their goods in order to pay off a settlement, or insurance rates will gradually increase. You won't notice it when you go to McDonald's and probably the effects of settlements like these take years to impact on prices, but eventually they do. You can bet on that.

>The setalment she recived was a little less than what McD's makes from one day of coffie sales.

>*First, learn how to spell. It's settlement, received, coffee.*

>I thought I made that clear in my post and if you would re-read the original post, you'll see that I say that the combined effect of frivolous lawsuits is to drive up prices. Maybe you're too thick-skulled to realize what "combined effect" means and, if that's true, then chalk up another mark against the American Educational System.

Net Resources

So you're anxious to see some wacky misspellings posted around the Internet? Well, spending five minutes in most any newsgroup is sure to give you an eyeful, but for quality misspellings, keep an eye on the following newsgroups: **alt.flame. spelling**, **rec.humor**, **alt.best.of.internet**, and **alt.humor.best-of-usenet**.

List Service

If you decide to flame someone else for a spelling goof, make sure you don't commit the dreaded self-flame set-up by perpetrating a spelling goof of your own in your spell-flame. Here are the most common self-flaming goofs we see:

1) Your so stupid you don't even . . .
2) Hey, stupid, you mispelled . . .
3) You need to buy a new dictionery . . .
4) Either you cna't spell or you haev a problem typing!
5) Don't you mean "seperate," not "separate"? Your so stupid . . .

Throw out your "dicshunaries" spell hard!!

An exchange from alt.flame.spelling (the names have been changed to protect the linguistically challenged).

>**Bobby and You suffer from a mental hang-up that is very annoying to us normal people. It is called Anal retention. Hence Danny has an symbolic cork in his . . .**

>*No, idiot-boy, read it again. You weren't raving at "Bobby", you were screeching at "Walter." At least get something right.*

>**BTW, I don't "wantabe" a teacher. Now, You want to feel superior!**

>*No, you simply feel inferior. Why do think that I am attacking you? Are you always this paranoid?*

>**I'm going to bring this group to its knees. I and my bad spelling brethren will, smash the baracades and drag every one of you pompus good spellers out of you ivory towwers and in to the mean streets of the NEt. Each one of you will be forced to drink a tall glass of Humliation in Public. And renunce Good grammer and right spelling.**

>*Subject: They Might Be Labotomized*

>**You know, They Might Be Labotomized.**

>*Does he mean "lobotomized?" Or does this have something to do with laboratories? But of course, being from AOL who am I to say? Surveys show that two out of three lobotomized USENET readers prefer laboratory lobotomies over, say, lavatory lobotomies. I am not making this up.*

>**I'd rather have a bottle in front of me than a frontal lobotomy. Of course both would be nice . . .**

Please E-Nail me if you v ish to talk further.

Posted to alt.personals

>**I am a single white bearded 5"11" brown haired, blue eyed male, I am smart, literate, funny. Please E-Nail me if you wish to talk further.**   ^^^^^^

>*Now there's an excellent freudian slip if I've ever seen one.*

Posted to alt.security, comp.security.misc, comp.security.unix

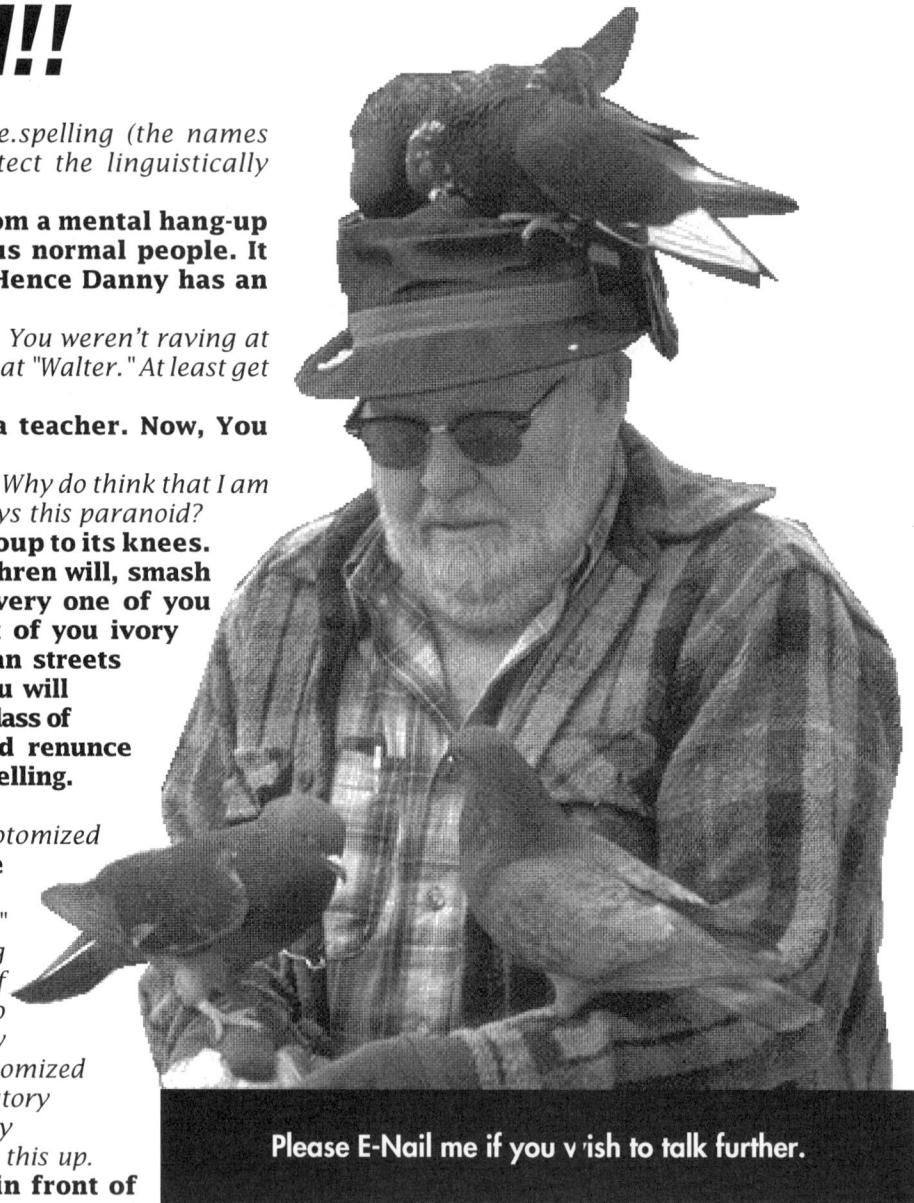

>**If by "Unix viruses" you mean "just any kind of computer virus, if it is found on a Unix machine," then there are much more cases. First, we regularly get report of Master Boot Sector infectors that have infected an IBM PC compatible, running som brand of Unix. Many people seem to ignore that the MBR infectors are not OS-specific and can infect *any* IBM**

PC, regardless of the OS it runs. Explain this for the uniformed, please.

^^^^^^^^^

>*For which branch of the armed forces do you want me to explain it?*

Posted to rec.arts.movies (subject: True Lies=facist propaganda)

>**Humiliating your enemy before you kill them is humerus.**

>*It's especially a giggle if you rap them smartly on the femur.*

>**(Our Motto: You brachium, we mendum.)** ■

THE USENET ORACLE HAS PONDERED YOUR QUESTION DEEPLY. YOUR QUESTION WAS:

What is it?

AND IN RESPONSE, THUS SPAKE THE ORACLE:

Well, the obvious answer is that it is a pronoun (more specifically, a neuter pronoun of the third person singular). But since you've gone to the trouble of asking the Oracle this question, instead of simply looking *it* up in the dictionary, you must be talking about the *it* of the ancient legends . . .

In the ancient days, when the earth and sky were young, war had not yet been invented. The young warriors sat around the council fire and grew restless, for they had nothing to do. So chief Jumping Eagle saw that the warriors were restless, and decided that they must occupy themselves with a game. So they played tag.

Chief Jumping Eagle was the first to be *it*, and he tagged Dancing Sparrow. And Dancing Sparrow tagged Running Bobcat. And Running Bobcat tagged Walking Horse and Walking Horse tagged Sleeping Moose. But Sleeping Moose was the slowest of all the warriors, and he could not tag anyone.

So Sleeping Moose said, "I will tag the west wind, so that the west wind will be it." And he tagged the west wind. But then on the next day, the wind blew from the east, and tagged Sleeping Moose right back. So then Sleeping Moose said, "I will tag the water in the river, so that the water will be it." And he tagged the water, and the water ran down the Big River, and the Big River ran down to the Big Sea. And many moons passed, and the water became the clouds, and the rain fell on Sleeping Moose, and tagged Sleeping Moose.

So Sleeping Moose said, "I'm sick of this. I will tag the big mountain, which does not blow as the wind, and does not run as the water. The big mountain will stay where it is, and will not tag me back. So Sleeping Moose tagged the big mountain, and the big mountain stayed where it was, and did not tag Sleeping Moose back.

And the big mountain was *it* for many, many seasons. The warriors had grandsons and their grandsons had grandsons, until the medicine man they called Oracle climbed the big mountain, to speak with the spirits of nature. And the Oracle said to the spirit of the big mountian "Big Mountain Spirit, will you speak to me?" And the spirit of the mountain said "Yes, I will speak to you, Oracle." Oracle said "What do you have to say to me?", and the big mountain said "Tag, you're it! Hahahaha!"

AND ORACLE WAS IT FOR MANY MORE SEASONS, UNTIL UNSUSPECTING SUPPLICANT CAME TO ORACLE. AND UNSUSPECTING SUPPLICANT ASKED ORACLE:

"What is *it?*"

AND ORACLE REPLIED:

"TAG!!! _You_ are it!!!! No Tag-Backs!!! Hahahahahaha"

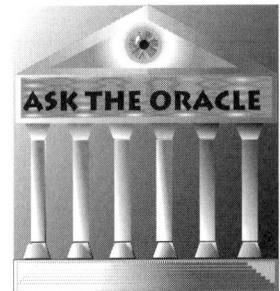

ARE YOU A SNAG?

By Dennis Hinkamp
(dennish@extsparc.agsci.usu.edu)

Like everything else cool, inane, or trendy, it has taken a bit longer for the Sensitive New Age Guy (SNAG) movement to reach this part of the world. After all, most people moved to the West to get away from the androgynous decay and gender cold-war stalemate that louds the rest of the country. Well, maybe I should only speak for myself.

Not the skinny wimp, Alan Alda type, the **SNAG** is the target audience for Cotton Dockers. He is likely to be someone who drinks espresso after working out on his Soloflex machine. He may still want to hold Cindy Crawford hostage for a weekend, but he keeps it to himself. **SNAG**s are popping up all over the West faster than Wal-Mart franchises.

Check this list to see if you or a loved one has been affected. Early warning signs of being a **SNAG** are

1) Have you said "you look like you could use a hug" or used the word "*snuggle*" in the last week?

2) Are you so conscious of being polite that you find yourself saying "*excuse me*," even when you walk into mail boxes and parked cars?

3) Have you ever described your clothes as "*fun*" (as in "this is really a fun tie, don't you think?") or borrowed an item of clothing from your father to wear in public?

4) Do you think those unplugged CDs by former drug-soaked, ear-splitting, blood-spitting rock bands "*are a much better forum for the true meaning of their lyrics.*"

5) You never use the word "*chick*" or "*hooters*" unless it is in reference to birds, and even then only if they are free-range or spotted.

The *Insider* offices are located in Los Angeles, but it's not what you think. We don't sit around at Spago or Mezalluna all day, sipping Pellegrino and munching pesto pasta. The *Insider* building is on, as they say, the other side of the tracks. Even still, we see our share of Sensitive, New-Age Guys (**SNAG**s). With their gentle compassion and restrained ruggedness, they're spoiling it for the rest of us. Women who date **SNAG**s impose **SNAG** standards on every man: they want us to beat up a mugger, then feel bad about how he's a victim of society. Get wise. Use the handy list here to spot **SNAG**s and take 'em out before they ruin everything!

INSIDE

OPINION

The right clothes and hair aren't enough to make you a SNAG. You have to have the *attitude*.

6) You named your drooling, hairy couch-hound or fur-spitting feline after a famous impressionist painter.

7) You breathe a sigh of relief when you approach one of those automatic opening doors, because heading towards a manual door with a woman throws you into emotional grid-lock. "*Do I open it for her to be polite? Is opening it for her condescending? Should I allow her to open it for me? What about the door, does it have feelings too?*"

8) You traded your pick-up truck for a "*sports utility vehicle.*"

9) You are confused by your conflicting impulses. You know that Supreme Court Justice Clarence Thomas was guilty, but you'd still like to know where you could rent those movies Sen. Orrin Hatch mentioned in the hearings. Or, while watching "Baywatch," you suddenly feel compelled to write a letter to the TV station complaining about their improper representation of CPR techniques.

10) You pronounce all three syllables of the word "*opera.*"

11) You sport a "pony nob." That is, not quite a tail, but a snippet of excess hair that makes you look something of a cross between an Edwardian prince and a rock musician.

12) You are starting to use these words interchangeably:

> **mow the lawn** / *landscape*
> **fix stuff** / *carpentry*
> **move stuff** / *remodeling*
> **coffee** / *espresso*
> **spaghetti** / *pasta*
> **movies** / *films*
> **Playboy magazine** / *sexist exploitive trash*
> **nude photography books**
> / *artistic rendering of the female form*

If you are feeling a little queasy right now, don't worry, hunting season is just around the corner.

Originally published in the "Slightly Off Center" *column in the* Logan Herald Journal *and the* Salt Lake City Event Magazine. ■

A celebrity who will remain nameless was involved in an incident no one will talk about involving another celebrity whose identity cannot be confirmed. Sources close to both parties are denying everything.

*Reporting from the edge of credibility, I'm Juan Bootsie.*Contact Juan Bootsie at: an31291@anon.penet.fi or check out his archives via FTP in the /pub/hamlet directory at ftp.netcom.com.

Bootsie Report

---

beverage containers on my desk

LIFE @ LARGE

haiku by John Perry (jpperry@oahu.cs.ucla.edu) posted to talk.bizarre

*lavendar plastic
cup I got from Grand Canyon
piece of trash, it leaks*

*cup with photo of
date at an amusement
park but no monorail*

*UCLA cup
half full of hot darjeeling
it's refillable*

*plastic coffee cup
"integrated solution"
is Art*Enterprise*

*black ceramic cup
one more Inference giveaway hot technology*

P.S. Bonus:
comestibles on shelf haiku

*case of Diet Coke
half a case of Dr. P.
and some cans in fridge*

Life, Death and the Internet

When people first start using the Internet, they're often shocked by its scope. They discover a computer network that stretches around the world, with tens of millions of users, all of whom can communicate with each other in the twinkling of an eye.

At first glance, it seems there isn't a corner of the globe that isn't reached by the Internet. But a closer look reveals we've still got a long way to go before the entire world is wired. And there are plenty of people in the world who would just as soon not be wired, thank you very much.

Take the natives of the Andaman Islands, for instance. The Andamans, a chain of about 200 small islands in the Bay of Bengal, off the coast of India, are not quite ready for the Internet. It seems they spend most of their time tending to their fires, which they never allow to burn out.

The problem, you see, is that the Andamans haven't yet figured out how to make fire. And they're not alone. Scattered groups of pygmies up and down the Congo river buy fire from nearby Bantu tribes, and it was only recently that the Tasadays of the Philippines figured out the fire trick.

The idea that some people have to constantly watch over a pile of burning sticks just to survive makes logging on to check your e-mail seem a little less urgent. It serves to put things in perspective. In fact, about the only things most of us share with Andamans are the absolute basics: birth, life, and death. Like the Andamans, we enter and leave this world alone.

No matter whether we are cyber-linked whiz-kids or stone-age fire-tenders, we all must face our own mortality. For many, these moments end up as personal narratives, essays, and stories shared across the Internet. Perhaps it's the Net's electronic anonymity that allows people to share thoughts and stories that they could never share face-to-face.

Whatever the reason, we are all the richer for it.

INSIDE
OPINION

My Own Blood

By Ellen Snell Adams (snelladams@aol.com)

It was the strangest thing. We were right behind the black truck and I knew it was going too fast. And I looked at Dan a second before it crashed. He was taking it all in, but he was placid, almost analytical: a raised brow was the only thing that betrayed anything out of the ordinary.

At the intersection, the driver should have turned left, but she was going way too fast. She jumped the curb and hit a light-pole. I heard the awful metal-clash: like a bulldozer scraping up bare pavement. The nose of the truck crumpled and the two opposing sides bent in toward each other.

"Oh, my God," Dan said. Then, more slowly, separating the three words as if they were separate sentences, "Oh. My. God."

I just sat silent. I had frozen. I was lead.

"We've got to help her," Dan said, and he was right.

But all I could think was, No, we don't. No, we don't.

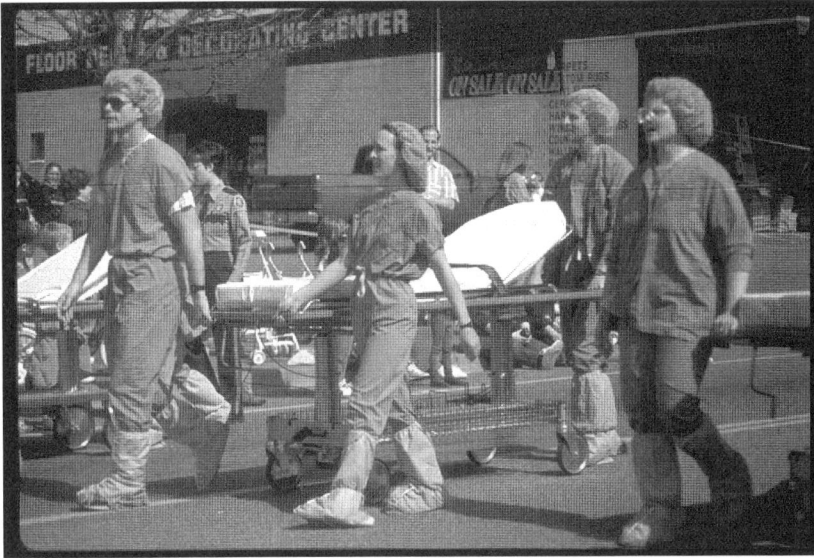

I said nothing, still.

We had gone through the light, and I was afraid Dan was going to slam on the brakes and we'd get hit.

"Oh, oh, look at that. Will you look at that," Dan said.

Dan pulled in the driveway of Pat's Snack Shack and drove out onto the grass, turning right toward the wreck. From this new vantage point, I could see the windshield was all smashed into a dangerous, sharp filigree. I couldn't see inside. But I knew she was in there. Dan got out first.

The ground seemed strange to me as I stepped down from our own little truck. I ran, but it seemed as if I was walking.

Dan was already pulling the woman from the cab when I reached the truck, which was popping and sputtering. He had his arms wrapped around her, as if she were a tipsy girlfriend who had just fallen backwards.

There was blood on her head, in a pulpy design, like a tiara that had slipped and cut her on the forehead. Her nose was smashed. I looked down. Her sweater was caught on something and was pulling up on her stomach. Her white skin and pink flowered brassiere were exposed. I ran over to pull her sweater down. She grabbed my head.

"Get my keys," she said, "I don't want nobody to steal my truck."

The truck was ticking and smoking like a bomb. Her legs were stuck in the cab.

I untangled myself from her grasp and stepped back. "Get her away from the . . . " I paused. I was going to say "car."

No, that was wrong, I thought. "The thing," I said. I started to cry. I felt so waifish. I was being no help at all.

"I'm doing my best," Dan said, suddenly terse, yanking on the woman and simultaneously trying to push his glasses up the bridge of his nose. "See what her legs are stuck on."

Her legs seemed to disappear into the wreckage. I pulled at her jeans. I saw the cuff of one leg and tugged.

"Ow. Bitch," the woman said.

I started to cry harder. Dan looked at me as if he didn't under-stand. He kept pulling backwards.

By now, other people had stopped to help or to gawk. A man who looked like my father came running up. He had parked his stationwagon in the lot at the Snack Shack, and had run through the weeds. I could see a woman and three small kids getting out of the car.

"Should I call 911?" he asked.

"Yes, please," Dan said, finally pulling her legs free. Her Wrangler jeans were soaked with long vertical stripes of blood.

I should have been calling 911, I thought. I stopped crying and looked at the sky. It was starting to cloud up. It was going to rain.

"Just put her, just lay her here on the grass," I said, pointing.

Dan nodded and put her down very gently. She was a big-boned woman, and Dan found it difficult to support her weight. He was relieved to set her down.

I went over to our truck and grabbed my white windbreaker and my purple umbrella. The jacket was too big for me. I had worn it when I was pregnant and stretched it all out. Now I bunched it up and made a pillow for the woman. She smelled like alcohol and carnations. I tried to straighten out her limbs, like she was some big doll I had found.

"Don't do that. She might have a spinal injury, and you could paralyze her," Dan said. He had taken his glasses off, and was mopping his sweaty forehead with his arm. Suddenly Dan sounded like a physician. I wanted to cry again. But I didn't.

Her head was lolling back and forth. I was worried about the stickers in the grass pricking her head. Her legs were crushed, and her nose was broken, but I was worried the stickers would hurt her.

From far away, I heard the siren. It began to thunder, too, and a light rain began to fall, misting the blood and the smoking truck. I crouched down and put up the umbrella, and held it over the woman's face.

"You kids, stay back. Back by the car. I mean it," said the woman from the stationwagon, who was shouting at her children as she walked slowly towards us. The kids all looked very scared. They didn't make a move towards the crash.

The ambulance jumped the curb and hurtled toward our little crowd. I thought they'd mow us all down. But instead, with crisp efficiency, the three-member emergency team jumped out and sized up the situation. They each began peeling out bandages and cutting away her clothes. One of them produced an oxygen tank. It clanked towards us noisily. They moved me and the umbrella out of the way.

"What happened, sir?" one of them asked Dan.

"I think she's drunk. I think. I mean, I don't know. She was going too fast. She should have turned. " Dan couldn't articulate.

A police car drove up. An officer began putting flares in the intersection. I thought that was stupid. The crash wasn't in the intersection.

Dan came over and put his arm around me. "Oh, honey," he said.

I let the umbrella fall to the ground. For a moment, I buried my head on his shoulder. The woman's blood was on Dan's shirt. We looked at the traffic bunching up on the freeway. People were slowing to look.

As they loaded her in the ambulance, I heard the woman say, "Hey. I can taste my own blood."

Originally published in the Nerdnosh Story Digest *mailing list. Reprinted here by permission.*

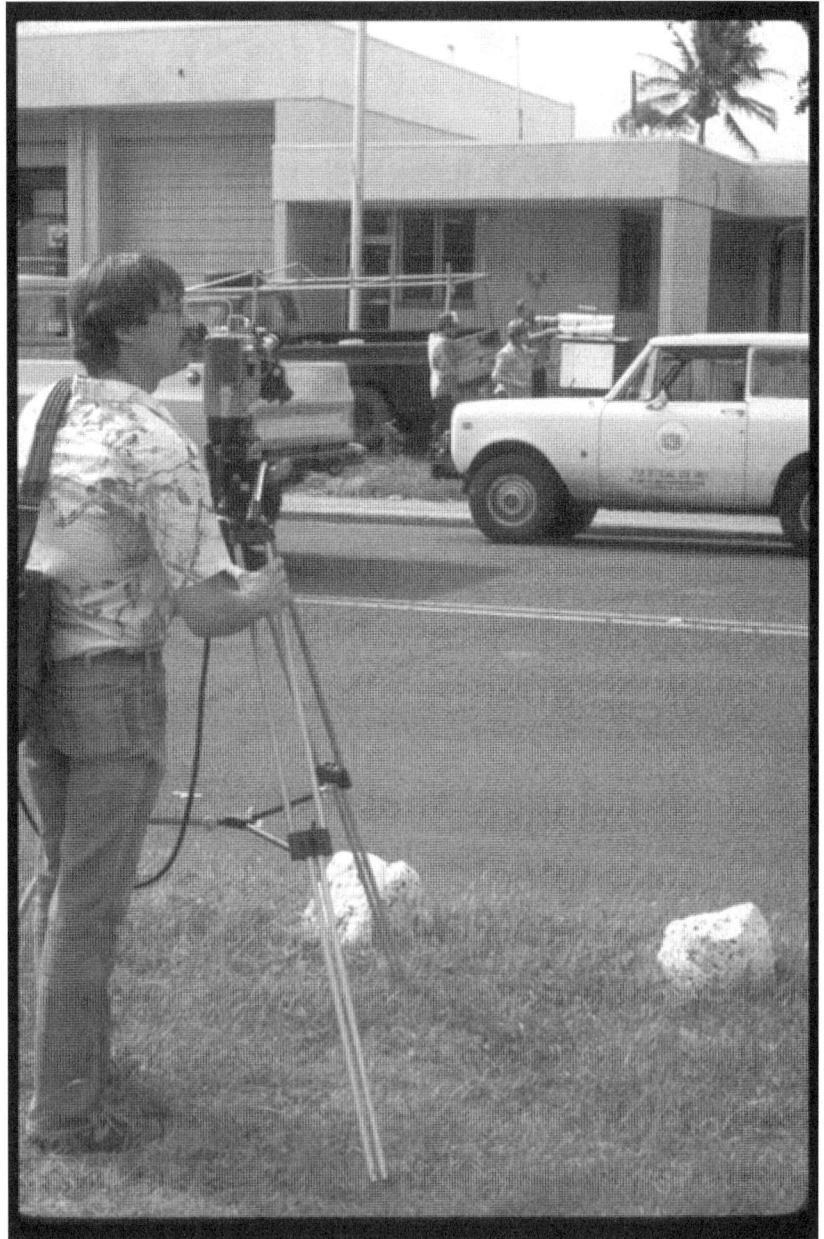

La Mort de Ma Mère

By Sean Sheehhan (bossman@iaccess.za)

It's 12:05 a.m. Time to come. They said so.

I wrestle my mutinous machine over the mountain until we hit the motorway on the other side. It's dead straight now. Full Wellie. No prisoners.

100. I'm jailbait. 120. So what? 140. So the fuck what? At 150 m.p.h., I move the car over to straddle the white line separating the twin lanes. I'm flying; inches from living. She's lying; inches from death.

My father is waiting on the sidewalk outside his house. He eases his bulk into the passenger seat and sighs. He doesn't say much. He never does.

The high-care ward is small: two opposing rows of two beds. She's lying in the right-hand corner—a tiny, withered figure trapped in a web of plastic piping and electrical wiring. The room is darkened, lit by the monitors and the nurse's small desk lamp. Her oxygen supply hisses balefully from the hole in the mask. I glance up at the monitoring machinery as the ubiquitous hospital smell irritates my sinuses and dries out my lenses.

BP 64/31; Mean Arterial Pressure (MAP) 43. Pulse 100. Heart

is steady; short, sharp spikes on the display. Cardiac barbed wire against the Reaper. BP sucks. BP sucks live rats through a straw.

We go to opposite sides of the bed. I arrange the mask which was pushing hard against eyes jammed tightly shut. A waterlogged, puffy hand each. Heavy and lifeless.

She hated the physiotherapy; a high-risk attempt to drain the twin swamps in her chest when the pipe through her back into her left lung provided insufficient seepage. I look down at the jar at my feet. The level of the evil green liquid rises and falls. Rises and falls. Slightly.

My father tried to stop the physiotherapy. Since her session yesterday she hasn't opened her eyes. The machines say she's alive. They should know. Tori slips into my mind, uninvited, the red-head from hell:

[whoo hoo . . . her time is getting nearer . . .]

May was monosyllable month after a rollercoaster year. Hi. Drink. Sore. The daily shopping basket of IVs and drugs from the dispensary. Now it's morphine. Insidiously; just another needle in her arm.

They're very understanding. Unlimited visiting time. Unlimited time to stare at one another and refine our non-communication. I flirt with the nurses. I'm like that.

I look up at the bank of monitors: BP 63/27, MAP 42, Pulse 95. Just slightly worse than stable. Tori, voice rising, keening:

[wooo hooo . . . her time is getting closer wooo hooo . . . her time to be a ghost]

Two hours pass. I drift in and out of dream sequences. Opening trapdoors in my mind. I shiver a lot. It's not cold. The damn tune won't leave me alone.

She tried to light a cigarette while wearing an oxygen mask. They watched her more carefully after that. Was that a month ago?

She demanded the Last Rites. When they said it was Time, I reluctantly made the call to the priest. That was a fortnight ago.

What's left of the family flew in, said their au revoirs to the husk ensnared in the web, and left. That was last week.

The IC nurse takes her readings and writes them. In case of later litigation, she confides. She tells me that my mother can sense our presence. Otherwise she'd have "slipped away" hours ago.

Time to take a walk.

The nurse calls to us in the garden. When we enter the room the cardiograph is a chaotic semi-sine wave; her defenses are breached. I look up. BP 52/26. MAP 33. Pulse 47. I'm not ready for this. Is that relevant?

The nurse has pulled a screen around the bed. A sop to the other patients, I guess. My mother doesn't appear to care much. We hold her swollen, heavy gray hands again as the nurse inserts some sort of vacuum into her mouth. She tells me it's usually quite ugly if they choke.

The attendant machinery gracefully records her steepening decline. It too, in its turn, becomes disinterested. Flatline. Electronic indifference.

My father leaves the room. He doesn't say much. He never does. I walk around the bed and take the waterlogged corpse into my arms. It's remarkably heavy now. I kiss its forehead. Replace it gently. Silence the oxygen-snake.

It's 4:15. Time to go. They said so.

Originally published in the Nerdnosh Story Digest *mailing list. Reprinted here by permission.*

Former head of MGM Louis B. Mayer rose from the dead this week and demanded his old job back. Mayer, gaunt, hollow-eyed and wearing a dusty suit way, way out of style explained, "Hey, with all the moolah that's being tossed around these days, I couldn't stand not getting my cut of the pie." Doctors and theologians are monitoring developments.

Reporting from the edge of credibility, I'm Juan Bootsie.
Contact Juan Bootsie at: an31291@anon.penet.fi or check out his archives via FTP in the /pub/hamlet directory at ftp.netcom.com.

Bootsie Report

Maggie's Loss

By Julie Parameter (jparment@indiana.edu)

Margaret lives across the street from me. She's young and pretty, with thick brown hair and dainty teeth that look too small for her mouth. She lives in a neat little white house with her husband and six-year-old son. She's a stay-at-home mom who volunteers at kindergarten and is careful about keeping her yard tidy. By looking at her, you'd never be able to tell the terrible sorrow that she has endured.

Five years ago, right after we'd moved into our house, I got a call at work from my husband. He was freaked. Something horrible and unspeakable had just happened. Maggie's three-year-old son, Jacob, lay dead in the street. It was a freak accident. The little boy had snuck out of the house and had been run over by Maggie's brother. He died instantly.

My husband was right there. He heard the crying and the sound of the ambulance. He heard Margaret's husband arriving home screaming, "What the *hell* happened?" But worst of all is the memory of the little blanket-covered bundle lying in the street. The police and the coroner came and went. The boy's body was removed. When I came home, there were bloodstains on the street.

After that, we didn't see much of Maggie for a long time. A couple of years ago, she began to talk about it. She says that after it happened, she stayed in her room for a long time. She thinks that she was in shock for two whole years. Then she just started putting one foot in front of the other, for the sake of her other child. She says that she is better now. And she is.

These days, Maggie and I are very close in the way that women get when their children play together. Together, we complain about men. We talk in great detail about her attempts to conquer infertility. We discuss kids and fashion and housework. We gossip extensively about the other neighbors. She tells me that she knows that she is an overprotective mother. Who can blame her? Sometimes we talk about Jacob, sometimes we don't. But it doesn't matter what we discuss, because behind everything we say stands the shadow of that little lost boy.

Originally published in the Nerdnosh Story Digest *mailing list. Reprinted here by permission.*

Netcops Mete Out Cyberspace Justice

by Hank Nussbacher
(hank@vm.tau.ac.il)

I eased the unmarked cruiser out onto the highway, its 424 cubic-inch, VJ engine purring. Traffic was heavy that day, as convoys of Usenet semi-trailers barreled their way down the Information Superhighway. Biker gangs using Crack steered clear of our sedan, searching instead for Internet tourists in Bermuda shorts

Netcops are ready to reach out and touch someone.

One summer, before joining the *Internet Insider* team, I lived and worked in rural northwestern Wyoming as a reporter-photographer for a small community newspaper. (A big howdy to my pals on the staff of the *Powell Tribune!*) Life in Wyoming (at least during the summer) is about as good as it gets.

There was plenty of room for everyone, and folks were about as friendly as you can imagine (but without being nosy or the least bit uppity). It's a cliché, but in the little town of Powell, Wyoming, I never locked my doors.

It's a fact: people in the wilds of Wyoming are as likely to handle their own legal problems (along with their friends: Smith, Wesson, Colt, and Remmington) as they are to call the constable. Fortunately, it's a rare instance when vigilante justice is called for, but it's always an option when the sheriff is two hours away as the crow flies.

When it comes to law enforcement and the service of justice, the Internet is a lot like rural Wyoming, only without any sheriff at all. Sometimes described (and accurately, I think) as the world's largest functioning anarchy, the Internet somehow manages to take care of its own problems, without any central authority figure or tin-badged referees.

A lot of newcomers to the Internet haven't the faintest idea of what the rules are (or even if there *are* any rules). And when it comes to justice, most Internet transgressors are about as ignorant of the dire consequences as Michael Fay was of Singapore's penalties for spray-painting cars.

I'm not going to spoil your voyage of discovery by laying a long (and questionable in some quarters) list of Internet rules on you. In general, though, keep in mind these two guidelines (also known as the "Woodstock Rules") offered by Internet veteran (and my good friend) Michael Fraase: try not to hurt anyone and clean up your own mess.

If you step out of line, there'll be plenty of cyber-cowboys, net-cops, and digital deputies to guide you back to the straight and narrow path, as Hank Nussbacher will gladly tell you.

INSIDE

OPINION

and Nikon cameras around their necks. The Internet was no longer a safe place for innocents. My partner, Friday, sat next to me, playing with his IRC CB, channel surfing for trouble.

"Unit 7, unit 7. Woman reporting a 426. Over," came the printout on the Netcops IRC channel.

Friday turned to me and gave me that look. The look that he gets when he wants to tear someone's head off. Friday is 6'6" and 230 pounds. He enjoys inflicting pain when necessary. "It's guys like this who give the Internet a bad name. Let's go see what we can do to help," Friday said as he placed the flashing blue Kojak on the top of the sedan. I popped the car into fifth gear and

slashed by the Usenet truckers hauling their load of pornographic magazines and political soapboxes.

We arrived at a Holiday Inn where the lady was staying. Her eyes were red and she looked like a Mac had hit her. Under the hurt she was actually quite pleasant to look at, kind of like the girl next door. Her name was Mary, and in between sobs we sat her down and ordered espresso from the lounge bar. "It was terrible. I feel so violated. I'd like to kill the bastard," spat Mary with a vehemence that only Friday could understand.

"Just the facts, ma'am," said Friday.

"I'm here overseas for nine weeks on assignment for my company. My husband is back home with our daughter and we decided to stay in contact via the Internet. I carry my subnotebook with me every time I travel. My husband and I get along great, but nine weeks away from each other is just too long, so we engage in cyber-sex. You know, private IRC channel, getting undressed behind locked doors and describing in intimate detail what we are doing to each other. We've been doing it almost daily for the past 3 weeks."

YOU CAN'T RUN FROM THE LONG-DISTANCE ARM OF THE LAW

"But this last time was different. My husband asked me to do all sorts of weird and kinky things—and I agreed—but it just seemed wrong. After we finished our three-hour session, my husband called later that day saying that his Internet system was under ICMP redirect attack and that he hadn't been able to get Internet access for the past 24 hours."

Friday cut her off, "Do you use any protection?"

"I normally would have used PGP (Pretty Good Privacy), but I forgot to install it on my computer before I left home. Listen, this guy at the other end must have been listening in on my previous sessions with my husband, because he knew all the right things to say to me so as to not arouse my suspicions." Her lip trembled as she tried to hold back her tears, but both Friday and I knew that while time may heal all wounds, the scar remains.

It was my turn now to bring down the hard facts. "Mary, it looks like you are the victim of a 426: net-rape. There are no laws on the Internet, no police, no govern-ment to turn to. Friday and I act as volunteers in this neck of the woods, along with thousands of others like ourselves throughout the world who mete out our form of frontier justice. What would you like done once we catch the perp?"

She didn't hesitate for a moment, "I want nine of his fingers broken."

"Why nine?" I asked.

"There's no greater torture than using the Internet with one finger."

Friday smiled. Mary had made herself a lifetime fan.

Epilogue

We were able to track down the perp via the historical data sampling we collect daily with our RMON probe. We just correlated the packets with Mary's known IP address and the time of day that the incident happened. Once we had the perp's IP address, we contacted our fellow "cowboys" in that area. They worked with the sysadmin who backtracked through the Unix logs and found the guy. Needless to say, he will never type fast again. ∎

New Jersey Enacts Stringent New Eco-Laws

by Steve Masticola
(masticol@cs.rutgers.edu)

I've never been a big fan of moderation. As far as I'm concerned, a moderate is typically someone who lacks the energy to be an extremist. We only move forward (or backward) as a society through extremism. I'm sure that you have heard wise old sayings like "everything in moderation" and that you are familiar with "the golden mean." Poppycock!

But when it comes to the environment, I'm a strident moderate. (Actually, I'm an ill-informed ambivalent do-nothing, but I'm going to use the term "moderate" because it makes me feel better.) I love the great outdoors and understand the need to protect the natural habitat of various critters and preserve the occasional fragile ecosystem and what-not. But I do enjoy a wild weekend tearing through the hills in a mechanized four-wheeled buggy of destruction, even if it means a few rare species of animal and vegetable get trampled in the process.

And to be honest with you, I bet that's the way most Americans think. Sure, have your parks and preserves, but let's have a place where we can raise hell too. We're all for clean water and fresh air, but we can't be expected to do without air conditioning, two cars in every garage, and a Salad Shooter (unused since the Christmas of '89) in every kitchen.

So it's refreshing to see someone take an extremist stand on the environment. No, I'm not talking about spiking trees or booby-trapping bulldozers. I'm not referring to the folks who chain themselves to spotted owls or go out every weekend planting baby blue whales in the clear-cut forests. I'm talking about the folks in New Jersey: the Garden State.

I've been to New Jersey. Once (I doubt I'll be returning). It's a state where people adopt a highway (and then christen it with their very own litter collection). Don't take my word for it. Just listen to Steve Masticola, who, in the great tradition of extremism, drafted a manifesto and posted it to the Net, entreating his fellow statesmen to adopt and follow his suggestions in the name of environmental extremism.

INSIDE

OPINION

Some day soon, perhaps the citizens of New Jersey will help make the moon's environment "better."

The following eight-point manifesto has been developed by the environmentalists of New Jersey to help maintain the quality of life here in the Garden Apartment State. Due to our constant vigilance and deep concern, we no longer have problems like the endangerment of the spotted owl and the salmon. In fact, we don't have any birds or fish to give us problems at all. New residents should memorize this manifesto and put it into practice in their daily lives.

1. Litter

The New Jersey Environmentalist throws it out his car window, whereupon it becomes someone else's problem. (And who cares about them, anyway?) After all, you'd have to *walk* (EECH!) to get to a trash can.

2. Open Space

Found inside malls. (The really big ones, of course.) Building malls is a good way to conserve space that would otherwise go to waste in some useless woods or farm.

3. Fresh Air

Comes from central air conditioning. Best if kept at 64 degrees or below. It's normal to wear sweaters in the middle of a heat wave. The New Jersey Environmentalist keeps all windows tightly closed at all times, so that the Fresh Air is not contaminated by anything from The Outdoors (see below).

4. The Outdoors

This is the space you have to *walk* through (EECH!) to get from the air-conditioned buildings to the air-conditioned car. That is, unless the car is in an air-conditioned parking deck. The true New Jersey Environmentalist supports the latter, because then he's always inside in the Fresh Air.

5. Plants

The New Jersey Environmentalist realizes the need for plants. Plants have two uses, depending on their size. The little ones are useful for spraying with ChemLawn. (Make sure your children stay inside in the Fresh Air after you have done this.) The big ones (i.e. trees) should be cut down to make room for more strip malls, to conserve Open Space.

6. Energy

The New Jersey Environmentalist conserves his energy by driving everywhere he has to go, and many places he doesn't. Otherwise, he'd have to *walk* (EECH!) to get places. It's dangerous walking in The Outdoors, because there are so many cars there. The bigger your car is, the better, because there's more Open Space and Fresh Air inside.

7. Recycling

Why bother? Nobody else does. New Jersey residents don't want a bottle bill, because it would inconvenience everybody and result in more than six layoffs in the bottle industry around Glassboro. The New Jersey Environmentalist recycles his garbage, old tires, and dead refrigerators by converting them into Litter (see above).

8. Wetlands

This usually means the Shore, where they've gotten rid of a lot of yucky marshes to build beautiful condos and strip malls. Every Friday, the New Jersey Environmentalist joins the traffic jam on the way to the Shore, so that he can have more time in the Fresh Air inside his car. He does the same thing on Sunday, but this time in the opposite direction. Once at the Shore, the New Jersey Environmentalist *never* goes Outdoors, since the freon from the air conditioners has destroyed the ozone layer and he'd get skin cancer.

If you must go outside, remember that the proper way to enjoy the environment is to do so on one square yard of sand, along with half a million other New Jersey Environmentalists and their boom boxes. Watch out for the syringes! ■

The Power Tool Rite of Passage

"Being a really big hit with the babes, next being a sports legend, and then remodeling a home" is how my grandfather explained the context of this home ownership phase I've been going through. "It's nothing to worry about, you're just entering the third stage of manhood," he said. Is it possible I just skipped straight through to stage three? How many stages are there? I wondered. I can't deny that for some unexpected, sick reason, I am enjoying this whole remodeling thing. Maybe it is hormonal. The joys are many, but these are the six most prominent rewards of home ownership:

1) You get to use toxic, possibly hallucinogenic chemicals indiscriminately. Even though I successfully traversed most of the illicit temptations of the '60s, I was not prepared for paint stripper. This ought to be considered a controlled substance. After several hours of stripping what I thought was a mural of a sunset, I realized that I was, in fact, trying to strip a window. Luckily the sun went down about the same time the paint stripper fumes wore off. Needless to say, I'm not going to do any more stripping unless music, money, and screaming women are nvolved.

2) You get to use violent, dangerous power tools indiscriminately. There is almost nothing you can't do with power tools. In fact, I suspect Black and Decker and Makita are missing

INSIDE OPINION

When I was a kid, my dad had not one, but *two* workshops. The main one was in the basement, where we stored the spare bricks and lumber, but there was a smaller, backup workshop in the garage, and even an emergency satellite work area in the laundry room. Each site had its own set of screwdrivers, hammers, pliers and other manly tool-and-dye accessories.

Nothing pissed the old man off more than me or my brother using the claw hammer from the garage workshop and "returning" it to the emergency satellite drawer in the laundry room—or worse still, leaving it in the yard or in the tree or under the culvert where we were using it.

He finally secured all the tools with combination locks, but my brother and I always found the scraps of paper where he wrote down combinations (when we couldn't guess them outright). We had even sneakier ways to get tools when we needed them. No mere lock can keep a boy from a power tool when he needs one. It's a rite of passage—part of becoming a man.

out on a lot of business by limiting their marketing to carpenters. While you're locked in the home improvement mode, I've found that you can make a passable raspberry shake with an electric drill and a paint-stirring attachment; a jigsaw makes short work of slicing those three-day-old bagels; and you can flash-fry a hot dog with one of those wallpaper-removing steam guns.

3) You get to lay waste to former owners' dreams and aspirations indiscriminately. That cute wallpaper with the duckies on it . . . paint over it. The ever-attractive cement lawn animals . . . sledge-hammer croquet with their little heads. The juni-

pers trimmed to look like poodles . . . Texas Chain Saw Massacre.

4) You get to hang all sorts of stuff on your belt. You can re-enact the old West if you are fortunate enough to have a cordless drill and a belt holster. For the more modern look, you can pretend you are Batman with "all those wonderful toys" at your fingertips. However, the crowd-pleasing favorite comes from hanging enough heavy objects to your belt, to achieve the look that I like to call "carpenters' butt." If you've been around a few construction sites, you know what I mean. Nothing like a little rump cleavage to attain that rugged man look.

5) You discover a whole new area of the store. There is a thing for everything. The problem is that most of us don't know the proper names of these things. So, we end up wandering through the store trying to find a "thing-a-ma-bob about the size of a baby's thumb that attaches to a do-dad next to the whatcha-ma-call-it." Fortunately, most helpful hardware men can translate this gibberish. Unfortunately, this tiny part usually costs more per ounce than gold.

6) You get to watch home improvement shows on television. In my pre-home ownership days, I used to enjoy the quaintness of shows such as Bob Villa's "This Old House." After actually buying an old house, I have come to realize that the name of this show should have been "This Damn House!" I think old Bob has been sniffing the paint stripper too long if remodeling is his idea of fun. Or, maybe he's just perpetually stuck in the inevitable third stage of manhood.

Originally published in the "Slightly Off Center" *column in the* Logan Herald Journal *and the* Salt Lake City Event Magazine. ∎

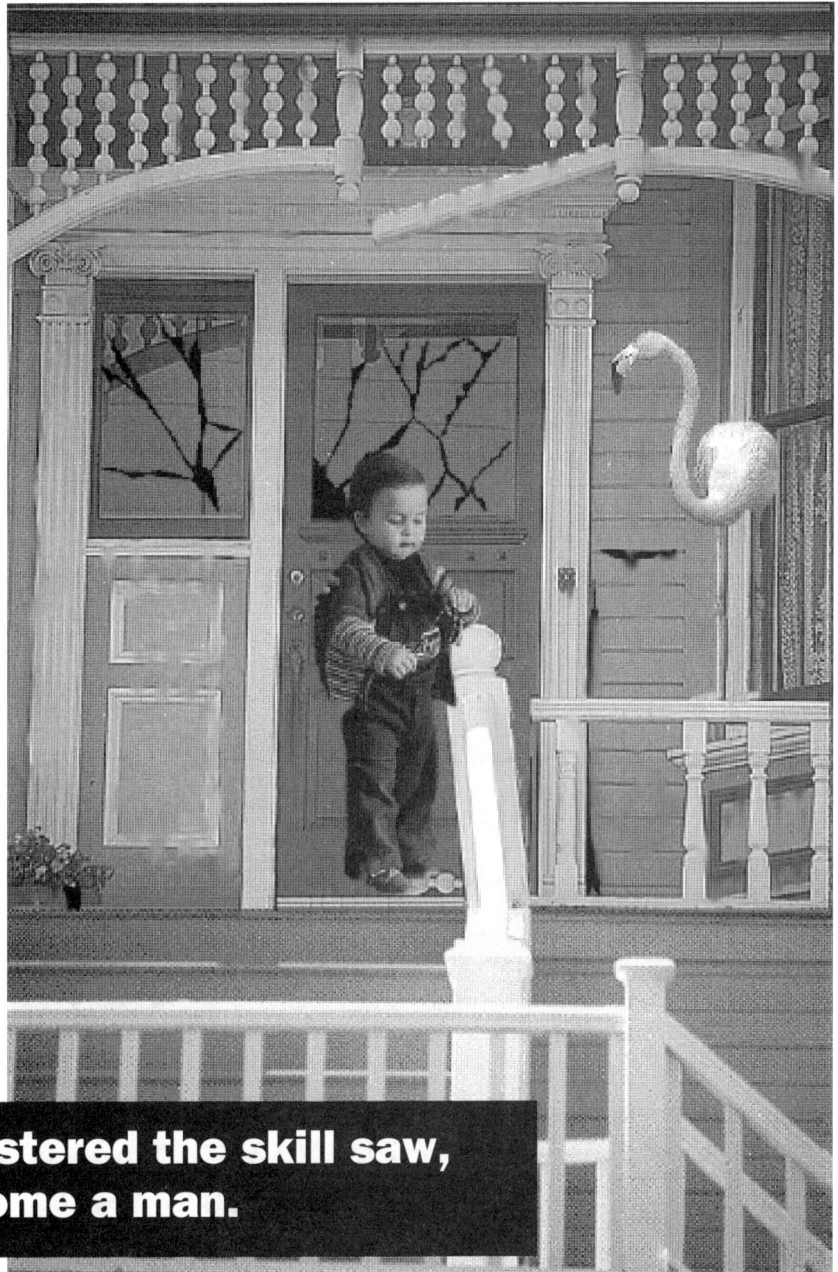

When he has mastered the skill saw, the boy will become a man.

Woman Ages Seven Years While On Hold

By Marianne DeMarco (demarcom@cs.bu.edu)

In the olden days, before modern technology, people had to vent their frustrations face-to-face. Now, thanks to the Info-fangled Hoopla-Skyway, folks can just log on to the Net and share their petty miseries with millions of people at once—electronically.

It may not be as satisfying as drinking a pint of stout with the mates in the local pub, or screaming at a busload of tourists at the beach, or spouting off with a mouthful of vitriolic gossip at the office water cooler, but hey, whatever works, right? Marianne DeMarco has the right idea; you're not gonna find her at the top of the bell tower, picking off co-eds across the quad. She goes online to vent, and our lives are richer for it.

I,for one, vote that we should nuke that godforsaken island known as Manhattan, once and for all. I recently had the opportunity (snort) to witness first-hand (tee-hee-hee) the wizardry and wonder of the World's Greatest City On Earth! (baaaa haaa haaaa haaaa haaaaa)

Why New York City should be used as a nuclear testing site:

Reason #12: It really wouldn't change much there.

Reason #13: The following phone conversation...

RING, RING, RING, RING, RING

—female voice which sounds like Johnny Most with a nasty accent:

"DepahtmuntaConsumaAhfaihs — Hold please."

(28 minutes later)

"DepahtmuntaConsumaAhfaihs, howcanihelpya?"

Me: "Ummm, yes, hi. Um, I am trying to get information on the application procedure for motion picture operators..."

Her: *"Okaaay, you need da depahtmunta city licenses. I'll transfer you."*

(31 minutes later)

—female voice which sounds like Ethel Merman on smack:

"Depaaaahtmunta Consuuuumahfaaaaihs, licin'cin' bureah."

Me: "Uh...Um, I'm trying to get an application for the motion picture operators' test, and I was wondering when tha---"

Her: *"Aaaaaaalright you need the Depaaaaahtmunta Completely Useless People. Hold please."*

Me: "Department of Compl--- but, but" (sputter, sputter)

Her: *"I'll transfer ya."*

(2 minutes)

—cheerful male voice clearly on massive amounts of cocaine:

"HI! Department of Really Nice But Completely Useless People! My name is Jimbo! What can I do for ya today?"

Me: "uh, hi, uh, I was ju---"

Him: *"Just call me Jimbo! It's short for Jim!"*

Me: "Ah, Okay...Jimbo. Well, I was just trying to get some information on the application proce- dure for becoming a licensed motion picture operator..."

Him: *"Ho - Ho! Big Hollywood Director, Huh?"*

Me: "Ah, no, I'm just trying to get a job as a projectionist..."

Him: *"Don't forget that Jimbo helped you get your start!"* (self-contented chortle) *"You know, my sister-in-law saw Robert DeNiro in the Bar-be-Que Restaurant in Tribeca two and a half months ago... Do you know Bobby?"*

Me: "Uh, no. Uh, is this really the right department for me, Jimbo?"

Him: *"You know, I really have no idea. Lemmee ask Diane— she's the smart cookie around here."* (barely muffled voice) *"Hey Diane! Some kid wansta know about showin' movies...issat us?....Oh, okay...I'll tell her....oh, and are you going to that company shindig next Saturday?......yeah, well I'm bringing? potato salad.....no, I'll get my mom to make it.....ooooh, that sounds good, where'dya get that recipe...really?"*

Me: (shouting): "Uh, Jimbo? Hey Jimbo!"

Him: *"Hangon, Diane...."* (into phone) *"No, I'm sorry, that's not our department, but I'll transfer you to the right department...hang on, I can never figure this damn phone system out... I think what you do is hit this button here, and then you dial the extension. Wait, lemmee ask Diane again."* (yelling) *"Hey Diane! Howdoya transfer a call again?.......okay, yeah........and then you hit what button?.....okay.......uh-huh....okay ....okay, thanks! I think I got it now, tha---"*

dial tone

Well, all in all it was about a seven-and-a-half-hour phone call, and I still don't have an application. Gosh, I just can't wait to start Grad School so I can have experiences like this one daily.

So now I know where snipers come from. ∎

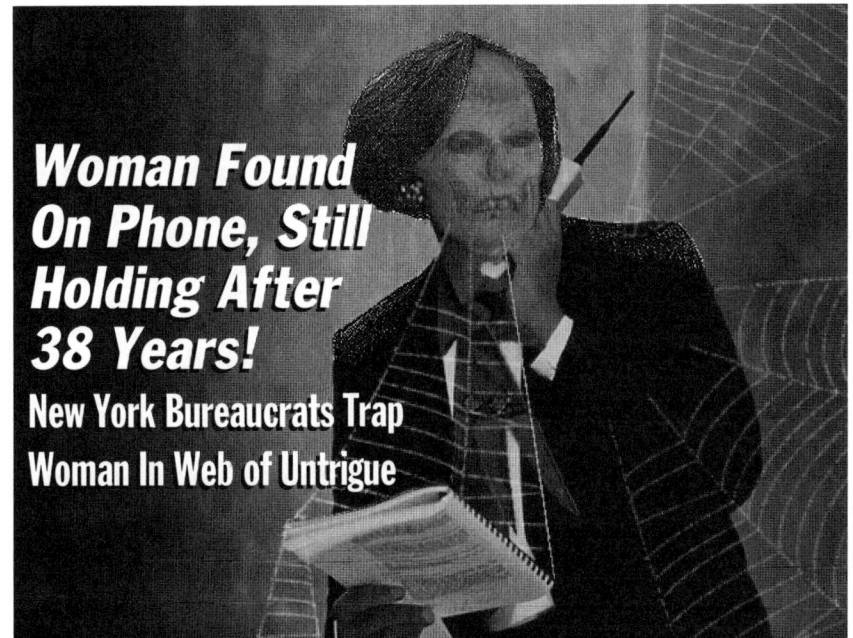

Woman Found On Phone, Still Holding After 38 Years!
New York Bureaucrats Trap Woman In Web of Untrigue

Twisted Genius Mangles Metaphors, Makes Malapropisms

Short man on a totem pole

By Noel Giffin (noel@reg.triumf.ca)

Well, I have been collecting these screwed-up expressions for a number of years now, and it has become an interesting list. They are all uttered by one of my coworkers, T. P. Moskven. He has achieved legendary status within our group, and it has become a game to pick up on the next fractured phrase. They are all malapropisms, mixed metaphors, spooner-isms, or some twist of this kind. I think he is an unconscious genius. We catch ourselves utter-ing our own now, and don't know whether they are a universal plague on the language, or if he has affected only his immediate surroundings. There have been lots we've missed, I'm sure, but here is a short list of his best ones. They are in no order, except a loose chronological one. I have placed translations beside them to lend some aid in understanding, since they're presented here out of context. I post them for your enjoyment.

T. P. Moskven's "Semiotics"

MOSKVENESE	ENGLISH
(What he said)	(What he *probably* meant)
movie Mongol	movie mogul
the sitcom satellite	satcom satellite
getting sedimentary	sedentary
obnoxious gas	noxious gas
groper	grouper (fish)
art decor	art deco
the "cloverleaf" is the vegetable of Ireland	"shamrock" is symbol/potato is vegetable
sheet metal music	sheet music/heavy metal music
Jacob's shirt of many colors	Joseph's coat . . .
malamutt	malamute
old gizzards	buzzards/geezers
the movie Rear View Mirror	Hitchcock's Rear Window
a sesame seed phone	Sesame Street phone
3 of 1, 2 of the other	6 of 1, half a dozen . . .
dead man's space	no man's land
armchair case	basket case
out of mind, out of sight	out of sight, out of mind
klutzomaniac	an inept person
the "Piaf" sewing machine	a "Pfaff" or a "Singer"
commuting with nature	communing with nature

IT'S TRUE!!

RIGHT HANDS

MOSKVENESE	ENGLISH	MOSKVENESE	ENGLISH
popular tree	poplar tree	aproxaminus one or two	plus or minus one or two
laughing at the bank	laughing all the way to the bank	a Burjeleaux	a Burgundy, Beaujolais, Bordeaux?
the battle of runamock	the battle of Tippecanoe	someone with a dark voice	a deep voice
he's got it down pitter pat	got it down pat	don't knock till you try it	don't knock it till you try it
hitchhiking in Europe is risqué	risky	a whole riffraff of stuff	a whole raft of things
		a brandy sniffer	a brandy snifter
that's a hairball idea	harebrained idea	the Colonel Boogie march	the Colonel Bogey march
Norwedish	Swediegian (Scandinavian)	that's a real pile of crock	that's a crock of . . .
he smokes like a fish	smokes like a chimney / drinks like a fish	hydroglyphics	hieroglyphics
	goes without saying	eating with your mouth full	speaking with your mouth full
that just goes without reason		it's an acquired smell	an acquired taste
he wouldn't give you the light of day	...the time of day	like an Offside cartoon	Gary Larson's "Far Side" cartoons
my jacket fits like a match	it fits like a glove	don't ruffle the boat	don't rock the boat/ ruffle his feathers
you buy what you pay for	you get what you pay for	no use beating dead wood	no use beating a dead horse
you buy what you get	you get what you pay for	throw in the hat	throw in the towel /throw your hat in the ring
whatever grinds your crank	whatever turns your crank		
count people with a turnbuckle	a turnstile	Riding Miss Daisy	The movie Driving Miss Daisy (X-rated?)
using an antideodorant	an antiperspirant	cutting out the driftwood	cutting out the deadwood
roughriders in the sky	the song Ghost Riders In the Sky		
garnishee his wages	garnish his wages		
put the floor to the metal	put the pedal to the metal		
put the metal to the pedal	put the pedal to the metal		
I'll fix his shorts	fix his wagon		
that beats the cake	that takes the cake		
gossiping bittersnipe	guttersnipe		

Smokes like a fish

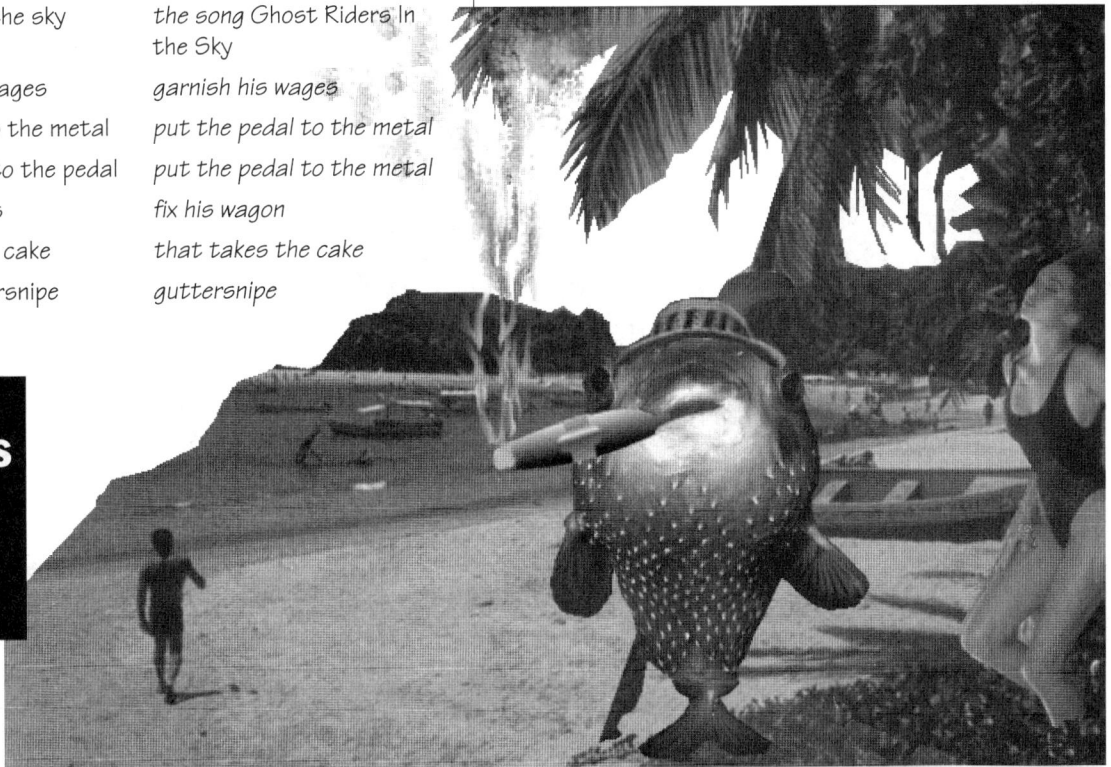

MOSKVENESE	ENGLISH
feeling a little sperky this morning	feeling perky, spunky
the movie Two Left Feet	My Left Foot
short man on a totem pole	low man on a totem pole
the Club Scouts of America	Cub Scouts/Boys Club
the government will quake in	. . . cave in (landslide?)
karramesh	Marrakech
trying to blame the finger at me	point the finger/pin the blame
I'll see it when I believe it!	seeing is believing/I'll believe it when I see it
The Man from Windy River	The Man from Snowy River
snoring like a trooper	swearing like a trooper
stuff it up your overcoat	button up your overcoat
the oddest ball people	oddball people
it was riveted with holes	riddled with holes
worst weather on recorded record	worst on record
he's got his finger on the thumb of it	his finger on the pulse of it/got it under his thumb
playing "Begin the Benign"	the song "Begin the Beguine"

MOSKVENESE	ENGLISH
studying the writings of Pluto	the writings of Plato
you're barking up a dead tree	barking up the wrong tree
people without left hands don't live as long	left-handed people don't live as long
my stereo speakers have a passover network	a crossover network
soldiers armed to the core	an army corps armed to the teeth
going at it like beavers	going at it like rabbits
put your ax to the grindstone	nose to the grindstone/have an ax to grind
he was hot as a toad	hot as a firecracker/cold as a fish/cool as a cucumber
you can't change an old horse	you can't teach an old dog new tricks
the extension of the dinosaurs	extinction of the dinosaurs
money is no expense	money is no object

The oddest ball people

WHEEEE!!

WHEEE!!

I Told You Never to Call Me During Jury Selection!

By Dennis Hinkamp (dennish@extsparc.agsci.usu.edu)

"Call Waiting!"

Pyramid Sales Telemarketers

It's OK to be rude to pyramid sales telemarketers. They deserve it!

Will my vegetarian friends be offended if I serve large slabs of near-bleeding beef at my dinner party? How should I feel about call waiting? Can I compost that old flowered couch? It's not easy being a consumer these days. The pressure to simultaneously exhibit political correctness and proper etiquette can cause undue anxiety. The following list is meant to solve this dilemma by providing rules of thumb for the '90s consumer:

Most of the reporters here at the *Insider* aren't real big on etiquette. "*Please*" and "*thank you*" are signs of weakness to the average reporter. As they'll be the first to tell you, everyday etiquette is tough to master. But the proliferation of new technologies makes it even tougher! Clearly, as **O.J.**'s attorney, **Robert Shapiro**, found out, taking cellular phone calls in open court is a no-no. But what about calling a pal in a restaurant? If only there were a handy-dandy guide to the manners problems of life in the modern world. Well now there is, and you'll find it on the Internet.

INSIDE

OPINION

Avoid "open containers" while driving.

Banking/Teller Machines

There is yet no established polite distance for standing in line behind somebody extracting money from an automated teller machine. However, the emerging custom in most big cities is approximately the length of a gun barrel—especially for evening withdrawals. For most other areas and times of day, the old bumper sticker adage, "*If you can read this, you're too damn close,*" applies to teller machines.

Cellular Phones

It is considered extremely tacky to call other cellular phone owners across the restaurant, even though it is possible. It is equally impolite to ask others to "*leave the room*" when you are taking a personal call on your car cellular phone.

Call Waiting

This is the electronic version of "*I've got a pie in the oven.*" It is a polite excuse to get out of a conversation with just about anyone. If you are

RUMOR CONTROL

When lead Simpson attorney **Robert Shapiro** received two phone calls in quick succession during preliminary hearings in Simpson's murder trial, Judge Lance Ito quipped, "*A third time, and it's mine.*" (Ito eventually seized the offending phone when it rang a third time.)

The incident lead netizens to ponder just who needed to speak to Shapiro so badly. The current scuttlebutt—and the Insider makes this claim with some confidence—is that it was none other than gab-show host and political king-maker **Larry King** ringing Shapiro for a date on **CNN**!

King's camp has confirmed that the cream-puff chat-meister had tried to reach Shapiro on his cellular phone at about that time, but couldn't confirm that it was, in fact, Larry. When asked about rumors that bug-eyed Larry King was, in fact, a reptilian alien from Zeta Reticuli, King spokesfolks had no comment.

> **"Never, ever compliment persons of either gender on their fanny pack!"**

the person being put on hold, it is appropriate to give this person's phone number to the **National Association of Pyramid Sales Telemarketers**.

Recycling
Throwing an aluminum can into the trash is likely to draw angry glances, so it is permissible to carry around empty cans in the back seat of your car, in your pockets, backpack, or purse. Empty beer cans in your car, however, will still be considered "*open containers*" in accordance with liquor laws.

Compost Piles
Whereas it would normally be considered obnoxious to talk about garbage at a social function involving food, compost piles can be discussed and admired for their environmental attributes. Your own **Personal Landfill** (PL) can be discussed at nearly all social occasions. For the inhibited, try these conversation starters: "*You ought to*

see mine rot!" or "*Look at the steam rising off that baby,*" or, lastly, "*The worms really love it.*" (Etiquette clarification: An old couch piled high with newspapers *isn't* recognized as a legitimate PL.)

Meat Eating
Bringing a bowl of meatballs to a Sierra Club meeting may be as repugnant as having a Happy Hour at an Alcoholics Anonymous meeting. Vegetarianism has become a status symbol in some circles. You can break the ice at predominantly vegetarian social gatherings with the statement: "*Is that tofu or did somebody accidentally chop up a dish towel in the stir fry?*"

DINK Pseudo-families
Due to the increased number of DINK (**Double Income No Kids**) families, it is now socially acceptable to substitute photos and humorous stories of your dog's Frisbee-catching exploits in the

absence of baby pictures. However, if your friends' dog starts sending Christmas cards to your dog, somebody should seek professional help.

Fanny Packs
Never, ever compliment persons of either gender on their fanny pack unless you are absolutely sure they're wearing one.

*Originally published in t*he "Slightly Off Center" *column in the* Logan Herald Journal *and the* Salt Lake City Event Magazine. ∎

"When humor writer Dennis Hinkamp is working on a new piece for his column, he tests his material by posting it to talk.bizarre.newsgroup."

"**Whereas it would normally be considered obnoxious to talk about garbage at a social function involving food, compost piles can be discussed and admired...**"

LIFE @ LARGE

Have you ever noticed how many sitcoms feature wacky young folks who used to work as stand-up comedians? **Jerry Seinfeld**. **Roseanne Barr**. **Tim Allen**. **Brett Butler**. **Elen Degeneres**. Prime time is littered with babbling heads that once spent most of their time in smoky comedy clubs tossing one-liners to indifferent boozers.

Now, big-time TV executives are prowling the comedy clubs for talent, while stars like **Seinfeld** use the comedy circuit to test out ideas for their shows.

Kinda weird, huh?

Well, believe it or not, the same thing happens on the Internet. Well, sort of. When humor writer **Dennis Hinkamp** is working on a new piece for his "Slightly Off Center" column in the *Logan Herald Journal*, he tests his material by posting it to the **talk.bizarre** newsgroup. Other comedy writers have been known to post humorous pieces to places like **rec.humor** to see what folks think.

The *Insider* predicts it won't be long before the next **Dave Barry** rises from the ranks of **alt.fondle.vomit**. We suspect the hot-shot comedy scouts from *Cracked, Mad, Boy's Life* and *Reader's Digest* are already prowling the Net in search of fresh young talent. So keep in mind that if you post something funny on the Internet, it may be your ticket to the big time.

Tormenting Telemarketers—A Game

By David L. Cathey (davidc@montagar.com)

Everyone has gotten a call from a telemarketer—the new scourge of the telephone system. Previously, when the phone rang, you always wondered whether it was someone you knew or someone with something to sell. Well, the time has come to turn the tables. We need to take control of our own phones. We need to take the "market" out of telemarketing.

Strike Back Against Evil Phone Sales Scum

Premise: Telemarketers take the brute force approach to making sales. If you talk to a whole bunch of people, someone will buy what you are selling.

Counter-Tactic: Waste as much of their time as you can. Each minute that you waste means several potential customers who will not be reached. Make telemarketing unprofitable. Hanging up only increases the chances for them to make a sale. Don't let this happen!

Hints: Most of the preliminary stuff is done by someone making minimum wage who's reading a script. Let them finish. It's easy points, and you were watching Star Trek and weren't using your phone anyway. It's easy to keep them interested using "attentive grunting," similar to when your mother calls.

Scoring

Basic Point System

For each minute spent on the phone—10 pts.

Getting transferred to someone who makes more than minimum wage—15 pts.

For each minute spent on the phone with person making more than minimum wage—25 pts.

Bonus Points

Getting them to repeat part of the "script—5 pts. each time.

Getting answers to stupid questions—15 pts. each question.

Changing the subject—50 pts./each time.

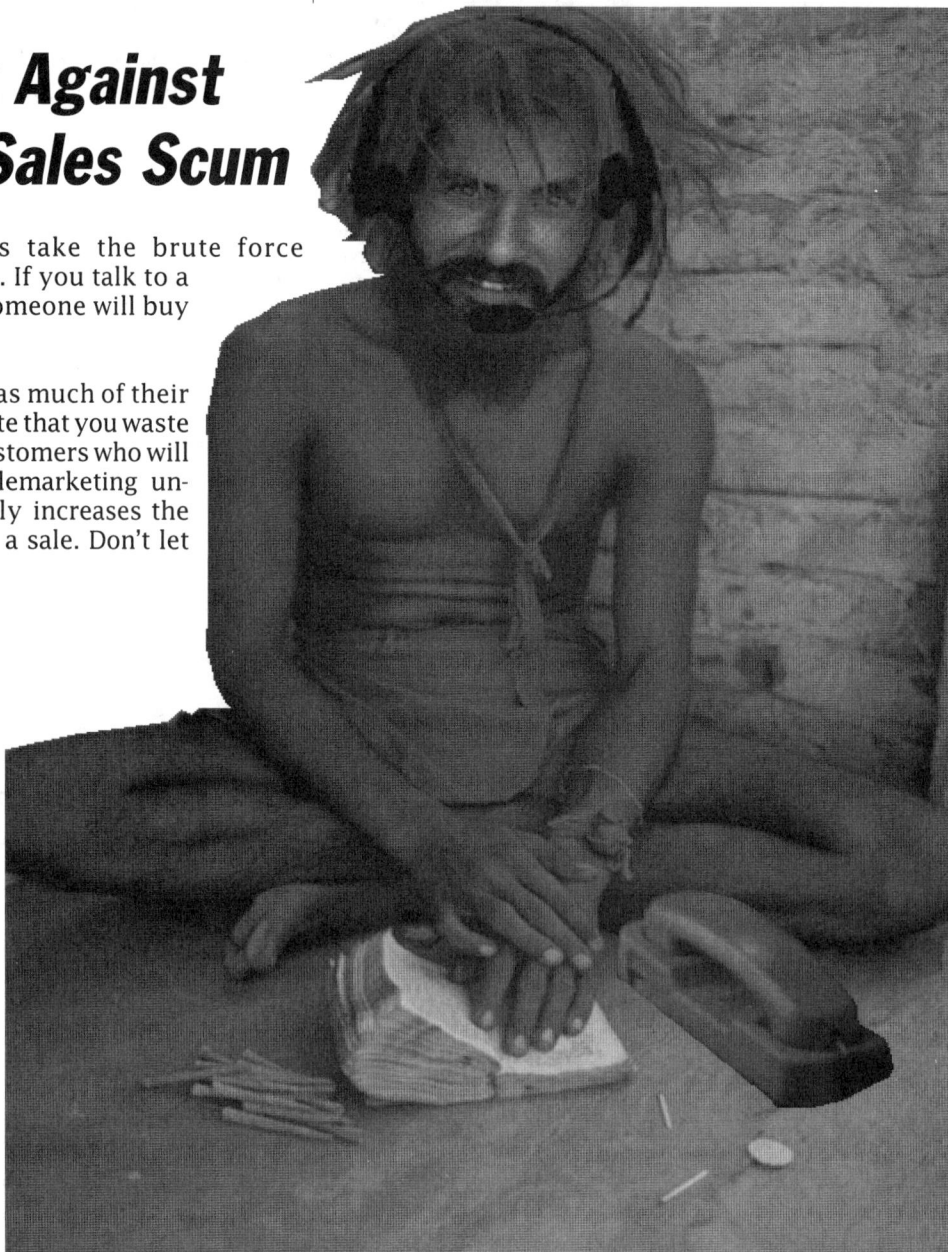

226

You Can Play at Home!

For each minute spent on the phone with person making more than minimum wage—25 pts.

Bonus Points:

Getting them to repeat part of the script—5 pts. each time

Getting answers to stupid questions—15 pts. each question.

Changing the subject—50 pts. each timeMaking the salesperson angry—175 pts.

Making the salesperson use profanity—750 pts.

Getting their boss on the phone, and telling them the salesperson used profanity—1,500 pts.

Getting their 1-800- number—10 pts.

Posting their 1-800- number to **alt.sex** as a free "Phone Sex" line—50 pts.

Checking the number a week later and finding it is busy or disconnected—5,000 pts.

Here's an example of how a typical game might go:

<Ring>
Me: Yes?
Them: Hi, I'm with Fly-By-Night Carpet Cleaning and we're in your area... *[start clock]*...would like to know if you are interested?
Me: Sure...
Them: Well, we are currently offering...depending on the size of the rooms.
Me: Well, how much for the whole house?
Them: Let me transfer you to Bob. [15 bonus pts.!]
Them: Sir?
Me: Yes?
Them: How large is your house? [25 pts./min!]
Me: Oh, about 2,000 square feet.
Them: Well, that would be about *$XXX.*
Me: It won't hurt the floor, will it? [stupid question]
Them: Oh, no! We use a [...this usually takes some time!...] and it is completely safe.
Me: Even with my pets? [stupid question]
Them: Oh, yes. The chemicals we use...
Me: Do you have to pre-treat, since I have pets?
Them: Yes, and we do that with...[repeat!]
Me: But the original offer was for $39.95. Does that include treating for pets?
Them: Uh...
Me: Well, it is kind of dirty. The guys were over for the game. Did you see the

Play the Telemarketing Game

Cowboys vs. the Rams? [subject change]
Them: Yes.
Me: What a game! That last touchdown pass! Wasn't that a great play?
Them: Yes, well, back to your house...
Me: Oh yes, what about moving the furniture?
Them: Uh...
Me: Do you clean furniture, too? Those guys spilled some beer. Have you smelled old beer on furniture before? But what a game, eh?! I couldn't believe that they couldn't move the ball in the second quarter...[subject change]
Them: Ahem... Would you like us to come out? [angry]
Me: Well, when could you come out?
Them: How about next week?
Me: Hmmm... Morning or afternoon?
Them: Either would be fine.
Me: Do you have anything the week after?
Them: Sure, can I put you down for Tuesday? [Okay, let's try for those last big bonus points]
Me: Well, I don't think it matters, since I have all hardwood floors here!
Them: Damn it! *<click>*[Yes! 750 points!] ∎

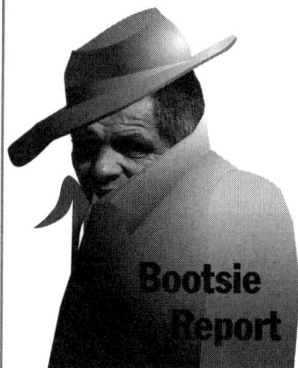

Bootsie Report

Lisa "Burn Baby Burn" Lopes, also known as "Left-Eye" of the rap group TLC, is reportedly in good condition at an unnamed Washington hospital after a slap fight with Chelsea Clinton at a White House function on Saturday. Clinton, who claims to be "the biggest TLC fan ever," was reported to be very excited at the prospect of meeting one of her favorite stars. Her excitement turned sour, however, when Lopes stormed into the reception (which also featured Flavor Flav of Public Enemy and Ice T) and accused Chelsea of trying to "steal my Andre!" Lopes then proceeded to pull Clinton's hair and to scratch at her face with fingernails. Chelsea responded with a stunning roundhouse right, which gave Lopes another reason to be called "Left-Eye." Lopes then proceeded to slap at the First Daughter, who responded with some slick Kung Fu moves that would have made Bruce Lee

"After several backflips, Chelsea went into a crane position, then launched a kick that left Lopes sprawled on the floor."

proud. After several backflips, Chelsea went into a crane position, then launched a kick that left Lopes sprawled on the floor.

Afterward, one of the secret service guys was overheard to have said, "That was pretty wild. Someone should have tried to break that up!"

No one at the White House would comment on the incident, but promoter Don King is said to have made several calls to the switchboard in an attempt to sign Chelsea to a contract.

Reporting from the edge of credibility, I'm Juan Bootsie. Contact Juan Bootsie at: an31291@anon.penet.fi or check out his archives via FTP in the /pub/hamlet directory at ftp.netcom.com.

Spice Up Your Prom with These Wacky Themes

Why are prom themes always so lame? How many times must we sit through yet another 70s night, or Roaring 20s event without falling asleep? Here are some suggestions to wash the prom blues away.

Theme: *An Evening in the Gulag.*

Song: *"We Gotta Get Outta This Place,"* by The Animals.

Meal: *Lumpy gruel for first five couples, everyone else sits on the floor and starves.*

Decor: *Hard labor, solitary confinement, dirt, fake snow storm; principal shoots at people who try to escape.*

Theme: *Medieval Banquet.*

Song: *"Aqualung,"* by Jethro Tull.

Meal: *Roast joint, mead, pigs-in-a-blanket, rice pilaf (no utensils).*

Decor: *Roving bands of wild dogs, torture devices (racks, iron maidens, stockades), King and Queen of prom joust for supremacy, large sharp objects, wandering wenches, black plague. Get splashed in the face with hot oil when your ticket is checked.*

Theme: *Polka! Party USA.*

Song: *"Hotel California,"* by Lenny Gamulka and Polka Java.

Meal: *Bratwurst, knockwurst, buttwurst, wiener schnitzel, sauerbraten, pork strudel, punch.*

Decor: *Polka dots, inflatable suspended accordions, free kisses from hairy German men.*

Theme: *Inside the Human Heart.*

Song: *"Barracuda,"* by Heart.

Meal: *Fried stuff.*

Decor: *Four rooms, red tuxedos, chaperones dressed as white blood cells.*

Reprinted from the e-zine Ooze. *For subscription information, e-mail DrBubonic@aol.com.* ■

Maybe one day America will be reserved for Americans, dang it, and everybody who has ancestors from a foreign land will just have to leave!

We've Got

A in't it great to be American? Sure, we are up to our necks in debt and, since we are the fastest gun in town, every two-bit punk with a surface-to-air missile wants to pick a fight with us. And, of course, it now seems our main responsibility as a nation on this planet is playing puzzled assistant principal to the world's schoolyard squabbles.

Don't get us wrong. The situation makes for bombastic headlines, which keeps the editors here at the Insider happy. Besides, the world loves us. Everyone loves an American! What's that? You're not so sure? Well, OK, maybe not the French. Oh, all right, everybody hates us.

What does all of this have to do with the Internet? Well, not much, unless you consider that the Internet—a network of some 25 million computer users who are mostly American and communicate primarily in English—also reaches

INSIDE

OPINION

about 100 other countries, none of which are America, and few of which use English as the primary language.

So watch what you say on the Net. Be polite. Don't think of the Internet—as one newbie so poignantly described it—as a means of exporting our culture and views to the rest of a captive world. Instead, consider it—as one Australian politely pointed out to that newbie—as a means of importing the views and opinions of other countries all over the world. Keep in mind that the Internet is a global forum.

Otherwise, you are likely to wind up looking a little jingoistic, or at least mildly politically incorrect, like Mutt in the exchange that follows. Mutt, whose comments were pulled from a mailing list (we're not saying exactly which one), agreed to let us reprint his comments provided we didn't divulge his real name (Barry).

Spurs That Jingo-Jangle-Jingo

I was in D.C. over the weekend—I came at the last-minute request of a friend who had decided to tie the knot (yet again), and I was wondering exactly what combination of mixed drinks would talk him out of it.

Anyway, I dropped by the **Museum of American History**. I haven't gone there since I was a child, and in the new spirit of patriotism that our discussions have inspired in me, I thought I would go and revel in the words and wisdom of Washington, Paine, Jefferson, and the gang.

Well, I never found them, though I did manage to fight through the crowds to see the harmonica that James Cotton played, and a photograph of the saxophone that Lester Young played. And I saw a demonstration of how printing works. Boy, was that ever educational.

There was a cool photo essay of the fight for civil rights. My favorite moment was when I was standing behind a family from Mississippi. The photo was of a civil rights leader, shot in the chest, lying on the ground, bleeding. The mother pointed to the ground beside the bleeding man and said, "Look, that's Mississippi! In the picture!"

I went to the **National Archives**, stood in line to see the Constitution (a must-see every time I visit), and got pushed out of the way by some freaking foreigners who cut in line! I wanted to beat the living crap out of them, but the stern guard was looking at me (with hand on gun) as if to say, "They're only Germans. They have enough pain." I was overall amazed at the lack of manners that all foreign tourists displayed. Sure, maybe the ugly American stereotype is true, but like all other things that are American, everybody seems to be imitating us.

I also went to the **Air & Space Museum**, where some redneck was reading aloud every dang placard in the Apollo exhibit, but getting key facts wrong. "**Alan Shepard**, he's the first man in space," this guy kept repeating to his kids, pointing to the picture. "That's the first man in space!" I really, really, really wanted to casually say: "Actually, **Yuri Gagarin** was the first man in space," but I don't think I would have been very casual if I'd actually said it.

That's my story and I'm sticking to it. ∎

The rest of the world may hate Americans as a people, and they may fear and despise us as a nation, but boy do they love our money!

According to the Federal Reserve, 60% of all the official governmental financial reserves held by countries around the world is in American dollars. The Fed estimated that in 1991, seven of every ten $100 bills in existence were physically located outside the U.S. That number, the Fed maintains, is sure to be even higher today.

But rumors abound on the Net that Americans, and the world at large, are in for a big surprise sometime in late 1995 or early 1996. That's when the U.S. Treasury switches to new paper money. The rumor, first reported by the PBS show *"Nova"* and now exposed as fact by the sluggish mass media, contends that the Treasury Department is nervous that our paper currency is susceptible to counterfeiting.

Yet Secret Service statistics demonstrate little or no significant threat of counterfeiting for the past 50 years, so why change the currency? Rumor-hounds and so-called "conspiracy theorists" on the Net are convinced the Federal Reserve Board—the secret cadre of appointed and unaccountable private bankers and businessmen who control the nation's money supply—is planning to devalue the old bills, and only those elite American financiers who have their holdings stashed in overseas banks will be able to exchange their cash at true market rates.

America's hard-working public, the rumor contends, will be stuck. Thus, the *Insider* recommends a two-tiered precautionary plan: First, keep an eye on **alt.conspiracy** (and be sure to listen to William Cooper's "Hour of the Time" broadcast on WWCR short-wave radio). Second, put your money in gold and silver.

Foreign Exchange

Does Socks Ride in Bulletproof Kitty Caddy?

In this episode, President Clinton decides the rough-and-tumble White House press corps has become too tough to face. Instead, he's facing a well-coifed Canadian news reader and a gaggle of youngsters in the ABC news show "Answering Children's Questions." Kids want to know: Does Socks travel in a bulletproof box? What does the President eat at McDonald's? After facing the kids, is Clinton anxious to take on Sam Donaldson and Lisa Myers again? Let's listen.

Mr. Jennings: Good morning everybody. Good morning especially boys and girls. Good morning, Mr. President.

The President: Good morning, Peter.

Mr. Jennings: Thank you for having us back, sir.

The President: I'm glad you're back.

Q: I had a fun question to ask you; and I was wondering, Mr. President, in elementary school, we had to pass a physical fitness test to pretty much get an A, and you got a President's award, or a certificate. And I was wondering if you've ever tried or ever thought of passing the test, or if you've even looked at the test that we have to pass?

The President: I haven't but I probably should. I imagine that I could pass it since I jog every day, and do a little work on my weights, and do some other things. I probably could, but I'll do it. I'll

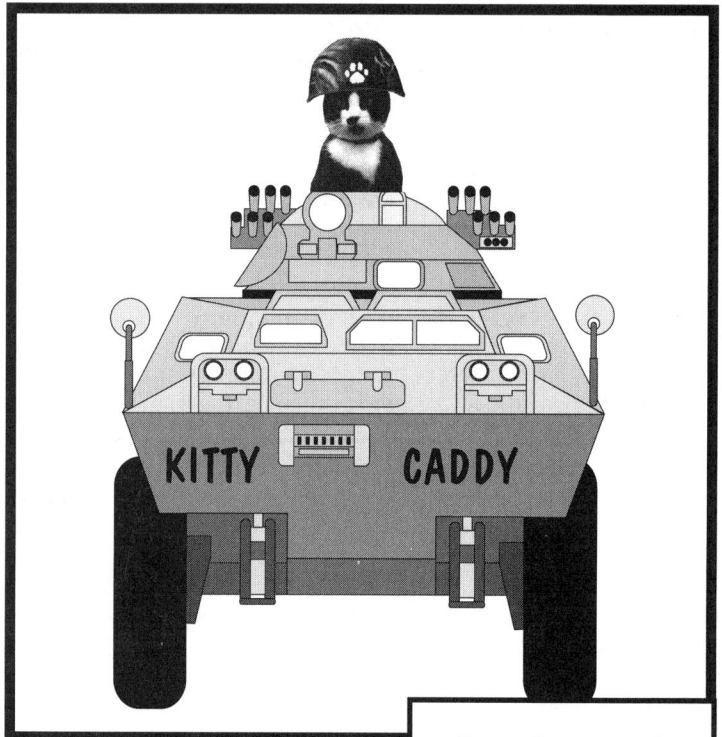

check on it. If I don't make it, then I'll have to get myself in shape.

Q: I read a book called **Socks in the White House**, and it said that **Socks had a bulletproof case**. Does he really?

The President: He can stand behind something that's bulletproof, but most of the time he's just out in the open. That's just a funny thing to say. It was a joke.

Q: Good afternoon. My question is going towards inner city kids. We feel as though the baby boomers

The place: The White House's East Room.

The time: March 19, 1994; 11:30 a.m. E.S.T.

The players: President Clinton, ABC News TelePrompTer reader Peter Jennings, and a host of inquisitive kids.

have forgotten that the chaos that we create was given to us by you all. We want the problem to be stopped, but we need help. A lot of us are tired of hearing that we are a lost generation when we are not. We are a generation of renewal. And we want to know, what steps are you going to take to give us the hope, the pride, and the strength that we need to succeed in the future, and to become strong—black, white, Chinese, African American—people in the society 10 and 20 and 30 years in the future?

Mr. Jennings: Tanya, can I ask you a question before the President answers? Do you think the President can do a lot about that? Do you think he makes a really enormous difference here?

Q: He makes a very enormous difference, but one thing a lot of people fail to realize, if you don't come into the communities on positive notes, when you come for negative notes, it really angers a lot of people. It's angered me a lot. And I want the media and you, also, to know that I wanted to leave Mr. Gore very baffled, and I'm glad I left him baffled because I want him to understand that you need to come when positive things happen, and not just come when negative things happen.

The President: I agree with that. Let me just make two comments about that, and then I'll try to answer your question.

We, at least, do come. He and I have been out there. My wife has been out there. We have been in inner city communities. We have walked streets that you don't normally see the President walking. We have been to places you don't normally see the President go. And I agree that we should support success stories.

I was in Detroit last week, and sure, Detroit has a lot of inner city problems. They also have, perhaps, the best job training program of its kind in America for inner city kids, putting them in very high wage, high tech jobs. So I visited that program because it's a success story. It proves that all children can learn. So I agree with that. We shouldn't just show up when something terrible happens.

The second thing I want to say to you is that, essentially, everything that I do is designed to try to give young people like you some hope and some structure and some opportunity back. I agree that generations ahead of you have left you a pretty lousy situation. You've got all these kids that are born into families where there was never a marriage. You've got all these neighborhoods where the jobs have disappeared. You've got all these places where the schools have, in effect, been given up on. And that's not your fault. You just showed up. You're a child; you shouldn't have to deal with that except to do your best.

The Socks Chronicles

In this ongoing series of behind-the-scenes looks at the inner workings of the White House, the *Internet Insider* follows Socks, America's First Cat, through another harrowing press conference. In this official White House document obtained exclusively by the *Insider*, you'll see how the White House press corps is once again sidetracked from the real issues facing our government to consider the life and times of that lovable kitty, Socks.

Why the media obsession with the President's cat? Is there something the White House doesn't want us to know? Is "Socks" a secret code word that sends reporters into a trance of distraction and diversion? Why does the press offer only a 30-second sound bite from a 30-minute meeting? Does Socks prefer frolicking in the Lincoln Bedroom or on the South Lawn? These questions and more are answered as we present another installment of *The Socks Chronicles*.

photo courtesy of The White House

Q: Well, I have a fun question for you. And I know you used to run in Arkansas so I think you will like it. My favorite restaurant is McDonald's, too. What do you get when you go there? (*Laughter.*)

The President: What do I get when I go there? Normally, an Egg McMuffin or something for breakfast. Those are the big meals that I eat at McDonald's. My daughter and I used to go there sometimes on Sunday morning before Sunday school, and then Hillary and I would go and pick her up and we'd go to church. But we love to have McDonald's Egg McMuffins on Sunday morning.

This excerpted transcript from an actual White House media event was downloaded from official archives of Clinton Administration documents available from a number of sources: via gopher: gopher.tamu.edu or sunsite.unc.edu; via anonymous FTP: ftp.spies.com; via World-Wide Web: http://english-server.hss.cmu.edu/WhiteHouse.html; via e-mail: publications@whitehouse.gov. ∎

Ever Get the Feeling You're

Did you hear the one about the libidinous sailor who got tired of always having sex the way the prostitute wanted it? "Can't we just do it my way once?" he asked. "Well, how would you like to have sex?" she asked. To which the sailor replied, "Ba perqvg!"

Sorry about that last bit being unreadable. The *Insider* is a family paper, and we're not allowed to print off-color jokes, particularly the punch lines. If you want to find out the punch line, (which isn't really that naughty at all), you'll have to decode the words using the ubiquitous Rot13 encoding standard.

Rot13 is a public-domain "encryption" method (free and widely available online) used by netizens to scramble the letters of messages or comments that others might find offensive or objectionable. For instance, when posting a slightly racy comment or joke to an otherwise straightlaced newsgroup, it's a decent idea to Rot13 encode the message first. Those with faint hearts, a low tolerance for expletives, or virtually no sense of humor can choose not to decode the message, and thus never be offended. As far as encryption goes—the idea of making something unreadable to all but those who are intended to read it—Rot13 isn't too formidable a method.

But then again, the idea behind Rot13 is that it allows anyone who wants to read the text to be able easily to decode it. On the other hand, there are plenty of people on the Internet who are very concerned about making sure their information is only read by those to whom it is addressed. Oddly enough, this grassroots quest for digital privacy tends to greatly annoy a lot of people in the government

and certain areas of big business. Encryption opponents in government and law enforcement maintain that only criminals, deviant pornographers, and terrorists are making a stink about privacy and computers.

This, of course, has us here at the *Insider* wondering just whom the people at the Harris polling company are choosing for their public opinion interviews. In a 1992 Harris poll, 78 percent of Americans expressed concern about their personal privacy. That number is certainly larger among Internet inhabitants, and it no doubt reaches the 100 percent mark among those who refer to themselves "cypherpunks" or "crypto anarchists."

In short, the cypherpunks believe that the same expectations of privacy and anonymity enjoyed in the physical world should be extended to cyberspace. To that end, they're dedicated to making powerful encryption technology available to everyone, not just spies and multinational corporations. At the Insider we not only agree with their efforts, we applaud them. (Our public key is available upon request.) As the old saying goes, "You can have my encryption key when you pry it from my cold, dead fingers."

But what drives a cypherpunk or crypto anarchist to spend so much time on the issue of free and easily available cryptography? We'll let them tell you in their own words.

> *"Civilization is the progress toward a society of privacy. The savage's whole existence is public, ruled by the laws of his tribe. Civilization is the process of setting man free from men." Ayn Rand,* The Fountainhead *(1943)*

Being Watched?

Don't Fear Encryption, Fear Secrets

A Cypherpunk's Manifesto

By Eric Hughes (hughes@soda.berkeley.edu)

Privacy is necessary for an open society in the electronic age. Privacy is not secrecy. A private matter is something one doesn't want the whole world to know, but a secret matter is something one doesn't want anybody to know. Privacy is the power to selectively reveal oneself to the world.

If two parties have some sort of dealings, then each has a memory of their interaction. Each party can speak about his or her own memory of this; how could anyone prevent it? One could pass laws against it, but the freedom of speech, even more than privacy, is fundamental to an open society; we seek not to restrict any speech at all. If many parties speak together in the same forum, each can speak to all the others and create an aggregate of knowledge about individuals and other parties. The power of electronic communications has enabled such group speech, and it will not go away merely because we might want it to.

When we desire privacy, we must ensure that each party to a transaction have knowledge only of that which is directly necessary for that transaction. Since any information can be spoken of, we must ensure that we reveal as little as possible. In most cases, personal identity is not salient. When I purchase a magazine at a store and hand cash to the clerk, there is no need for the clerk to know who I am. When I ask my electronic mail provider to send and receive messages, my provider need not know to whom I am speaking or what I am saying or what others are saying to me; my provider only need know how to get the message there and how much I owe in fees. When my identity is revealed by the underlying mechanism of the transaction, I have no privacy. I cannot here selectively reveal myself; I must *always* reveal myself.

Therefore, privacy in an open society requires anonymous transaction systems. Until now, cash has been the primary such system. An *anonymous* transaction system is not a *secret* transaction system. An anonymous system empowers individuals to reveal their identity when desired and only when desired; this is the essence of privacy.

Privacy in an open society also requires cryptography. If I say something, I want it heard only by those for whom I intend it. If the content of my speech is available to the world, I have no privacy. To encrypt is to indicate the desire for privacy, and to encrypt with weak cryptography is to indicate not too great a desire for privacy. Furthermore, to reveal one's identity with assurance when the default is anonymity requires the cryptographic signature.

We cannot expect governments, corporations, or other large, faceless organizations to grant us privacy out of their beneficence. It is to their advantage to speak of us, and we should expect that they will speak. To try to prevent their speech is to fight against the realities of information. Information does not just want to be free, it has to be free. Information expands to fill the available space. Information is Rumor's younger, stronger cousin; Information is fleeter of foot, has more eyes, knows more, and understands less than Rumor.

We must defend our own privacy if we expect to have any. We must come together and create systems that allow anonymous transactions to take place. People have been defending their own privacy for centuries with whispers, darkness, enve-

lopes, closed doors, secret handshakes, and couriers. The technologies of the past did not allow for strong privacy protections, but electronic technologies do.

We, the Cypherpunks, are dedicated to building anonymous systems. We are defending our privacy with cryptography, with anonymous mail forwarding systems, with digital signatures, and with electronic money.

Cypherpunks write code. We know that someone has to write software to defend privacy, and since Cypherpunks can't get privacy unless we all do, we're going to write it. We publish our code so that our fellow Cypherpunks may practice and play with it. Our code is free for all to use, worldwide. We don't much care if you don't approve of the software we write. We know that software can't be destroyed and that a widely dispersed system can't be shut down.

Cypherpunks deplore regulations on cryptography, for encryption is fundamentally a private act. The act of encryption, in fact, removes information from the public realm. Even laws against cryptography reach only so far as a nation's border and the arm of its policing power. Cryptography will ineluctably spread over the whole globe, and with it the anonymous transactions systems that it makes possible.

For privacy to be widespread it must be part of a social contract. People must come together and deploy these systems for the common good. Privacy only extends so far as the cooperation of one's fellows in society. We, the Cypherpunks, seek your questions and your concerns and hope we may engage you so that we do not deceive ourselves. We will not, however, be moved out of our course because some may disagree with our goals.

The Cypherpunks are actively engaged in making the networks safer for privacy. Let us proceed together apace.

Onward.

Carter Calms Cypherpunks

Long before the advent of nuclear weapons, there were widespread rumors and dark fantasies about "doomsday devices": various bombs, ray-guns, or other devices so powerful they could destroy virtually any opponent, perhaps even entire populations. As we move from the nuclear age to the digital age, these rumors have transformed to frightened whispers about the "doomsday database."

So-called "conspiracy nuts" have warned of the danger of huge, centralized information bases for decades, with such ranting usually being dismissed as paranoid delusions. But paranoid delusions didn't bring about the death of journalist Danny Cassalaro. Found dead in his hotel room, days away from publishing a story he'd come to call "the Octopus," Cassalaro—whom some claim committed suicide, while others assert he was murdered—had been investigating the fantastic PROMIS software created by Inslaw, Inc. This revolutionary software seems the stuff of fables. Supposedly, the PROMIS software could track and cross-reference virtually unlimited amounts of information, which it would then compile into database form so that practically any question about any person could be answered instantly.

Some dismiss PROMIS as a harmless specter created by deluded minds, while others see it as a very real and potentially dangerous example of a federal government shockingly overstepping its bounds. Whatever the case, the facts of the matter are that the government has seized vast amounts of software source code from Inslaw, Cassalaro died under extraordinarily questionable circumstances, and many questions about PROMIS remained unanswered.

Now might be a good time to download and begin using a reliable encryption program.

net.speak

The world of cryptography is full of complex and confusing words and sketchy buzzwords. A glossary of cryptographic jargon is a much-needed aid to sorting out the matter. The terms below are excerpted from a crypto-glossary (crypto.dic) available in the via anonymous FTP in the library/document directory at ftp.spies.com.

crypto anarchy The economic and political system after the deployment of encryption, untraceable e-mail, digital pseudonyms, cryptographic voting, and digital cash. A pun on "crypto," meaning "hidden," and as when Gore Vidal called William F. Buckley a "crypto fascist."

cryptography Another name for cryptology.

cryptology The science and study of writing, sending, receiving, and deciphering secret messages. Includes authentication, digital signatures, the hiding of messages (steganography), cryptanalysis, and several other fields.

digital signature Analogous to a written signature on a document. A modification to a message that only the signer can make but that everyone can recognize. Can be used legally to contract at a distance.

National Security Agency (NSA) The largest intelligence agency, responsible for making and breaking ciphers, for intercepting communications, and for ensuring the security of U.S. computers. Headquartered in Fort Meade, Maryland, with many listening posts around the world. The NSA funds cryptographic research and advises other agencies about cryptographic matters. The NSA once obviously had the world's leading cryptologists, but this may no longer be the case.

public key encryption The use of modern cryptologic methods to provide message security and authentication. The RSA algorithm is the most widely used form of public key encryption, although other systems exist. A public key may be freely published, e.g., in phone book-like directories, while the corresponding private key is closely guarded.

Excerpted from a file compiled by Timothy C. May (tcmay@netcom.com) and Eric Hughes (hughes@soda.berkeley.edu)

The Crypto Anarchist Manifesto

By Timothy C. May (tcmay@netcom.com)

A specter is haunting the modern world, the specter of crypto anarchy.

Computer technology is on the verge of providing the ability for individuals and groups to communicate and interact with each other in a totally anonymous manner. Two persons may exchange messages, conduct business, and negotiate electronic contracts without ever knowing the true name, or legal identity, of the other. Interactions over networks will be untraceable, via extensive re-routing of encrypted packets and tamper-proof boxes that implement cryptographic protocols with nearly perfect assurance against any tampering. Reputations will be of central importance, far more important in dealings than even the credit ratings of today. These developments will alter completely the nature of government regulation, the ability to tax and control economic interactions, and the ability to keep information secret, and will even alter the nature of trust and reputation.

The technology for this revolution—and it surely will be both a social and economic revolution—has existed in theory for the past decade. The methods are based upon public-key encryption, zero-knowledge interactive proof systems, and various software protocols for interaction, authentication, and verification. The focus has, until now, been on academic conferences in Europe and the U.S., conferences monitored closely by the National Security Agency. But only recently have computer networks and personal computers attained sufficient speed to make the ideas practically realizable. And the next ten years will bring enough additional speed to make the ideas economically feasible and essentially unstoppable. High-speed networks, ISDN, tamper-proof boxes, smart cards, satellites, Ku-band transmitters, multi-MIPS personal computers,

The Crypto Anarchist Manifesto

and encryption chips now under development will be some of the enabling technologies.

The State will, of course, try to slow or halt the spread of this technology, citing national security concerns, use of the technology by drug dealers and tax evaders, and fears of societal disintegration. Many of these concerns will be valid; crypto anarchy will allow national secrets to be traded freely and will allow illicit and stolen materials to be traded. An anonymous computerized market will even make possible abhorrent markets for assassinations and extortion. Various criminal and foreign elements will be active users of CryptoNet. But the reaction to this will not halt the spread of crypto anarchy.

Just as the technology of printing altered and reduced the power of medieval guilds and the social power structure, so too will cryptologic methods fundamentally alter the nature of corporations and of government interference in economic transactions. Combined with emerging information markets, crypto anarchy will create a liquid market for any and all material that can be put into words and pictures. And just as a seemingly minor invention like barbed wire made possible the fencing-off of vast ranches and farms, thus altering forever the concepts of land and property rights in the frontier West, so too will a seemingly minor discovery in an arcane branch of mathematics come to be the wire clippers that dismantle the barbed wire around intellectual property.

Arise, you have nothing to lose but your barbed wire fences! ■

THE USENET ORACLE HAS PONDERED YOUR QUESTION DEEPLY. YOUR QUESTION WAS:

I accidentally deleted a Most Important Project from the disk, and I don't have a backup. My boss is expecting a (now deleted) project soon. What should I do?

AND IN RESPONSE, THUS SPAKE THE ORACLE:

First, clear your mind of the illusion that it was you who deleted the project. It was Dharma. He deleted the project as a test to see whether you are ready to undertake your destiny.

When your boss next asks you when the project will be completed, tell him or her, "It is complete."

BOSS: "Oh? When did you finish it?"
YOU: "It is not yet finished."
BOSS: "Well, when can you get it to me?"
YOU: "You already have it."
BOSS: "I do? Where is it?"
YOU: "It is inside you."
BOSS: "What?"
YOU: "The report is a part of you, and of me. We are a part of the Universal All. When we are finished, All shall be finished."
BOSS: "The Universal All?"
YOU: "The beginning is the end. Hesitate. Be lost. Consider the Lotus."
BOSS: "Lotus . . ."
YOU: "Om."
BOSS: "Om."

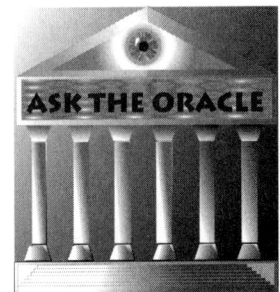

If you get the conversation to this stage, Dharma will be very satisfied with you. As you can tell, it is your destiny to get your butt canned in the near future. You owe the Oracle a backup of your latest project.

The Usenet Oracle has pondered your question deeply.

The Truth Behind the Krispie Conspiracy

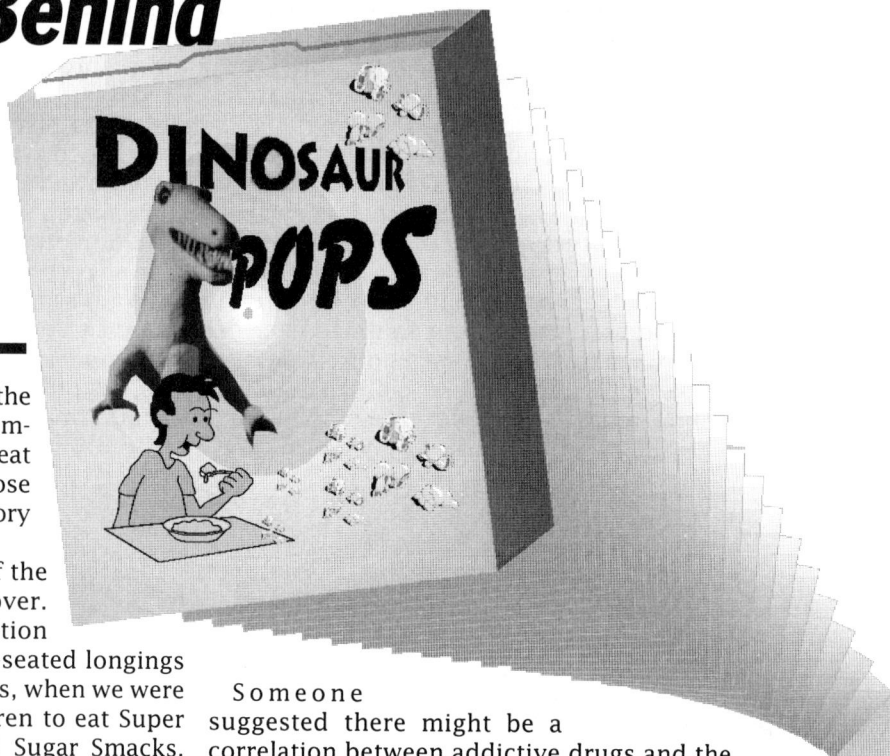

There are two kinds of people in the world: those who eat cereal that resembles twigs and leaves and those who eat cereals coated in sugar. (Sorry, but those who don't eat cereal from either category do not qualify as "people.")

News flash: *everyone* on the staff of the *Internet Insider* is a sugary cereal lover. (It's actually an employment condition here.) Maybe it stems from the deep-seated longings we all associate with our younger days, when we were denied our sovereign rights as children to eat Super Sugar Crisps, Sugar Corn Pops, and Sugar Smacks. (Alas, today's anti-sugar zealots have forced these cereals to be re-named "Golden Crisps," "Corn Pops," and merely "Smacks"—we're wondering when the anti-heroin lobby will take umbrage with that last name.)

On the Net, there's a group of folks who take their cereals very seriously. In **alt.cereal**, most of the discussion revolves around fond memories of sugar-coated breakfasts, with the occasional mention of a "healthy" cereal. The two groups have coexisted peacefully for years, but recently something odd happened in **alt.cereal**. Something very strange, and rather frightening.

Someone suggested there might be a correlation between addictive drugs and the way sugary cereals are advertised. The group soon erupted into a long-lived, vitriolic stream of flaming bickering so heated and vicious that one member suggested the group change its name to **alt.flame.cereal**. To protect the "innocent," we've changed the names of the combatants, and since the *Insider* is a family paper, we've *@!&%BLEEEPED * @!&% out any unsavory language.

In the end, the debate died out, and no one seemed entirely sure why things got so out of hand. We suspect it has something to do with the deep rift between healthy cereal advocates and those in the sugar-coated camp. Or perhaps it was a deeper, older hatred—the mistrust and prejudice that has always existed between cereal-eaters and non-cereal-eaters. Frankly, we're glad it's all over. Folks were acting like monsters for a while. We're happy things are back to normal, and we're thrilled to be spending time with our other favorite monsters: Franken Berry, Count Chocula, Boo Berry, Fruit Brute, and Yummy Mummy.

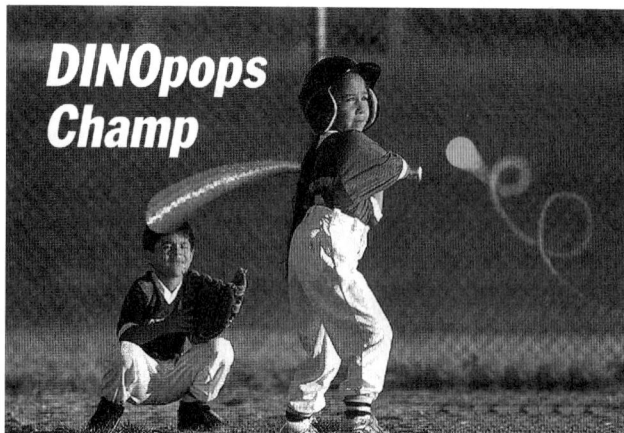

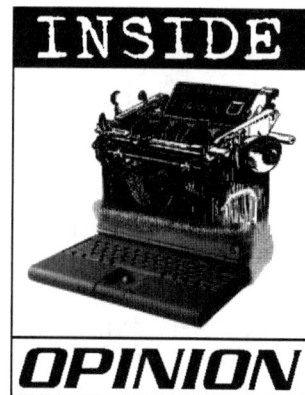

DINOpops Champ

INSIDE

OPINION

240

LIFE @ LARGE

The fantastic and taste-tempting world of modern-day breakfast cereals that we take for granted is the result of a long and colorful history. According to Jonathan Crawford's **alt.cereal** FAQ and Thomas J. Schlereth's *Victorian America: Transformations in Everyday Life*, cereal was once considered an oddity of the strange domain of early health advocates.

Apparently, something strange and wonderful was going on in Battle Creek, Michigan in the 1890s, when **John H. Kellogg** and **C.W. Post** began advocating that Americans abandon their typical breakfast of steak, potatoes, porridge, and eggs for a healthier meal. In fact, Post's first cereal wasn't even a cereal: **Postum Cereal Food Coffee** was a coffee substitute concocted of bran, wheat, and molasses. In 1906, Post introduced a corn flake cereal he called Elijah's Manna, but following an outcry from religious groups, he renamed the cereal **Post Toasties**.

Net Resources

If you're searching for more info about cereal on the Internet and you find a resource besides the **alt.cereal** newsgroup, please let us know. The only other spot we've found is the Web page where the alt.cereal FAQ resides. Web-surfers can find it at: http://www.halcyon.com/irving/alt.cereal.faq.html.

If you're hankering for a few real-world cereal resources (and hey, who isn't), try contacting these major cereal producers:

General Mills, Minneapolis, MN 55440 (800) 328-1144

Kellogg Company, Battle Creek, MI 49016 (800) 962-1413

Post/Kraft General Foods, Inc., White Plains, NY 10625 (800) 431-7678

Quaker Oats Company, Chicago, IL (312) 222-7111

Ralston Purina Company, St. Louis, MO 63164 (314) 982-1000

Still mad at your mom for throwing out your comic books? (No, mom, this isn't a snipe at you . . . but don't even *think of* touching my comics—you don't need the closet space that badly!) Miffed that you could have sold that cigar box full of baseball cards for enough to buy a Mercedes, only Aunt Hilda sold them all at a yard sale for 50 cents? Well you better lock up your cereal box prize collection before Bowser starts chewing on it. According to the alt.cereal FAQ, some of those pieces may be worth $2,500!

Ralph (a.k.a "Quisp&Quake") collects some cereal toys. If you've got trinkets from the following cereal boxes, send Ralph the good news (ralphe@ux1.cso.uiuc.edu) and maybe he'll make you rich:

List Service

Quisp

Quake

Quangaroo

Cap'N Crunch and his cohorts

Grins, Smiles, Giggles, and Laughs

Major Moonstones

Freakies

Baron VonRedberry and Sir Grapefellow

CoCo Puffs/Sonny

Rocky, Bullwinkle, or Dudley premiums

Funny Face drink mixes

Trix Rabbit

Sugar Bear

Who knows how nasty rumors get started, or why? Some begin as manifestations of our worst fears, some result from government disinformation campaigns, while others are simply wild speculation and fantasy, aimed at eliciting a specific response from a particular group of people. Just such a rumor (spread by one rkerber@dolphin.upenn.edu) made it's way into the **alt.cereal** group:

"I once heard from someone that they had toured a big cereal factory. The vats of bubbly, mushy cereal batter (or whatever substance it was) was a major turn-off for them, and they swore off cereal for a while. They were huge, and they looked as if debris was falling in. Just thought I'd let you all know."

Luckily, cooler heads prevailed, and a clear-thinking member of the alt.cereal group (mcdonoug@elvis.rowan.edu) came forward to put an end to the ridiculous tale of massive, contaminated cereal vats.

"Lies! Lies! Lies! Everyone *knows* that our cereal supply is brought to us by benevolent yet powerful aliens that Mr. Kellogg contacted while in a meditative trance. That secret air force base in Nevada is where the alien cereal delivery ships land. Duh!"

Tough-Guy Krispies Muscle In On Cereal Market

By Scott H. Reece (sreece@nmsu.edu)

Could this be Tony The Tiger?

OK. Has anyone else noticed that Snap, Crackle, and Pop are out to take over cereal-land. Let's review a few important facts here:

1) Cocoa Krispies

What happened to the cool little brown elephant that used to be the mascot? Gone. Snap, Crackle, and Pop (SCP) took over that outlet, then subcontracted it out to whatever the name of that arrogant monkey is. He is obviously an elf cousin of SCP in disguise, placed there to do their bidding.

2) Frosted Krispies

These guys got serious here. They took out the big guy's son, Tony Jr., in order to gain control of that outlet. Poor Tony was so devastated by this blow that he let the reigns slip out of his hands. He is merely a figurehead now. A poor shell of a tiger, going through the motions for the sake of his fans. SCP retain control of this outlet.

3) Marshmallow Krispies

Krispie Treats, and now what is it Apple-Cinnamon Krispies? With their original outlet, that makes six that they control, far surpassing other industry big-wigs like Captain Crunch (3 regular titles and one seasonal—Christmas Crunch) and Fred Flintstone (3 titles). That's three titles for Fred, but with one of them being run by his pet dogasaurus—reminds me of Caligula making his horse a general. Not a bright move in this blood-thirsty business, what with

Barnaby and Friends

Barney always attempting hostile takeovers.

I see Fred being spread very thin with the release of the movie and all. Ripe for invasion, especially since these are puffed rice cereals, a known favorite of SCP and a proven market winner for them. Watch out Fred. Also, keep an eye on newcomer Popeye, making his bid for a market share with at least 2 and some reports of 3 new titles. Although basically knock-offs of popular favorites, Popeye's cereals ship in reduced packaging (bag only), which is sure to be a hit with green consumers. Sure hope he doesn't incur the wrath of SCP, or we might find Olive floating with the soggy marshmallows.

Sugary Gathering Spontaneously Combusts

From Cynthia:

Hi everyone! I have been reading this group recently and haven't seen anyone comment on the disturbing aspects of certain children's cereal commercials. The two series of commercials that I find most disturbing are the "Coo-Coo for Coco Puffs" ads and the "Trix are for Kids" ads. Both these ads feature "birds" that are addicted to cereal which either causes them to hallucinate and see many colors (*a la* LSD) or to freak out and wreak havoc on the nearby area (*a la* PCP).

What kind of message is this sending our children? When the cereal doesn't give them the desired effect, will they seek this sort of drug-induced hysteria through illegal narcotics? I am presently getting ready to start a petition to have these ads taken off the air. The implications scare me, and I do not allow my little ones to eat these cereals because of it.

Have a nice day!

From Ed:

Have you seen the free hypnotic eyes you can get now as a premium with a box of Trix! The kids can eat the cereal then put the eyes on and authentically look high!! Also, I haven't seen a Sonny or a Trix Rabbit ad in a long time, do they still run them??

From Cynthia:

That's the new line of commercials that makes me believe in this strange connection between drugs and certain cereals all the more! You have the Trix bunny going to hypnotherapy to relieve him of his insane addiction. And yes, they still run these ads quite a bit. The newest ad that I saw today while watching Jenny Jones was for some new Captain Crunch fruity cereal. It showed a young boy (animated) visibly upset because he had no vacation plans. Quite suddenly, out of his wading pool, no less, the good Captain gives him this fruity cereal which becomes a "trip" unto itself with its many "bright colors." Why is it that we teach our children at an early age that they must have a tool for escaping reality? We start them with cereal until they are old enough to drink or obtain drugs. But it seems to begin with the cereal.

From Jeff:

I totally agree with you. I have noticed this for a long time and have never said anything because it didn't affect me personally. I think that our nation needs to put a stop to this. They are subliminally telling our youth to go out and try drugs. Do you remember when Mighty Mouse used to snort the white powder? It gave him strength and powers. Well we are dealing with the same thing. We need to act now!! Lets move on this.

From Cynthia:

I don't find this at all funny, Jeff. You seem to think I'm making some sort of joke with your sarcastic tone. I have a serious point in all this and it has nothing to do with tacos. This is a serious problem that somebody in the FCC is just allowing to go on uninhibited. I wish they could do something, but they won't, so I'll do my best to make a small impact.

From Jeff:

Listen Cynthia! Did I say one *@!&% word about tacos? NO, I DIDN'T, so why don't you get your head out of your *@!&% and read what I wrote. Mighty Mouse used to snort a white powdery substance, presumably cocaine. Mighty Mouse was a cartoon meant for kids. For this reason he was not allowed to snort any more. I was trying to make a point: that you might have a chance in trying to make your impact. AND I SAID I AGREED WITH YOU!! So think before you go make a judgmental call on what I believe in!

From Jason:

Cynthia wrote: "I am presently getting ready to start a petition to have these ads taken off the air. The implications scare me and I do not allow my little ones to eat these cereals because of it."

Well, I dunno here, Cynthia . . . I grew up watching violent Bugs Bunny cartoons, and I don't go around trying to squash people (or cartoon characters) with anvils. Well, at least not recently. There are more important "bad influences" in the world to concentrate on than cartoons and commercials. Besides, if you don't let them eat the cereal now, they'll just end up hating you when they're older, taking PCP, and eating the cereal anyway.

From Deborah:

Cynthia wrote: "I am presently getting ready to start a petition to have these ads taken off the air. The implications scare me and I do not allow my little ones to eat these cereals because of it."

Um, Cynthia? I don't know how old you are or what philosophies you subscribe to, but here's a friendly suggestion . . . relax!

I am 21 years old and no longer eat sugary children's cereals, but I remember eating the aforementioned cereals as a kid. When I used to see those commercials, I did not think, "Wow, they look like they are having fun with drugs." Instead, I thought, "Gee, those kids are mean not to let the bunny have his Trix." And when I was eating my cereal, I did not think, "Hmmm, how come I'm not hallucinating?" Instead I was thinking, "Oh no! I better hurry up and finish eating or I'm gonna be late for school!"

I know the world is a scary place, but I think some people are too nervous, especially parents. I'm not saying that parents shouldn't worry (I plan on being a parent in a few years, and I know I'm going to worry, a lot), but in this case I feel you're overdoing it. We already have warning labels on music to indicate "explicit" lyrics and a rating system for movies. We have "Just Say No" and sex ed programs in our schools. All this accounts for nil if parents don't talk to their kids. (For example, I gained nothing useful from my school's sex ed program, and I wish my parents had talked to me about it more, but they were too embarrassed about it).

Instead of adding more censorship to the world, I suggest you spend the energy (that you would have exerted writing to whomever is "in charge") talking to your kids; don't preach, but actually start a dialogue in which you say something and they say something and you say something and they say something (you get the idea), and really try to listen to them.

From Jason:

Once upon a time, Cynthia wrote:...a lot of stuff, some valid, some rather nasty.

I have a coupla suggestions here.

1) Don't expect to make friends by name-calling. I understand you want to talk about this seriously, and that it means a lot to you for personal reasons, but you're not going to get any support talking like this.

2) This is an alt group, featuring fairly recreational discussions on a fun topic: Cereal. I think you'd be better served bringing your topic up in a media group, or something like that. Or a drug-related group. Or something. You can't flame anyone for being here for fun.

From Rob:

What is happening to this group? Only a couple of weeks ago, I considered it relatively normal. Now we have people like Larry, Jeff, and Cynthia. Yes you Cynthia! You're as bad as the rest of them, for flaming everyone whose opinion differs from yours. Maybe this group should be renamed **alt.flame.cereal.**

From Cynthia:

I take offense at this attack against me. It seems to have become fashionable in this group to do so lately and it really pisses me off. I have not been arbitrarily "flaming" people for disagreeing me. I have been voicing my dismay at the personal attacks being leveled against me. My posts have been discussing a serious topic that is relevant to this group. I am *not* joking. And what is your post, Rob? It is a flame. Everything I have posted other than defending myself has been CEREAL RELEVANT. Your post is a whiny little flame. None of you seem to see the big picture I am addressing here. Instead, you are all content to ignore what is in front of your face and, instead, crack little jokes about me. You all have a little growing up to do.

From Larry:

OK, that's it! I'm so sick and *@!&% damn tired of the freaks on this group. I have been reading this group for a while myself. Never posted, but always read the news. Then some freak named Jeff came on here and I'm like "I can take care of this guy," and now, you dirty rotten stinky *@!&%'s are telling me that I'm kinda abnormal. Well *@!&% YOU, *@!&%. That's the last time I do anything for this newsgroup. I have a better idea about newsgroups. why don't you go and make one up named alt.I'm.an.*@!&%!

From Barnaby:

Larry, better lay offa the chocolate cereals in chocolate milk . . .

From Scott:

[In response to suggestions that some posters should be banned from alt.cereal for profane bickering:]

I think we shouldn't kick anybody out for providing entertainment, profane as it is. Let these two jerks flame each other all they want. It's a helluva lot better reading than some weenie who thinks cereal ads should be banned because the characters therein experience altered states of consciousness. (To which I reply in a Pee-Wee Herman voice, "How would you know?")

From Cynthia:

Scott, let me begin by saying that you are an *@!&%. I was posting on a serious and disturbing topic, but you would rather be "entertained" by an idiot rambling about his taco. If you are not interested in what I have to say, don't read it. But please refrain from insulting me, as I, unlike many others around here, have a serious point to make about the state of advertising and its effects on our children.

And to answer your question, I am in my seventh year of sobriety from alcohol and narcotics. I probably have done more hallucinogens in my time than the rest of this newsgroup combined, so DON'T TELL ME WHAT I DON'T KNOW. Go back to junior high, *@!&%.

From Norris:

I'm OUTRAGED when I see the cruel and inhumane treatment that the Trix Rabbit has to endure at the hands of his human oppressors. The kids don't have to be so freakin mean! It's just cereal, after all. Would it be so bad to let him have just one bowl? But NO, it's just sooooo funny to mock the little bunny rabbit. Forget about his feelings. He's not HUMAN, after all. America's youth is going to hell for this.

P.S. I am an active member of P.E.T.A. and am going to bring this up at the next meeting. Hopefully we will pursue legal action against the kids.

From Chuck:

Hey, man, wake up and smell the cereal. Oppression of good-natured cartoon characters has been the norm for this country for a long, long time. Think about it . . . Lucky's always running from those little monsters who steal his cereal and force him to make new marshmallows to satisfy their mad design. Or how about the honey bee? Sure, they all get a laugh as long as the kid gets the darn cereal and the bee gets a door slammed in his face. Fruity Pebbles? Once best friends, now turned mortal enemies, Barney, a seemingly good-natured fellow, uses his malicious cunning to take advantage of his chum's gullibility. I think that the only character who's gotten revenge is Sonny.

In the beginning, the kids would torture the poor mutant bird into going cuckoo, but sometime, without anybody noticing, the tables have turned and Sonny is surely succeeding in making all the kids in the world go cuckoo for Coco Puffs.

It's a tough market out there; if you wanna sell kid's cereal, somebody's gotta get hurt. How 'bout the Cookie Crook? Is trying to get just one damn bowl of cereal his only crime? Oh the humanity! And what of the Cookie Crook's dog? Why should he go to jail in every commercial? He's a *dog*, for Christ's sake! I'll tell you why: people are ruthless. Sure, you think you're a pretty nice guy . . . you never get in anybody's way, you never start any trouble, you'd help a guy in trouble if you could, right? Wrong!

You start with maybe some Lucky Charms, and watch the commercials . . . mmm. You know, those kids may use the wrong means, but I sure do like these new marshmallow chartreuse station-wagons they persuaded Lucky to make. I think I'll have some more.

After three bowls, you're flying so high on a marshmallow-sugar binge that you're wondering why no one has thought to tear out Lucky's fingernails one by one until he turns the whole of *@!&%ing Ireland into a giant marshmallow for you to eat. Yeah, bash the bee on the head pour hydrochloric acid on his wings, ha ha ha, just as long as I get my tummy tempted by the taste of nuts and honey! I'll put a hatchet in the head of my own parents if they keep me from my beloved corn pops. Think about it—is it worth all this? Can't we all just get along?

The End Is Nigh, the Beast Is Anxious for Your Soul

People have always believed they were living in the end times. Since before the earliest rumblings of organized religion—beginning, perhaps, with primitive pagan rituals—folks have been convinced the end of the world would come within their lifetime. People today are no different: they, too, are convinced these are the last days. They are different, though, in that they are correct.

Yeah, that's right, we're living in the end times. Don't tell us you're surprised to learn this. As if harnessing the atom, walking on the moon, and Ted Koppel's hair weren't scary enough to wake you up, there's this whole "mark of the Beast" thing. You'll recall, of course, the Bible prophecy that the Beast (or Antichrist) will show up in town and force us all to bear its mark, without which we'll be unable to buy, sell and/or travel, depending on which version of the Bible we're using.

A number of folks on the Net seem to be taking these predictions seriously, while others are at least hedging their bets, prophetically speaking. Regardless of the degree to which they buy into the mark of the Beast idea, thousands of netizens are aware of the prophecy and are keeping an eye out for someone sporting a "666" on his forehead or hand.

The folks at BeastNet, for instance, have come up with the idea that the Beast is already here, hiding out on Madison Avenue or along Hollywood Boulevard, or lurking in the halls of the Capitol or in any number of places where least expected. They're using the Net to spread the word about the Beast, and they want your help in identifying and eradicating it—which isn't as crazy as it sounds. As the specter of a scary new millennium bears down on us all like a sumo wrestler with a jockstrap full of hornets, we might do well to hold back our scoffs and keep at least one eye open in search of the Beast.

INSIDE

OPINION

Net Resources

In an exclusive interview with the Insider, one of BeastNet's founders described the group as a "loosely affiliated private coalition of sovereign citizens dedicated to fighting the Beast and its agents in all their manifestations. An electronic champion for free speech, civil liberties, and Constitutional rights, BeastNet offers an open forum where information, opinion, and speculation about the nature and activities of The Beast can be freely exchanged. BeastNet is privately funded by its members and receives no funding or other support of any kind from government or corporate sources."

For more details on BeastNet or to volunteer your time and efforts in the war against The Beast, write to **BeastNet@farces.com** or download further information from the Beast-Net site at **ftp.farces.com**.

Still vague on the whole "mark of the Beast" thing? From a message sent to the *Insider* offices by a concerned reader, we offer the nitty-gritty of the prophecy, taken directly from Revelation 13, which describes the whole scenario in detail. Needless to say, it isn't a positive outlook on the impending future.

From Revelation 13:15
And he had power to give life unto the image of the beast, that the image of the beast should both speak, and cause that as many as would not worship the image of the beast should be killed.
13:16
And he causeth all, both small and great, rich and poor, free and bond, to receive a mark in their right hand, or in their foreheads.
13:17
And that no man might buy or sell, save he that had the mark, or the name of the beast, or the number of his name.
13:18
Here is wisdom. Let him that hath understanding count the number of the beast: for it is the number of a man; and his number is Six hundred threescore and six.

The Net works in wonderful ways. When someone in the **alt.conspiracies** newsgroup asked for information on an article about the mark of the Beast, a fellow Beast-buster responded quickly with the vital details.

LIFE @ LARGE

Query:
Someone posted to **alt.conspiracy** an article from *Nexus* magazine, entitled "666 is coming," which told of chips being implanted under the skin. I'm trying to find out the truthfulness of this article. I received a copy from a local BBS. The posting stated it came from the *Nexus* magazine, sometime in June. I've called several magazine stands and they've never heard of *Nexus* magazine. I would like to get a copy of this article, if possible. If anyone knows more info on this article, has a copy or knows about *Nexus* magazine, please send me an e-mail.

Response:
Nexus Vol. 2, #20
June/July 1994
Nexus
P.O. Box 177, Kempton, IL 60946-0177
Fax: 815/253-6300; Vox: 815/253-6464

Titled: *"The Microchip and the Mark of the Beast"*; pages 14-15; discussions with Dr. Carl W. Sanders; transcript edited from *"The Good News Paper,"* Vol. 4, #12 1993.

Contact details for further information and audio tapes:
93213 Division St. #140
Spokane, WA 99218 USA
509/623-6285

A Call to Arms for the 21st Century

BeastNet Mission Statement
4 July 1994

Throughout history, people have struggled to achieve more than their predecessors, to create for themselves and pass on to their children a world that is better in every way than the one they inherited. Whether through individual efforts or cooperative endeavors, it is an inherent drive of all people to engender a human experience more positive, fulfilling, and enlightening than that which previously existed.

Yet, for every bold step forward taken by individuals, organizations, societies, and nations, there has always been an opposing force that would seek to halt mankind's progress, to arrest human development at every opportunity. This opposing force—this dark, contrary, beastly aspect of human nature—has manifested itself in many forms throughout the ages, and it is often only with the perspective of history that we can see this dark power—this Beast—for what it truly is.

The great challenge facing humanity is not so much to use the hindsight afforded by current circumstances to understand what this Beast has done in the past, as it is to identify the Beast in current times and to act to counter its influence on all that is decent and noble in the world.

The great social experiment known as the United States of America that was begun two centuries and 18 years ago has brought to the citizens of the world new standards of freedom, prosperity, and justice, striking a devastating blow at the very heart of the Beast. Yet since the founding of the United States of America, the inalienable rights, liberties, and responsibilities implicit in the covenant of American citizenship have drastically changed. Many of those duties that were once the sole obligation of individuals have now become the burden of government, while rights that once belonged to the states or the citizens are now claimed by a self-sustained federal bureaucracy.

In short, the utopian republic envisioned by our forefathers, which was in large part realized through decades of hard work, innovation, and self-sacrifice, has been slowly auctioned off in small, seemingly insignificant pieces to the highest bidders, which are always agents of the Beast. The unfortunate result would seem to be an impending dystopia that would rival the darkest days of human existence.

Yet this ostensible and progressing dystopia has not arisen overnight. Rather, it slowly grew like a cancer, fed by an unwitting conspiracy of complacency, ignorance, apathy, and arrogance. Sometime, somewhere along the way, something happened in America. Her citizens forgot their hard-learned lessons of liberty, abandoned their principles of freedom, and surrendered their ideals of independence. The very fundamentals of life and the qualities of character that made the United States the envy of the world are now all but forgotten, and a once-proud nation of pioneers, creators, and risk-takers has lost its collective confidence, giving way to a land of sycophants, cowards, and parasites.

Our United States of America are not alone in their struggle with the Beast and its agents. Yet, while other nations may enjoy higher standards of living, safer streets, or more efficient public works programs, there is no state on earth where individuals are as free to pursue their dreams and follow their own aspirations. If America's torch of liberty is extinguished, it is unlikely that the flames of freedom will long burn elsewhere.

While the situation is grim, a world devoid of individual liberty, personal responsibility, and singular creativity is not a foregone conclusion. Though we are to some great extent at the mercy of others in our society, we still each control our own destiny by the individual choices we make every day. Since all power lies with the people, and the governments of the world can derive their authority only from those rights and freedoms that their citizens voluntarily or involuntarily surrender, it is up to us as individuals to realize the Beast for what it is and work to counter its influence in every corner of the world.

To that end:

BeastNet has been created to inform and educate the American people and the rest of the world about the true nature of the Beast, and to serve as a guiding light for those seeking the freedom, liberty, and justice they so righteously demand. By serving as a clearinghouse for information, a reliable source of news, and a powerful means of communications, BeastNet aims to combat the Beast by exposing its actions, illuminating its motivations, and providing effective methods of opposition to all who would work to oppose the Beast.

By using the Internet as a central communications infrastructure, BeastNet can reach millions of people around the globe. Through soliciting information from as many independent sources as possible, BeastNet strives to provide an accurate

Help Slay the Beast

and comprehensive account of the actions of the Beast based on first-hand observations from individuals in hundreds of nations and thousands of cities. Successful tactics for combating the Beast can be shared with any interested party with only a few computer keystrokes.

The mission of BeastNet includes, but is by no means limited to, an effort on the part of freedom-loving individuals to:

- Identify and annihilate, through words and actions, all servants and deeds of every manifestation of the Beast, which is that capacity for evil that lurks in the hearts of men and women everywhere.

- Work for a society in which all people are free to exercise their inalienable human and civil rights, with no exceptions or conditions, and to create and foster a society in which all people are free and equal in the eyes of the law.

- Resist all attacks on the American people and the United States Constitution from enemies both domestic and foreign.

- Educate our fellow American citizens about the destruction of our Constitutional republic and the rise of a police state.

- Establish an economic system in which the sovereign citizens of the United States are viewed not as cattle or slaves, but as active and valuable participants.

Top 10 Ways to Starve The Beast

By John DiNardo (jad@nyxfer.blythe.org)

It isn't surprising that the New World Order Beast is rapidly growing to gargantuan proportions. It isn't surprising that The Beast is now attacking us more viciously than ever before. The larger it grows, the more brazen it becomes, devouring our ever-dwindling wealth, liberties, and human dignity.

It isn't so surprising when you realize that YOU and I have been feeding this Beast . . . no, "feeding" does not accurately describe it; "engorging" is the accurate term. We engorge The

Don't Feed the Hand That Bites You

Beast with money for the oil that it sells us. We engorge The Beast when we buy its adulterated, toxified, pesticide-ridden foods. We engorge The Beast when we fall prey to its myriad TV advertising enticements.

Can you imagine how The Beast would shrink to less threatening proportions if we systematically starved it instead of feeding it?

Each day that is squandered as we run our rat races for the bankers and corporate executives of the global New World Order dictatorship . . . each of these squandered days immerses us ever deeper in our own enslavement and guarantees the future enslavement of our children.

World Ends, Beast Devours All, Film at 11:00

Remember our children. Save the children, for otherwise, they will suffer far more than we will, clearly because they will live deeper in the pit of the oppressive twenty-first century—in the belly of The Beast.

The remaining time in which we can control our own society and our own lives is fast running out. So let us now actuate the vast dormant power of our minds to produce the creative ideas that will lead us to overcome and overwhelm the growing Beast of freedom's doom.

Here are a few ideas on how to starve The Beast, but you too must help by following up with creative ideas of your own.

1. Starve The Beast by growing at least some of your own vegetables and fruits or by buying non-pesticide-ridden, nutritionally rich grains like rice, rye, oats, and barley produced by small companies and sold at health food stores. If you eat health foods and shun the refined, toxified, nutritionless junk foods that The Beast pushes on you in the supermarket, then you will surely look radiant and you will feel vibrant.

2. Starve The Beast by asserting your rights and fulfilling your duties as a sovereign citizen of the United States of America. Your rights and responsibilities as a citizen are clearly delineated in the U.S. Constitution. Make sure you own at least one copy and by all means study it. It contains simple answers to the myriad problems we are experiencing as a nation.

3. Starve The Beast by turning OFF your TV set and stop watching the perpetual psychological warfare designed to numb your sensibilities and excite your desires for more material possessions. (nyt@nyxfer .blythe.org)

4. Starve The Beast by being an Artist at EVERYTHING you do. Create, create anew. (Keith Sorensen, ksorensen@college .antioch.edu)

5. Starve The Beast by buying things second-hand, thus gaining a 75% raise, as well as avoiding sales taxes. It's rewarding fun too. Only drawback is you don't support working Americans, but there aren't going to be many of those soon if we don't do something. How about learning how to reload your own ammo? (Bob Cathar, fi017@cleveland.freenet.edu)

6. Starve The Beast by bartering for whatever goods and services you can, whenever you can. This is the most effective and purist form of capitalist exchange, circumventing the use of worthless Federal Reserve Notes and denying the illegal and unconstitutional Internal Revenue Service another chance to steal money from working people and deliver it to international bankers.

7. Starve The Beast by paying off all consumer debts and avoiding them in the future. Avoid especially using credit cards as a lazy form of high-interest loan to yourself or a method to live beyond your current means. Every dollar of credit card debt you incur each year results in 15-20 cents going into the pockets of The Beast.

8. Starve The Beast by refusing to accept the propaganda of fear and demagoguery of hate. The Beast and its politician servants want you to fear and hate your neighbor. Get to know your neighbors and get involved in your community—don't count on the government to clean up your streets or solve your problems—take responsibility for them yourself.

9. Starve The Beast by questioning authority and thinking about what you're told. Don't accept as fact whatever you read in the paper or see on TV. (Avoid TV in general for that matter.) Don't assume that authority figures, from law enforcement agents to politicians, are acting in your own interest. Think for yourself and verify questionable information.

10. Starve The Beast by alerting others to its actions. Most people are generally shocked and horrified to learn of the extent and nature of its activities. Most people, if approached in a friendly and sympathetic manner and given hard facts about The Beast, will appreciate your efforts to educate them.

Now it's your turn to present ideas on how to starve The Beast. Begin with the words, "Starve The Beast by . . ." and e-mail your ideas to John DiNardo at (jad@nyxfer.blythe.org). I will append it to the growing "starve-the-beast" list.

Portholes '95?

Microsoft Logo Is Mark of the Beast

By Philip Heggie (heggie@rmit.edu.au)

The Windows logo is the image of the beast received in your right hand by mouse and in your forehead from eyeball to visual cortex.

```
......----- 
......|_|_|   3 rows of six black dots = 6 6 6 connected
......|_|_|   to an image of a window.
```

The win.com startup logo has 7 rows of 6 dots in several colors, but 3 of the rows of 6 dominate the image in the "color" black. So 6 6 6 is embedded and dominant in the software's color logo's image.

That sneaky devil Gates has duped you all to run your life, the Universe, and everything through Windows. He will control your life on the super info highway by his 6 6 6 Windows interface. You won't be able to travel, buy, or sell without a Windows license in the near future.

Whosoever receives the virtual reality glove in their right hand or virtual reality mask on their forehead of 6 6 6,

who is ASCII: BILLGATES 3 (CONTROL-C),

shall not perish, but have everlasting life in the fast lane of the super info highway. Lost in Cyberspace forever, riding on a satellite beam to infinity.

Enter the number of the beast: press CONTROL-F CONTROL-F CONTROL-F to ACKnowledge your fate now.

Brought to you by your computer that blasphemes the church of fawny case shun.

6 6 6 in ASCII is an ACKnowledge ACKnowledge ACKnowledge command. 6 6 6 is to acknowledge a buy, to acknowledge a sell, and to acknowledge travel. A triple acknowledge transaction by computers is predicted in the bible.

6 6 6 = sum of ASCII codes for "BILLGATES" + 3, which is ASCII 'End of Text,' meaning the beginning of the Graphics User Interface with Windows for PC's using an Icon that is the image of the beast. I CON you not.

Modified quote: The real name of Bill Gates is William Henry Gates III. Nowadays he is known as Bill Gates (III), where "III" means the order of third (3rd.).

By converting the letters of his current name to the ASCII-values and adding his (III), you get the following:

B	66
I	73
L	76
L	76
G	71
A	65
T	84
E	69
S	83
ack	3 ACKNOWLEDGE transaction

6 6 6!!

Some might ask, "How did Bill Gates get so powerful?" Coincidence? Or just the beginning of mankind's ultimate and total enslavement??? YOU decide! ∎

It's A Conspiracy!

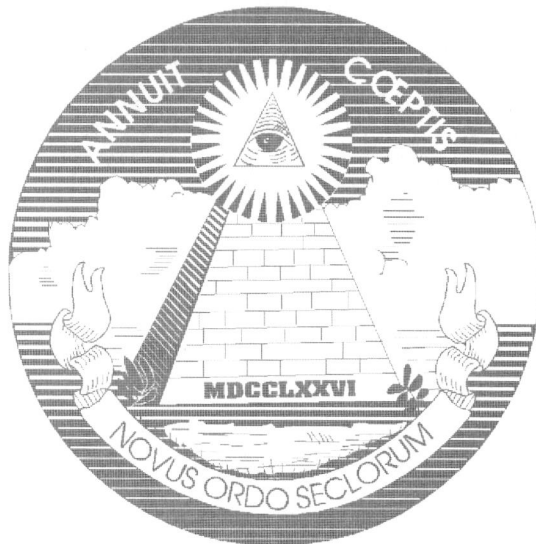

The word "tabloid" hasn't always been such an expression of derision. It used to simply mean a newspaper of a certain size and format. But tabloid has gone the way of so many other words: Marxist, fur, liberal, radiation, fundamentalist, compromise, intellectual, violence, secular, victim, meat, responsibility, covert, benefit, dependent.

Like *tabloid*, these words—previously innocuous, or at least only slightly tainted—have come to elicit the shame and scorn of Hester Prynne's scarlet *A*.

"Conspiracy" is another such charged word. For years, anyone who believed in a conspiracy was painted as a shut-in, a subversive or a mental weakling. Conventional wisdom dictated that conspiracies just didn't happen. This was America—we do business in the open. There's no need for conspiracies.

But events ranging from the Kennedy assassination to Watergate through BCCI and Iran-Contra have brought about a marked change in the connotations of the word "conspiracy." With more and more Americans convinced that the government (regardless of which party controls it) is not only ignoring the people's wishes but acting contrary to them, "conspiracy thinking" has gained a new acceptance.

Combine rampant cynicism with a complete distrust of the press—the traditional guardians of truth and watchdogs of democracy—and you've created an atmosphere where yesterday's "conspiracy buffs" are today's political visionaries. And the Net is the central exchange of such skeptical information.

In fact, it's no surprise to see an obscure "crackpot" theory from **alt.conspiracy** turn up as the latest plot twist in an episode of *The X Files*. So if "conspiracy theories" are now not only accepted, but hailed—at least on the Net—what does it all mean? Don't ask us. After all, we're only a *tabloid*.

Power Rangers Stamp Out Individuality

By Animesh Karna (karna@pobox.upenn.edu)

Now, *here's* a topic worthy of a conspiracy!

Consider . . . every now and then, they talk about how fighting isn't the only way to solve problems, but it's the only method the Power Rangers seem to ever use. In the middle of a battle, they never seem to stop and say to a monster: "You seem to have a lot of anger . . . tell me about your childhood." Nah, it's just bash bash kick.

About 90% of the episodes follow this plot: Rita/Lord Zed sends down a monster, Power Rangers go and fight it, Rita/Lord Zed makes the monster huge, they get their Dino-Zords, form MegaZord, and nuke the monster. This is a LOT like Voltron. What is the theme of MegaZord and Voltron? Individuals can't succeed, give up your identities and become cogs in some machine if you want to win.

Besides, Lord Zed should give a major apology to Rita. He was rather mean to her regarding her inability to defeat the Power Rangers, yet he's not doing any better.

My son loves this show . . . sigh . . .

(BTW, this is meant to be a lighthearted conspiracy, folks; considering that I used to watch "He-Man and the Masters of the Universe," I don't think I have the right to complain.)

If you're going to hang around the **alt.conspiracy** newsgroup, do everyone a favor and brush up on the lingo. Trying to join the Net-driven discussions of what's really going on in the world without knowing a dupe from a patsy is like trying to talk baseball without knowing a fly ball from a grounder.

black helicopter—Netizens around the U.S. are reporting sightings of sinister "black helicopters" bearing no markings or lights, or with insignias that don't match any known government agency.

black op—A covert or "black" operation carried out without the knowledge of the general public and without conventional government oversight.

Constitution Party—Political party (PO Box 7565, Beverly Hills, CA, 90212) dedicated to furthering the cause of the United States Constitution as the basis for government in America.

dupe—Someone in power who has been unwittingly "duped" into supporting a hidden agenda. Differs from a "patsy" in that a patsy is set up to take a fall, whereas a dupe is continually and systematically manipulated.

FEMA—Federal Emergency Management Agency. A strangely powerful government organization invested by executive order with supreme powers during times of national crisis.

mark of the Beast—Any of dozens of various "marks," ranging from bar codes to credit cards to Norplant-style implants that may represent the "mark of the Beast" described in the Bible's book of Revelation.

militia—Loosely affiliated group of citizens organized to defend their families, homes and property against threats both domestic and foreign. Citizen's militias are springing up across the country in response to what their members consider a growing police state and threat to U.S. sovereignty and individual liberties.

MJTF—Multi-Jurisdictional Task Force. An amorphous and unaccountable federal entity made up of several "goon-squad" enforcement arms of other agencies, such as the DEA, FBI, BATF, and so on.

New World Order—Phrase used by former President George Bush following the Gulf War (also found in Latin on back side of U.S. dollar bill) to describe an emerging single governing body that will rule over all nations. Believed by many to be a code word for secret plot by internationalists to install a single totalitarian world government.

patriot movement—Grass-roots political phenomenon marked by strong local organization, bipartisan membership, and cynical distrust of government in general and the federal government in particular. The patriot movement aims to excise special interests, reduce the size of government, and restore the Constitution as the supreme law of the land.

puppet-master—Someone who pulls the strings of a dupe, sets up a patsy, or otherwise manipulates political puppets to achieve a hidden agenda.

secret societies—Groups such as the Illuminati, Freemasons, Trilateral Commission, Bildebergs, Bohemian Grove Society, Council on Foreign Relations, Rosicrucians, Propaganda Due, Knights Templar, or McGraw-Hill Board of Executives, which are considered by **alt.conspiracy** regulars to secretly control the economies and governments of various nations.

spook—A spy or former operative for any number of clandestine and unaccountable federal agencies, including the Federal Bureau of Investigations, the National Security Agency, the Central Intelligence Agency, the Defense Intelligence Agency, and so on.

United Nations—Global organization of about 150 member nations, considered by **alt.conspiracy** regulars to be a pawn/enforcer of those seeking to establish a New World Order, or totalitarian one-world government.

walk-in—A political figure who inexplicably reverses his/her position on a key issue. Term arises from the explanation that the "real" person is gone and an "alien" or "controlling" power has "walked into" the re-animate body. ("Man, Bob Dole's flip-flop on GATT only proves that he's a total walk-in.")

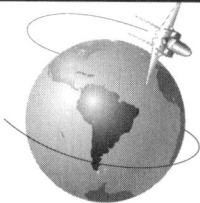

Net Resources

For the most up-to-date conspiracy information, check out the **alt.conspiracy** newsgroup. While this group serves as a strong attractor for net.kooks of all varieties, plenty of reasonable albeit conspiracy-minded folks hang out there. Also, keep an eye on alt.illuminati, alt. freemasonry, alt.masonic.members, alt.conspiracy.jfk, alt.activism, alt.censorship, and alt.law-enforcement,as well as the various alt.politics and alt.current-events groups.

A number of independent archives are maintained across the Net, each of which contains a healthy catalog of conspiracy-related material. Via anonymous FTP, you can access archives at **mary.iia.org**, **tezcat.com**, and **ftp.spies.com**. Many other sites around the Net are also host to various "patriot" archives, which usually contain a wealth of conspiracy files.

If you have a shortwave radio, check out WWCR, broadcasting at 5.810 MHz. WWCR shows are the topic of much discussion on **alt.conspiracy**, particularly William Cooper's *The Hour of the Time* show, running nightly at midnight Eastern.

BeastNet is an independent group of netizens out to eradicate "the Beast" in all its incarnations, from Madison Avenue mind control techniques to fascist police-state tactics. Check out the BeastNet archives at **ftp.farces.com** or send e-mail to **BeastNet @farces.com** for more information.

People's Spellbreaker is an electronic newsletter covering the growing rise of the American police state and the accompanying New World Order, as well as the presence and plans of United Nations troops inside the U.S. For more information or to subscribe, send e-mail to **jad@nyxfer.blythe.org** or **pnpj@db1.cc.rochester.edu**.

Conspiracy Nation is a daily electronic bulletin (formerly titled "Conspiracy for the Day") covering conspiracies and strange goings-on of all sorts. To subscribe to *Conspiracy Nation*, send e-mail to **bigxc@prairienet.org**, with "subscribe" followed by your e-mail address as the body of the message.

Full Disclosure covers matters of personal privacy and oversight into government operations. You can check out the *Full Disclosure* radio show via shortwave (WWCR at 5.819 Khz) every Sunday at 7 p.m. Central time. Check you local public access cable schedule for details on the *Full Disclosure* cable show, or e-mail *Full Disclosure* editor Glen L. Roberts at **glr@rci.ripco.com** for information.

Schr0dinger's Radio describes itself as "a schizoid digest for schizoid times, with news and features on the panoply of the confounding...[including] conspiracy, military intelligence, UFOlogy, psychedelics, experimental arts, the paranormal, mindcontrol, and anthropology." To subscribe, send e-mail to **majordomo@tezcat.com** with "subscribe schr0dingers" as the message. (We should point out that it's a zero—not an "o"—in "schr0dingers".) Back issues of *Schr0dinger's Radio* are available via anonymous FTP

Terminator Slaughters His Way to White House

By Eddy Davis (ekd@feenix3.com)

A lot of you may be wondering about the circumstances surrounding the numerous "suicides" among soldiers stationed in Haiti. I myself find it rather mysterious that we've got so many unhappy soldiers down there, anxious to blow their brains out in a foreign land. It smacks of Vince Foster to me. But the Foster "suicide" is but one in a series of odd and unexplainable deaths attributable to the Clinton administration. While a number of those relegated to the rolls of the "Clinton Body Count" can be explained as part of his efforts to cover up the Whitewater fiasco or the cocaine and arms coming in and out of Mena, Arkansas during his terms as governor, I'm still unsure why all these people were killed.

Linda Thompson of the American Justice Federation (AJF) has detailed the "Clinton Body Count" quite convincingly, and it's my thinking that we should all do our best to help her figure out what the hell is going on. About 30 people who've been connected to Clinton have died mysteriously over the past five years. Consider the mysterious and GOPHER at **tezcat.com** in the publications directory or via the Web at **http://tezcat.com/publications/**. Check out "The Octopus Archive" at the same addresses for further conspiracy info.

The *New York News Transfer* offers independently produced news articles covering topics outside the focus of the mainstream. For more information on the *New York News Transfer* and the related Workers World Service, send e-mail to **info@blythe.org**.

The EPIC project, which covers matters of Constitutional importance as well as matters concerning technology, is run by the Fund for Constitutional Government and Computer Professionals for Social Responsibility. For more information, send e-mail to **sobel@epic.org**.

The *Covert Action Quarterly* covers various "black ops" that are almost entirely ignored by the mainstream press. For subscription information and other details, send e-mail to **caq@igc.apc.org**. (Prisoners receive a discount on subscriptions!)

The Citizens Committee to Clean Up the Courts covers the latest news on court actions, banking matters, espionage agencies, and political assassinations. It maintains a telephone hotline whose contents are often transcribed and posted to the Net by various organizations. You can check the hotline (new messages released every Saturday) by calling (312) 731-1505.

A-albionic Research is a private research and publishing firm based in Ferndale, Michigan. They maintain extensive files online and offer a number of informative publications via mail-order. Access their book catalog or check out their New Paradigms Project via anonymous FTP at **ftp.a-albionic.com**, or via gopher at **gopher.a-albionic.com 9006**, or via mail server by sending the message "info prj"tomajordomo@mail.msen.com.

Purchasers of the highly recommended Name-Base, a microcomputer database with 166,000 citations and 76,000 names, receive regular e-mail updates via the NameBase NewsLine. Name-Base is a 3 MB database (available on floppy disks) used by over 650 journalists and researchers around the world. For more information, contact Public Information Research, PO Box 680635, San Antonio TX, 78268, fax: 210-509-3161.

The Committee for Waco Justice is a group dedicated to investigating and prosecuting any of those suspected of wrongdoing in the raid on the Branch Davidian home and the suspected subsequent destruction of evidence regarding the raid. Contact the Committee for Waco Justice at P.O. Box 33037 Washington, DC, 20033, or send e-mail to Alan Forschler **alanf@cap.gwu.edu** for more information.

circumstances of Vince Foster's death:

He was found in a park he was never known to visit. He supposedly used a gun that was not his to shoot himself through the roof of the mouth. The gun contained only two bullets, and no one has been able to account for where the gun or bullets came from. The left-handed Foster shot himself with his right hand, which was still clutching the gun when he was found—very uncommon in self-inflicted gunshot wounds. There were no marks, chipped teeth or other injuries in or around his mouth. Judging from his body position, he would have bled "uphill" at some point to explain the blood patterns.

Consider then that the White House instructed the Park Police, and not the FBI to investigate the "suicide." The White House also seized Foster's briefcase and removed items (evidence) from it. They first denied removing various papers, including Foster's diary, but now admit they have it and promise to return it, but still have not. Hillary Clinton instructed her private secretary to ransack Foster's office and shred apparently any paperwork she found. Intense paper-shredding also took place soon after Foster's death at the Rose Law Firm in Arkansas, where Foster and Hillary Clinton had worked (as well as Thomas "Mack" McLarty, chief White House legal counsel and Webster Hubbell, associate attorney general).

Compound this with the mysterious recent deaths of another 30 people associated with Clinton and his administration and I'm convinced we have a massive conspiracy on our hands that has connections to the Reagan and Bush administrations and the October Surprise scandal, the Iran-Contra affair, the Inslaw matter, the guns and drugs coming in and out of Mena, Arkansas, and the obvious connections via Whitewater to the Madison Bank and the Arkansas Development Finance Authority.

According to John DiNardo, editor of the *People's Spellbreaker* net newsletter, Executive Order 11647 signed by Richard Nixon on Feb. 10, 1972, sets up the structure for carrying out Executive Order 11490, which establishes 10 Federal Regional Councils to govern 10 Federal Regions made up of the various states. Ostensibly created to help the Federal Emergency Management Agency (FEMA) govern the country in times of widespread disaster, these 10 federal regions will be imposed soon when the federal government declares martial law, many readers of **alt.conspiracy** suspect.

As described in Rexford G. Tugwell's *The Emerging Constitution* (Harpers Magazine Press, Harper and Row), the 10 regions are listed here. Play along at home by finding out which region you live in and by learning what your new totalitarian regional capitol will be. (Scoff now, but don't say we didn't warn you.)

List Service

The 10 Federal Regions

- REGION I: Connecticut, Massachusetts, New Hampshire, Rhode Island, Vermont. *Regional Capitol:* Boston
- REGION II: New York, New Jersey, Puerto Rico, Virgin Islands. *Regional Capitol:* New York City
- REGION III: Delaware, Maryland, Pennsylvania, Virginia, West Virginia, District of Columbia. *Regional Capitol:* Philadelphia
- REGION IV: Alabama, Florida, Georgia, Kentucky, Mississippi, North Carolina, Tennessee. *Regional Capitol:* Atlanta
- REGION V: Illinois, Indiana, Michigan, Minnesota, Ohio, Wisconsin. *Regional Capitol:* Chicago
- REGION VI: Arkansas, Louisiana, New Mexico, Oklahoma, Texas. *Regional Capitol*: Dallas-Fort Worth
- REGION VII: Iowa, Kansas, Missouri, Nebraska. *Regional Capitol*: Kansas City
- REGION VIII: Colorado, Montana, North Dakota, South Dakota, Utah, Wyoming. *Regional Capitol:* Denver
- REGION IX: Arizona, California, Hawaii, Nevada. *Regional Capitol:* San Francisco
- REGION X: Alaska, Oregon, Washington, Idaho. *Regional Capitol:* Seattle

RUMOR CONTROL

Are the Russkies up to something dark and sinister? Sure, we know it's popular these days to view those former enemies as a shattered, defenseless, and mostly harmless nation. But we ask you, does a psychotronic brain-melting shock-wave ray gun sound harmless?

According to the Reuters news service, the *Fortean Times* and the online newsletter *Schrøedinger's Radio*, the Russkies are developing a weapon that would do a lot more than pollute our precious bodily fluids and violate our purity of essence.

In February 1994, speaking in Podgorica, Montenegro, Vladimir Zhirinovsky casually mentioned that Russian soldiers had disrupted the life forces of a dozen Moslem soldiers near Belgrade in what used to be Yugoslavia. Zhirinovsky—the fire-brand leader of Russia's Liberal Democrat Party,whom some describe as Russia's answer to Jesse Helms—said that the soldiers were killed by Russia's new "Elipton" device.

"It's a sonar effect. It's a very big noise impossible for man," Zhirinovsky proclaimed in broken English. He claimed the sonic weapon kills by emitting a massive sound pulse. Months later during a confrontation with a group protesting his dictatorial style and anti-emitic rhetoric, Zhirinovsky spit into the group before threatening to kill them with an "atomic pistol."

Writer Wants to Tell World the REAL Story

By

Charles Platt
(cp@panix.com)

I am a writer whose work has dealt with libertarian themes. I have had forty books published, including two that were nominated for the Prometheus Award, sponsored by the Libertarian Futurist Society. I am considering writing a book about the Patriot movement and other activists who are concerned about erosion of liberties. The purpose of this book would be to portray such activists in a sympathetic (but realistic and accurate) way, to encourage the general public to listen to the content of the message instead of dismissing the activists as "extremists."

If anyone has opinions on how I should proceed with this project, or wishes to suggest people who should be included in the book, please send me e-mail at cp@panix.com.

Thank you.

List Service

In John DiNardo's *People's Spellbreaker* electronic newsletter, a federally licensed firearms dealer described some of the more harrowing details of an unexplained raid he suffered at the hands of the Bureau of Alcohol, Tobacco and Firearms (BATF). His story is only one of thousands on the Net that never reach the public via traditional media outlets. Yet the Net is changing the power structure by giving everyone a voice, and citizens are calling for a re-examination of the need for a number of federal agencies, or at the very least, a careful look at how these agencies carry out law enforcement operations.

After reading accounts like the one below, it's easy to see where the Net-driven outrage comes from:

[During the raid] federal agents threw lit cigarettes wherever they landed. They burnt the carpet in my home and the carpet in my son's home.

They confiscated the following:

- the read-outs from my cancer tests
- my marriage certificate
- the document of my will
- my insurance cards
- my insurance policies
- my registrations
- birth certificates
- baptismal papers
- [school] report cards
- my cancer emergency phone number list
- my gun show promoter's license
- fictitious [business] name records
- my mailing list for gun shows
- my medical records of my spinal tests
- my medical records of my foot injury
- my records of doctor's appointments
- my lists of phone numbers of family and friends
- 30 to 40 Percodan [prescription pain pills]
- six timer watches
- my gun show admission stamps
- my [gun show] exhibitor badges
- my bank deposit bags

These federal agents also broke the lid off my jewelry box, and they broke the cabinet door off my copier machine. Toward the end of the federal agents' rampage, they told my son: "Your father is upset right now. Tell him not to call anyone by phone and not to tell anyone at gun shows that we were here. Otherwise, he is of no use to us."

Upon exiting my house, a female federal agent stomped and kicked my kitten to death! For almost eight hours, my wife, my son, and I were terrorized, threatened and humiliated. As recently as June 11th 1994, my wife was threatened in [a] supermarket parking lot by a federal agent. They have committed a lot more acts and threats against my family, and they have also stalked us. We have pictures and videotapes of the damage that these Federal agents did to my home and property.

My goal is to get a Congressional inquiry so that the BATF and the IRS will stop these assaults and other crimes against law-abiding people.

We challenge anyone to prove that we have committed any crime.

Citizens Demand Justice After Waco

On January 28, 1994, in a letter sent to President Bill Clinton, the Committee for Waco Justice—an independent group of American citizens—called for the President to direct Attorney General Janet Reno to appoint an Independent Counsel to investigate evidence of official misconduct, violations of rights, and excessive use of force culminating in negligent—and possibly intentional—homicide in the federal government assaults on the Branch Davidian religious group in Waco, Texas. More than a year later, nothing has been done to address the concerns of the American people in this very serious matter. Make your voice heard by contacting Alan Forschler of the Committee for Waco Justice via e-mail at alanf@cap.gwu.edu or write to Carol Moore (cmoore@cap.gwu.edu) for a complete electronic copy of the Committee's report. Write to President Clinton at (president@whitehouse.gov) and stress your demand that justice be served and that a full and complete investigation of the events at Waco be undertaken immediately. The Committee's letter, as posted to the Net, appears here.

January 28, 1994

President Bill Clinton
The White House Washington, D.C.
Dear President Clinton:

Enclosed is the Committee for Waco Justice's report, "The Massacre of the Branch Davidians: A study in Government Violations of Rights, Excessive Force and Coverup." We are distributing copies of our report to members of Congress, major media and columnists, political and religious organizations and tens of thousands of Americans over national computer networks.

Although our small Committee's research has been limited largely to public sources—government reports and hearings, news accounts and other published materials—we have discovered abundant evidence of official misconduct, violations of rights, excessive use of force, and even negligent—and possibly intentional—homicide. We consider the Treasury Department's September 30, 1993 and the Justice Department's October 8, 1993 reports to be little more than coverups of possible criminal acts by government agents and officials. Neither Department's "review team" even was authorized to take testimony from agents and officials under oath.

Pages 2 to 4 of our report list disturbing evidence of crimes which has been withheld from the people of the United States and their Congressional representatives. Some of the most disturbing are:

It was revealed in the Branch Davidian trial that BATF raid commanders planned to use force and expected a shootout—something not revealed to Treasury Department officials before the raid, nor men-

List Service

For decades, the privately operated Council on Foreign Relations (CFR) has met in secret, presumably to discuss U.S. government policies on various issues of national and international importance. While the organization in and of itself is not illegal, a quick glance at its membership roster tends to support even the most paranoid ravings of strident "conspiracy theorists." Excerpted from a much larger list posted to **alt.conspiracy**, the individuals below are all current or former members of the Council on Foreign Relations. As for what the CFR is up to, we here at the *Insider* will leave you to draw your own conclusions based on the list below, which is far from a complete roster of CFR membership.

Lloyd Bentsen, Secretary of the Treasury
Roger C. Altman, Deputy Secretary of the Treasury
R. James Woosley, Director of Central Intelligence
Adm. William Studeman, Deputy Director of Central Intelligence
Joseph S. Nye, Jr., Chairman, National Intelligence Council
Bruce Babbit, Secretary of the Interior
Henry G. Cicernos, Secretary of Housing & Urban Development
Donna E. Shalala, Secretary of Health & Human Services
Carol Bellamy, Director, U.S. Peace Corps
Joseph D. Duffey, Director, U.S. Information Agency
Ruth Bader Ginsburg, Associate Justice, U.S. Supreme Court
Karin M. Lissakers, U.S. Executive Director International Monetary Fund
Ricki Rhodarmer Tigert, Chair, Federal Deposit Insurance Corporation
George Stephanopoulos, White House Spokesman and Policy Advisor
David R. Gergen, Policy Advisor
W. Anthony Lake, National Security Advisor
Samuel R. Berger, Assistant National Security Advisor
W. Bowman Cutter, Economic Policy Advisor
Adm. William Crowe Jr., Chairman, Foreign Intelligence Advisory Board
Laura D'Andrea Tyson, Chairman, Council of Economic Advisors
John H. Gibbons, Director, Office of Science & Technology Policy
Alice M. Rivlin, Deputy Director of Office of Management & Budget
Gordon M. Adams, Assoc. Dir. for National Security & Internat. Affairs
Ronald H. Brown, Secretary of Commerce
Jeffrey E. Garten, Undersecretary of Commerce
Les Aspin, Former Secretary of Defense
John M. Deutch, Underscty. of Defense for Acquisition & Technology
Sarah Sewell, Dpty. Ast. for Peacekeeping/Peacemaking Policy
Gen. Gordon R. Sullivan, Joint Chief of Staff, Army
Gen. Merrill A. MacPeak, Joint Chief of Staff, Air Force
Gen. Carl E. Mundy, Jr., Commandant, Marine Corps
Vice Adm. L.W. Smith, Jr., Deputy Chief, Plans, Policy & Operations
Vice Adm. W.A. Owens, Deputy Chief, Resources, Warfare
Warren M. Christopher, Secretary of State
Strobe Talbott, Deputy Secretary of State
Peter Tarnoff, Undersecretary for Political Affairs
Princeton N. Lyman, Director, Refugee Programs
Madeleine Albright, Ambassador to the United Nations
Irvin Hicks, Deputy Ambassador to the United Nations
Geraldine A. Ferraro, United Nations Human Rights Commission

tioned in either the Treasury Department report or by BATF officials in testimony before the House Judiciary or Appropriations Committee hearings.

Attorney General Janet Reno has not completed an investigation into 911 tapes whose time sequence was re-ordered so that Branch Davidians' claims helicopters were firing at them appeared on the tape after the helicopters had left the scene. Two raid commanders who lied to the Treasury Department review team were in those helicopters.

Richard M. Rogers, the FBI Hostage Rescue Team Commander at Waco who repeatedly sabotaged negotiations by pushing for pressure tactics, may be indicted for his overly aggressive tactics in the 1992 standoff with Randy Weaver in Idaho.

The FBI and Justice Department covered up FBI reliance on "cult busters," including a long-time FBI advisor, for information and advice. Such individuals are committed to destroying new religious movements like the Branch Davidians.

The FBI convinced Attorney General Reno to approve its plan to gas and demolish Mount Carmel Center by evidently withholding from her David Koresh's very credible April 14th letter promising to surrender. Evidently this letter also was withheld from the press, the public, Congress and even Justice Department outside experts during Justice Department and FBI briefings.

Despite both FBI and Justice Department statements to the contrary, news footage clearly shows FBI agents outside their tanks just feet away from Mount Carmel Center before the fire. Under the FBI rules of engagement in force at the time, agents had the authority to shoot Branch Davidians. Many speculate they may have done so and are now covering up their acts.

The Justice Department and FBI are refusing to admit that there was an order to begin the demolition of Mount Carmel Center right before noon on April 19, 1993. They have not revealed who—FBI ground commanders or FBI or Justice Department officials—gave that order. Associate Attorney General Webster Hubbell was the highest ranking official in the FBI's Operation Center when that order was given. Questions remain about whether Hubbell contacted you directly after the April 19th fire.

Independent Counsel Robert B. Fiske is now investigating if there was any "obstruction of justice" regarding illegal financial dealings engaged in by you, Vince Foster, and possibly Webster Hubbell.

Since you and your associates were also top decision-makers in the Waco incident, we believe Mr. Fiske should investigate whether any possible coverup in the "Whitewater" matter extended over into efforts to cover up any errors or criminal actions which resulted in the deaths of 86 or more Branch Davidians. We are sending a copy of our report to Mr. Fiske.

Mr. President, if you could direct that Attorney General Janet Reno appoint an Independent Counsel to investigate these suspected illegal financial activities, we believe it is incumbent upon you to do the same regarding fatal assaults by government agents acting under your authority. The Committee for Waco Justice therefore calls on you to direct Attorney General Janet Reno to appoint an Independent Counsel empowered to identify and prosecute government agents and officials responsible for any crimes against the Branch Davidians, and any coverup of those crimes. The Independent Counsel would have full powers to subpoena witnesses to give testimony under oath and to grant immunity in exchange for evidence of criminal wrongdoing.

The Committee for Waco Justice is committed to ensuring that the U.S. government never again initiates or participates in another massacre like that of the Branch Davidians.

signed: Carol Moore
Alan Forschler

cc: Attorney General Janet Reno; Members of the House and Senate Judiciary Committees; Other Members of the U.S. House of Representatives and U.S. Senate; Louis Freeh, Director of the Federal Bureau of Investigation; John W. Magaw, Director of the Bureau of Alcohol, Tobacco and Firearms; Robert B. Fiske, Independent Counsel ■

THE USENET ORACLE HAS PONDERED YOUR QUESTION DEEPLY.

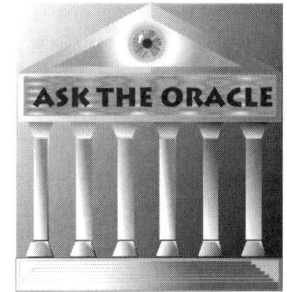

YOUR QUESTION WAS:

A question that has puzzled me for ages, O Oracle, most wise. I shall be most grateful for the answer to this:

Two people pull into a parking lot into two adjacent spaces, 100 feet from the door. They see two spots 30 feet closer to the door. Driver A starts the car and drives that extra 30 feet. Driver B sez "Nah, too much hassle to re-start the car and drive, I'll just walk the extra 30 feet." Which of the two drivers is lazier?

Thank you for the consideration of this most unworthy question. Be secure in the knowledge that I will provide service to the Oracle commensurate with the answer!

AND IN RESPONSE, THUS SPAKE THE ORACLE:

Not a bad question, as far as it goes, but you forgot to include a few other relevant drivers.

Driver C: The *New York Driver*; attempts to pull into driver A's space before driver A can reach it, despite the fact that there is a perfectly good empty space next to it.

Driver D: The *Boston Driver*; attempts to pull into driver A's space ahead of driver A, and then parks parallel to the curb, taking up driver A's space, the space next to it, and a good ten feet of sidewalk.

Driver E: The *New Jersey Driver*; is willing to swear before a grand jury that there never was a parking space, besides which he didn't take it, and anyway, he doesn't know nything about an unfortunate "accident" that befell driver A involving several tons of concrete and a sawed-off shotgun.

Driver F: The *Texas Driver*; pulls into the space closer to the shop, then decides that, in the interests of his family, he ought to take the one farther away, but then concludes that his supporters really want him to take the first space, which he'll do if they can validate his parking ticket in all fifty states.

Driver G: The *College Student Driver*; puts off deciding where to park until all the spaces are taken, then decides it's too late, and goes off to get a beer.

Driver H: The *Internet Driver*; decides that picking a space on his own is too much effort, and therefore posts a query to "rec.auto.parking" asking, "Which space should I take?" prompting a five-month long thread, the content of which breaks down as follows: 15% instructions to read the FAQ; 54% flames; 30.999% asking "How many parks could a parking lot lot if a parking lot could lot parks?"; and .001% providing relevant (if erroneous or misleading) information.

To answer your question, the laziest of all is driver I, who is so lazy that he does not even bother to finish answering the

(answer by Jacob Weinstein; jacobw@cap.gwu.edu)

Wacky Kids Speak Secret

Some people just don't get it. This is especially true on the Net. Keeping the *Insider* staffed with people who "get" the Net can be a challenge. (It also means we've got a lot of smart-mouthed 14-year-old "reporters" who think they can push around the old boys. Well, it's not gonna happen! You don't get to be king of the mountain just to have some snot-nosed punk come in and brush you aside like some dried-up raisin!! Oh, sorry . . .)

Anyway, one newsgroup that you either "get" or you "don't get" is **alt.adjective.noun.verb.verb.verb**. The group's name also describes its posting syntax. If you want to post a message in alt.adjective.noun.verb.verb.verb, you'd better follow the format and make sure your post begins with "alt." and then follows with an adjective, then a noun, then three verbs. It goes something like this:

alt.descriptive.example.appears.demonstrates.clarifies

Kinda strange, huh? Don't ask us to explain it; these kids with their Nintendo video games and crazy rap music and baggy pants! Now it's this goofy computer network gibberish language. What the hell is the world coming—oh, sorry again. Anyway, reading through a collection of postings to alt.adjective.noun.verb.verb.verb can give you a pretty good idea of what life in that group is like. Strange? Sure. Crazy? Probably not. (Damn kids.)

---

alt.self-referential.postings.stagnate.languish.exhaust
alt.occasional.topics.expand.incite.introduce?

> —*Andrea Missias* (cm@pharmdec.wustl.edu)

alt.last.test.finished.endured.regurgitated
alt.lousy.prof.despise.curse.vilify
alt.smartass.eyes.poke.poke.poke
alt.grinning.mouth.foam.foam.foam
alt.relaxing.vacation.anticipate.need.demand
alt.mindless.tv.watch.stare.drool
alt.morphin.rangers.flip.flip.flip
alt.busty.baywatch.drool.foam.[delete]
alt.still.sunlight.exists.endures.rises?
alt.never.daylight.see.greet.revel
alt.next.post.compose.create.send

> —*Stephen Garry Calder* (scalder@fraser.sfu.ca)

alt.various.magazines.fret.fume.worry
alt.most.stories.contradict.misrepresent.fudge
alt.greenhouse.effect.postulated.predicted.mentioned
alt.new.ice-age.postulated.predicted.claimed
alt.editors'.short-term-memory.lost.gone.pickled?
alt.general.public.confused.confused.confused
alt.overall.impact.lost.dissipated.negated
alt.real.issues.obscured.muddied.untouched
alt.worried.environmentalist-Angela.sigh.sigh.sigh

> —*Angela Gunn* (agunn@pipeline.com)

alt.worldwide.coverage.increase.detail.describe
alt.local.awareness.broaden.inform.worry

> —*Andrea Missias* (acm@pharmdec.wustl.edu)

alt.lame.Time-Magazine.wrote.suggested.postulated
alt.new.ice-age.begin?.commence?.start?
alt.California.ground.rumble.quake.shake
alt.Mississippi.river.flood.drench.soak
alt.Bosnian.crisis.kill.die.die
alt.Rwandan.people.die.die.die
alt.our.environment.destroy.mutilate.ruin
alt.other.people.joke.kid.wonder
alt.final.Armageddon.coming?.arriving?.existing?
alt.strong.disbelief.have.remains.exists
alt.curious.coincidences.were.are.will-be

> —*Brent Parker* (brent@netnews.upenn.edu)

alt.subversive.agents.conspire.plot.scheme
alt.trilateral.commission.cause.create.engineer
alt.nosey.brent.snoop.uncover.reveal
alt.nosey.brent.die.die.die

> —*Peter Steiger* (psteiger@ns1.unicomp.net)

alt.damn.CIA.discovered.found.exposed
alt.silly.post.believed.misunderstood.enhanced
alt.tragic.life.ended.finished.done

> —*Brent Parker* (brent@netnews.upenn.edu)

Code Language

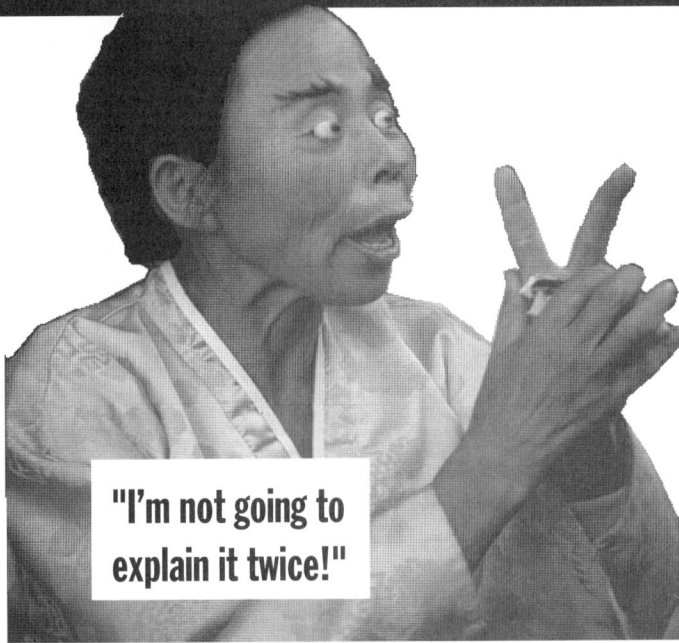

"I'm not going to explain it twice!"

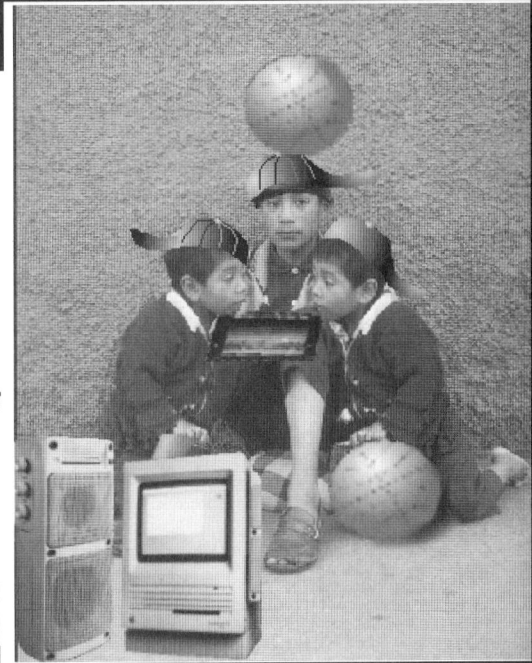

"Hey, quit hogging the Internet! Dangit!"

Brent Parker (brent@netnews.upenn.edu) wrote:
> alt.now.summer.come.exist.is

alt.wrong.part-of-speech.post.place.emit
alt.serious.violation.commit.commit.commit
alt.abject.forgiveness.seek.beg.secure
alt.right.life.live.seek.endure
alt.sarcastic.me.pick.snivel.carp
alt.erring.Brent.respond.recant.repost!

—*Michael F. Howard* (mikeh@netcom.com)

alt.glaring.error.made.created.performed
alt.mental.breakdown.had.occurred.happened
alt.profuse.apology.prepare.give.deliver
alt.sincere.promise.make.promise.declare
alt.clearer.thoughts.have.express.elaborate
alt.sacred.format.adhere.maintain.uphold

—*Brent K. Parker* (brent@mec.sas.upenn.edu)

Stephen Garry Calder (scalder@fraser.sfu.ca) wrote:
> alt.never.daylight.see.greet.revel

alt.inappropriate."never".used.posted.broadcast
alt.appropriate.words.use.share.compose
alt.wonderful.format.enjoy.appreciate.share
alt.correct.form.observe.enforce.police
alt.relaxing.break.take.have.experience!
alt.bated.breath.waiting.watching.anticipating

—*Michael F. Howard* (mikeh@netcom.com)

Michael Howard (mikeh@netcom.com) says:
>alt.serious.violation.commit.commit.commit
>alt.abject.forgiveness.seek.beg.secure
>alt.proper.usage.demand.protect.police!
>alt.correct.form.observe.enforce.police

alt.terrified.me.shake.tremble.post
alt.intimidated.poster.beg.plead.attempt
alt.gentle.police.be.be.be
alt.terrible.grammar.forget.botch.apologize
alt.pathetic.marks.attained.skipped.fooled-around
alt.hopeful.wrath.avoid.escape.run-away!

—*Janine Jean* (ak344@rreenet.carleton.ca)

Michael Howard (mikeh@netcom.com) says:
>alt.wonderful.correction.made.seen.posted
>alt.prompt.comprehension.observed.noted.appreciated
>alt.perspicacious.poster.welcomed.approved.anticipated
alt.brilliant.guru.police.protect.serve
(alt.subtle.flattery.brown-nose.reap.reward)
alt.perspicacious.dictionary.lookup.read.return

—*Janine Jean* (ak344@rreenet.carleton.ca) ∎

A Few Short

By Alan Silverstein (ajs@ajs.fc.hp.com) and Nathan Mates (nathan@cco.caltech.edu)

A couple sandwiches short of a picnic.

A few beers short of a six-pack/a six-pack short of a case.

A few bombs/bricks short of a full load.

A few french fries short of a Happy Meal.

A few open splices.

A few peas short of a casserole.

A few pickles short of a jar.

A few screws loose.

A few tiles short of a successful re-entry.

A few volts below threshold.

A few yards short of the hole.

A flying buttress short of a cathedral.

A photographic memory, but the lens cover is glued on.

A room temperature IQ.

A victim of retroactive birth control.

All crown—no filling.

All his eggs in the same basket.

All the lights don't shine in her marquis.

All the sex appeal of a wet paper bag.

Always in the right place, but at the wrong time.

Always sharpening his sleeping skills.

An ego like a black hole.

An experiment in Artificial Stupidity.

As bright as a nightlight.

As quick as a corpse.

As sharp as a marble.

As thick as two short planks.

Attic's a little dusty.

Back burners not fully operating.

Been napping in front of the ion shield again.

Been short on oxygen one time too many.

Blew his O-rings.

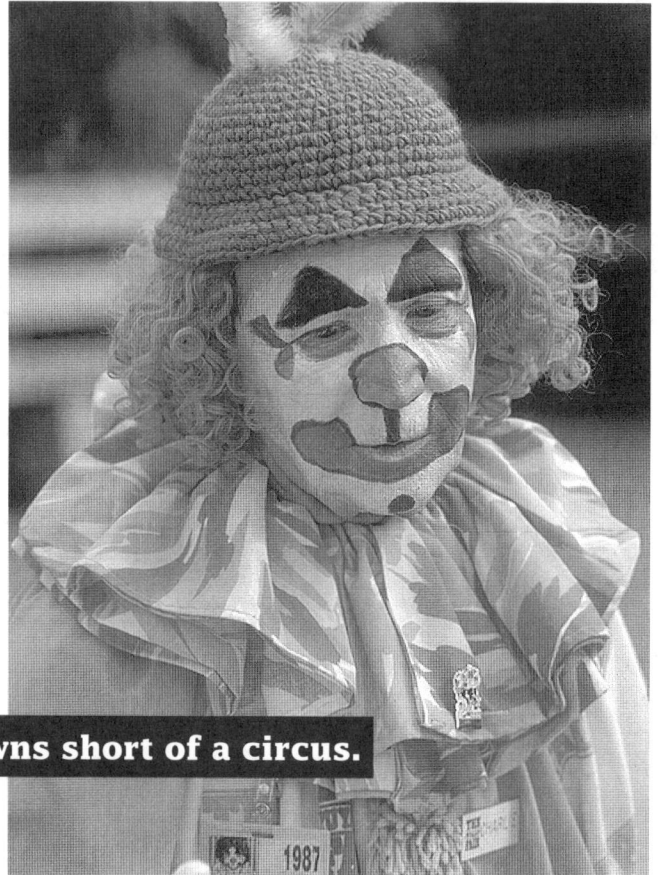

A few clowns short of a circus.

Born a day late and like that ever since.

Both oars in the water, but on the same side of the boat.

Bright as Alaska in December.

Bubbles in her think tank.

CPU not connected to the bus.

Can be outwitted by a jar of Marshmallow Fluff.

Car's only got three wheels, and one's going flat.

Chimney's clogged.

Contributes to the population problem.

Couldn't pour water out of a boot with instructions on the heel.

Diarrhea of the mouth—constipation of the brain.

Doesn't have all the dots on his dice.

Donated her body to science . . . before she was done using it.

Driving with two wheels in the sand.

Dumb as a stump.

Dumb as a sack of hammers.

Dumb as a box of rocks.

Echoes between the ears.

Fired from McDonald's for having a short attention span.

Fired her retrorockets a little late.

Flying on one engine.

Four cents short of a nickel.

Full throttle, dry tank.

Gates are down, the lights are flashing, but the train isn't coming.

Gavel doesn't quite hit the bench.

Gyros are loose.

Had a head crash.

Half a bubble off plumb.

Has a leak in his ceiling.

Has a one-way ticket on the Disoriented Express.

Has all her bricks, but no cement holding them together.

Has his solar panels aimed at the moon.

Has it floored in neutral.

Has no upper stage.

Has signs on both ears saying "Space for Rent."

Has the Grand Canyon under the crew cut.

Has the IQ of a salad bar.

Has the attention span of an overripe grapefruit.

Has the mental agility of a soap dish.

Has two brains; one is lost and the other is out looking for it.

Hasn't got all his china in the cupboard.

Hasn't got the brains God gave a cat.

He's diagnosable.

Her caboose pulls her engine.

Her dialing thumb must be broken.

Her memory is truly random-access.

His antenna doesn't pick up all the channels.

His buffer is full.

His head whistles in a cross wind.

His picture is in the dictionary under "zero."

If brains were dynamite, she wouldn't have enough to blow her nose.

If brains were lard, he'd be hard pressed to grease a small pan.

If brains were water, hers wouldn't be enough to baptize a flea.

If he had another brain, it would be lonely.

If her brains were put in a hummingbird, it would fly backwards.

If his IQ was two points higher he'd be a rock.

A few planes short of an Air Force.

If she was any dumber, she'd be a green plant.

If what you don't know can't hurt you, she's practically invulnerable.

If you give him a penny for his thoughts, you get change back.

If you stand close enough to him, you can hear the ocean.

In need of a ROM upgrade.

Infinite space between her ears.

On the batting end of a no-hitter.

One bit short of a byte.

One board short of a porch.

One boot stuck in the sand.

One sentence short of a paragraph.

One shingle shy of a roof.

One side short of a pentagon.

Too many birds on her antenna.

One taco short of a combination plate.

One tree short of a hammock.

One weight short of a shipwreck.

Only one oar in the water.

Only playing with the jokers.

Parked his head and forgot where he left it.

Playing hockey with a warped puck.

Plays solitaire...for cash.

Racing fifty yards with a pregnant woman, he'd come in third.

Informationally deprived.

Intellectually challenged.

Knitting with only one needle.

Left his booster on the launch pad.

Left the store without all of his groceries.

Little red choo-choo's jumped the track.

Living proof that nature does not abhor a vacuum.

Lug nuts rattling in the hubcaps.

Mainspring's wound too tight.

Metronome needs winding.

Mind like a steel sieve.

Mind like a steel trap—rusted shut.

Needs another brain to make half-wit.

Nine pence in the shilling.

Nineteen cents short of a paradigm.

Not digging in the same ditch with the rest of us.

Not firing on all cylinders.

Not the sharpest knife in the drawer.

Nothing between the stethoscope.

Oil doesn't reach his dipstick.

Reading from an empty disk.

Renewable energy source for hot air balloons.

Runs squares around the competition.

Sat under the ozone hole too long.

Seven seconds behind, and built to stay that way.

She wears a pony tail to cover up the valve stem.

Skating on the wrong side of the ice.

Skylight leaks a little.

Slinky's kinked.

So slow he has to speed up to stop.

Some drink from the fountain of knowledge, but he just gargled.

Someone let the air out of her lock.

Surfing in Nebraska.

Swimming in the shallow end of the gene pool.

Teflon brain—nothing sticks.

The cheese slid off his cracker.

Thick as a brick.

Trying out for the javelin retrieval team.

With one more neuron he'd have a synapse. ∎

Couldn't Hear You– I Needed A Fish In My Ear

Fans of Douglas Adams' Hitchhiker's Guide to the Galaxy books (and their companion adventure games for computers) will be interested to hear the rumor of a mental patient who had confounded doctors for months until they discovered the key to his strange code language.

On the basis of unconfirmed speculation on the Net, the *Insider* has pieced together a report of what appears to be a patient obsessed with the popular science fiction/satire books. When a man in a bar said to a friend, "Here, put this fish in your ear," a psychiatrist sitting instruction that matched the deranged ramblings of his patient.

The patient reportedly only responds to questions and answers couched in the ridiculous nonsense of Adam's *Hitchhiker* series, but apparently doctors are at least now able to communicate with him. ∎

INSIDE
OPINION

The Net offers a perplexing dilemma to law enforcement officials. Writing and posting messages to an electronic forum generally can't be considered a crime. There are a few instances (threatening the president's life, for instance) where posting a specific message is itself a crime, but such messages represent an incalculably tiny percentage of the traffic on the Net.

So what to do? The government can't be everywhere on the Net all at once. (They're on the Net, they claim, because they're "only trying to help.") But if some net.subversive is plotting a heinous crime spree, they'd better know about it. So, should agencies like the F.B.I. or the Secret Service be snooping around the Net, or private bulletin boards for that matter? Should they be setting up their own bulletin board systems in search of subversives? Should they be developing a massive search-and-retrieval system to scan millions of computer files for incriminating words and phrases? What is the role of G-men and shade-wearing super spooks online?

United States Representative Don Edwards (D-Calif.) wondered the same thing, so he decided to write the Secret Service and ask them a few questions. Luckily, he was open with his questions and the Secret Service's answers, and the Computer Professionals for Social Responsibility (CPSR) posted the Secret Service's response to the Net. Their answers may surprise you.

If you buy the government's logic, then you'll believe they review thousands of potential "dangerous" computer files every day, but keep virtually no records of such reviews. You'll also believe they use special software and hardware tools to electronically snoop through your files, but it's nothing you couldn't buy at your corner Ye Olde Komputer Shoppe.

If you buy that logic, please send us your name, address, home phone and credit card numbers, because we'd like to run a check of your information to make sure it's accurate. We're only too glad to help.

Is Big Brother Reading Your E-Mail?

DEPARTMENT OF TREASURY
UNITED STATES SECRET SERVICE
WASHINGTON, D.C. 20223

April 30, 1990

The Honorable Don Edwards, Chairman
Subcommittee on Civil and
  Constitutional Rights
Committee on the Judiciary
House of Representatives
Washington, D.C. 20515

Dear Mr. Chairman:
  Thank you for your letter of April 3, 1990, concerning your committee's interest in computer fraud. We welcome the opportunity to discuss this issue with your committee and I hope the following responses adequately answer your questions.

Question 1:
Please describe the Secret Service's process for investigating computer related crimes under Title 18, United States Code, Section 1030 and any other related statutes.

Response:
The process by which the Secret Service investigates computer related crimes is similar to the methods we use to investigate other types of criminal investigations. Most of the investigative techniques are the same; surveillance, record checks, witness and suspect interviews, etc. The primary difference is we had to develop resources to assist in the collection and review of computer evidence.

To provide our agents with this expertise, the Secret Service developed a computer fraud investigation course

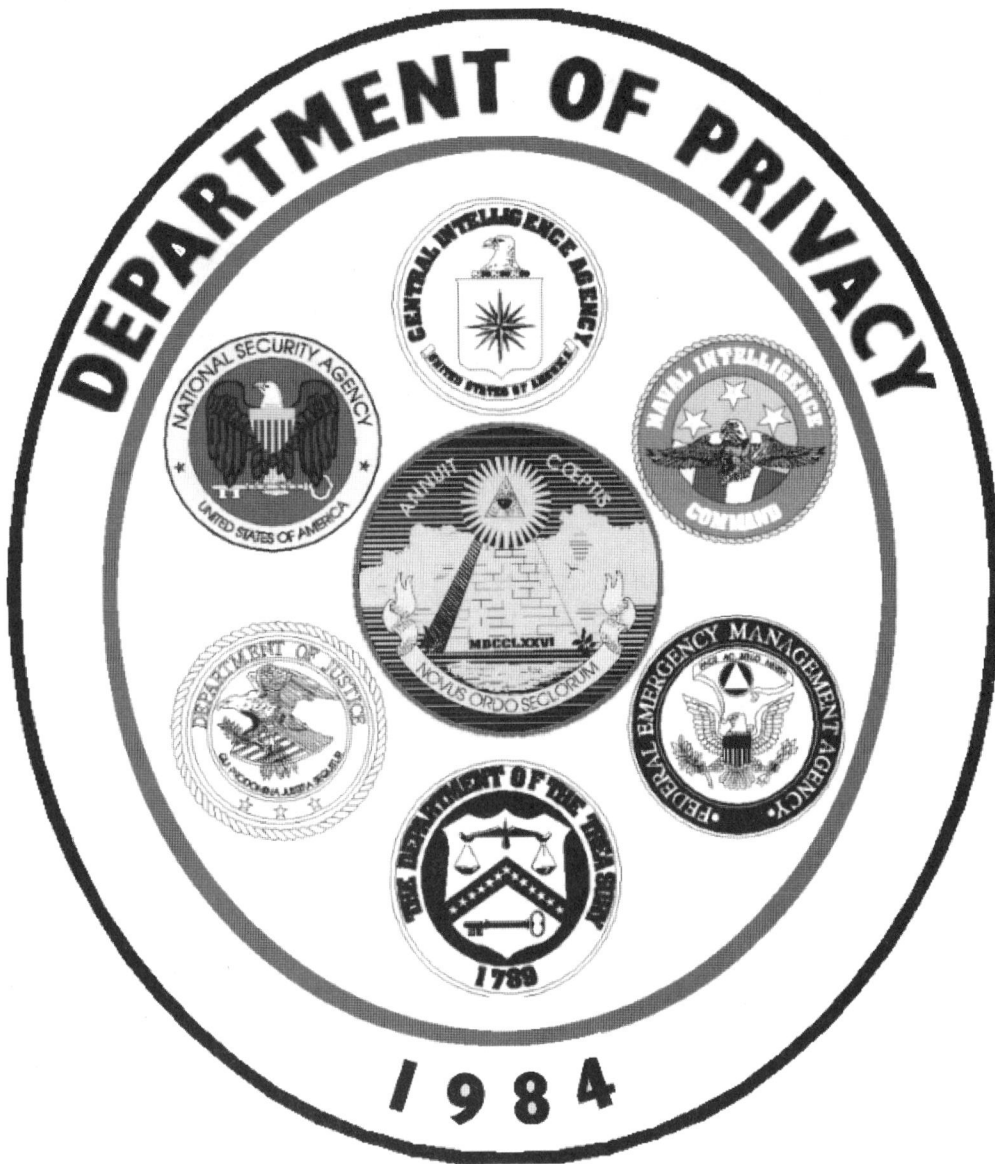

DEPARTMENT OF PRIVACY

1984

which, as of this date, has trained approximately 150 agents in the proper methods for conducting a computer fraud investigation. Additionally, we established the Computer Diagnostics Center, staffed with computer professionals, to review evidence on computer systems.

Referrals of computer related criminal investigations occur in much the same manner as any other case. A victim sustains a loss and reports the crime, or, a computer related crime is discovered during the course of another investigation.

In the investigations we do select, it is not our intention to attempt to supplant local or state law enforcement. We provide enforcement in those cases that are interstate or international in nature and for one reason or another are beyond the capability of state and local law enforcement agencies.

When computer related crimes are referred by the various affected industries to the local field offices, the Special Agent in Charge (SAIC) determines which cases will be investigated based on a variety of criteria. Each SAIC must consider the economic impact of each case, the prosecutive guidelines of the U.S. Attorney, and the investigative resources available in the office to investigate the case.

In response to the other portion of your question, the other primary statute we use to investigate computer re-

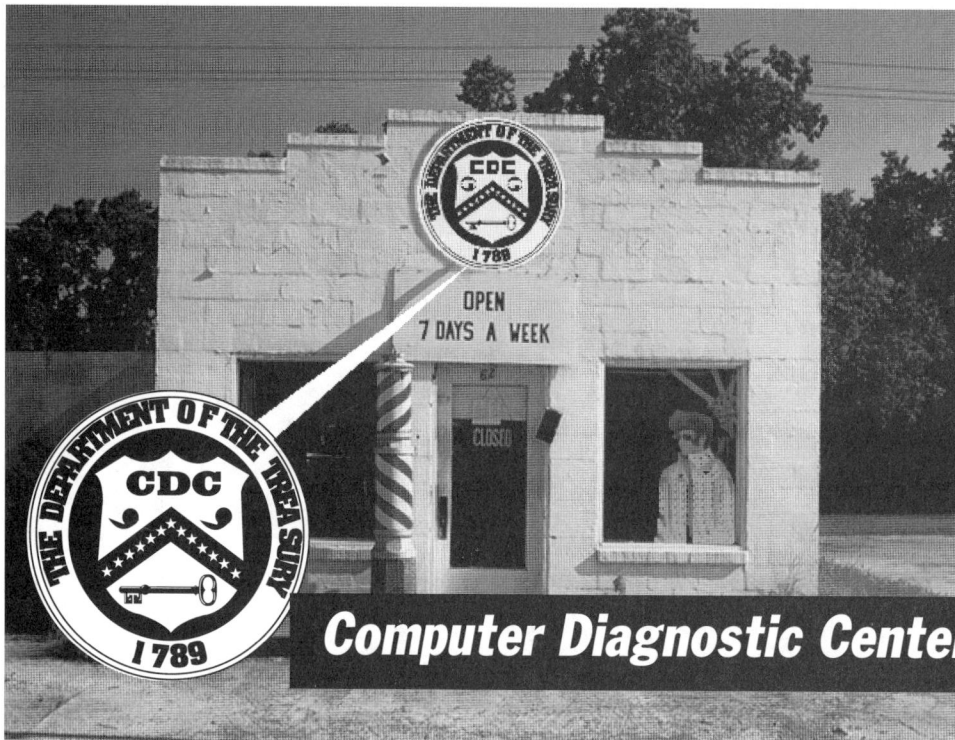
Computer Diagnostic Center

lated crimes is Title 18, United States Code, Section 1029 (Access Device Fraud). This service has primary jurisdiction in those cases which are initiated outside a bank and do not involve organized crime, terrorism, or foreign counterintelligence (traditional responsibilities of the F.B.I.).

The term "access device" encompasses credit cards, debit cards, automatic teller machine (ATM) cards, personal identification numbers (PINs) used to activate ATM machines, credit or debit card account numbers, long-distance telephone access codes, computer passwords and logon sequences, and, among other things, the computer chips in cellular car phones which assign billing.

Additionally, this service has primary jurisdic-

tion in cases involving electronic fund transfers by consumer (individuals) under Title 15, United States Code, Section 169n (Electronic Fund Transfer Act). This could involve any scheme designed to defraud EFT systems used by the public, such as pay-by-phone systems, home banking, direct deposit, automatic payments, and violations concerning automatic teller machines. If the violations can be construed to be a violation of the banking laws by a bank employee, the F.B.I. would have primary jurisdiction.

There are many other statutes which have been used to prosecute computer criminals but it is within the purview of the U.S. Attorney to determine which statute will be used to prosecute an individual.

Question 2:
Has the Secret Service ever monitored any computer bulletin boards or networks? Please describe the procedures for initiating such monitoring, and list those computer bulletin boards or networks monitored by the Secret Service since January 1988.

Response:
Yes, we have occasionally monitored computer bulletin boards. The monitoring occurred after we received complaints concerning criminal activity on a particular computer bulletin board. The computer bulletin boards were monitored as part of an official investigation and in accordance with the directives of the Electronic Communications Privacy Act of 1986

(Title 18, United States Code 2510).

The procedures used to monitor computer bulletin boards during an official investigation have involved either the use of an informant (under the direct supervision of the investigating agent) or an agent operating in an undercover capacity. In either case, the informant or agent had received authorization from the computer bulletin board's owner/ operator to access the system.

We do not keep records of the bulletin boards which we have monitored, but can provide information concerning a particular board if we are given the name of the board.

Question 3:
Has the Secret Service or someone acting under its direction ever opened an account on a computer bulletin board or network? Please describe the procedures for opening such an account and list those bulletin boards or networks on which such accounts have been opened since January 1988.

Response:
Yes, the U.S. Secret Service has on many occasions, during the course of a criminal investigation, opened accounts on computer bulletin boards or networks.

The procedure for opening an account involves asking the system administrator/operator for permission to access the system. Generally, the system administrator/operator will grant everyone immediate access to the computer bulletin board but only for lower levels of the system. The common "pirate" computer bulletin boards associated with most computer crimes have many different levels in their systems. The first level is generally available to the public and does not contain any information related to criminal activity. Only after a person has demonstrated unique computer skills, been referred by a known "hacker," or provided stolen long-distance telephone access codes or stolen credit card account information, will the system administrator/operator permit a person to access the higher levels of the bulletin board system which contains the information on the criminal activity.

As previously reported in our answer for Question 2, we do not keep records of the computer bulletin boards on which we have established accounts.

Question 4:
Has the Secret Service or someone acting under its direction ever created a computer bulletin board or network that was offered to the public? Please describe any such bulletin board or networks.

Response:
No, the U.S. Secret Service has not created a computer bulletin board nor a network which was offered to members of the public. We have created an undercover bulletin board which was offered to a select number of individuals who had demonstrated an interest in conducting criminal activities. This was done with the guidance of the U.S. Attorney's office and was consistent with the Electronic Communications Privacy Act (ECPA).

Question 5:
Has the Secret Service ever collected, reviewed, or "downloaded" transmissions or information from any computer network or bulletin board? What procedures does the Secret Service have for obtaining information from computer bulletin boards or networks? Please list the occasions where information has been obtained since January 1988, including the identity of the bulletin boards or networks, the type of information obtained, and how that information was obtained (was it downloaded, for example).

Response:
Yes, during the course of several investigations, the U.S. Secret Service has "downloaded" information from computer bulletin boards. A review of information gained in this manner (in an undercover capacity after being granted access to the system by its system administrator) is performed in order to determine whether or not that bulletin board is being used to traffic in unauthorized access codes or to gather other information of a criminal intelligence nature. At all times, our methods are in keeping with the procedures as outlined in the Electronic Communications Privacy Act (ECPA).

If a commercial network was suspected of containing information concerning a criminal activity, we would obtain the proper court order to obtain this information in keeping with the ECPA.

The U.S. Secret Service does not maintain a record of the bulletin boards we have accessed.

Question 6:
Does the Secret Service employ, or is it considering employing, any system or program that could automatically review the contents of a computer file, scan the file for key items, phrases, or data elements, and flag them or recommend further investigative action? If so, what is the status of any such system? Please describe this system and research being conducted to develop it.

Response:
The Secret Service has pioneered the concept of a Computer Diagnostic Center (CDC) to facilitate the review and evaluation of electronically stored information. To streamline the tedious task of reviewing thousands of files per investigation, we have gathered both hardware and software tools to assist our search of files for specific information or characteristics. Almost all of these products are commercially developed products and are available to the public. It is conceivable that an artificial intelligence process may someday be developed and have application to this law enforcement function, but we are unaware if such a system is being developed.

The process of evaluating the information and making recommendations for further investigative action is currently a manual one at our CDC. We process thousands of computer disks annually as well as review evidence contained in other types of storage devices (tapes, hard drives, etc.). We are constantly seeking ways to enhance our investigative mission. The development of high tech resources like the CDC saves investigative man-hours and assists in the detection of criminal activity.

Again, thank you for your interest. Should you have any further questions, we will be happy to address them.

Sincerely,

John R. Simpson,
Director

cc: Honorable Charles E. Schumer ∎

Resource Index

Finding what you're looking for on the Net is seldom easy. In fact, it's often difficult and can sometimes be a downright dangerous proposition. That's why we recommend leaving the hard-core net-surfing to trained professionals like the staffers of the *Internet Insider*.

But if you've noticed something in this edition that you'd like more information on, this handy quick-reference index is a great place to start. While most entries feature their own Net Resources sidebar, the various articles are listed here along with their accompanying sources for easy reference.

Be warned, however, that if you're searching for a specific article or posting like one you've seen in here, you're not likely to find it. The Internet's information distribution system is strictly a here today, gone tomorrow situation. (Unless, of course, some eagle-eyed reader sends in the net.gem to the editors of the *Insider*.)

Many of the items in this edition won't be sourced in the list below because they were sent directly to us by our numerous correspondents in the field, or to reveal their origins would be a violation of the sacred trust between reporter and source. But most of the major public resources covered in the *Insider* are listed below.

So use this index (arranged alphabetically according to the section title as it appears in the Table of Contents) as a guide to help you find related articles and information resources. Good luck, be careful, and happy hunting!

America's Love Affair with Hate
Newsgroups: alt.fan.oj-simpson, talk.rumors, alt.current-events

Ask the Oracle
Anonymous FTP: cs.indiana.edu
E-mail: mailserv@cs.indiana.edu
Newsgroup: rec.humor.oracle.d

Bloated Beast Named "Fed" Grows Out of Control
Anonymous FTP: ftp.spies.com
E-mail: faq@whitehouse.gov, congress@hr.house.gov
World-Wide Web: http://gopher.nara.gov:70/7g/register/laws, http://www.nara.gov/, http://wings.buffalo.edu/geogw, http://galaxy.einet.net/e-periodicals/ushous.html

Bootsie Report
Anonymous FTP: ftp.netcom.com (/pub/hamlet directory)
E-mail: an31291@anon.penet.fi
Newsgroups: talk.rumors, talk.bizarre, alt.showbiz.gossip, alt.timewasters

Clinton, Gore Stuck in Slow-Moving World-Wide Web
E-mail: faq@whitehouse.gov
World-Wide Web: //http:whitehouse.gov

Close Encounters of the Net Kind
Anonymous FTP: phoenix.oulu.fif
E-mail: mcorbin@paranet.org, psychospy@aol.com
Newsgroups: alt.alien.visitors, alt.paranet.ufo

Elvis Sightings
Newsgroup: alt.elvis.sightings

The End Is Nigh, the Beast Is Anxious for Your Soul
Anonymous FTP: ftp.farces.com (BeastNet directory)
E-mail: beastnet@farces.com

Ever Get the Feeling You're Being Watched?
Anonymous FTP: ftp.spies.com, gate.demon.co.uk, ftp.eff.org
E-mail: info@eff.org
Newsgroups: sci.crypt, talk.politics.crypto, alt.privacy, alt.security.pgp, comp.org.eff.talk

If You Pave It, They Will Come
Newsgroup: alt.pave.the.earth

Internet Foils Coup
E-mail: rferl-daily-report-request@admina.refrl.org, surean-l@ubvm.bitnet
Newsgroups: soc.culture.soviet, alt.current-events, alt.activism, soc.rights.human

Internet Report on MEXICO
E-mail: activ-l@mizzou1.missouri.edu
Newsgroups: soc.culture.mexican, soc.culture.mexican-american, alt.activism, soc.rights.human, alt.politics, alt.politics.radical-left, soc.culture.native, alt.native

Internet Serves as Modern-Day Babble-On
Anonymous FTP: sspp.gsfc.nasa.gov
E-mail: tuning@varese.mills.edu, mailserv@sspp.gsfc.nasa.gov.
World-Wide Web: http://sspp.gsfc.nasa.gov/

It's a Conspiracy
Anonymous FTP: mary.iia.org, tezcat.com, ftp.spies.com
E-mail: pnpj@db1.cc.rochester.edu, bigxc@prairienet.org, glr@rci.ripco.com, majordomo@tezcat.com ("subscribe schr0dingers"), info@blythe.org, sobel@epic.org, caq@igc.apc.org, majordomo@mail.msen.com ("info prj"), alanf@cap.gwu.edu
Newsgroups: alt.conspiracy, alt.conspiracy.jfk, alt.alien.visitors, alt.illuminati, alt.freemasonry, alt.politics

The Kool-Aid Cure for the Common Cold
e-zine contact: Chris (chriscon@njcc.wisdom.bubble.org)

Millions Suffer from Angstrom Syndrome
Newsgroups: alt.angst, alt.bitterness, alt.atheism
World-Wide Web: http://www.cs.indiana.edu/hypian/krawling/angst.html

More Losers Than Winners in Net Spelling Bee
Newsgroups: alt.flame.spelling, rec.humor, alt.best.of.internet, alt.humor.best.of.usenet

My Secret Shame
Newsgroups: talk.rumors, alt.showbiz.gossip

The Socks Chronicles
Anonymous FTP: ftp.spies.com
E-mail: publications@whitehouse.gov
Gopher: gopher.tamu.edu or sunsite.unc.edu
World-Wide Web: http://english-server.hss.cum.edu/WhiteHouse.html

Spontaneous Combustion
Newsgroups: alt.flame, alt.aol-sux, alt.my.stupid.job, alt.flame.roomates

Today's Kook is Tomorrow's Genius
Anonymous FTP: wuarchive.wustl.edu (pub/msdos_uploads/cyberpunk directory)
E-mail: philip@rmit580fs1.hais.rmit.edu.au
Newsgroups: alt.conspiracy, alt.conspiracy.jfk, alt.usenet.kooks, alt.alien.visitors, talk.bizarre, alt.discordia, alt.paranet.skeptic, alt.paranormal, alt.prophecies.nostradamus, comp.ai.fuzzy, info.firearms, rec.arts.sf.fandom

The Truth Behind the Crispy Conspiracy
Newsgroup: alt.cereal

What's Your Takeaway?
Anonymous FTP: ftp.infonet.net (/showcase/dmorris/nerdnosh directory)
E-mail: listserv@clovis.felton.ca.us

Index

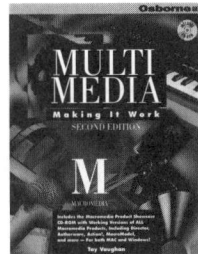

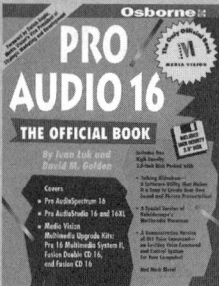

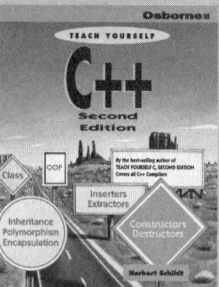

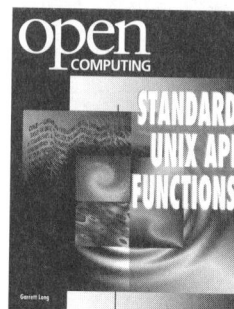

ORDER BOOKS DIRECTLY FROM OSBORNE/McGRAW-HILL

For a complete catalog of Osborne's books, call 510-549-6600 or write to us at 2600 Tenth Street, Berkeley, CA 94710

Call Toll-Free: *1-800-822-8158*
24 hours a day, 7 days a week
in U.S. and Canada

Mail this order form to:
McGraw-Hill, Inc.
Blue Ridge Summit, PA 17294-0840

Fax this order form to:
717-794-5291

EMAIL
7007.1531@COMPUSERVE.COM
COMPUSERVE GO MH

Ship to:

Name _____

Company _____

Address _____

City / State / Zip _____

Daytime Telephone: _____
(We'll contact you if there's a question about your order.)

ISBN #	BOOK TITLE	Quantity	Price	Total
0-07-88				
0-07-88				
0-07-88				
0-07-88				
0-07-88				
0-07-88				
0-07-88				
0-07-88				
0-07-88				
0-07-88				
0-07-88				
0-07-88				
0-07-88				
0-07-88				
		Shipping & Handling Charge from Chart Below		
		Subtotal		
		Please Add Applicable State & Local Sales Tax		
		TOTAL		

Shipping & Handling Charges

Order Amount	U.S.	Outside U.S.
Less than $15	$3.45	$5.25
$15.00 - $24.99	$3.95	$5.95
$25.00 - $49.99	$4.95	$6.95
$50.00 - and up	$5.95	$7.95

Occasionally we allow other selected companies to use our mailing list. If you would prefer that we not include you in these extra mailings, please check here: ☐

METHOD OF PAYMENT

☐ Check or money order enclosed (payable to Osborne/McGraw-Hill)

☐ AMERICAN EXPRESS   ☐ DISCOVER   ☐ MasterCard   ☐ VISA

Account No. ☐☐☐☐☐☐☐☐☐☐☐☐☐☐☐☐

Expiration Date _____

Signature _____

In a hurry? Call 1-800-822-8158 anytime, day or night, or visit your local bookstore.

Thank you for your order   Code BC640SL

If You Liked the Book, You'll LOVE What's Online!

The Internet Insider brought you a strange new world of deadly guide dogs, Canadian love slaves, and bizarre lunatics who are determined to pave the earth. But only the electronic version of **The Internet Insider** can bring you instantly up-to-date on the shocking news from the edge of cyberspace!

Browse through the extra information! Read the twisted tales and sordid stories that *almost* made the first edition! (Don't think of it as the news that didn't make the cut—consider it the news that's fit to print, but didn't fit.)

But wait! There's more!

➤ **Get the latest updates:** Late-breaking news and timely bulletins are posted regularly online. Don't wait for the morning paper to find out how shockingly strange your world really is. Log on any time for the *Inside* story.

➤ **Go behind the scenes:** Learn the secrets and explore the hidden forces that shape the world's only digital tabloid. Get the straight dope on how we put **The Internet Insider** together.

➤ **Join the *Insider* staff:** Submit your own net.finds for inclusion in the next edition of **The Internet Insider**. Original material is best, or forward your favorite discoveries, but be sure to include the original author's name and e-mail address.

Use your local World-Wide Web browser to check out the **Insider** home page. Subscribe to the **Insider**'s e-mail updates. Download back issues and extra editions via anonymous FTP. Facing the shocking horrors and exhilarating thrills of the unchartered Internet has never been easier!

Experience **The Internet Insider** online. It's quick. It's easy. But best of all, it's free! For more information, send e-mail to ruffin@cerf.net. ■